THE BOOK OF THE
CHOW CHOW

BY
DR. SAMUEL DRAPER
AND
JOAN MCDONALD BREARLEY

FRONT COVER: Canadian and American Ch. Mi-Pao's Timang, owned, bred and handled by F.P.A. Odenkirchen, Mi-Pao Kennels, Ontario, Canada.

FRONTISPIECE: A classic Tauskey photograph of one of the top-winning Chow Chows and sires in the history of the breed, Ch. Eastward Liontamer of Elster.

BACK COVER: A dry-brush watercolor of the incomparable Ch. Eastward Liontamer of Elster rendered by Heidi Choquette for owners Dr. Samuel Draper and Mr. and Mrs. Robert Hetherington, Jr.

Book Designed
by
Joan McDonald Brearley

ISBN 0-87666-653-5

Distributed in the U.S.A. by T.F.H. Publications, Inc., 211 West Sylvania Avenue, P.O. Box 27, Neptune City, N.J. 07753; in England by T.F.H. (Gt. Britain) Ltd., 13 Nutley Lane, Reigate, Surrey; in Canada to the book store and library trade by Clarke, Irwin & Company, Clarwin House, 791 St. Clair Avenue West, Toronto 10, Ontario; in Canada to the pet trade by Rolf C. Hagen Ltd., 3225 Sartelon Street, Montreal 382, Quebec; in Southeast Asia by Y.W. Ong, 9 Lorong 36 Geylang, Singapore 14; in Australia and the South Pacific by Pet Imports Pty. Ltd., P.O. Box 149, Brookvale 2100, N.S.W., Australia. Published by T.F.H. Publications, Inc. Ltd., The British Crown Colony of Hong Kong.

Table of Contents

ACKNOWLEDGMENTS 6
ABOUT THE AUTHORS 8
1. ORIGIN OF THE CHOW CHOW 11
2. THE COMING OF AGE OF THE CHOW CHOW IN THE WESTERN WORLD 16
3. THE HISTORY OF THE CHOW CHOW IN GREAT BRITAIN 20
World War I Calls a Halt. . . The Golden Years in British Chowdom. . . Minhow—
One of the Biggest and One of the Best. . . Stud Dog Records. . . Brood Bitch Records
. . . Notable All Breed Chow Wins. . . Present Day Record Holders. . . Chow Chow
Registrations in Great Britain. . . Other Chow Chow Activities
4. THE CONTINENTAL CHOW CHOW 93
The International Chow Chow Congress. . . Judging and Championships. . . Chow
Chow History on the Continent. . . Chow Chows in Belgium. . . The Chow Chow in
Holland. . . The Chow in Luxembourg. . . Chow Chows in France. . . Chow Chows in
Italy. . . The Chow Chow in Denmark. . . Chow Chows in Switzerland. . . Chow Chows
in Germany. . .Chows in Other European Countries. . . Chow Chows in Norway and
Sweden
5. THE CHOW CHOW IN THE UNITED STATES—THE BEGINNING 167
6. THE CHOW CHOW IN THE UNITED STATES—KENNELS OF TODAY 247
Ah Sid. . . Audrich. . . Autumn-Sun. . . Betmar. . . Carchow. . . Carlee. . . Chang-Shi
. . . Charmar. . . Cherokee. . . Chia Hsi. . . Cheng Lee. . . Clar-Ell-Mo. . . Don-Lee. . .
Don-Ray. . . Dre-Don. . . Eastward. . . Ellwanger. . . Fa-Ci. . . Farresdale. . . Five Ash
. . . Gotschall. . . Jon-Ell. . . Keesaman. . . Ky-Lin. . . Lakeview Kennels. . . Lli Haven
. . . Liontamer. . . Luck-ee. . . Magi. . . Mardi Me. . . Martonge. . . De La Moulaine. .
Nor-Ton. . . Pandee. . . Plainacre. . . Ru-Bil. . . Shanglo. . . San Kee. . . Shamrock. . .
Soo-Z. . . Scotchow. . . Tag-El. . . Tamarin. . . Tsang-Po (the Allens). . . Tsang-Po
(the Norths). . . Wu San
7. THE CHOW CHOW IN CANADA 362
BuDynasty. . . Champad. . . Chi-Kwang. . . Foo H'Sing. . . Hanchow. . . Keba-Yan. . .
Mi-Pao. . . Mi-Tu. . . SinKiang. . . Suyan
8. THE CHOW CHOW STANDARD 383
The American Standard. . . Interpretation of the Standard. . . European Standards
9. BUYING YOUR CHOW CHOW PUPPY 407
The Puppy You Buy. . . Male or Female?. . . The Planned Parenthood Behind Your
Puppy. . . Puppies and Worms. . . Veterinary Inspection. . . The Conditions of Sale. . .
Buying a Show Puppy. . . The Purchase Price. . . The Cost of Buying Adult Stock
10. THE SOCIALIZATION OF THE CHOW CHOW 423
Rules for the Socialization of the Chow Chow
11. GROOMING THE CHOW CHOW: THE ADULT AND THE PUPPY 433
Three Positions for Grooming the Chow. . . Basic Grooming or Brushing. . . Bathing. .
Grooming the Puppy

12. GENETICS 442

13. BREEDING·YOUR CHOW CHOW 444
The Health of the Breeding Stock. . . The Day of the Mating. . . How Much Does the Stud Fee Cost?. . . The Actual Mating. . . Artificial Insemination. . . The Gestation Period. . . Probing for Puppies. . . Alerting Your Veterinarian. . . Do You Need a Veterinarian in Attendance?. . . Labor. . . The Arrival of the Puppies. . . Feeding the Bitch Between Births. . . Breech Births. . . Dry Births. . . The Twenty-Four-Hour Checkup. . . False Pregnancy. . . Caesarean Section. . . Episiotomy. . . The Power of Pedigrees

14. BREEDING AND NUTRITION 456
Feeding Puppies. . . Weaning the Puppies. . . Feeding the Adult Dog. . . The All Meat Diet Controversy. . . Obesity. . . Orphaned Puppies. . . How to Feed the Newborn Puppies

15. TRAINING YOUR CHOW CHOW 466
When to Start Training. . . The Reward Method. . . How Long Should the Lessons Be? . . . What You Need to Start Training. . . What to Teach First. . . The "Down" Command. . . The "Stay" Command. . . The Stand for Examination. . . Formal School Training. . . Advanced Training and Obedience Trials

16. THE CHOW CHOW IN OBEDIENCE 474

17. SHOWING YOUR CHOW CHOW 482
Match Shows. . . The Point Shows. . . The Prize Ribbons and What They Stand For. . . Qualifying for Championship. . . Obedience Trials. . . Junior Showmanship Competition. . . Dog Show Photographers. . . Two Types of Dog Shows. . . Benched or Unbenched Dog Shows. . . Professional Handlers. . . Do You Really Need a Handler? . . . The Cost of Campaigning a Dog With a Handler

18. TOP-WINNING CHOW CHOWS AND THEIR RECORDS 496
Partial List of Chow Chow Winners at Westminster. . . The Chow Chow Club's Specialty Winners. . . Top Ten Chow Chows—1960-1973

19. GENERAL CARE AND MANAGEMENT 506
Tattooing. . . Outdoor Housebreaking. . . Other Important Outdoor Manners. . . Geriatrics. . . Dog Insurance. . . The High Cost of Burial. . . In the Event of Your Death. . . Keeping Records

20. THE BLIGHT OF PARASITES 513
Internal Parasites

21. YOUR DOG, YOUR VETERINARIAN AND YOU 519
Aspirin: A Danger. . . What the Thermometer Can Tell You. . . Coprophagy. . . Masturbation. . . Rabies. . . Vaccinations. . . Snakebite. . . Emergencies. . . The First Aid Kit. . . How Not to Poison Your Dog. . . Symptoms of Poisoning. . . The Curse of Allergy. . . Do All Dogs Chew?. . . Bones. . . Hip Dysplasia. . . Elbow Dysplasia. . . Patella Dysplasia. . . HD Program in Great Britain. . . The Unites States Registry

22. PURSUING A CAREER IN DOGS 550
Part-Time Kennel Work. . . Professional Handlers. . . Dog Training. . . Grooming Parlors. . . The Pet Shop. . . Dog Judging. . . Miscellaneous

23. CHOW-MANIA 559
About Birgit Nilsson and "Little Louie". . . Virginia Woolf and Chows. . . Georgia O'Keeffe visits the Chows in Monroe. . . From Our Nostalgia Department. . . How to Photograph a Chow Correctly

APPENDIX 574

INDEX

Dedication

To my beloved parents,
Samuel Brice Draper and
Mary Lee Dukeminier Draper
who love all God's creatures,
and especially my Chow Chows!
S.D.

and

To Robert R. Shomer, V.M.D.,
incomparable veterinarian,
extraordinary human being,
unforgettable friend,
who shared many happy years with
his devoted Chow San-Kee Sineath.
J.B.

Acknowledgments

The authors wish to express their deep appreciation to Percy Whitaker, the most outstanding Chow Chow authority in England, whose unparalleled experience and knowledge made possible the chapter on the Chow Chow in Britain, and likewise their thanks to Henk van der Wouw of van Mongolie Kennels in the Netherlands, whose scholarly thoroughness as well as unlimited knowledge was responsible for the chapter on the Continental Chow Chow. Their contribution will serve as an undying monument to their painstaking industry and eternal love of the Chow Chow. The authors' words are insufficient to express their gratitude to these eminent authorities.

They wish to thank Mrs. Georgia King, founder and editor for many years of *The American Chow Chow*, and certainly the leading Chow authority in the United States today; Mrs. King's support is much appreciated for the countless ways she assisted us. . . a photo needed here, a fact or record needed there, a never-failing response when help was sought. She provided much of the statistical background for the chapter on the "Top Ten" Chow Chows. And her encouragement was always an inspiration.

To Joel and June Marston and Clif and Vivian Shryock, who were supportive and assisting in the gathering of material both old and new, the authors express their thanks.

The authors are grateful to all concerned in regard to the Greenacre contribution. Without the specific assistance of Mrs. Sally Beneville and Mr. and Mrs. Ormond Deignan, the Greenacre Kennels of Mrs. E.K. Lincoln, Mrs. Beneville's mother, would not have been represented as well as it should be. Greenacre was one of the illustrious and most important kennels of the early days.

While mentioning important kennels of the past, the authors wish to thank Mr. Ralph Hellum of Mrs. David Wagstaff's famous Ledgelands' Kennels in Tuxedo Park, New York. Mr. Hellum put at the authors' disposal all of his scrapbooks and clippings of 30 or more years at Ledgelands'.

They wish to single out also Miss Kathleen Staples, who gave them several important photos of her Chows and those of Mrs. L.W. Bonney, with whom she was associated for so many years at Tally-Ho. Had it not been for the generosity of Dr. JoAnne Schmidt O'Brien and Dr. Imogene Earle, the Linnchow Kennels of the early days and some photos belonging to the late Agripinna Anderson, given to Dr. Earle, would not have appeared. And the authors appreciate the cooperation of Mr. and Mrs. Howard Kendall, Mrs. Hazel Grey and Mrs. Madaline Ferguson for their assistance in preparing the history and photographs of the early days in California.

Thanks to Mr. H. Kenneth Stine for pertinent information about Dr. and Mrs. A.V. Hallowell, important breeders, and to Miss Iris de la Torre Bueno for newspaper clippings concerning some early Chow Chows. And, of course, special thanks to Robert R. Shomer, V.M.D. for expert counsel through the years for which co-author Joan Brearley attributes the good health of the occupants of her Sahadi Kennels over the decades. Dr. Shomer has been for many years a Chow Chow owner and admirer of the breed.

The authors wish to thank Mr. John Peter de Meritt, connoisseur of art and world traveler, for occasioning one of the greatest pieces of good fortune we've had, the small Egyptian statue of two Chow Chows (based on a Chinese drawing) shared as a gift with Dr. Draper and presented especially for inclusion in this book. How can one properly thank the owner of such a sumptuous gift? The National Gallery of Art, Washington, D.C., must be mentioned for sending the valuable reproduction *The Dog,* which was a gift to the National Gallery from Edgar William and Bernice Chrysler Barbisch for inclusion in this book.

Thanks also to Miss June Goldsborough for her unique drawings of the Chow Chow; the authors wish to express special gratitude for such works of art. Also they wish to mention how enthusiastic Miss Goldsborough became about the breed as she worked with so many friendly and beautiful Chows to accomplish her art work. To Mrs. Sharon Breitweiser for her impeccable typing of much of the manuscript and to Desmond Murphy for the reading of proof, the authors offer sincere thanks.

Also we wish to mention and acknowledge with thanks the cooperation of the Canadian Chowists, especially for the assistance of Mr. and Mrs. Herbert Williams and Mr. John C. Frederick Peddie of Toronto for all they did to encourage the book. And to Don Drennan and Bob and Jean Hetherington for their aid in many ways. For assistance in preparing the chapter on Westminster Winners, the authors thank the charming and efficient Miss Lucette Savoie, Secretary to the Committee of the Westminster Kennel Club. To Irene Castle Phillips Khatoonian, dogdom's distinguished scholar and expert on purebred dog statistics, we owe a special debt of gratitude for her research on certain facts needed to complete the section on the "Top Ten" Chows.

Without the expert knowledge and practical experience of Prudence Baxter, the chapter on the Chow Chow in Obedience would not have been as complete, and for the encouragement and assistance of Colonel Gerald Sterling and his lovely wife Lucile, both ardent Chowists for many years, the authors' task would have been more arduous.

Professor Draper wishes to thank his academic colleague and friend, Dan Masterson, the poet, a light in many lives, who was so encouraging during the three years of preparing this book.

To Harry M. Blackmer, of Athens, Greece, the authors are especially indebted for his presentation to them of one of the most interesting curios in the history of the Chow Chow in western culture, a copy of *The Memoires of Chi-Chi the Chow,* written for Chi-Chi himself with the help of his mistress, Mrs. E. Berry Wall, who in Mr. Blackmer's copy wrote a few words to Mr. Blackmer's grandfather's wife, the well-known Norwegian opera singer Eide Norena, a friend of the Walls and of Chi-Chi.

The authors also wish to acknowledge their appreciation to Alexander C. Schwartz, Jr. for his excellent photographs of the proper way to groom a Chow Chow.

Certainly the authors wish to express their gratitude to all the many Chow breeders, fanciers and exhibitors who believed in *The Book of the Chow Chow* from the very beginning and who shared their knowledge and precious photographs with us to help make this book the informative and valuable "bible" to all of us who love the Chow Chow.

About the Authors

SAMUEL DRAPER

Sam Draper grew up in Modesto, California, in the middle of the great San Joaquin Valley, where land, crops and animals are important. At the Drapers' place in the country there were always several cats, an occasional horse, chickens, rabbits, pigeons, hogs now and then, and from 1936 on Cairn Terriers and other pure-bred dogs.

When Sam enrolled at the University of California at Berkeley after he had come back from World War II, he took with him his last Cairn, Champion Credheil, called "Cree," who was very popular among the campus undergraduates and thoroughly enjoyed life as a freshman as much as Sam did!

After graduation from the University of California at Los Angeles in 1950, Sam began to raise and show Cocker Spaniels, as he was unsuccessful in his attempts over a period of years to purchase a Chow Chow with an excellent show potential. He had seen his first Chow at a neighbor's in Modesto in the 1930's and has been intrigued by the breed ever since. Sam believes his interest in dogs was fulfilled when his long search for a Chow Chow ended with the acquisition of Ch. Ah Sid the Avant Garde in 1965. Since then there have been many Chows, including a co-ownership of Ch. Eastward Liontamer of Elster; owning "Louie" with Bob and Jean Hetherington has represented a life-long desire—to own a truly great show dog and sire.

After teaching in college for four years, Sam began his doctoral studies at Columbia University in New York City in 1957. Sam lived in Brussels and Paris during 1959 and '60, where he studied the life and drama of the superb Belgian playwright Michel de Ghelderode in preparation for Sam's translations of *The Strange Rider and Seven Other Plays by Ghelderode*, published in 1964. Sam is still working on a biography of the Belgian author. While in Europe, Sam attended many dog

shows and visited many kennels housing various breeds. He thought the Continental Chows were magnificent.

Sam has taught English and comparative European literature at Columbia, Manhattanville and the University of California at Berkeley, and since 1971 he has been a full Professor of English at Rockland Community College, State University of New York, Suffern, N.Y., where he is in charge of English 220-221, Honors Literature Seminar. He has also lectured at Princeton, the University of Texas, Yale, Harvard and the University of Michigan.

In the 1974 edition of *The Dictionary of International Biography*, the entry concerning Dr. Draper includes not only all his academic accomplishments but also his interest in opera (co-founder of the Kirsten Flagstad Memorial Collection in San Francisco and co-chairman of the Committee for the Kirsten Flagstad Commemorative Plaque at the new Metropolitan Opera House, New York City) and Sam's fascination with abstract painting (patron of the Modern Museum of Art in New York City).

JOAN McDONALD BREARLEY

Joan Brearley has loved animals ever since she was old enough to know what they were. . .

Over the years there has been a constant succession of dogs, cats, birds, fish, rabbits, snakes, turtles, alligators, squirrels, lizards, etc., for her own personal menagerie. Through these same years she has owned over thirty different breeds of pure-bred dogs, as well as countless mixtures, since the door was never closed to a needy or homeless animal.

A graduate of the American Academy of Dramatic Arts, Joan started her career as a writer for movie magazines, actress and dancer. She also studied journalism at Columbia University and has been a radio, television and magazine writer, writing for some of the major New York City agencies. She was also a television producer-director for a major network on such shows as *Nick Carter, Master Detective*, and she has written, cast, directed, produced and, on occasions, starred in television film commercials. She has written material for such personalities as Dick Van Dyke, Bill Stern, Herman Hickman, Dione Lucas, Amy Vanderbilt and many others prominent in the entertainment world.

Her accomplishments in the dog fancy include being an American Kennel Club approved judge, breeder-exhibitor of top show dogs, writer for various dog magazines, author of many breed books including *This is the Afghan Hound, This is the Shih Tzu, This is the St. Bernard, This is the Bichon Frise, This is the Old English Sheepdog, This is the Siberian Husky* and many others. For five years she was Executive Vice-President of the Popular Dogs Publishing Company and editor of *Popular Dogs* magazine, the national prestige publication for the dog fancy at that time.

Joan Brearley is just as active in the cat fancy, and in almost all the same capacities. She is editor of the Cat Fanciers Association Annual Yearbook and writes for

the various cat magazines as well. Joan Brearley speaks at kennel clubs and humane organizations on animal legislation and has received many awards and citations for her work in the field, including an award from the Morris Animal Foundation.

At present Joan lives in a penthouse apartment overlooking Manhattan in New York City with three dogs and a dozen or more cats, all of which are Best in Show winners and have been professional models for television and magazines. Joan is proud of the fact that in her first litter of Afghan Hounds she bred a Westminster Kennel Club Group winner, Champion Sahadi (her kennel prefix) Shikari, the top-winning Afghan Hound in the history of the breed.

In addition to her activities in the world of animals, Joan Brearley is a movie buff and spends time at the art and auction galleries, the theatre, creating needlepoint (for which she has also won awards), dancing, the typewriter—and the zoo!

The King! English Champion Ukwong King Solomon wears his crown well! Solly is one of the most important all-breed winners in England! He was named England's Top Dog of the Year for 1971 and 1972, and in 1974 he became the all-breed Champion Certificate record holder when he captured his 63rd C.C. at the Three Counties show. Percy Whitaker had the very great honor of handling King Solomon on the auspicious occasion when he broke the record. Solly is owned by Joan and Eric Egerton.

1. ORIGIN OF THE CHOW CHOW

Scientific research indicates that the Chow Chow originated in China as long as 3,000 years ago, according to some canine historians. On the other hand, some scholars believe that the Chow came first from the Arctic Circle and then migrated to Mongolia, Siberia and China. The American Kennel Club's publication *The Complete Dog Book* (1972) states that the Chow came about through a crossing of the old Mastiff of Tibet and the Samoyed from the northern parts of Siberia. However, other scholars claim that the Chow was the original ancestor of the Samoyed, the Norwegian Elkhound, the Pomeranian and the Keeshond.

However, the following datum has been agreed on universally: the Chow as it is known today is easily recognizable in pottery and bas-relief sculpture of the Han Dynasty (206 B.C. to 220 A.D.); this period was marked by bureaucratic monarchy, a revival of letters and the introduction of Buddhism. It is said to be the era in which modern China was born. Other artifacts indicate that the Chow was a distinct breed in China as early as 1000 B.C., a conservative estimate, certainly.

Two distinct theories exist concerning the name Chow Chow. The word *chow* or *chou* is a slang Chinese word meaning edible. The short-haired or smooth Chow is more usually eaten in China than the long-coated variety. According to one authority, both the Chinese and the Koreans have bred Chows to be eaten in place of lamb or mutton.

A British historian, an authority on China, visited Canton in 1878 and reported that he had counted about twenty-five restaurants that specialized in the delicacy of Chow meat. The public buying and sel-ling of Chow meat was prohibited by law in China in 1915. Dr. Margaret Mead has written that dog meat was eaten as a delicacy by many different peoples, including the American Indian.

Will Judy wrote in his memorable work *The Chow Chow* the following concerning the Chow's name: "The breed was commonly described not as the chow, but as the edible dog of China. However, as the

This Chinese statue of the Chow Chow is estimated to be over 3,000 years old. Fu dogs, as the statues are called, are usually sold in pairs, and there are thousands of variations on the theme.

An outstanding Chow, Champion Win Sum Min T'Sing, bred by Franklin Hutton of Win Sum Kennels, Long Island, New York. Mr. Hutton had earlier imported Min T'Sing's sire, English Champion Ackum, who became a foundation sire of Win Sum Kennels. Min T'Sing himself became the most important and influential sire of the early period in U.S. Chow history. In 1915 Mr. Hutton sold Min T'Sing to Mr. and Mrs. E.C. Waller. Min T'Sing was the father of several important champions, including Ch. Clairedale Son Too, likewise a valuable sire. If one Chow of the early days in America should be singled out as the greatest who had the most influence, it would be Min T'Sing.

word chow means food in English, and as at one time the trade in spices and mixed pickles was known as chow chow, the chinaman himself was alluded to by Europeans as a Chow or Chink. Any Chinese commodity was called chow. Therefore, it was natural that in time the edible dog of China acquired the name of Chow Chow."

Another theory has also been put forth, perhaps not as logical or as scholarly as the concept about the Chow's being edible. Nevertheless, it should be reported. In the early 1800's when the clipper ships sailed regularly from England to China, the hold of the ship where miscellaneous objects were stored was called the "chow chow" hold, chow chow meaning bits and pieces of this and that, or the general miscellany. When the Oriental dog was first brought to England in the 1830's, he made the trip in the "chow chow" hold because he had no usual or regular quarters. Eventually, the dog took on the name of the place where he had lived for several months on the sea voyage from **China**.

In reading a book on the Chinese breeds (Pekingese, Chow Chow, Pug, Shih Tzu and Lhasa Apso) the authors discovered that the experts on the Pekingese, Shih Tzu and Lhasa were very quick to point out that their breeds were the "Royal Dogs of China" and that the Chow Chow was relegated to a somewhat more plebian environment and use. The Chow Chow, admittedly, was the only native Chinese "hunting dog." Before the Chinese used firearms for hunting, the Chow was essential as a "retriever" or even a "pointer." (Those of you well familiar with the breed have seen a Chow "point" in his own inimitable fashion.) Indeed, the Chow is an outdoor dog capable of great stamina, a dog that can hunt and even pull a sled. He was also used as a cattle dog for tending sheep and cows. One should constantly keep in mind the original purpose for which the Chow was originally bred and used. He is an outdoor dog with enough size and power to work, and he must have enough leg and rear drive to make his way through the snow as if pulling a sled or hunting.

However, one does admit that the show Chow of today is much more a product of what happened to the Chow in England and later in the United States than he is of his original heritage.

A figurine from the Han Dynasty clearly depicting the image of a Chow Chow dog. The figurine is on display in the Berlin Museum.

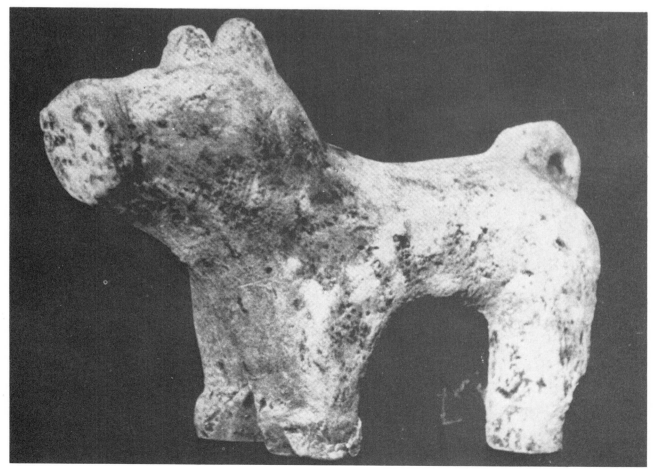

A hanging scroll in ink and color on silk titled *Palace Concert* dating back to 937-975 A.D. of ten court ladies and two maids making music and drinking. A Chow Chow sleeps under the table. The artist is anonymous, and the work can be attributed to the Southern T'ang period of Chinese art.

Below: A detail from the *Palace Concert* scroll clearly showing a dog of the Chow Chow type asleep under the table. Photo courtesy of Percy Whitaker, England.

Opposite—

This little figurine of two Chow Chows in the act of copulation, perhaps the rarest and most unexpected pictorial treasure of the entire book, is a truly lucky find. Authenticated by Pierre Laport, Paris, registered French antiquities expert, as an Egyptian piece of terra cotta based on a Chinese drawing, it was made in Egypt in the Roman period between the second and third centuries A.D. The figurine is co-owned by John Peter de Meritt, Paris and Athens, and Dr. Samuel Draper, co-author of this book. Mr. de Meritt bought the statuette in Egypt and presented it to Dr. Draper as a gift. Of enormous value, it will eventually be presented to a museum. Photo by Studio Marion-Valentine, Paris.

2. THE COMING OF AGE OF THE CHOW CHOW IN THE WESTERN WORLD

Although France and England had shown considerable fascination with "things Oriental" —Chinese porcelain, rugs, jewelry, painting—in the 18th century, the Chow Chow did not make its appearance in Western Europe until very late in the 18th century and in greater numbers in the early part of the 19th century. The "Chinoiserie" of the 1700's in England had awakened a profound fascination with China so that the Chow Chow, the Chinese Dog, was heralded with enthusiasm when the breed first arrived about 1780 and later in 1820, brought from China by the clipper ships.

The first reliable allusion to the Chow Chow was made in *The Natural History of Selborne in the County of Southampton* by the Rev. Gilbert White, born in Welborne, Hants, England in 1720, dying there in 1793. This astonishing book is made up of a series of letters to two gentlemen, Thomas Pennant, Esquire, and the Honourable Daines Barrington, concerning many birds and beasts that the author had seen. In the index to his work, he lists Letter LVIII **(58)** under "D" — Dogs, *Chinese* from *Canton*. This historical antiquity is addressed to the Honourable Daines Barrington and is quoted here almost in its entirety.

"LETTER LVIII"

"My near neighbour, a young gentleman in the service of the *East-India* Company, has brought home a dog and a bitch of the *Chinese* breed from *Canton*; such as are fattened in that country for the purpose of being eaten: they are about the size of a moderate spaniel; of a pale yellow colour, with coarse bristling hairs on their backs; sharp upright ears, and peaked heads, which give them a very fox-like appearance. Their hind legs are unusually straight, without any bend at the hock or ham, to such a degree as to give them an awkward gait when they trot. When they are in motion, their tails are curved high over their backs like those of some hounds, and have a bare place each on the outside from the tip midway, that does not seem to be matter of accident, but somewhat singular. Their eyes are jet-black, small and piercing; the insides of their lips and mouths of the same colour, and their tongues blue. The bitch has a dew-claw on each hind leg; the dog has none. When taken out into a field the bitch showed some disposition for hunting, and dwelt on the scent of a covey of partridges till she sprung them, giving her tongue all the time. The dogs in *South America* are dumb; but these bark much in a short thick manner, like foxes; and have a surly, savage demeanour like their ancestors, which are not domesticated, but bred up in sties, where they are fed for the table with rice-meal and other farinaceous food. These dogs, having been taken on board as soon as weaned, could not learn much from their dam; yet they did not relish flesh when they came to *England*. In the islands of the *Pacific* ocean the dogs are bred up on vegetables, and would not eat flesh when offered them by our circumnavigators."

"We believe that all dogs, in a state of nature, have sharp, upright fox-like ears; and that hanging ears, which are esteemed so graceful, are the effect of choice breeding and cultivation. Thus in the Travels of *Ysbrandt Ides* from *Muscovy* to *China*, the dogs which draw the *Tartars* on snow-sledges near the river *Oby* are engraved with prick-ears, like those from *Canton*. . ."

"Now we are upon the subject of dogs, it may not be impertinent to add, that spaniels, as all sportsmen know, though they hunt partridges and pheasants as it were by instinct, and with much delight and alacrity, yet will hardly touch their bones when offered as food; nor will a mongrel dog of my own, though he is remarkable for finding that sort of game. But when we came to offer the bones of partridges to the two *Chinese* dogs, they devoured them with much greediness, and licked the platter clean. . ."

No further occidental record appears to exist concerning the Chow dog and bitch referred to by the Rev. White; perhaps they were not bred or did not desire to mate since they were in a strange land.

Some forty years later than the references by the Rev. White, an English newspaper account of May, 1820 concerned with exotic wild animals imported from China, Japan and India mentions an oriental dog that has a thick red coat and a blue-black tongue which attracted widespread attention. Some early reports of the Chow in England mention that several Chows were housed in the London Zoological Gardens and were identified as "the wild dog" of China, exotica like the monkeys, snakes and parrots.

It is known that Queen Victoria was given a Chow Chow about 1865, a Chow imported from China; Lytton Strachey, an eminent authority on the life of Queen Victoria, mentions the Chow along with many other pets of Her Majesty, including several Skye Terriers, but he does not use the Chow's name.

None of the major biographers of Queen Victoria deals with the story concerning the "Teddy Bear" theory. It was said that Victoria loved the Chow puppy, its cuddly quality and its "stuffed doll" appearance so that several courtiers had a dressmaker design and sew a stuffed Chow puppy as a gift to her. That plaything pleased the Queen immensely and became known finally not as the Chow Dog or Bear, but the "Teddy Bear." Probably apocryphal, the anecdote nevertheless lives on because Chow puppies are even cuter than teddy bears. They are unique.

All reliable extant sources agree on the date of the commencement of Chow history in England: 1880. In that year, Chinese Puzzle, a black Chow bitch, was exhibited at the Crystal Palace show in London. Her weight was thirty-two pounds

Queen Victoria and Prince Albert are shown here with some of the Queen's Skye Terriers in this portion of Landseer's famous *Windsor Castle in Modern Times.* The painting was made about 1840.

R.M. Moore's rendition of Peridot, owned by Lady Granville Gordon and daughter, Lady Faudel Phillips. The black dog in the portrait is Ch. Blue Blood.

and her height sixteen inches at the shoulder. Her owner was W.K. Taunton. But it was the Marchioness of Huntley who was the pioneer of the breed in England. In the late 1880's (one source says 1887, one 1888), she imported a male who she called Periodot. From a union of one of her bitches with Periodot (also called Peridot, in fact sometimes spelled that way by Lady Faudel Phillips herself), she bred Periodot II, whom Lady Granville Gordon bought and with whom she established a celebrated Chow kennel. Lady Gordon's daughter, Lady Faudel Phillips, became the leading breeder and exhibitor in England until about 1898.

According to Will Judy, "...the first Chow to be recorded in the English Kennel Club Stud Book was recorded in 1894. In July 1895, the English Chow Chow Club was organized and from this date, the modern history of the Chow begins. The first show held by the club was in 1895 at Westminster in London. In the following year 1896, the Kennel Club in England granted Challenge Certificates for the breed. The first challenge or Championship Certificates were won by the imported male Blue Blood owned by Lady Granville Gordon, and by the home bred bitch Blue Bell, owned by W.H.R. Temple."

"The great patriarch of the Chows was Chow VIII," Judy goes on to say, "imported in 1895 by Miss Bagshaw. Many consider him the supreme model. The only fault was perhaps the large round eyes. Chow VIII, exhibited in 1897, was offered in the catalog at a hundred guineas and sold—the highest price ever paid for a Chow to that time. He soon became a famous champion and his get carried on his record."

Some of the Chows imported in the early period to England were: Yum Yum, Ah Wang, Chinese Junk, Kaio, Ah Wonk, Mighty Atom, Princess Tung, Black Bess, Ah Woo, Kei Tan, Ching Foo, Ah Sin Woo, Pekoe II and Ruddigore.

Premier Ch. Chow VIII, imported to England from China by Miss Bagshaw in 1895.

This 8-week-old puppy, Ch. Psawanli, was born in 1924 and owned by Mr. H. Routledge of England.

3. THE HISTORY OF THE CHOW CHOW IN GREAT BRITAIN

As early as the 1860's a few Chow Chows had arrived in England. These unusual-looking dogs came to England via various ship captains and voyagers who brought them back with them from their visits to the Far East. We know the Chow Chow is a very ancient breed and possesses qualities, such as the blue tongue, evident in no other breed. While those early English dogs certainly did not totally resemble the Chow Chow as we know it today, they did bear many of the characteristics that unmistakably identified them as Chows and established the fact that they had come from the Orient.

Breedings in their native land could hardly have been regarded as being pure. The Chows had more than likely mixed with the Pi dog, a much lighter and somewhat smaller dog which was purebred for centuries to protect the dwellings in the hills of China. The Pi dogs, like other oriental breeds, were not sold, but on occasion they were given as gifts to visiting dignitaries of great importance. It was in this manner that they found their way to the cities along the China seacoasts, where they were crossbred with the Chow Chows and found their way into the hands of seafaring men who took them to other parts of the world.

By 1880, therefore, some relatively good-looking specimens were getting themselves known and admired in England; as a result, the first attempts at serious breeding began. Additional stock continued to come to England via the wealthy travelers and diplomats as world travel became more common and as the popularity of the breed began to spread.

The first, and perhaps most memorable, Chow Chow devotee was Lord Hugh, Earl of Lonsdale. He was well known for his round-the-world travels and possessed a keen interest in the breeding of animals of all kinds, including horses, cattle, pigeons, dogs, etc. His name soon became synonymous with all forms of livestock.

It is a matter of record in the annals of Chow Chow history that on one of his many visits to the Far East, he was presented with what was said to be a purebred specimen of the breed. At that time it was known in China as the Chou Chou, the edible dog. As unpleasant as it may be to most to think of eating dog flesh, it must be remembered that since earliest times man has eaten, as well as domesticated and worked with, animals, and the dog was no exception. Almost all of the ancient cookbooks contained recipes for dog meat, and our "chubby Chinamen" must have been particularly good eating.

It must also be recognized that even today, around the world, dog meat is eaten. During the World Wars it was a common practice all over Europe, and it still occurs today in the starving nations of the Orient. Dog meat is sold quite openly in Chinese butcher shops, and returning servicemen stationed in the Orient will attest to the fact that it was not safe to leave a dog in the backyard unwatched!

Upon his return to England with this delightful "edible dog," the Earl of Lonsdale presented his Chow Chow to his relatives, the Marquis and Marchioness of Huntley. The dog created quite a stir within their family. Plans were immediately put underway to bring back more of these dogs for breeding purposes on the Earl's very next trip. Despite complications this was done, and breeding within this aristocratic English family began in earnest.

Ch. Blue Blood, born in 1892, was owned by Lady Faudel Phillips of England.

Some of the Chow Chows found their way to other members of their family who became interested also in breeding. Lord and Lady Granville Gordon began a serious breeding program. Lady Granville Gordon, a beautiful woman, did much to popularize this rare breed. Her interest was later shared by her equally beautiful daughter, Miss Armyne Gordon, and it was they who produced the first English-bred champion male Chow Chow. This was the blue dog Ch. Blue Blood. While he was bred from red stock, he obviously carried the genes of the much prized blue hue, found in only small numbers even in China.

Miss Gordon, later to become Lady Faudel Phillips, inherited all her parents' Chows upon their demise and formed the celebrated Amwell Chow Chow Kennel, which continued to breed these dogs for

over 50 years and with a few other kennels played an important part in the history of the breed, shaping its destiny for all time.

The Amwell Kennel was managed from 1919 until the day Lady Faudel Phillips died by Percy Whitaker, who inherited all her trophies, most of her dogs, five massive volumes of photographs and records including thousands of articles and reviews on the history and progress of the Chow Chow the world over. These date from 1883 until her death in 1943. It is these records which are relied on here and the cooperation of Mr. Whitaker to whom the authors are eternally grateful for this chapter on the breed in Britain.

The Earl of Lonsdale, or "the sporting Earl" as he was popularly known, was a keen Chow Chow enthusiast also until the day of his death. He was a frequent visitor to Lady Faudel Phillips' estate and spent

Ch. Pei-Woong of Amwell, born in 1919, was owned by Lady Faudel Phillips of England.

much of his time at the kennels with Percy Whitaker giving freely of his most knowledgeable opinions on the breeding progress of the Chow Chows. Mr. Whitaker tells us that it was the Earl of Lonsdale who was the first to proclaim that the Chow Chow would get to be heavier in build as time went on. Today we do have a sturdier, heavier-boned Chow Chow, just as he predicted.

In addition to the Lonsdale belts given as boxing awards, the Earl shall forever be remembered in Chow Chow history for the presentation of the Lonsdale Trophy, a massive silver and gilt replica of a Chow Chow which is in the possession of the Chinese Chow Club. On the base are inscribed words to the effect that in the event that the Chinese Chow Club became defunct,

the trophy would be returned to the Earl's heirs or successors. What its value would be today is undetermined, but at the time of its initiation it was appraised at 600 pounds, or about three thousand dollars at the then-prevailing rate of exchange. It is for many reasons the most prized trophy in the Chow Chow world.

With the breed in the hands of the British titled and wealthy, (who could well afford the expenses of breeding and the hiring of capable and experienced people to care for their dogs) the Chow Chow began to grow in number and popularity. The first Chow Chow club was formed in 1896 and recognized by The Kennel Club. But before that, on July 1, 1895, a meeting was held in London with Mr. W. Temple in the chair, and other devotees of the breed such as Lady Granville Gordon, her daughter Armyne Gordon, Mrs. Arthur James, Mrs. Fitswilliam, Mrs. Burgess, Mr. and Mrs. Janvrin Dickson, Miss Ella Casella, and Mrs. Onken who came together to call to order their first meeting. On this same day a scale of points was drawn up which has lasted, with only the slightest amendments to this very day. While the Standard was vague in some respects, it has maintained the breed over the years in good order.

For some years prior to the formation of this club, dogs of "Chow-like description" had been seen in the show rings, but the first mention of a Chow Chow which adhered to the Standard was the bitch named Chinese Puzzle, referred to in the preceding chapter. This dog had been im-

ported directly from China by a Mr. W. Temple, who later became known as a foreign dog expert. By 1890, just a decade later, over 200 Chows—or what were said to be true specimens—had been registered in the Stud Book. Many others were bred and shown, of course, but for lack of merit were not included in the Stud Book.

Until 1893 these dogs competed in classes for foreign dogs, but in 1893 the first class for Chow Chows was scheduled. At the London Aquarium on December 10 and 11, 1895, the Chow Club Show had 54 present. In one of Lady Faudell Phillips' scrapbooks there is the actual silk ribbon and prize card won by her Chow Chow Periodot II as Best in Show at the Ladies Kennel Club championship show held at Ranelagh on June 8, 1895. This was the

Ch. Pusa of Amwell, born in 1912 and owned by Lady Faudel Phillips of England. Photographed by Thomas Fall of London.

first recorded really big win at a show with the Chow Chow competing against all breeds. However, the biggest winner at the time was the famous Ch. Chow VIII, a red dog on which it is said the Standard of Points was drawn up in England.

Chow VIII was an imported dog and had several owners during his career. According to written reports he was of good type and build though somewhat lacking in profuse coat. He was also a "maneater," according to Percy Whitaker. Various references to this unfortunate trait appear in the reports of the Chow shows, with some judges reporting that he could not be handled by them at all. Some of the judges put him down for this, but most of them put him up in spite of it, recognizing his great merit. His tendency to bite is also believed to be one of the reasons for the dog's changing owners so often during his lifetime. However, it did not discourage one of them from paying 100 pounds for him.

Jack Holgate handled Chow VIII for various owners during his show ring career and attests to how "difficult" he was to handle. He was at stud at Holgate's Kennel at Hook in Surrey for many years, and while he did sire one champion, his influence on the breed cannot be said to be as significant as his show record. It was this same Jack Holgate who later became a top judge of all breeds, judging all over the world, and was the agent and "go-between" in the sale of many famous dogs.

While Ch. Chow VIII was the first Chow Chow champion in England, the first English-bred Chow Chow champion was Ch. Blue Blood. A blue bitch, Ch. Leyswood Blue Bell, became the first bitch champion. The first red champion bitch was Ch. T'ien, owned by Miss Ella Casella. She was not only a highly respected lady, but also one of the best-loved of all Chow Chow owners and knew more than most of her generation about the breed.

Miss Casella resided in an apartment in London, near Hyde Park, so she could never keep more than one or two Chows at a time, but her advice was sought by many of the older breeders and newcomers alike. It was from Miss Casella and Lady Faudel

Phillips that Percy Whitaker gleaned much of his knowledge of the breed, and he is about the only one today still active in the Chow Chow breed who reaped the benefits of this valuable link with the past and early beginnings of the breed in England.

It was about the time when Ch. Chow VIII was causing such a stir in the show ring that another dog came along and created also quite a furor. At a Ranelagh championship show a judge faulted Mr. Bosco II, a well-known winner who had always been shown in "any other colour" classes. This bronze or off-red dog was said to have been fully of type and well made; he had defeated a great number of excellent dogs, including Ch. Chow VIII. But at this particular show, the judge disqualified him for "not being whole coloured." This action quite naturally raised a storm of comment, and the matter of his color was brought before the Committee of the Chow Chow Club. They decided that the dog could not be shown again. This was the only time such an occurrence had taken place in England, although another color controversy came up in the 1900's and

Ch. Pu An of Amwell, black dog born in 1924, owned by Lady Faudel Phillips.

caused such dissent in the breed that the effects of it can still be felt today.

From about 1906 on, the flashy light reds with almost white breechings began to make their appearance, and then, as now, they were full of quality and type. When in full bloom, there is no denying that they do catch the eye. But the "dark red, and nothing but dark red" enthusiasts protested and for many years held sway, with the dark reds doing most of the winning. They won on color over quality at times, much to the distress of the true Chow lovers. Since the reds had shorter legs and shorter leg hair, these traits can still be seen in some of the

Ch. Yung Cheng of Amwell, born in 1931, was owned by Lady Faudel Phillips of England.

Ch. Hildewell Chincherinchee, owned by Lady Faudel Phillips of England, was born in 1922.

25

Ch. You Si, a blue Chow Chow born in 1934 and owned by Lady Faudel Phillips, England.

Eastern Saga of Kut Sang, a winning daughter of the famous Wong Tung dog owned by Lady B. Royle of England.

Lee Wu, Best of Breed at the 1926 Crufts show in England. Owned by Lady Faudel Phillips.

Ch. Chang Fu of Amwell, a British winner born in 1925.

Ch. Peng T'Se of Amwell, born in 1928 and owned by Lady Faudel Phillips of England.

Ch. Li Chin of Amwell, dam of Champions Yung Cheng and Pu Yi of Amwell, winning British dogs.

Chow Chows of today, and not just in England, and are a direct result of this controversy.

In 1898 a Mrs. Scaramanga returned to England after a long stay in India and brought with her a black male Chow Chow named Hak Kwhy. He won his first certificate on his second appearance in the show ring and won a total of 14 C.C.'s during his ring career. He was the first of many top Chow Chows with the Kwhy kennel name for Mrs. Scaramanga. She made a tremendous impact on the breed with her Ch. Red Craze, who sired two full champions and two other get with C.C.'s. She also owned Ch. Theem Kwhy, Ch. Wiggles, Ch. Fi Fi of Newlands, winner of 18 C.C.'s, and Ch. Foo Kwhy. In 1901 Ch. Fu Chow made his debut, and this red import made quite an impression, even though he was a little on the small side. While he himself sired only one champion, and another with a Challenge Certificate he is behind a very dominant line still popular today. He was known for his good eyes and expression, and he had a very hard coat.

The sire of Mrs. Scaramanga's Ch. Red Craze was a very light red dog, Ch. Shylock. Before he came to the United States, he sired three champions and six others which won champion certificates. This line, however, has been over-shadowed by others since that time, though they continued to dominate the scene until about 1911. About this time other outstanding Chows started to appear. For instance, Mrs. F.B. Moore of the Hildewell Kennels presented her Ch. Hildewell Kwong and her Ch. H. Chow. Another name to make headlines was Miss Anna Peck, who showed Ch. Duchess of Nona. Lady Faudel Phillips appeared on the scene and was very successful with her Ch. Papoose, Ch. Queen of Hearts and Ch. Pouchong.

WORLD WAR I CALLS A HALT

1914 brought the outbreak of World War I, and the dog shows came to a resounding halt. All was quiet until 1919, when shows started anew and two outstanding Chow Chows made their bid for fame. One was the black dog Ch. Pusa of Amwell; the other was a red bitch owned by a Mr. Allright, Ch. Pickles. Pickles was by another well-known dog, Ch. Sinbad, and she proved to be his most successful offspring.

Ch. Pusa was bred by Lady Faudel Phillips in 1913. Ch. Pickles was also whelped in 1913, and when she and Pusa were mated in 1919 they produced what was probably the most influential litter up to that time. In this litter were three Chow Chows, each of which set a distinct winning line of its own; these three lines for the most part have lasted up to the present day, not only in England, but abroad as well. There was the red dog Ch. Lemning, the dark red dog Ch. Hildewell Ba-Tang, and the light red bitch Ch. Pei-Woong of Amwell.

Ch. Lemning was the sire of four full champions, and three others of his get were winners of Challenge Certificates. Ch. Hildewell Ba-Tang sired four champions and one other winner of a C.C. Ch. Pickles was the dam of four full champions and one winner of a C.C. This was a record which stood for many years, until after World War II. Ch. Pusa of Amwell was the sire of five full champions and six others which won Challenge Certificates, a record which stood for over 30 years. Challenge Certificates, we remind you, are awarded to the best of each sex at each show.

THE GOLDEN YEARS IN BRITISH CHOWDOM

Following World War I came the Golden Years in Chows, and some truly remarkable dogs from the aforementioned breeding burst into prominence; these Chows will be remembered forever. In 1920 Mr. William Scriven began to show again and met with immediate success with his Mulfras dogs. He will always be recalled for producing dogs with true Chow type and especially good heads and coats. While his dogs might have been small by today's Standard, they were remarkable enough for him to have finished eight champion bitches. He won two of the three required Challenge Certificates with his Mulfra Sar-

Int. Ch. Choonam Brilliantine of Manchoover, the great English and American champion, contributed greatly to today's modern Chow Chow. Originally owned by Mrs. Manooch of the world-famous Choonam Kennels in England, this Chow was sold to Mrs. Earl Hoover in the United States.

Four champion Chow Chows owned by Mrs. Scaramanga. Left to right: Theem Kwhy, Red Craze, Wiggles, Hah-Kwhy. From the painting by Maud Earl.

ahb, a red dog which he had brought back with him after a judging assignment in the United States, one of the few Chow Chows owned by Mr. Scriven which he had not bred.

Until 1925 Ch. Pusa of Amwell and his sons Ch. Ba-Tang and Ch. Lemning had virtually all the wins captured. Only Ch. Foo Kwhy, a black dog, Ch. Kowa Seke and Ch. Ragavarno did any other winning. But late in 1925 a new star appeared on the horizon and was what many considered to be the best Chow dog produced up to that time. It was Miss Anna Peck's Ch. Akbar.

Percy Whitaker was responsible for this dog to a great extent. Akbar's dam, Cheefoo, later a champion in her own right, was sent to Mr. Whitaker to be bred to Ch. Pusa of Amwell. Pusa would not look at Cheefoo, and the choice of an alternative mate was left to Mr. Whitaker. He chose a red dog, Lee Wu, a well-bred dog sired by Ch. Lemning out of Ch. Susan of the East. Lee Wu was awarded the male championship C.C. and Best of Breed at the 1926 Crufts show in London before being sold to Madame Ely in France. While Ch. Akbar created a sensation when he first appeared, he was even better known after siring some of the best Chow Chows seen up to that time. He won 22 championships, placing second only twice. His son Ch. Choonam Brilliantine won seven championships in England before being exported to the United States for a record sum of 1800 pounds, or over 9,000 dollars at the then-existing rate of exchange. His record in the United States in both the show ring and as a sire is told elsewhere in this book and is a matter of Chow Chow history. His litter sister, Ch. Brilliantina, was also a famous Chow Chow, and two other of his offspring were Ch. Chinnery and Ch. Rochow Akbella, described at the time as one of the best ever seen. These last

Mrs. E. Roberts with Ch. Sweet Jadworth at the Bath Championship show in 1932; Percy Whitaker handles Ch. Yung Cheng of Amwell.

Ch. Wan-Li of Amwell with a friend, photographed in England in 1929. Wan-Li was owned by Lady Faudel Phillips of England. On the day this photo was taken, Wan-Li was First in a class of 352 red bitches!

two were owned by Mr. C.D. Rotch, an antique dealer and Chow Chow enthusiast.

Ch. Choonam Brilliantine and Ch. Brilliantina were bred by Mrs. Violet Mannooch, whose kennel prefix (Choonam) is her name spelled almost exactly backwards. She got interested in Chow Chows after observing the dogs of one Johnny Hartwell while living in quarters above his gunsmith's shop. Her first purchase became Ch. The Lotus Flower, a typey bitch although light in bone by today's Standard. She had a wonderful coat and gained a reputation for being put down well. Mrs. Mannooch was to become the biggest-winning owner of her time, having won over

Wigwam of Wu Wang, owned by Lady Faudel Phillips.

Text continues on page 52

Lady Faudel Phillips, a great Chowist, with Ch. Peng Tse of Amwell. Photographed in 1929.

Trophy. Presented by The Earl of Lonsdale
To the Chinese Chow Club. 1911.

CHINESE CHOW CLUB.
"LONSDALE"
CHALLENGE TROPHY.
FOR THE BEST DOG IN THE SHOW.

Won by "Sidonia". Nov: 10. 1915.

From the
Lady Faudel Phillips Scrapbook

Sidonia.

Born June 21. 1911. Shasi of Amwell. Destroyed. June 1918.
Bred by Self. Prizes Won. None.

Blue Battle. A son of Pusa

Blue Battle.

Blue Charm of Amwell.
By Blue Blood of Amwell. Bred by
Self. Prizes won. 1. First only time
shown. Sold to America. For £63

From the
Lady Faudel Phillips Scrapbook

Born March 28. 1905. Ch. Papoose. Died May 9. 1914.

Bred by Mrs Scott. Prizes won. 16 firsts. 5 seconds. 5 Thirds. 9 Specials. 4 Championships.

Born March 28. 1905.   Pouchong. Died Jan: 23. 1915.

Bred by Mrs Scott. Prizes won. 13 firsts. 4 Seconds. 5 Thirds. 10 Specials. 2 Championships.

From the
Lady Faudel Phillips Scrapbook

Lob. Litter by Yong Chang - Ko-Fan. 6 weeks old.

Lob. Born Nov. 19. 1908.

From the
Lady Faudel Phillips Scrapbook

Born July 27-20.   Maru Chow Lo Sing
Bred by Mrs Barragry- Prizes Won.

Born Sept: 10·16. Ch: Su of A. Died Aug: 12·25. Bought for £3·10
      Prizes Won 21 Firsts · 10 Seconds · 9 Thirds 3 Cham-

From the
Lady Faudel Phillips Scrapbook

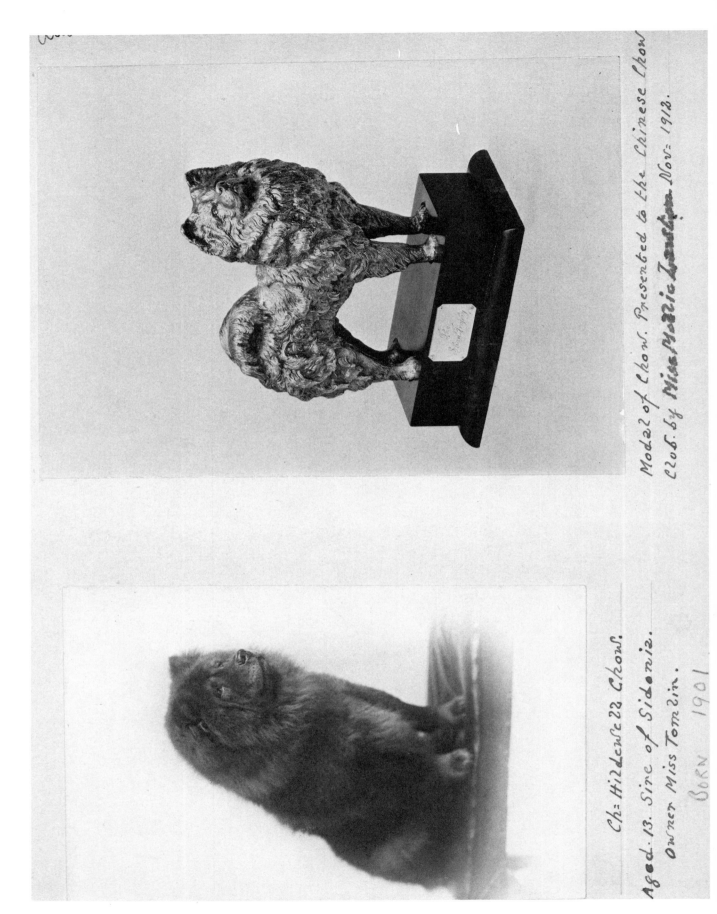

Model of Chow. Presented to the Chinese Chow
Club by Miss Mollie Lambton Nov: 1913.

Ch: Hildense 22 Chow.
Aged. 13. Sire of Sidonia.
Owner Miss Tomlin.

BORN 1901

Born. Jan: 23. 1906.   Poyang. Died June 3. 1914. Boosht for £10.10.
Bred by M⁰ Webb. Prizes won. 20 Firsts. 15 Seconds. 6 Thirds. 7 Specials.

Owned by Lady Faudel Phillips

Born April 7. 1902.   Ch= Queen of Hearts. Died Dec= 8. 1913. Boosht for £31.
Bred by M⁰ Sawbell. Prizes won. 21 Firsts. 10 Seconds. 8 Thirds. 10 specials.
4 Championships— 1 Reserve.

From the
Lady Faudel Phillips Scrapbook

Born. Aug: 11. 1905.   Red Monarch.   Died July. 1909. Bought for £4

Bred by Mr Johnson. Prizes Won. 4 Firsts. 3 Seconds. 1 Third. 3 Specia

Bought

for

£12. 12.

Sold

for

£31. 10 -

Born. Jan: 11. 1908.   Ko Fan.   Sold to Mr Clerkson. America. Feb: 19

Bred by Mrs Rawson. Prizes Won. 6 Firsts. 7 Seconds. 4 Thirds. 4 Specia

From the
Lady Faudel Phillips Scrapbook

Blue Devil.

Born July 21. 1907. Bongo. Shot April 1911
Bred by Mr Guibell. Never shown by me.

Born Nov. 19. 1908. Lob. Given Dr Adler. Nov. 1913. Born Dec. 17. 1909. You-Linn. Sold to Mr Armstrong
Bred by self. Prizes won. 7 Firsts. 8 Seconds. Dec. 12. 1909. Died. May 1912. Bred by self.
4 Thirds. 6 Specials. Prizes won. 2. Firsts. 3 Seconds. 2. Thirds.

From the
Lady Faudel Phillips Scrapbook

Bought
for £17.
March 1910.

Sold
for
£21.
April 19..

Born. July 29. 1903.   Hildewell Pooh Bah. Sold Mᶜ Vickers. U.S.A. April 1911.
Bred by Miss Wilkins. Prizes won. 12. Firsts. 2 championships, 3 Seconds. 8. Thirds.

Owned By Lady Faudel Phillips

Hildewell Pooh Bah. Died in America
1912.

10

A Son of Ch: Pusa.

Peridot of Amwell

Ch: Pao Jan. Sold to America
A Son of Chuggie of Amwell.

B. 1922

Bred by
Lady Faudel
Phillips

Ch: Pao Jan.

From the
Lady Faudel Phillips Scrapbook

Pu An of Amwell. Aug= 1926.

From the
Lady Faudel Phillips Scrapbook

Two Blue Bitches by Ch: Pusa - Chuggie Both sold to America - 1 Cream Dog Ting -

Blue Moon of Amwell - Sold May 1926 - £210. By Ch: Pusa - Chuggie

From the
Lady Faudel Phillips Scrapbook

Trophies Won with Chows. 1909 — 14.

Born July 26. 1912.   Sidonia. Bought for £50. Feb: 1915.
Bred by Mᵉˢ J. Stuart. Prizes Won. 20 Firsts, 17 Seconds, 12 Thirds.
5 Specials. 2 R. championships. At 25 Shows.
Died Heart Disease. March. 1917.

From the
Lady Faudel Phillips Scrapbook

Born Sept: 19. 1911.   Blue Blood of Amwell. Destroyed. Feb: 1918.
Bred by Mr Fishbourne. Prizes Won. 16. Firsts. 1. Second. 3. Specials. 1 R. Champ.
At 9. Shows—

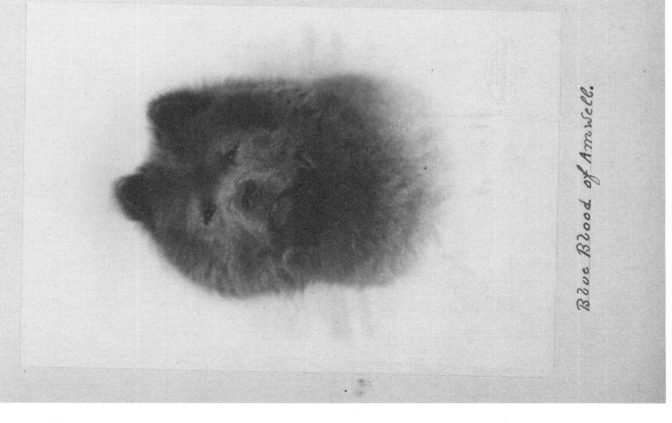

Blue Blood of Amwell.

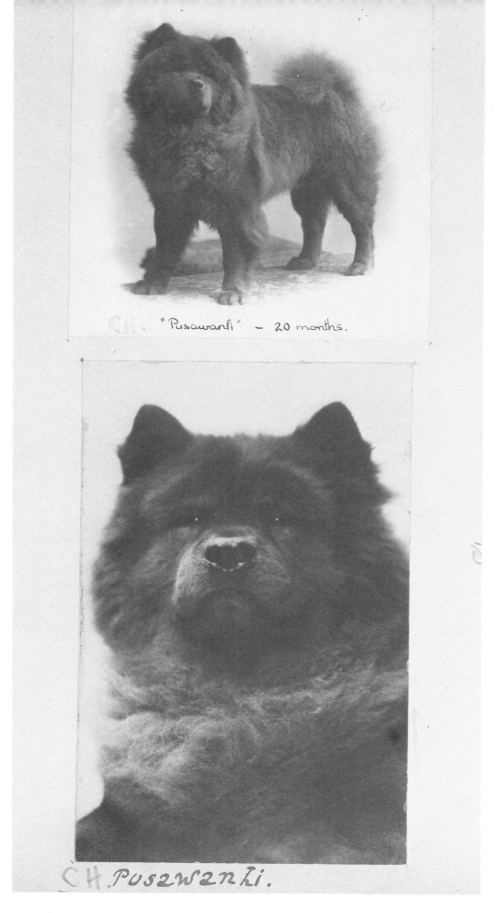

CH. "Pusawarli" — 20 months.

CH PUSAWARLI.

From the
Lady Faudel Phillips Scrapbook

Born March 28. 1905. Papeete. Died June 1915. Bought for £6.6.
Bred by Mrs Scott. Prizes Won. 8 Firsts. 7 Seconds. 4 Thirds. 7 Specials.

Born Oct= 2.1910. Pei Lou of Amwell. Destroyed. 1916.
Bred by Miss Fishbourne. Prizes Won. 11 Firsts. 2 Seconds. 2 Thirds.
4 Specials. At 5 Shows—

From the
Lady Faudel Phillips Scrapbook

This Photo appeared in The Daily Telegraph
Dec: 1923.

Ch: Blue.

BIGGEST WINNING Bitch
BITCH " " 1912.

From the
Lady Faudel Phillips Scrapbook

134 Challenge Certificates, finishing six dogs and ten bitches to championship; six others had C.C.'s also.

The 1920's saw another black dog go to the top. He was Ch. Pu An of Amwell, bred by Lady Faudel Phillips and sired by the aging Ch. Pusa, then in his 12th year; Pu An was the result of a father/daughter mating. Mr. Routledge's red dog Ch. Pusawanli, bred as the name suggests by Ch. Pusa of Amwell out of Ch. Wan Li of Amwell, saw great success. He won a record number of classes at all types of shows. He himself was the sire of Ch. Peng Tse of Amwell, who in turn was the sire of the top-winning bitch in England of all time.

Between 1935 and 1939, the legendary Ch. Pu Yi of Amwell won 32 Challenge Certificates. She was a red out of a famous cream bitch, Ch. Li Chin of Amwell. This grand show and brood bitch was also the dam of another champion, Yung Cheng of Amwell, and her litter sister, Pudi of Ttiweh, was the winner of the bitch Challenge Certificate at the Kennel Club championship show in 1933 when Mrs. Flora Bonney of the United States judged there. Pudi was bred by Lady Faudel Phillips and was given to Mrs. Hewitt Pitt, known all over the world as the originator of the modern Cavalier King Charles Spaniel. Mrs. Pitt had bred Li Chin and sold her for a small sum to Lady Faudel Phillips, and Pudi was given to Mrs. Pitt to compensate for the wonderful investment made with the acquisition of Li Ching, who made her championship and produced champions of her own, including the record-winning bitch to date.

Another great Chow Chow fancier and breeder who came into prominence about that time and is still an avid Chowist today is Mrs. Mabel Fryer, now Mrs. M. Cliff. A descendant of another very old family, the Selby Bowndes, she was deeply involved in horses and dog lore. In 1933 she showed Ch. Huzzar of Chungking and in 1938 the famous Ch. Trumpeter of Chungking. Trumpeter suffered somewhat from being shown at the same time as another great dog, Ch. Choonam Hung Kwong, who amassed 44 C.C.'s; however,

Trumpeter was shown from March, 1934, through June, 1939, and did remarkably well. Another Chow shown at the time who left his mark on the breed was Ch. Rochow Dragoon, winner of 36 C.C.'s, and purchased by Mr. C.D. Rotch. When Dragoon first made his appearance at a small evening variety show, he was spotted by Mr. Rotch, who did not have his checkbook with him at the time, but wrote out a check for 20 pounds on the back of a cigarette packet! Mr. Rotch was so intent on having Dragoon that he did not want to wait until he could get his checkbook! Dragoon became a big winner and finished with the distinction of having defeated Ch. Hung Kwong more times than any other Chow, and indeed many more times than Hung Kwong defeated him.

Other winners at this same time were Mrs. M. Nicholl's Ch. Niclos Marksman; Lady Faudel Phillips' blue dog Ch. You Si, who sired the first champion after shows were resumed in 1945 after World War II; and the great black dog Ch. Sabu Layo Wu, owned by Nana Corelli. He only won one C.C. but was well thought of. There was Ch. Rochow Adjutant, owned by Mr. C.D. Rotch, who figures much in today's history of the Chow Chow. Others were Ch. Choonam Ho Tung, Ch. Chinky Chuw and another red which did much winning, Ch. Poo Bah of Thasew. The last championship show to be held in England in 1939 was at Harrogate the day prior to war being declared, when Charles Harrison awarded the C.C.'s to Ch. Chinky Chuw and a blue bitch, Tchin Quan of Pekin. Due to the war restrictions, Tchin Quan never did attain her championship.

Other bitches which figured prominently in the early years were Sandringham Loo Choo, owned by Her Majesty Queen Alexandra. At the Kennel Club show in 1906 judge Mr. J.S. Turner awarded her the C.C. for bitches, and the dog certificate went to Ch. Red Craze for his fifteenth win. Another to make an impact was Miss Lawton's Ch. Shoo Shan, a kennel mate of Ch. Foo Chow. In 1916 Ch. Lodmore Ching was a top-winning bitch. After World War I only one bitch, Ch. Bluet, re-

On the last page of Lady Faudel Phillips scrapbook is a photograph of Queen Alexandra and Queen Marie of Russia, photographed at the 1914 Ladies Kennel Association Show in Chelsea, England. Her Majesty Queen Alexandra owned the Chow Chow Sandringham Loo Choo.

turned to win. Born in 1912 and bred by Lady Faudel Phillips, Bluet won 15 championships. Unfortunately, like so many other champion bitches, she was never bred.

Mrs. Graham Williams produced a lovely red bitch, Ch. Susan of the East, whose name appears in many lines of big winners. A black bitch, Ch. Topsy Wang, made a great impact. Percy Whitaker believes that when in full coat she would have gone to the top among our present-day winners. She had excellent conformation and deep black coat. A blue bitch, Ch. Ridgy, won under judge Lady Faudel Phillips when she judged her first show in 1925, at which time Ridgy won her first C.C. and

soon after gained her championship title. The Mulfra dogs and bitches made their appearance in the 1920's and included Ch. Mulfra Zula in 1929, a bitch with lovely head and eyes. There was also Ch. Mulfra Rachel and Ch. Mulfra Blossom.

In 1929 Percy Whitaker did well with Ch. Wan Li of Amwell. He had seen Wan Li on the bench at Crufts, and although she was seven years of age and entered in the novice class, he liked her very much and managed to purchase her for 30 pounds from her owner, a Mr. Powell from Torquay. She was bred by Mrs. B. Moore and sired by Ch. Hildewell Ba-Tang. Later that year Mr. Whitaker brought her out at the Taunton show under judge Mrs. Lid-

Above: Ch. Talifu Hesperides, owned by Mrs. Joan Egerton, Whaley Bridge, Cheshire, England. Below: International Ch. Illustrious Lad of Ukwong, famous English dog.

When Mr. Rotch gave up his kennel, Ch. Adjutant was sold to the Comtesse de Changy, who was then living in Brussels. Unfortunately, the Comtesse and her family suffered greatly during World War II, and only a handful of her dogs survived. As a complete contrast to the small bitches being shown at the time, Ch. Josephine of Nee Pa appeared on the scene. A big bitch even by modern standards, she was shown by Mr. J. Hurst, a great admirer of the Choonam dogs. As a matter of record, there was only one occasion during his judging assignments when he did not award them a Challenge Certificate. Ch. Chu Chow of Amwell also did her share of winning, but by and large, until the outbreak of the second World War, Ch. Choonam Hung Kwong and Ch. Pu Yi of Amwell did most of the winning. This war also brought to an end this most colorful period in Chow Chow history in England, not only because of the records then, but because of the dogs that were beginning to be exported to other countries, changing the picture of the breed abroad.

don, who awarded her Best Bitch and her first C.C. Another win followed at Darlington and then she was bred. She produced in this litter a champion named Ch. Hildewell Chincherinchee.

About this time Mrs. Mannooch brought out her Ch. Choonam Moonbeam. She was perhaps the smallest of all the Choonam dogs, weighing 42 pounds on the scales at the 1930 S.K.C. show. A litter sister to Ch. Choonam Toto and sharing with him excellent head type, she was never bred. Toto made his full championship and died shortly thereafter, but not before having sired two of the most influential Chow Chow champions England ever produced. They were Ch. Choonam Hung Kwong and Ch. Rochow Adjutant. The former became the biggest winner of C.C.'s in England, with his total of 44, and the latter became the sire of dogs that created a winning line not equalled in the breed up to that time.

The famous Ch. Conorada Hector Hercules as an old dog at his kennel in England. He was owned later in his career by Miss E. Buckley.

Ch. Sing Tong of
Silverway, owned by Mrs.
M. Bird of England.

Ch. Chu Chow of Amwell, born in 1930 and owned by Lady Faudel Phillips of England. Photographed by Thomas Fall, London.

BREEDING DURING WORLD WAR II

Chow Chow breeding continued in England during the war, even though only small shows were permitted. Unlike what happened during World War I, when breeding could continue only under permission of license, many of the small Chow Chow kennels continued on a somewhat restricted basis, and the Chow Chow Club managed to hold three Specialty shows each year. The winners of these shows became champions almost immediately after the end of the war with the resumption of **the all-breed shows.**

One of the winning bitches during this war period was the light red bitch Ch. Peach of Silverway. She won a Best of Breed, that is, a Best in Show, under Percy Whitaker when he judged the Midland Club show at Tamworth on December 27th, 1943, with 151 entries in 12 classes.

At the first post-war open show in Birmingham there was the staggering total of 539 all-breed entries in 32 classes. The 66 Chow Chow males were judged by Mr. J. Hurst and the 46 bitches by Mrs. M. Cliff. The Best of Breed award went to Anthea of Barwick; best dog was Choonam Mong Yen. Both became champions when the championship shows were resumed. Another open show, put on by the Northern Counties Chow Club at Leeds, drew 325 entries in 32 classes for Mr. G.W. Browning and Mrs. A. Pitt to judge. Peach of Silverway was again Best in Show, and the best male was a black, Sabu, owned by Mrs. Stanley Barrett. This show was followed by the Midland Chow Club's event with 359 entries, and Peach and Sabu were once again the winners.

As the championship shows resumed, some additional good Chow Chows were seen. Viking of Barwick, owned by Mr. A.J. Beets, quickly gained his title against some stiff competition, including Sabu,

Ch. Choonam Mong Yenm, Ch. LI Wu Fa, Ch. Bbormot L-Sau, and Ch. Linterless Boy Blue. Competition increased still more when the Comtesse de Changy sent over the never-to-be-forgotten Int. Ch. Chang Shi Ukwong. This was the dog destined to change completely the picture in England. He came from pre-war English bloodlines mainly, most important of which was Ch. Rochow Adjutant.

Percy Whitaker was the man selected to care for and handle Ukwong in England for the Countess of Kilmorey, and Ukwong eventually found his way to the late Mrs. M. Bird of the Silverway Chows in Burton-on-Trent. Percy Whitaker was also showing a daughter of Ukwong, the beautiful red bitch Ch. Chang Shi-Y-Azdig of Amwell, bred by the Comtesse and sent over to the Countess of Kilmorey as a young puppy. She made a sensational debut, winning the C.C. and Best of Breed at the L.K.A. show and then went on to Best in Show, all breeds, over 9,000 entries. Later the same year Mrs. Bird injured her leg and Owen Grindey asked Percy Whitaker to show Int. Ch. Kwong under the late judge May Pacey. He did this and won the C.C. and Best of Breed and went on to Best in Show on the second day, runner-up to the Afghan Hound, the Supreme Best. Both Chow Chows became champions, and later Percy Whitaker took Kwong all the way to a Best in Show the following April at the West of England Ladies Kennel Society.

Another great Chow Chow bitch was Mr. Reg Holland's red, Ch. Pu Yi Tao. Percy Whitaker was a handler for the Hollands over the years and was constantly scouting for a show winner for them. While dining with them one day, a local dog shop in Edmonton called to say a woman had brought in a litter of Chow Chow puppies to be sold. Since the shop was only four

Ch. Pu Yi of Amwell, pictured here at 12 months of age, was born in 1933 and owned by Lady Faudel Phillips of England. Pu Yi was at one time the holder of the largest number of CC's in Britain.

Ch. Tempest of Nitram, born in 1954, was owned by Mrs. J. Martin of England.

Ch. Chowlaw Hector Hercules, born in 1957 and owned by Mr. Eric Egerton, Ukwong Kennels, Cheshire, England.

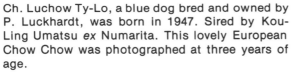

Ch. Luchow Ty-Lo, a blue dog bred and owned by P. Luckhardt, was born in 1947. Sired by Kou-Ling Umatsu ex Numarita. This lovely European Chow Chow was photographed at three years of age.

Ch. Sungod of Nitram, born in 1946, owned by Mrs. J. Martin of England.

Ch. Chanoya Xmas Carol of Nitram, owned by Mesdames Martin and Diamond of England.

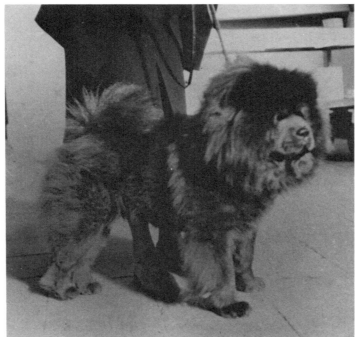

miles away, they all went to take a look at the puppies. The moment Percy Whitaker saw the smallest of the red bitches, he purchased her for 16 pounds, then about $75. Two years later she was ready to be shown and was taken out under judge Mr. J. Blake at an Olympia show. There were ten champions entered, but she went through to Best of Breed. Her championship was completed with six C.C.'s; she won all of the 26 classes in which she had been entered. She was retired for breeding at this point but failed to produce a litter even after many tries. At ten years of age, Percy Whitaker has written, she looked as marvelous as she did in her prime.

Percy Whitaker gave Miss Corelli's Ch. Black Anna of Limone her qualifying win at the Bath Championship show in 1924. There were also show winners from the kennels of Miss Ethel Buckley and Mrs. Lydia Ingleton. Miss Buckley had two champion bitches, Ch. Choonam Mei-Su-Tang and Ch. Heyville's Black Magic. Later Ch. Dogs Mandarin of Adel and still later Ch. Chowlaw Hector Hercules came to her kennel. Just after the war, Mrs. Lydia Ingleton and her sister came to the winners circle with Robin Roi, who won best Chow male at Cardiff in 1926. Later came Ch. Wy Wing Wa.

With the passing of the Amwell and Choonam kennels, the Kin Shan dogs took over, and quite a stream of winners came from them. Ch. T'sai of Kin Shan and Ch. Chang T'Sao of Kin Shan were among them. Chang T'Sao was believed by some to be the most "extraordinary" Chow to become a champion! He had a good head and good back legs but was so small and otherwise unbalanced that he resembled a huge frog. It was understood that "Froggie" was his kennel name for quite obvious reasons. Also bred at the kennel was Ch. Wong T'Sung of Kin Shan, a most likeable dog, and the black Ch. Wupei Nagyur Tut, later exported to the United States by Joseph Hartley Baileff. He was good in type and conformation, but his expression was spoiled somewhat by a rather light eye. He won several specialty shows, several groups and a Best in Show for his owner, Mrs.

Ch. Black Anna of Limone, born June, 1950 and bred by N. Corelli of England. The sire was the smooth Chow Chow Ralmoss Recamier *ex* Lilo of Limone, a black bitch.

David Wagstaff of Ledgelands' Kennels, Tuxedo Park, N.Y. Quite a number of dogs from the Kin Shan kennel made championships in other countries also.

Another popular kennel which made its claim to fame by using some of the Kin Shan dogs were the Brinchows, owned by Mrs. Brind. In one litter there were three champions, Cherub of Brinchow, Una of Brinchow and Manda of Brinchow.

When Mrs. Ingleton died in 1964, her passing created a large void in the Chow Chow ranks. However, a kennel which had been associated with the Kin Shan bloodlines continued to forge the way for the breed. This was the Junggwaw Kennel, owned by Mr. and Mrs. Stan Smedley. They had acquired a bitch named Phillida of Barwick from Miss Collett. When she produced a litter sired by Int. Ch. Chang Shi Ukwong, the English Chow scene took on an exciting new aspect. From this litter came three notable red brothers, Ch. Edward of Junggwaw, Int. Ch. Emperor of Junggwaw and Ch. Enrico of Junggwaw. And these three themselves produced a stream of top-winning Chows unsurpassed by any other strain up to that time.

Ch. Edward of Junggwaw was acquired by Frank Watkinson, who had gathered

Ch. Chang-Shi Y Zadig of Amwell photographed after winning Best in Show in England in 1950 over *ten thousand entries* at the Ladies Kennel Club. Zadig was owned by the Countess of Kilmorey.

Eng. Ch. Nu-Huang Cobweb and litter sister Eng. Ch. Nu-Huang Peaseblossom, photographed in 1952. Mrs. H.W. Dunk of Rotherham, England, owner.

Ch. Cottam Bo-Bo of Melching, English dog born in 1955.

Kwaisay Yum Yum, winner of two CC's, owned by Mrs. P. Westley and Dr. T. Kemp-Homer of England.

Ch. Renee of Ukwong, born in 1957, is owned by Mrs. Joan Egerton of England.

Int. Ch. Astom with his handler, Percy Whitaker, and the judge, the Countess of Kilmorey, as Astom goes Best of Breed at the 1958 Crufts show.

Ch. Mairim Blue Marianne, born in 1958 and owned by Mrs. M. Simpson of England.

his knowledge of the breed from the late Mr. W. Scriven of the Mulfra kennels and later from Miss Alice Brackenbury, who had long been associated with the Mulfra dogs as well. Ch. Edward of Junggwaw was not only a big winner at the shows but also further enhanced his reputation as a supreme stud dog. At one time he was the sire of no fewer than ten English Chow Chow champions, which captured for him the top stud title from the noted Int. Ch. Chang Shi Ukwong, who sired nine during his short stay in England. All three of the Junggwaw Chows sired champions leaving a lasting influence on the breed in modern history.

At this time Mr. and Mrs. Eric Egerton became interested in the breed. Enjoying a picnic in Sherwood Forest one day, they met, not Robin Hood, but Mrs. J. Boot of the Talifu Chow Chows. They purchased a red puppy dog from her and thus began what has proved to be the biggest winning kennel of all time in England. Eric Egerton went into a partnership with Mr. and Mrs. Boot and their bitch, Tinka-Belle of Talifu, started them off. She was bred to Int. Ch. Chang Shi Ukwong and a litter of four was born on October 25, 1952. These three bitches and one male proved to be a record litter of champions.

There had been three champions in a litter before this, but never four champions from a single litter. They were Ch. Talifu Handsel, Ch. Talifu Hesperides, Ch. Morning Glory of Talifu and Ch. Talifu Golden Glory.

They were first shown in the Puppy Class at Blackpool in 1953 under judge

Ch. Talifu Handsel, English Chow Chow.

Opposite: Ch. Minhow Edward of Junggwaw, born February, 1953, was bred by Mr. S. Smedley. Owner: Frank Watkinson of England. The sire was Int. Ch. Chang Shi Ukwong *ex* Phillida of Barwick.

Ch. Nu-Huang Deidre, born in 1959, was owned by Mrs. Joan Egerton, Ukwong Kennels, Cheshire, England.

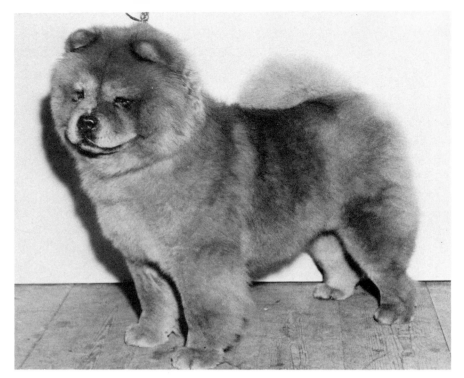

Ch. Leading Lady
of Ukwong, England.

Mr. Eric Egerton of England with Int. Ch. Astom, Int. Ch. Emperor of Junggwaw and Ch. Talifu Hesperides. The fourth dog is unidentified.

International Ch. Chieftain of Ukwong, owned by Mrs. Joan Egerton of England.

Ch. Lynne of Ukwong, bred by Mrs. Joan Egerton of Cheshire, England.

Int. Ch. Chang Shi Ukwong, England.

Int. Ch. Emperor of Junggwaw, top-winning English Chow Chow.

Percy Whitaker, who placed Handsel first, Morning Glory second and the other two third and fourth. Though he predicted championships for them all at the time, he did not know then that later he would be handling them to their championships.

The Egertons' next big winner was Int. Ch. Emperor of Junggwaw, mentioned though the wins were often shared with his litter brothers, as they did their share of winning also. Then followed in rapid succession Ch. Renee of Ukwong, sired by Emperor, Ch. Doll Tearsheet, Ch. Rowena of Ravensway, and soon after Int. Ch. Astom was imported from Belgium and shown under the joint ownership of the Comtesse de Changy and Eric Egerton.

Astom was a great success in England, and his record was a long run of top wins in the show ring, earning ten championships

and no less than three Supreme Championships at all-breed shows including one at Glasgow, Three Counties and Leeds. Astom came to England with the explicit proviso that he not be used at stud outside the Ukwong Kennel. The name "Ukwong" was used by the Egertons as their kennel name with the permission of the Comtesse, since it was the name of her most celebrated male!

Astom sired three champions before he went back to Belgium after twelve months of winning in England. He was a dog of great character and was known for his substance and excellent front. He did much for the breed, and his influence can be seen to this day, though like many other successful dogs he did evoke some adverse comment. . . but not enough to stop his winning. His son, Int. Ch. Illustrious Lad of Ukwong, became a champion in England and before going to Pakistan won the Supreme Championship at the Bath championship show. At this time also, the strength of these Ukwong Chow Chows was made evident by the fact that the kennels housed, all at one time, Ch. Emperor, Ch. Astom and Ch. Illustrious Lad, all three of which had won Supreme Championships, a feat for any breed, and unique in Chow Chows.

A champion bitch sired by Astom was the light red Ch. Dollar Maid of Ukwong; she went as high as Best Bitch at an all-breed show and runner-up for Best in Show at a Three Counties championship show. However, she will probably be best remembered as the dam of the much-talked-about Jackpot of Ukwong. Never shown, but much admired, he sired two litters, each of which had a full champion in it. When mated to Ch. Rowena, he sired Ch. Viking of Ukwong. When he was bred to Countess of Ukwong in 1959 a truly remarkable litter resulted, all of which were

Ch. Dollar Maid of Ukwong, owned by Mrs. Joan Egerton of England.

Jackpot of Ukwong, sire of two important British Chows, Ch. Wat-A-Gal of Ukwong and Ch. Viking of Ukwong.

Int. Ch. Illustrious Lad of Ukwong, sired by Int. Ch. Astom and owned by Mrs. Joan Egerton of England.

Ch. Viking of Ukwong of England.

big winners, perhaps the best being the light red bitch Ch. Wat-A-Gal of Ukwong. She achieved her full championship at the age of seven months and six days. She was handled throughout her career by Percy Whitaker, who in his capacity as kennel manager for the Ukwong Kennels at this time entered her in 29 classes which resulted in 29 first placings. She was later acquired by Mr. and Mrs. Arthur Westlake of the Baytor Kennels, where she became a top brood bitch and is behind most of the present-day Baytor champions.

Another important red dog was produced when Mrs. Shaw bred Ch. Chieftain of Ukwong from two Ukwong Chows, Lucky Star of Ukwong *ex* Wonga of Ukwong. Ch. Chieftain became the sire of Ch. Fairwood Adam, who in turn sired Ch. Attaboy of Ukwong, a frequent winner of championships and Groups, and now owned by Mr. Ron Moss. Ch. Chieftain was also the sire of Ukwong Hermes, a top winner also, though not a champion, and he was the sire of many winning dogs at that time.

When the Ukwong Kennels were disbanded, the majority of the Chows were sold, with only a few given as gifts to friends. They went all over the world. Ch. Viking of Ukwong went to Mrs. Hazel Davis in Wales. He had already won one C.C. and had also been a runner-up for Best in Show at Cardiff. When the Ukwong Kennels resumed operation once again sometime later, Viking returned and rapidly finished his title. But it was while he was residing with Mrs. Davis that he sired a red dog which was to mark another milestone in English Chow Chow history. This was the great dog Ch. Fairwood Fu Simba, whelped in May, 1962.

As a small puppy Simba was given to Mrs. Cleveland Smith. He was shown under judge Percy Whitaker at Cardiff in July, 1963 and was awarded a first in both puppy and novice classes. Mr. Whitaker said of him that he was "clearly of championship grading, although still immature." When he did not win as time went by, Mrs. Smith wrote to Mr. Whitaker and asked why. After another look at Simba, it was decided that he would go under a joint

Ch. Wat-A-Gal of Ukwong, a full champion at seven months and six days of age. Her sire was Jackpot of Ukwong, who also was the father of Ch. Viking of Ukwong. Viking sired Ch. Fairwood Fu Simba.

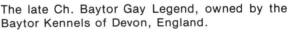

The late Ch. Baytor Gay Legend, owned by the Baytor Kennels of Devon, England.

Ch. Baytor Winter Wonder, owned by Mrs. Anita Westlake of the Baytor Kennels in Devon, England.

Ju-Dee of Rhiwbina, born September 5, 1964, sired by Ch. Fairwood Fu-Simba *ex* Hi-dee of Rhiwbina. Winner of one CC and three Reserve CC's.

ownership between the Smiths and Eger-tons. Shown again at Crufts, he won only a third prize in Open Dog class, but at his next shows won his championship, going on to win Groups and finally a Best in Show among all breeds at Bath in 1967. He had won 15 C.C.'s and was "Chow of the Year" that same year. He has been acknowledged as one of the greatest stud dogs of all time and has become a legend in his own era. He set a "type" in his progeny that stamped them as his very own get. He passed on great substance, right texture of coat, outstanding fronts and smaller ears. Final figures of the numbers of winners Simba produced as sire or grandsire in England or abroad are not readily available, but it is well over 20 champions in all.

Crufts, 1968. Left to right, Mrs. Egerton's Ch. Ukwong Saul of Weircroft, Ch. Fairwood Fu Simba, and Mrs. R. Bullows's Ch. Simon of Kukim. The judge is Mrs. Antrobus.

Ch. Minhow Martini, born in March, 1960, was bred and owned by Mr. F. Watkinson of England. The sire was Ch. Minhow Edward of Junggwaw *ex* Minhow Jacqueline of Wongtung.

Mr. Eric Egerton with Ch. Fairwood Fu Simba, shown winning Best in Show at Bath, England over nine thousand entries.

Mr. Eric Egerton of the well-known Ukwong Kennels in Cheshire, England with Jackpot of Ukwong.

Ch. Pei-Ming of Silverway, a winner at Crufts at the 1959 show. Owned by Mr. N. Hart of England.

His best known son was perhaps Ch. Ukwong Saul of Weircroft, winner of 19 C.C.'s, who was defeated only by two of his own kennel mates, Simba and the really outstanding young dog Alfie of Ukwong. After winning Best Chow at Manchester, Alfie unfortunately died very suddenly. Saul was bred by Mrs. Ivy Bancroft from two Ukwong Chows and went to Ukwong as pick of the litter. Saul was a remarkable Chow in many ways and, like most of his line, was slow to mature; he was kept back until he was ready for the really big wins at the shows. He won nine first placings at his first show, going second only to his sire, Simba, for Best of Breed, at the Chow of the Year show in 1967.

Ch. Saul was sold to Japan for a large sum of money, and it was only after he had left that it was realized just how potent a stud he had been. Three of his get became full champions. They were Ch. Marsay Ming, Ch. Marsay Delilah and the well-known Ch. Ukwong King Solomon.

Many kennels were founded on the Ukwong dogs in addition to these just mentioned. Mr. and Mrs. Alan Ramsay of the Marsay Chows, who also owned another champion bitch in Ch. Red Magic of Shawcross; Mr. and Mrs. Terry Wright of the Termade Chows own Ch. Termade Star, sired by Simba and Ch. Termade Renata, a red bitch who was once placed over Ch. Solomon for Best of Breed at the Chow Chow Club's championship show. She was in the breed for many years and has had several outstanding Chows such as Ch. Weircroft Venture Boy, Ch. Weircroft Lovely Coleen and Prince Paul of Weircroft, just short of a single win for his title. Several other good Chows have been bred at this kennel, which is known both in England and abroad.

Opposite:

Ch. Weircroft Saul of Ukwong, English winner owned and bred by Mr. and Mrs. Eric Egerton of the Ukwong Kennels.

Ch. Tiko-Ling of Hanoi, owned by Mrs. Dulcie Smith, Hanoi Chow Chows, England.

Ch. Rosemary Rose of Nitram, born in 1966 and owned by Mrs. J. Martin of England.

Hanoi Kennels, owned by Dulcie Smith, was another kennel known in England for many years. Their stock won a great deal between the two world wars, but since World War II the Hanoi Chows have not been shown to any extent. Perhaps the best known of their dogs was Brutus of Ho Ping, winner of two Challenge Certificates. He was an outstanding red dog by any standard. After Brutus there was Ch. Tiko Ling of Hanoi. He was a great winner of many C.C.'s and was a Best in Show dog, with the Supreme Champion title. He was also a potent sire and has left his mark both in England and abroad. Perhaps the best-known Hanoi Chow since World War II was the red bitch Ch. Una of Hanoi. Another well-known Hanoi Chow was the red dog, Ch. Hanoi Damon of Kalamunda.

Ch. Hanoi Damon of Kalamunda, winning English Chow Chow, bred and owned by Dulcie Smith, Hanoi Kennels.

Anna May Wong of Kut Sang and Eastern Saga of Kut Sang photographed at 6 months of age. Owned by Lady B. Royle of England.

Golden Jubilee of Kut Sang. Goldie was exported to South Africa; bred by Lady B. Royle of England and whelped in January, 1960.

Ch. Cindylu of Briercliffe, winner of many CC's and Bests of Breed in England in the 1970 to 1972 show season, is owned by Mrs. I. Bowker of Bradford, Yorks., England.

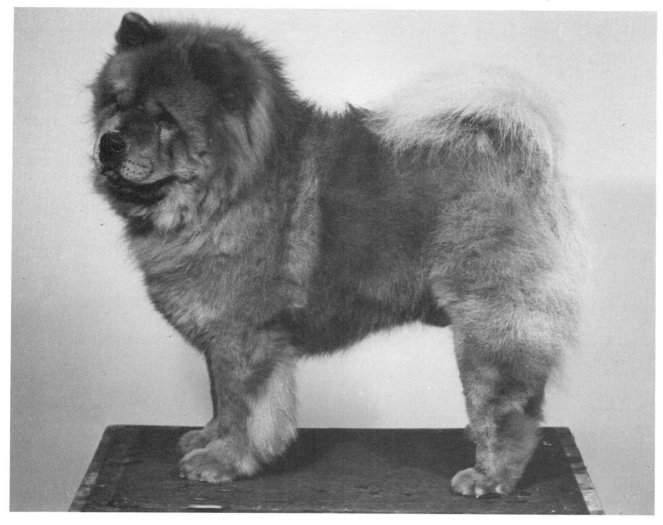

Int. Ch. Hussar of Ukwong, bred and owned by Mrs. Joan Egerton of England.

Ch. Simon of Kukim, born in England in 1962.

Litter brothers. . . Hwang Ti Che Kwong and Hwang Ti Chao Chun, born in 1949. Bred by Mrs. F. Pieterse-Hummel and sired by Int. Ch. Chang Shi Ukwong *ex* Bonnie van Nunatak.

MINHOW—ONE OF THE BIGGEST AND ONE OF THE BEST

One of England's biggest and best kennels in both activity and numbers of top specimens produced is the Minhow Kennels owned by Mr. and Mrs. Frank Watkinson. Their first big winner, Ch. Edward of Junggwaw, was mentioned earlier in this chapter. Edward was a prolific sire and also produced the light red bitch Ch. Minhow Charmaine. She was always presented in top condition by the late Pem Kingsbury, who was largely responsible for her success. Pem Kingsbury was a Chow Chow person himself, being the owner of Ch. Li Wu Fa. He was associated with other prominent Chow Chow people also, including Mrs. Stanley Barrett of the Westwoods Kennels and Mrs. Montefiore, who owned the noted red dog Li Po, the sire of Ch. Li Chin of Amwell, Ch. Choonam To To and Ch. Choonam Moonbeam.

Other top Chows from the Minhow Kennels were Ch. Minhow Mi-Boi, a fawn dog, Ch. Minhow Gem of Ukwong, Ch. Minhow Mohican, Ch. Minhow Blue Queen of Silverway, Ch. Minhow Mustang (winner of over 20 championships) and Minhow Martini, born in 1960, who held the postwar record of the most C.C.'s won with a total of 27. These and many others are pictured in this book along with the latest of their great dogs, born in 1971, Ch. Minhow Mings Moon, already a Group winner in show competition. Many great Chows have come from this kennel, and many others have been sired by dogs from the kennel and are winning for other British breeders. Perhaps the best known of these winners, Ch. Van Lee of Kai-Oko, owned by Mrs. Harold Cromptons, was sired by Edward. This dog not only won 25 C.C.'s but also won a Group at Crufts. Unfortunately he left no progeny, a loss since he obviously had a great deal to offer.

Also prominent in show circles was the red dog Ch. Simon of Kukim, owned by Mr. and Mrs. Bullows. Another successful dog around Simon's time was the red dog Ch. Heyvilles Ambassador of Wong Tung. Bred by Mr. C. Hey out of Ch. Rowena of Ravensway, Ambassador came into his possession after the break-up of the Ukwong Kennels. He was acquired by Mrs. Ethel Downsborough, who was perhaps one of the best "spotters" of top Chow Chow quality ever in the breed. Mrs. Downsborough showed at least seven champions with the Wong Tung name, most of which were acquired while still young. Her best-known winner was Ch. Kian Chang of Wong Tung. He was known for his lovely head, but unfortunately he never sired a litter. Other Wong Tung dogs of note were Ch. Wong Tung Bula of Philmagee, Ch. Wong Tung Chang of Canton, Ch. Brette Lee of Wong Tung, Ch. Anna of Wong Tung and Ch. Georgina of Wong Tung. There were several others; Chang became sire of four English champions, and his influence can be seen in some of the present-day stock.

Another important kennel was the Westwood line by Mrs. Stanley Barret. While she is now interested in another breed, during the post-war period a great stream of winning Chows handled by the late Pem Kingsbury appeared from the Westwood Kennels. The first was the famous black Chow Ch. Sabu, a great winner; he was followed by Ch. Great Westwood Black Pansy and the blue dog Ch. Linterlee Boy Blue. They and many others made strong competition in their day. A few notable bitches also appeared at this time along with Pansy, and they included May Young's red, Ch. Mei of Adlung, and a truly fine bitch named Ch. Chuchin Wong, owned by Mr. E. Lumley of Blackpool. Percy Whitaker awarded her her first championship when she was nearly seven years old, and she finished very soon after that with a well-deserved championship.

The largest litter of Chow Chow puppies born in England was a litter of eleven born to Chuggie of Amwell, a blue bitch, in 1923. Another record litter was of ten born in 1926 to a bitch named Elizabeth owned by a Mrs. Duff. The average number of puppies in a litter is not usually above five.

A 1968 litter bred by Mrs. M. Cunliffe deserves mention, since it consisted of three champions. These were Mrs. Bowker's Ch.

Ch. Minhow Charmaine of Bramacres, born June 10, 1955, bred by Mrs. L. Paget. She was winner of 7 CC's, 8 Reserve CC's, and 2 Bests of Breed. Owned by Frank Watkinson of England.

Cindylu of Briercliffe, Mr. C.W. Regan's Ch. Russ Kandy of Briercliffe and Mrs. R. Quinss's Ch. Brentstevan of Briercliffe.

Other bitches which have produced more than one champion are Ch. Rowena of Ravensway, Minhow Jacqueline of Wong Tung and Countess of Ukwong. . . all since the end of World War II.

Fewer than thirteen bitches produced more than one champion per litter during the period 1895 to 1939. It is notable that over the years so many full champion bitches have never produced a litter. One reason for this, Percy Whitaker believes, is that they were kept in the show ring too long and therefore missed the perfect time for breeding. The byword in England has become, "Never sacrifice breeding for showing." Before its adoption, however, showing often did take precedence

Ch. Minhow Mustang, born in 1960, owned by Frank Watkinson of
England.

Chinese Chow Chow Club Open Show in March of 1963. Right to left, Ch. Minhow Martini, Perky Chow Pug's Poppet, Anna May Wong of Kul-Lang, Black Meg of Linore. The judge is Leon Packman.

Ch. Minhow Mings Moon, whelped in 1971, was bred and owned by Mr. Frank Watkinson of England.

Edlen Special Agent, winner of Best Chow Chow Puppy of the Year at a show in England with over 60 entries. Agent also has many Firsts at championship shows and a Best in Show at an open show, all-breeds. Sired by Weircroft Romeo *ex* Wendy Wu of Redstone. Owned by Edna and Carol Entwisle of Cheshire, England.

English Ch. Unalissa of Thursfield, whelped in 1970, and sired by Graeme of Thursfield *ex* Jessica of Thursfield. Owned by Edna and Carol Entwisle of Cheshire, England.

Wendy Wu of Redstone, whelped in March, 1970, is the dam of Edlen Special Agent, winner of many firsts at championship shows in England. The sire was Prince Palil of Weircroft *ex* Judy of Redstone. Owners are Edna and Carol Entwisle of Chesire, England.

Ch. Rowena of Ravenway, photographed at 10 months of age. Owner was Mrs. Joan Egerton of England.

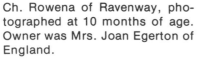

Mr. W. Thomas handles his bitch Ch. Si-Kong Katy of Shergay to Best in Show at Welks, England, in 1971. The judge is well-known Chow judge Owen Grindey. Mrs. J. Lee Gordon, president of Welks, presents the trophy.

Ch. Russ Kandy of Briarcliffe, whelped in 1968 and owned by Mr. C.W. Regan of England. Russ Kandy is one of three champions in one litter, the other two being Ch. Cindylu of Briarcliffe and Ch. Brentstevan of Briarcliffe.

Ch. Crispin of Kalamunda, winner of 33 Bests of Breed, 20 Group Firsts, 8 Reserve Groups, 10 Bests in Show, all breeds; he is a full brother to the famous Damon. The sire was Ch. Tiko-Ling of Hanoi *ex* T'Sai Chin.

STUD DOG RECORDS

The stud dog siring most full English champions is Frank Watkinson's Ch. Edward of Junggwaw, with a total of ten. Closely following in his footsteps is Ch. Chang Shi Ukwong, with nine. Ch. Fairwood Fu Simba has six to his credit, and some of the dogs being shown now are well on their way to equalling or perhaps topping these records.

BROOD BITCH RECORDS

The best Chow Chow brood bitch is Tinkerbelle of Talifu, with a total of four champions. Others which have produced three champions in a litter are Ch. Pickles, Mulfra Ning Ning and (in more recent times) Mrs. Cunliffe's Wendy Lulu Ling.

English Ch. Edlen Crisandra, sired by English Ch. U-Kwong King Solomon *ex* Edlen Crista. Crisandra was Puppy of the Year, all breeds, out of a world record entry of 2,109 top-winning Chow Chow bitches in 1973 at the championship shows. Her record is 8 C.C.'s, 1 Group and a Reserve Best in Show at Peterbough. Owners Edna and Carol Entwisle, Cheshire, England.

NOTABLE ALL BREED CHOW WINS

From 1945 on the following Chow Chows have scored all-breed wins in Great Britain:

Ch. Sitric Yung T'Sun — Best in Show at the 1949 Brighton championship show; owned by Mrs. M. Curtis.

Ch. Bbormot U-Sau — Best in Show, Altringham championship show in 1948; owned by Mr. W. Robbs.

Ch. Chang Shi Zadig of Amwell — Best in Show 1952 L.K.A. championship show; owned by Countess of Kilmoreys.

Ch. Ricky of Kai Oko — Best in Show 1957 Birmingham National; owned by Mrs. Reynolds.

Int. Ch. Chang Shi Ukwong — Best in Show at the 1953 W.E.L.K.S. championship show; owned by Comtesse de Changy and Mrs. Birds.

Int. Ch. Astom — Best in Show at 1957 Scottish Kennel Club show, 1957 Leeds show and 1956 Three Counties Kennel Club show; co-owned by Comtesse de Changy and Eric Egerton.

Int. Ch. Emperor of Junggwaw — Best in Show at Manchester championship show and Paignton championship show in 1957; owned by Mrs. Joan Egerton.

Int. Ch. Illustrious Lad of Ukwong — Best in Show at Bath in 1957; owned by Mrs. Joan Egerton.

Ch. Fairwood Fu Simba — Best in Show at Bath championship show; owned by Mrs. Joan Egerton.

Ch. Tiko Ling of Hanoi — Best in Show at Paignton championship show in 1962, owned by Mr. and Mrs. W. Smith.

Ch. Ukwong King Solomon — Bests in Show at Scottish Kennel Club, Bournemouth, Cardiff, Darlington, L.K.A. plus two others for a total of seven in 1971, and went on to win six more Bests in Show in 1972; owned by Mrs. Joan Egerton.

PRESENT DAY RECORD HOLDERS

There can be little dispute that the Chow Chow acknowledged as the greatest winner of all time in Britain is the fabulous Ch. King Solomon of Ukwong, owned by

Ch. Emperor of Ukwong, bred by Mrs. Joan Egerton of England, not to be confused with Ch. Emperor of Junggwaw.

Ch. Sitruc Yung T'Sun, born in 1946 and owned by Mrs. M. Curtis of England. He was the winner of 21 CC's, and a Best in Show, all-breeds, at the 1949 Brighton show.

Mrs. Joan Egerton. Bred by Mrs. Egerton from her own Ch. Weircroft Saul of Ukwong *ex* Ukwong Melita and whelped on June 21, 1968, he has produced a winning record in his own breed and against other breeds. His record is without equal in England.

To date Solomon has been awarded 14 Group Placings in 1971 with seven Bests in Show. He was named Dog of the Year in all-breed ratings for 1971, and in 1972 his record was 12 Group Placings and six times Best in Show; for the second consecutive time he was Dog of the Year in 1972, a feat without equal in any era! By November of

1972 his 44 wins made him joint holder of the record number of Challenge Certificates won by a Chow Chow. The co-holder of the record is Ch. Choonam Hung Kwong, owned by Mrs. V. Mannooch and bred by her in 1933. Hung Kwong was first shown in March, 1934 at the Manchester show and appeared until the shows stopped with the advent of the war in 1939. It is interesting to note that he took five and a half years to acquire his record, whereas Solomon attained his in only three and a half years. But it should also be noted that the record stood for 33 years before it was challenged, and it may well be another 33 years before a Chow tops the record set by these two fantastic dogs.

It is truly a remarkable honor held by the Egertons' Ukwong Kennels. In the 22 years they have been active they have produced 26 full champions acquiring over 200 C.C.'s, and at least seven of their dogs have won Best in Show, all breeds. Two of their dogs not mentioned before are Ch. Ukwong Flour and the only black they ever showed, Ch. Ukwong Chi Chi. Runner-up to this record would be that of the late Mrs. Mannooch, with her 16 champions and 128 Challenge Certificates.

The Egertons did not show Ch. Solomon during 1973 since Eric Egerton judged the breed at Cursts. Also they chose to play host to American judge Clif Shryock rather than exhibit when he traveled to England to judge at England's famous Manchester event in March, 1974. 97 Chow Chows presented 169 entries for Clif Shryock, with a total show entry of 12,255 representing 7,887 dogs. A record for Manchester, needless to say.

According to the June 21, 1974 issue of *English Dog World*, Champion Ukwong King Solomon became the all-breed

Every dog an English champion! Left to right, John Duxbury, Joan and Eric Egerton and Percy Whitaker; the dogs are Ch. Talifu Morning Glory, Ch. Talifu Golden Glory, Ch. Talifu Handsel, Ch. Talifu Hesperides, Int. Ch. Emperor of Junggwaw, Ch. Rowena of Ravensway, Ch. Renee of Ukwong, and Ch. Chowlaw Hector Hercules.

Ch. Brentstevan of Briarcliffe, born in 1968 and owned by Mr. R. Quinn of England.

Champion Certificate record holder when he won his 63rd C.C. at the Three Counties show. The record had previously been held by Bettie Farrand's Wire-haired Dachshund Ch. Gisbourne Inca, holder of 62 C.C.'s.

It is widely known that Percy Whitaker has been closely associated with King Solomon's career. On the occasion of Solly's breaking the C.C. record, Percy wrote: "It is a tremendous feat, a record that will not be broken, at least in the foreseeable future. What a boost for the Chow Chow! I was lucky enough to be on the end of Solomon's lead when he won his first C.C. at the big Scottish Kennel Club Championship show. And I had the honor of handling him when he broke the C.C. record at

the Three Counties event. It was a pity that Eric and Joan Egerton and their family were in the United States when Solly broke the record. I have a feeling that Eric would have liked to have been at the end of the lead when the record went. That's only natural, of course."

It should also be mentioned that Solomon was again B.I.S. at the 1974 Chow of the Year show. He is the sire of Ch. Cassandra, who was the 1973 Pup of the Year, all breeds. Solomon, even though he had reached six years of age at the time of this great victory, had never looked better.

The number of wins at the Open Shows and other lesser dog shows during the early 1970's are too numerous to record here, but it is indicative of the high stand-

Ch. Ukwong King Solomon pictured in a dramatic scene winning the Group at the 1971 Crufts Dog Show in England.

ard of merit in the Chow Chow produced in England during the post-war period. It must be remembered that the English General Championship shows, in which the entries in all breeds range from about 6,000 to as many as 15,000, make a Best in Show a truly coveted win. The Chow Chow entries average anywhere from 80 to over 200 at each event.

The Chow of the Year Show held annually in England attracts well over 400 entries and brings together "the cream of the crop" in the breed for this stellar event. The Best in Show Award carries high prestige and is usually won by what turns out to be not only the top Chow Chow at the show but also a top Chow Chow of the era. It is a unique show and well supported by all the Chow clubs of England, each taking a turn at sponsoring it to comply with the rules of the Kennel Club. The show is well attended, and it provides a yearly display of the greatest gathering of Chow Chows to be found anywhere in the world.

Ch. Ukwong King Solomon at 10 months of age.

CHOW CHOW REGISTRATIONS IN GREAT BRITAIN

Chow Chow registrations are nearing the 1,500 per year mark and are steadily climbing back to the so-called "Golden Years of Chowdom," when England saw in the early 1920's the registration of over 2,000 a year. Dedicated Chowists, such as Percy Whitaker, believe the breed today, with rare exception, to be in good, qualified hands. These people are in the majority and are truly dedicated to this marvelous breed; they will carry it on to even greater success and popularity.

OTHER CHOW CHOW ACTIVITIES

In addition to putting on record the history of the Chow Chow in England, we must of course include the activities in the breed in the rest of the British Isles, for there has been much support for the Chow in the past in Wales and Scotland. During the 1970's a Scottish Chow Club was formed. Together with the long-established Welsh Chow Club, its members look after the interests of Scottish Chowists.

An Irish Chow Chow Club was very active at one time when there were quite a few Chow Chows in that country. Unfortunately, there has been no word of late of any activity from the Irish group. It is sincerely hoped that with new records being achieved and surpassed, this new interest and enthusiasm for the Chow Chow will spread once again to Ireland!

Ch. Ukwong Fleur, bred and once owned by the Eric Egertons of England, now belongs to Mr. and Mrs. Clifton Shryock of Hawaiian Gardens, California. She was Best of Opposite Sex to Ch. Eastward Liontamer of Elster at the Chow Chow Club National Specialty in Dallas, Texas in March of 1973.

4. THE CONTINENTAL CHOW CHOW

When discussing the Continental Chow Chow, the reader has to realize at once that the structure of the dog world and the organizations that govern Chows in Europe are vastly different from those in the United States.

Individual countries have their own Kennel Clubs and their own stud books; some have their own breeding regulations, and all have rules for judging and showing. Each country has its own national breeds, some of which enjoy great popularity in other countries of the world, while others are in vogue only in their own country.

The countries behind the Iron Curtain are more or less separated by the political situation. Importation of dogs is possible but very rarely done, as it takes a long time to get the necessary licenses. Germany **requires** an "Export Pedigree" from the German Kennel Club if dogs are shipped out of the country. The Scandinavian countries have quarantine restrictions; Sweden's is the most severe. Some West European judges invited to judge in Russia need to get a special permit. Some judges from England, Holland and Luxemburg have been invited to judge in other European countries and have done so. Henk van de Wouw judged the special Chow Chow Club show in Leipzig, East Germany and reports entries of between 60 and 100 Chows. The East German dogs were nice specimens, though he reports they are not up to other standards on the Continent.

In some respects the Continental Chow Chow shows are similar to the English system of judging. They award Challenge Certificates, but the Continental requirements are more severe than for those won in England.

As far as the interpretation of the Standard is concerned, there is not quite the same way of thinking about it in England as on the Continent. The English Standard for the breed, for instance, is binding upon the member-countries of the **Federation Cynologique Internationale.** This only mentions "faults" and no "disqualifying faults". No dog can be sent out of the ring because of showing serious faults. However, in England as well as on the Continent, monorchids and cryptorchids are immediately disqualified.

THE INTERNATIONAL CHOW CHOW CONGRESS

As there were different opinions about the interpretation of the Standard in the Continental countries, it was believed desirable to try and come to more unanimity. Mr. Erich Buchner of West Berlin, one of the oldest Chow fanciers in West Germany, therefore initiated the idea of arranging a meeting between all the special Chow Chow clubs of Europe and those from England. As Holland had the closest international contacts and Amsterdam was situated most centrally, the Dutch Chow Chow Club, in cooperation with the Dutch Kennel Club, organized an International Chow Chow Congress, held on October 5 and 6, 1957. The Congress was held in the meeting room of the Kennel Club's building. The discussions were presided over by the chairman of the Dutch Kennel Club, Doctor W.K. Hirschfeld, Professor of Genetics, on the first day. On the second day it was Professor A.J.M. Holmer. The English delegation, representing several of the English Chow Chow clubs, was headed by the well-

Jowtrix Jadjucator, born in 1971 and photographed at 1 year of age. Bred by Mr. J. Trick of England and owned by Ulla-Britt Lundstrom of Norway. Sired by Shou Mong-Fu ex Jowtrix Java Rose.

Ch. Kansus Leo, whelped in 1970 and bred by Ulla-Britt Lundstrom. Owned by Y. and J. Lindberg. Sire was Ch. Jason of Junggwaw ex Ch. Kansus Inka.

Int. Ch. Jalu Mong-Fu, born in 1960, was bred and owned by Mrs. Irene Cottafavi. Pictured here at two years of age, he was sired by Int. Ch. Dalai Mong-Fu ex Int. Ch. Gwally de la Moulaine. A winning German Chow Chow.

Ch. Kansus Inka, whelped 1957, and photographed at 5 years of age. Bred and owned by Ulla-Britt Lundstrom. The sire was Int. Ch. Black Roi of Silverway ex Int. Ch. Skansabrons Queen Beauti.

known veterinarian, Chow Chow breeder and judge Miss Joan Joshua, F.R., C.V.S. The Comtesse R. de Changy and the Comtesse T. de Villegas de Clercamp represented Belgium. France was represented by Mr. Rene Hassenforder (de La Moulaine) and Madame L. Descamps, West Germany by its expert on Chow Chows, Mr. Erich Buchner, accompanied by Mr. W. Wohnrau. The Dutch delegation consisted of Mr. L.G. van den Broek and Mr. Henk van de Wouw. The basis for the discussion was the subscription of the Standard as laid down by Mr. van de Wouw in his Dutch book *The Chow Chow*. The meeting was attended by several well-known Chowists and judges, and throughout the two days there was serious discussion, penetrating far into many points of the breed: the type of the head, the mouth (West Germany and Switzerland are penalizing dogs for lack of premolars), hind legs and other characteristics of the breed, including the stilted gait. For instance, Henk van de Wouw objected to the term "the desired double-jointed hocks," as described in the Chow Chow Standard drawn up in England. In spite of the fact that every Chowist knows what is meant by it, he believed it is incorrect to ask for an impossibility in the structure of a leg. As this is the official Standard for the breed in a large part of the world, Mr. van de Wouw thought it wrong that an "anatomical nonsense" should be stated when this joint could not possibly bend both ways. Representatives of the other European countries agreed unanimously, and the English delegation was requested to present this problem to the Kennel Club. In 1965 the Kennel Club in England published its decision to change the Chow Chow Standard accordingly.

JUDGING AND CHAMPIONSHIPS

As in England, there is no point system on the Continent, nor does the number of entries at a show influence the progress to the title in any way. However, there are differences between the English and the Continental regulations for champion titles and the classes at shows. On the Con-

Quan van Majodo, born in the 1930's, was bred and owned by J. Doll. By Kou-Ling Umatsu *ex* Ninon van Majodo.

tinent black Chows are judged in separate classes and have their own champion titles, separate from "the other coloured" specimens. Reds, fawns (cinnamon in the United States), blues and whites are judged together in the same classes. Long-haired and short-haired specimens are judged together also.

Instead of points, the winning dogs of each sex get a National Championship Certificate C.A.C. (*Certificat d'Aptitude au Championat*), and at an international show a C.A.C.I.B. (*Certificat d'Aptitude au Championat Internationale de Beaute*) as well.

At most shows there are three or four classes for each sex of both blacks and "other colours": (1) Open Class (15 months and older); (2) Junior Class (9-24 months); (3) Champion Class (in some countries for dogs which already have one or more C.A.C.'s or C.A.C.I.B.'s. In Holland for full champions only); (4) Bred by exhibitor. The judge has to qualify every single exhibit. He has to express his opinion on the dog's qualities by characterizing it as excellent, very good, good or moderate. The first four dogs of each class have to be placed in order of merit. The winning dogs of the various classes compete for the Best of Sex. The best male and female get the C.A.C., and at international shows, the C.A.C.I.B. as well, but only if qualified as "excellent." The best of the sexes have to compete for Best of Breed at the end.

The judge has to write a judging report on every single dog; this report is published. In the Scandinavian countries it is written in the ring by a secretary and published at once. In other countries, like West Germany and Holland, the judge has to send his report to the Kennel Club within a month after the show. The qualification system assures that only "excellent" dogs can become champions. Instead of disqualifying a dog for serious faults or lack of quality, it leaves the judge the possibility to qualify it as "moderate." In smaller shows and at those where quality is not high, sometimes none of the exhibits in the classes is qualified as "excellent," and the certificate is withheld.

For the national champion title a dog needs four C.A.C.'s under at least two different judges. Moreover, there is the stipulation that the last certificate has to be gained after the dog has reached the age of 27 months. This means that the dog has to be fully matured to get the title. Since there are only four to seven shows a year in each of the Continental countries, it is obvious that there are few national champions. The requirements for the title are stiff, especially for brood bitches. For the title of International Champion a dog has to gain four C.A.C.I.B.'s in three different countries, and one of the certificates must be won in his own country. A dog has to be at least 15 months old to compete for the C.A.C.I.B., and there must be at least twelve months between the first and last C.A.C.I.B. In contrast to the C.A.C., however, the second best of sex may get the certificate if the winning dog already has an International Champion title.

This makes the International Champion title easier to acquire than the national championship title in many countries on the Continent. In Holland, for instance, a full national champion which wins its class may compete for the C.A.C. in spite of his title. Many feel that only the best dog should win, whether he is a champion or not. The only way to beat a full champion is to try to breed a better one. There have been Dutch champions with eleven C.A.C.'s to their credit. Needless to say, they were great champions.

The Federation Cynologique Internationale confers the international title. The F.C.I. binds most of the Continental countries. Their Kennel Clubs are members of the F.C.I., and they send their delegates to the annual F.C.I. congress. They have their representatives on the various boards, and the F.C.I. regulations are binding for the member-countries. The F.C.I. Committee appoints the number of international shows to be organized every year in each of the countries and sanctions the competition for the C.A.C.I.B. on these shows.

It was an F.C.I. decision to give champion titles for blacks separately. The intention was not only to judge them separately from the other colored specimens but also to have them bred purely (blacks to blacks only). In Holland and West Germany the clubs think this an absurd requirement, as breeding the blacks to reds and other colors would be conducive to good pigmentation and proper texture of the coat. Moreover the basis for breeding black to black would narrow down and might lead to having blacks become a "breed within a breed." The fact that so many blacks look "rusty," especially when between coats, was the reason that the French clubs put forward this regrettable proposal. It obtained a majority vote at a F.C.I. meeting there a few years ago.

The explanation of the organization behind the sport of dogs in Europe will give an idea of how champions are made on the Continent. It is obvious that it is a long way from the first step into the show ring to the coveted title of Full Champion.

CHOW CHOW HISTORY ON THE CONTINENT

It must be understood that not all

European countries have contributed equally to our breed. Some of them played hardly any part in Chow Chow history; others dominated during a particular period. It is remarkable that the smaller countries, such as Belgium, Holland and Luxembourg, not only put their mark on Chow breeding on the Continent, but even influenced the progress in breeding in other parts of the world. Of course, the importance of a particular country and its level of quality in a certain breed depend on whether it is the native country of one or more prominent breeders or the country where these breeders happen to be living. The first Chow Chows made their appearance on the Continent at the end of the nineteenth and the beginning of the twentieth century. They were occasionally brought from China via the East Indies, but mostly they were imported from England. At that time they were a sort of curiosity in the homes of the wealthy, the nobility, famous artists or just plain "snobs."

They were just pioneers and though in some cases a litter was bred, they are not of any interest in the history of the present day Chow Chow. After the Standard was made up in England in 1895, a few more Chows were imported occasionally, but still only by the "Continental Upper-Crust" as the mysterious "edible dog" from China. The wealthy paid extremely high prices to obtain a descendant from one of the English champions, but the dog fanciers did not pay much attention to the breed yet. It took another twenty years before Chows were entered at the dog shows. Communication was not so easy in those days, and traveling around was not very easy or comfortable. It took rather a long time before this "new breed" caught on and came into demand on the Continent. Moreover there was only sporadic contact between the Chow owners, and it was not until the late 1920's that dog shows drew foreign exhibitors now and then.

We must remember that the sport of dogs has never been commercial on the Continent the way it has become here in the United States. It was just a hobby with Chow owners and breeders; there have

Oe-Diang von Blucherheim, a cream dog born in 1935. Bred by G. de Bruyn and owned by Dr. A. Augustyn. By Bear *ex* Lee Chong van de Doorwerth.

never been really big kennels. The largest ones keep twenty to thirty dogs; others keep ten to twenty, but the majority of Chow fanciers own just a few dogs, for which they occasionally breed a litter. Prominent breeders, building up a kennel and contributing to the progress of the breed, slowly started in the 1920's. One of the first Chow Chow kennels that can be considered one of the pillars of Chow breeding on the Continent was in Belgium.

CHOW CHOWS IN BELGIUM

Madame E. du Bois de Roest started her 'T'Kell'Sie Kennels in her castle yard in Itterbeek. Madame du Bois, being a great horse-lover and a traveler crossing the Channel many times, probably became interested in Chow Chows in England. She imported many Chows from the leading kennels in England and became a well-

Chang-Shi Nit-Chan, born in 1938 and photographed here in 1939. By Ch. Rochow Adjutant *ex* Syrron Prudence. Bred and owned by Countess de Changy.

Int. Ch. Chang-Shi Rolly Polly (lying down) and Int. Ch. Chang-Shi Kitty Hawks. These two bitches were photographed in 1946.

Ch. Chang-Shi Up-To-Date, born in 1946, is shown here at nine months of age. Bred by Contess de Changy, she is owned by Henk van de Wouw. By Chang-Shi Snaff *ex* Chang-Shi Tanky.

Countess Mary de Changy in 1939 with Ch. Chang-Shi Neron and Chang-Shi Ruang. The Countess was a great European breeder of Chows.

Ch. Rochow Adjutant, by Ch. Choonam To To *ex* Rochow Alissa. Whelped in 1933, and shown here as he looked in 1938, Adjutant was bred by C.D. Rotch and was owned by the Countess de Changy

Int. Ch. Chang-Shi Ukwong, bred and owned by Countess de Changy. Born in 1946; by Chang-Shi Noch-Ka *ex* Chang-Shi Tamky. This photo was taken in 1948.

known exhibitor and judge for the breed. She had the honor of being the first Continental judge of Chows to judge in England, at the W.E.L.K.S. Show in 1934.

Amongst her importations were Red Peppin of Five Ash, from Mrs. L. Vickers, and Wigwam Jung Po, bred by Miss Brandes Ely. But her greatest success began later on when Madame du Bois imported her dogs from Mrs. V. Mannooch's world-famous Choonam Kennels. She brought many Choonams into Belgium. Among them were Ch. Choonam Yo-Ti-Ming, Choonam Fu-Shen and Choonam Black Jewel. In 1932 she purchased the full English champion Choonam Chi Foo, a dark-red male. Another interesting importation was the bitch Choonam Golden Dream, in whelp to Choonam Tai Kong. From this litter she kept a bitch, 'T'Kell'Sie Gin Fizz, a light-shaded red with a beautiful coat. The name of Gin Fizz is to be found in many of the old Continental Chow pedigrees.

In the meantime Madame du Bois had imported another dog, Ch. Rochow Brigadier, a dog that made himself a great name in Chow history. (He was a son of one of the most famous dogs, Ch. Rochow Dragoon, bred by Mr. C. Rotch, undoubtedly one of the most prominent Chow Chow breeders ever known in the history of the breed.) Brigadier's name is still a concept to be found in a countless number of pedigrees. He was used as a stud dog by many other Continental breeders and was no doubt one of the pillars of Continental Chow Chow breeding. He became an International Champion in 1934 and was one of the first Chows to gain this title. Madame du Bois had her 'T'Kell'Sie Gin Fizz bred to him (she bred several litters by this pair), and it has been proved that their puppies have been of great value to Continental Chow breeding. Some of the bitches were 'T'Kell'Sie Archue (which went to Holland), 'T'Kell'Sie Mouse (in the possession of Comtesse R. de Changy), 'T'Kell'Sie Duchess (sold to Mrs. A. Roes-Roes in Holland); the dogs were 'T'Kell'Sie Duke, 'T'Kell'Sie Tony, 'T'Kell'Sie Muso (sold to Holland), 'T'Kell'Sie Pfaffikon, 'T'Kell'Sie

Brigand. The last two dogs as well as the bitch Archue later came into the possession of Mr. Henk van de Wouw. 'T'Kell'Sie Brigand was sold again to Mr. W. Elbers in West Germany and can be found in many of the German pedigrees. No doubt all these dogs were the foundation of Chow Chow breeding in many of the Continental countries. Madame du Bois was the first in **Belgium to breed the famous English Choonam and Rochow lines together,** though several English breeders had done so before her. History has proved that from those two strains many famous dogs were produced, and Madame du Bois de Roset's name lives on in the history of Continental Chow Chow breeding.

THE CHOW CHOW IN HOLLAND

Some of the early Chow Chows in Holland had been brought along by sailors and people returning from the Dutch East Indies and China, since Holland had close ties with the Far East in the early days. Afterwards they were imported from England. They appeared at Dutch dog shows, and in 1918 the first Chow gained a championship title. It was not until 1933, however, that a second Chow Chow earned the championship title. These early Chows did not make Chow Chow history. The real Chow breeding started in Holland at Kennel of the Golliwogs, the affix of Mrs. F. Geitel de Lange, first in Velp, later on in Wageningen, Holland. She was the pioneer. The majority of her imports came from Mrs. Bernard Cutberth's Omar Kennel, the best known being Ch. Omar's Black Tower. The best one she bred was Ch. Ebony of the Golliwogs, a black dog owned by Mr. J. Dollee (Kennel van de Berenkuil). Ebony was the third Dutch champion but only the first Dutch-bred champion.

A few years after Mrs. Geitel de Lange started her Golliwogs, her cousin, Mrs. Roes-Roes, living in Oosterbeek (near Arnhem) took a great fancy to the breed. Her van de Doorwerth kennels developed into the largest existing in Holland until now, comprising twenty to thirty dogs. Mrs. Roes got her first imports from the Omars

Int. Ch. Rochow Brigadier, Continental Chow bred by C.D. Rotch and owned by Madame E. du Bois de Roest. Photographed in 1930 at one year of age. By Ch. Rochow Dragoon *ex* Red Che Kei.

as well but soon switched to other well-known kennels, choosing from the best English bloodlines as a foundation for her breeding. She bought Amwells, Rochows, Choonams and many Ttiwehs (Mrs. Amice Pitt) to raise her kennels' quality. She bought the same bloodlines the two countesses in Belgium had earlier purchased. In 1930 she imported Rochow Samson, a grandson of Ch. Chinnery on the sire's side, and of Li-Po on the dam's line. After that Pen of Amwell and Squiks of Amwell (daughter of Ch. Pusawanli, Ch. Pusa of Amwell's son) joined the Doorwerths. Mrs. Geitel de Lange bought in that same year

Miss-Chiff of Chifu, a granddaughter to Ch. Akbar. Thus more or less a family competition started, though Mrs. Geitel retired in the mid-1930's.

As Belgium was so near, Madame du Bois appeared at the Dutch shows, and her Ch. Rochow Brigadier became a full Dutch champion in 1935. In the same year Mrs. Roes finished two full champions: her importations Ch. Hilsum of Quernmore, bred by Mr. Prior, and Ch. Roebucks Aimee, from Mrs. L. Vickers, a light-shaded red with a lot of quality. Both were purchased as adults. Her breeding was Ch. Rochow Dragoon X Suye of Five Ash. The

Ch. Kwan Jin van de Doorwerth, born in 1938. Bred and owned by Mrs. A. Roes-Roes. By Chu Tong van de Doorwerth *ex* Mirdsa van de Doorwerth. Photograph taken when the bitch was 4 years old.

fourth Chow gaining the title in the same year was the bitch Angola van de Doorwerth, owned by Mr. J. Smit. Several other Ttiwehs were purchased, as well as two others with first class pedigrees and of great value to her breeding. They were Ch. Chu Tong of Ttiweh, Choonam Chu Tang, a self-red, very sound, well-balanced dog, and the bitch Choonam Kin-Sha, a Ch. Choonam Hung Kwong daughter, a light-shaded red one with extremely heavy bone, a beautiful coat and a nice big head. She was seldom shown, but her career as a dam was well known. It must be admitted that Mrs. Roes chose the bloodlines she bought very carefully. Another bitch added to the kennel was 'T'Kell'Sie Duchess, a Ch. Rochow Brigadier daughter bought from Madam Du Bois in Belgium. These bloodlines produced great effects on the quality of the Dutch Chow breeding in general at that time. Mrs. Roes exported now and then in the early and mid-1930's, and Doorwerths are to be found in several

of the old German pedigrees. She bred some really outstanding dogs whose names are still found on the pedigrees of some famous present-day Chows. Some of her best dogs which live on in history are: Ch. Angola van de Doorwerth, Ch. Kwan Jin van de Doorwerth, Ch. Wang Many van de Doorwerth (owned by Henk van de Wouw) and the two brothers Ch. Hoeng-Woe van de Doorwerth and Ch. Wong-Again van de Doorwerth, out of 'T'Kell'Sie Duchess.

The last four were sired by a beautiful dog named Chu Tong van de Doorwerth (Ch. Chu Tong of Ttiweh X Choonam Kin-Sha) a big dog with grand bone, a beautiful body and a very nice head. He was only shown twice but proved his value as a stud. In the late 1930's and early 1940's Mrs. Roes owned several excellent-quality dogs with beautiful pedigrees. She was on top in Chows, the most successful breeder and exhibitor in the country. World War II had started and her beautiful home was half an hour on foot from Arnhem, which in 1944 was the site of the Battle of Arnhem. Oosterbeek was in the middle of the front-line. Shells were flying all around Mrs. Roes's house, and it was hit several times. The situation defied description. The Roes family had to evacuate the house within a quarter of an hour but not before Mrs. Roes had to witness the horror of the shooting of her dogs, one by one. It was the end of the Doorwerth Kennels.

Apart from what this meant to this prominent Dutch Chow lover and breeder, it was a tremendous loss for the Dutch Chow fancy as well as for the whole Continental Chow breeding program. The two largest Chow Chow kennels had been destroyed. Again over twenty dogs from the finest English bloodlines had been killed. From the Doorwerth Kennels only one single bitch was saved. Mrs. Roes's daughter had taken Tsing-Pauw to the side of the house and fastened her to a tree. So Tsing-Pauw van de Doorwerth (in whelp) went with the Roes family to a safer part of the country. After the war Mrs. Roes bred one more litter, but with the memory of what had happened to her dogs, she didn't have the courage to start all over again. Her beautiful place was sold, and the family moved to Arnhem. Her last Chow Mrs. Roes kept just as a pet.

Undeniably, however, Mrs. Roes was the one who was responsible for the growing interest and quality of Chow Chows in Holland at that time. It is therefore no co-incidence that she is the aunt of Kitty van Donge (Ki-Dong), now Mrs. Kitty van de Wouw. Kitty had owned two Doorwerths and used to spend many weekends and holidays at the Doorwerth Kennels, ever since she was a school-girl. When she received a postcard informing her of the Doorwerth tragedy she went to see Mrs. Roes. As there were no trains or cars running during this terrible period of the war, she traveled eight hours by bicycle. Tsing-Pauw van de Doorwerth had had her litter (by Ch. Hoeng-Woe van de Doorwerth). She was a sister to the beautiful Chu-Tong, while Hoeng-Wou van de Doorwerth was his son. Kitty took a little bitch puppy home in her bicycle-bag. That little bitch was Adinda van de Doorwerth, a name found in many pedigrees on both sides of the Atlantic. Just after the war, she was mated to Chang-Shi Noch-Ka and produced the fine dog Ch.

Mrs. A. Roes-Roes with Tsing-Pauw van de Doorwerth. This red bitch was born in 1939 and was 3 years of age when this photograph was taken. By Ch. Chu Tong of Ttiweth *ex* Choonam Kin Sha.

Chutong van de Doorwerth, born 1937 and photographed at 2 years of age. Bred and owned by Mrs. A. Roes-Roes. By Ch. Chu Tong of Ttiweh *ex* Choonam Kin Sha.

Ki-Dong King. Another time, mated to Int. Ch. Kou-Ling Xolsky, Adinda produced Ch. Ki-Dong Cheng Wong.

Some pre-war breeders have to be mentioned together with some valuable imports because of their contribution to the breed. In 1933 Mr. J. Smit bred his Ch. Angola van de Doorwerth (A-Tjoe van de Doorwerth X Pen of Amwell) to Int. Ch. Rochow Brigadier. Thus a dog named Bear was produced; Bear is of interest as the sire of Pucka Sahib von Blucherheim, Oediang von Blucherheim and Ch. Ebony von Blucherheim. They were all bred by Mr. G. de Bruin in cooperation with Dr. A. Augustyn, who imported the bitch Li-Ru of Squerries from Mrs. Gerhold. This bitch, mated to Pucka Sahib von Blucherheim, produced the outstanding bitch Magna von Blucherheim. She was bred back to her sire Pucka Sahib, and a dog from that litter was the well-known black, Ch. Matjan. The Blucherheims show beautiful, heavy, very big typical heads, full of expression. In type they resembled (much later appearing) Chang-Shis and Kou-Lings. Ch. Matjan has proved his value to the breed.

Two more dogs which deserve mention are, first, the deep mahogany-red Kowa-Acajou by Mulfra Sarab (Saon the Strong X Am. Ch. Moosilauke Pao Yen) out of Lowenlu (a Ch. Rochow Brigadier daughter). He was a dog with a beautiful, typical head, owned by Mrs. Geytenbeek. An interesting story from that time concerns Miss Boudewijnse, a young English lady living in Holland. She owned an English bitch, Penglou Eastern Duchess (Ch. Rochow Dragoon daughter), that was mated to the Countess de Changy's Ch. Rochow Adjutant. A dog from this litter was

Ch. Hoeng Woe van de Doorwerth, born in 1938. Bred and owned by Mrs. A. Roes-Roes. By Chu-tong van de Doorwerth *ex* T'Kell'Sie Duchess. Photographed at 3 years of age.

Mirdsa van de Doorwerth, born in 1935 and bred by Mrs. A. Roes. She was owned by Kitty van Donge. By Ch. Hilsum Wundah of Quernmore *ex* Ch. Roebuck's Aimee.

sold to Mrs. Roes-Roes, but this male with such a valuable pedigree behind him produced only one litter. The second dog worth mentioning was Kim, who left the country for England with Miss Boudewijnse because of the war situation. He became the possession of the ladies Elam and Braye. As sometimes happened in England, his name was changed and he lived on as Ransom of Padua, becoming a popular stud dog in Britain.

Shortly before the Second World War several Belgian dogs were imported, such as 'T'Kell'Sie Pfaffikon, Ch. Kou-Ling Mouch-Ka, Kou-Ling Oli Thu-Fu, Chang-Shi Houplah and Chang-Shi A-Whang-Ti. From the last two the dog Shu-Lang-Leh was bred, owned by Mr. J. van Tuinen

(Nunatak), the owner of Ch. Matjan at the time. His father, P. van Tuinen (van de Oldenhove), also bred Chows. Son J. van Tuinen owned the bitch Joyce van de Oldenhove; mated with Ch. Matjan, she produced a bitch named Bonnie van Nunatak, which was sold to Mrs. F. Pieters-Hummal. She mated her to Int. Ch. Chang-Shi U'Kwong and got a beautiful litter which included Hwang-Ti Che-Kwong, the sire of the famous Int. Ch. Astom. During the first years of the war, breeders were not very active, as times were too uncertain. There were a few dog shows, though, and in 1942 the Countess de Changy's bitch Chang-Shi Nit-Chi gained her Dutch title and became the first of that kennel to be a full Dutch champion.

As Chows used to be called "Chinese Keeshonds" in Holland, the Chow fanciers joined the Keeshond Club. In 1941, however, the Dutch Chow Chow Club was founded. The only founder who is still active in Chows is Mr. Henk van de Wouw. One of the members of the first Dutch Chow Chow Club Committee was Mrs. M.

Wodan, blue dog born in the 1940's, was bred and owned by A.V. Hoof. By T'Kell'Sie Pfafikon *ex* Kou-Ling Zah-Zah. Photographed when the dog was 3 years of age.

Kloos-Dixon, grandmother of Mrs. Minnie Odenkirchen, well-known for the Mi-Pao Kennels in Canada.

During the first few years after the second World War, the Chow had the misfortune of becoming a "fashionable" dog, with all the consequences of that doubtful honor. Chows were second in popularity in Holland to German Shepherds, according to the number of pedigrees entered in the Dutch studbook. Tremendous production resulted that had nothing to do with what could be necessarily called good breeding. It was the mating of one Chow to another Chow, perhaps owned by somebody across the street. Fortunately, a small group of dedicated breeders who cared about lines and pedigrees carefully preserved their good stock. There were only a few dogs from the old strain left after the war. The Belgian breeders had a head-start in rebuilding their stock because they had been liberated earlier. When traveling was more or less possible again, Dutch breeders eventually profited from outstanding Belgian stock. A few good Dutch bitches were mated to Belgian males, and some fine puppies were imported. Thus the post-war Dutch Chows are mainly based on Belgian blood and therefore indirectly on English bloodlines. This is where the present-day "Dutch type of Chow" comes from.

In that early post-war period, the atmosphere was very friendly and there was real co-operation in contributing to the building up of the breed. It may be useful to mention the importations: Ch. Chang-Shi Up To Date (Henk van de Wouw), Kou-Ling Umatsu (Luckhard), and Dutch and Int. Ch. Kou-Ling Xolsky (Mr. Nuyen). As these dogs are much interwoven in the pedigrees of the majority of top Chows, one of the kennels that continued breeding and deserves a mention is Van Majodo, owned by Mr. and Mrs. J. Doll. They were first of all breeders and did not care much for exhibiting. They bred, owned and imported some high-pedigree dogs, beautiful specimens worthy of being champions. Majodo still occurs on pedigrees of their progeny in all parts of the world. The Dolls

Ch. Chang-Shi Vanguard, red dog born in 1947. Bred by the Countess de Changy and owned by Rene Hassenforder. By Kiwu Koo-Chih *ex* Int. Ch. Chang-Shi Rolly Polly. Photographed at three years of age.

Ch. Xilla van Majodo, born in 1954. Bred by J. Doll and owned by Mrs. A. Velder-v. Rooyen. This three-year-old bitch was by Li-Nu-Tsja's Golden Wong *ex* Quan van Majodo.

mainly kept six to seven Chows. They used top dog for their bitches and stressed head type in their breeding. To name a few of their breeding we mention Ch. Xilla van Majodo (Mrs. van Rooyen), Ch. Woolly van Majodo (van de Wouw) and Int. Ch. U'Milo van Majodo (Lou Nuyen).

The basis of the kennel was Quan van Majodo (Kou-Ling Umatsu X Ninon van Majodo), a heavy bitch with an extremely big head, really the limit for a female. She was a valuable brood bitch, and mated to Int. Ch. Kou-Ling Xolsky she produced not only Int. Ch. U'Milo van Majodo but also U'Kwa van Majodo (dam of Ch. Wooly van Majodo), and that beautiful dog Za-Chou van Majodo, a shaded red good-sized dog with plenty of bone, a magnificent head and wonderful expression. He was a born champion but was shown only twice at a club show. He was one of the finest sires of his time, as he stamped his type on his progeny. Though the van Majodo Kennel was a small one, it did much for the improvement of the breed.

Another breeder of importance was Mr. P. Luckhard, owner of the Luchow Kennels. He started in Chows in the early 1940's and knew very well what he was after. When the war was over he had his bitches mated to the best Belgian males, mainly Kou-Lings, and imported several Chow Chows from this kennel. One of the puppies he added to his kennel was Kou-Ling Umatsu (Kou-Ling Tcheou X Kou-Ling Saida). Later on the bitch Kou-Ling Saida was bought as well. She was a self-red with a beautiful head full of expression. Another well-known inmate of this kennel was Ch. Luchow Ty-Lo, a beautifully balanced blue dog with a magnificent head for a blue. Mr Luckhard selected his stud dog and bitches carefully, which resulted in a beautiful type of Chow. In the early and mid-1950's the kennel had consolidated an excellent group of about fifteen dogs from the best bloodlines. Then, on an ill-fated day, an epidemic struck the kennel, killing most of the dogs. The result of many years of great effort was lost, and the Luckhards stopped. The few remaining dogs were sold.

Tsjomoloengma Chi Pham, born in 1970, shown here at 1½ years of age. Her breeder-owner is Mrs. A. van de Saag. Sired by Ch. Tschiang Kai Tchek van Mongolie ex Rodeza's Petia.

Ukwa van Majodo, born 1952. Bred and owned by J. Doll. She was sired by Int. Ch. Kou-Ling Xolsky ex Quan van Majodo.

One of them, a bitch named Pei-Whangs Ti-Ni, came into the possession of Miss W. de Jeu (Mrs. Lamerus-de Jeu now). Ti-Ni was a daughter of Ch. Ki-Dong King out of Luchow Panja (a daughter of Int. Ch. Kou-Ling Rex). She was not a show bitch, but mated to Ch. Man-Chu van Mongolie she proved her value to the breed as the dam of the beautiful Wamchow Biyanka, a well-balanced red bitch with good bone and a gorgeous head, and her brother Wamchow Bhe-Tong, winner of two champion certificates. He had the biggest, heaviest head ever seen in a show, but he was not an easy dog to show. A sensational result, however, was the breeding of Wamchow Biyanka to Za-Chou van Ma-

Ch. Man-Chu van Mongolie, born 1956, was bred and owned by Henk van de Wouw of Holland. By King van Mongolie ex Ch. Woolly van Majodo.

jodo, producing, though not in the same litter, German, Dutch and Int. Ch. Wamchow Che-Foo, owned by Mrs. C. Hoffman-Rooseboom, West Germany.

Dutch and Int. Ch. Wamchow Goe-Neng was owned by Henk van de Wouw, who also owned Wamchow Chan-Ny, litter-sister to Che-Foo. These two dogs were undoubtedly among the most famous on the Continent. Another well-known dog, named Wamchow Fabian, owned by Mrs. Reyenga, came from Heyville's Honey Boi (Ch. Wongtung's Chang of Kanton X Ch. Rowena of Ravensway), imported by Mr. Goorkate. Fabian was a big deep self-

Ch. Shao Ying Tjio van Mongolie, born 1948. This red bitch was bred and owned by Henk van de Wouw of Holland. By Ch. Ki-Dong King ex Ch. Chang Shi Up To Date. This photograph was taken when she was four years old.

Kongo (a dog) and Karga (a bitch) vom Hendrickshof. Born in 1952 and photographed at five months of age. Breeder-owner, H. Borchardt. By Int. Ch.Kou-Ling Xolsky *ex* Ko-San-Lo Kwangsi.

Int. Ch. Regina van de Loumi-Hoeve, born in 1958, bred and owned by Lou Nuyen. By Ch. Enrico of Junggwaw *ex* Int. Ch. Choonam van de Loumi-Hoeve. She is pictured at the age of ten months.

Wamchow Biyanka, born 1958. Bred and owned by Mrs. W. Lamerus. She was photographed here at 2 years of age. By Man Chu van Mongolie *ex* Pei Whang's Ti-Ni.

red male with a beautiful body and a delightful mover. After losing Biyanka and having some other bad luck, this small but previously very successful kennel lost that beautiful bloodline. It has now started new activities.

The next kennel to be mentioned in Dutch Chow Chow history is the Loumi-Hoeve, owned by Lou and Miep Nuyen. They started with a pet Chow but a few years after the war built up a kennel consisting of twelve to fifteen dogs. In 1948 they bought a puppy from Mr. Bechet in Belgium that grew up to be the famous Dutch and Int. Ch. Kou-Ling Xolsky, a dog that gave the kennel its fame. Xolsky dominates the pedigrees of the post-war Chows in Holland and possibly even more so in West Germany. This was a result of a combination of circumstances. First of all, the dog itself: he was a small, well-proportioned dog with good bone and beautiful coat. Counting against him was lack of breadth in the back-end, but it was his magnificent head with glorious expression that made him so much admired. Since the Loumi-Hoeve kennel was situated in the southeastern part of Holland, close to the German border, Lou Nuyen exhibited Xolsky constantly in Belgium, France and Switzerland but especially in Germany, where there was a lack of quality in the Chows at the time. Of course, a dog full of type like Xolsky was in great demand as a stud dog, for even on bitches lacking in type of head he provided improvement. He was bred to over a hundred bitches all told, thus printing his name in countless numbers of pedigrees, including in England, when one of his sons, Dutchman, was sent to Mrs. Dulcie Smith of Hanoi Kennels in England.

Lou Nuyen bred a bitch, Int. Ch. Choonam van de Loumi-Hoeve, by Int. Ch. Kou-Ling Xolsky X Dutch and Int. Ch. Chin Yu of Hanoi. She was an importation, bred by Mrs. Dulcie Smith. She was sent to England in whelp to Int. Ch. U'Milo van Majodo and whelped her puppies in quarantine. The breeder of that litter was Mrs. Dulcie Smith. The bitch came out of quarantine three months after giving birth and stayed with Dulcie Smith. They called her the "puppy-box," since the next time she was in season she was mated to Ch. Enrico of Junggwaw and sent back home in whelp. From this litter Lou Nuyen kept Dutch and Int. Ch. Regina van de Loumi-Hoeve. When Chin-Yu's puppy U Mi of Hanoi was shown in England as an adult, she caused a lot of controversy over her type, which was referred to as the "exaggerated Dutch type." As a matter of fact she was so similar to Quan van Majodo that it was not the "Dutch type" but the Quan van Majodo type. It is understandable that this was strange to English Chow fanciers, as it was the limit to Continental opinion. But it improved the type of Mrs. Smith's dogs, which gained great fame abroad. Xolsky got his Dutch champion title at the show in Utrecht in 1950, under Countess de Changy, and won two more Championship Certificates. He received over thirty C.A.C.I.B.'s during his career. Bred to top Dutch bitches, he produced several valuable offspring such as Int. Ch. U'Milo van Majodo (a pick of a litter from Quan van Majodo), Ch. Ki-Dong Cheng Wong (owned by Mr. J. de Graaf), the famous King van Mongolie (owned and bred by Henk van de Wouw), Za-Chou van Majodo, U-Kwa van Majodo.

Yusung, red dog born in 1950. Bred and owned by J. Martin. By Int. Ch. Kou-Ling Xolsky *ex* Yula v.d. Doorwerth. A winner in 1951, he was photographed here at 3 years of age.

The kennel kept Int. Ch. U'Milo van Majodo. He was winning a lot abroad and got his International Champion title, but he never attained the Dutch title. He was a nice dog and showed his mother's type with the same big head, but he did not possess the fine nobility and dignity of his sire. After Lou Nuyen passed away, too early and too young, the kennel was reduced by slowly halting the breeding program. Miep kept the remaining dogs but retired from Chow activities. She is still interested in the breed, however, and keeps a Chow as a pet all the time.

After the Loumi-Hoeve Kennels, we mention the Liang-Ming-Keou Kennel. Mr. H. Steegmans founded this kennel mainly on Xolsky blood, even making intensive inbreeding on that line. He has been in Chows for many years and is the breeder of the famous black dog Dutch and Int. Ch. Kuang-Wu of Liang-Ming-Keou, sired by Mi-Ka-Lo van de Loumi-

Int. and Dutch Ch. Kai-Men-Ti Liweng, born in 1954, was bred and owned by Mrs. H. Wachholtz. By Hwang-Ti Tsjia Jen *ex* Kai-Men-Ti New O'Lan. Photographed at four years of age.

Hoeve (Mi-Ka-Lo was a beautiful blue Xolsky son that died early) X Joengkai van de Loumi-Hoeve (bred in on Xolsky). He was a middle-sized, beautiful black dog, well balanced and heavy-boned, with a big, gorgeous head. Another champion in the kennel was a son of this famous dog, named Ch. Popoff van Sebastopol (dam Matouscha van de Loumi-Hoeve, also Xolsky-line). With some new blood in his bloodline from the dog Henk van de Falkenweg (an Int. Ch. Wamchow Che-Foo son) and Vivianne van Mongolie (an Int. Ch. Wamchow Goe-Neng daughter), Mr. Steegmans is continuing successfully today. It may be of interest that Ch. Kuang-Wu of Liang-Ming-Keou is the sire of Ch. Yakimov, owned by Mr. J. Scholten, and also of You-Two's Commander-Black, owned

by the Mi-Pao Kennels in Canada and bred by the You-Two Kennels of Miss Martha Visser.

Miss Visser had been in Chows for a few years before she bred her first litter in 1962 from her bitch Ho-Thy von Meh-Thue (to Int. Ch. Emperor van de Tongelreep X Ch. Wing-Wa van Mongolie), bred by Mr. Erich Buchner from Berlin. She bred this bitch to Int. Ch. Wamchow Che-Foo and got only one puppy, but he was Canadian and American Ch. You-Two's Ganti-Biroe Aloes. She imported an English bitch, Zena of Junggwaw (Ch. Enrico of Junggwaw X Princess of Junggwaw), bred by Mr. Stanley Smedley. The present kennel is based and constantly bred in on Mi-Pao's stock, of which she imported Int. Ch. Mi-Pao's Piwa Rangan (Int. Ch. Chang-Shi Hong Kwong X Canadian Ch. Tiga) and Mi-Pao's Poetri (Ch. Djimat van de Martinhoeve X Canadian Ch. Tiga). Piwa was a beautiful self-red dog with a magnificent head. He died before he had finished his Dutch title but is a well-known sire found in many pedigrees. From both Mi-Pao dogs Martha bred her You-Two's Echo Emperor, a fine shaded red dog that won three Championship Certificates but had bad luck and has not won the title yet.

Wamchow Bhe-Tong, red dog born in 1958 and bred by his owner, Mrs. W. Lamerus. By Ch. Man-Chu van Mongolie *ex* Pei Whang's Ti-Ni. Photographed at two years of age.

Ch. Ki-Dong Cheng Wong, born in 1951, was bred by Kitty van Donge. Owned by J. de Graaf. Sired by Int. Ch. Kou-Ling Xolsky *ex* Adinda van de Doorwerth. Three years of age in this photograph.

Ch. Bbormot Dan Ul, whelped in 1950, bred by Tom Robb. Sired by Ch. Bbormot Yung-Li *ex* Fan Lei of Hishan. Owner, Rune Johnson of Holland.

King van Mongolie, born in 1950. Bred and owned by Henk van de Wouw. By Int. Ch. Kou-Ling Xolsky *ex* Ch. Shao Ying Tjio van Mongolie.

Int. and Dutch Ch. Pei Whang's Yang Moi, born in 1952, is shown here at ten years of age. Bred by W. Taale and owned by Henk van de Wouw. By Ch. Ki-Dong King *ex* Luchow Panja.

Another successful dog from this kennel is Swedish Ch. You-Two's His Highness (Int. Ch. Mi-Pao's Piwa Rangan X Mi-Pao's Poetri). The kennel now consists of twelve to fifteen dogs and is continuing to breed actively today.

Another kennel that must be mentioned is Kai-Men-Ti, owned by Mrs. H.

Int. and Dutch Ch. Wang Wei Chou King, born in 1956, is pictured here at five years of age. Bred by J. Tonnaer and owned by J. Schenk. By Int. Ch. Kai-Men-Ti Liweng *ex* Kai-Men-Ti Li-Li.

Wachholtz, who started in Germany in 1943 with the Von Der Waldmark Kennel. She came to Holland after she had founded the Kai-Men-Ti Kennel in 1948. The name of this kennel is synonymous with its most famous product: Dutch and Int. Ch. Kai-Men-Ti Liweng, sired by Hwang-Ti Tsjia Jen (Tsjoeng Kwa van de Bakenberg X Hwang-Ti Donka-Chang) out of Kai-Men-Ti New O'Lhan (Golf von Enztal X Mah-Ling Beauty). Liweng was a beautifully balanced red dog with a heavy body, good bone and a very nice head. He carried a good quality coat and was an excellent mover. Looking at his pedigree, you would not expect to see such a fine dog as Liweng. He holds the record for the most bitches mated to one dog. Far more than a hundred bitches were bred to this great sire, who undeniably put his stamp on his progeny. He proved his value as one of the top sires of champions by producing no fewer than 16 International or full National Champions, including his daughter and kennel mate, the beautiful black bitch Int. Ch. Beauty. Other champions included Int. Ch. Kai-Men-Ti Tay-Yun (Cottafavi, Luxembourg), Int. Ch. Kai-Men-Ti Wun-iang (Mr. Metzger, Germany), and Nordic Ch. Kai-Men-Ti Yuan (Mrs. G. Adner, Sweden). Liweng died in 1965, when he was eleven years old. Mrs. Wachholtz reduced activities slowly then. She bred a few more litters but did not show anymore. She

still owns some grandchildren of her great Liweng, who was almost a legend during his life and lives on in countless numbers of pedigrees of present-day Chows; many of his descendants still win constantly.

A small breeder who always cares for quality is Mrs. A. van der Saag of the Tsjomoloengma Kennels. She owned Anjalina, a beautiful bitch with a gorgeous head, by Int. Ch. Kai-Men-Ti Liweng X Brendana. This bitch was mated to Hwang-Ti Chao-Chun, producing the bitch Ch. Tsjomoloengma Aki-Mito, a magnificent red creature, perfectly proportioned, with great bone and a glorious head. It was Aki-Mito that was greatly admired by Mrs. Vivian Shryock of California when she judged at the Dutch Chow Chow Club Specialty in 1959 and put her up as Best Bitch in Show. Mrs. van der Saag owns a small kennel of usually about five dogs but always chooses the finest bloodlines for her breeding.

Now we come to the van Mongolie Kennel, owned by Henk and Kitty van de Wouw. It is one of the oldest and largest and also one of the most successful kennels in Holland during the past twenty-five years. These days the kennel has about twenty dogs. Henk van de Wouw started in 1937, cooperating with Mr. A. van Hoof in Tilburg in the Ho-Wo-Wonk Kennel when he was studying economics. At that time showing results were more successful than the breeding results; they won with the im-

Anjalina, born in 1955, owned by Mrs. A. van der Saag. By Int. Ch. Kai-Men-Ti Liweng *ex* Brendana.

ported dog T'Kell Sie Pfaffikon and later on with the bitch Ch. Wang-Mang van de Doorwerth.

In 1941 he started his own van Mongolie Kennel, founded on Doorwerth blood. During the war he bred some litters and showed his nice home-bred dog Edelknaap van Mongolie. Even more success came after the war. Henk was the very first going to Belgium and imported the beautiful bitch puppy that later became Ch. Chang-Shi Up To Date, by Chang-Shi Snaff out of Chang-Shi Tamky, a Ch. Rochow Adjutant daughter. She became one of the founders of the post-war van Mongolie Kennel. She was a very heavily built bitch with

Int. Ch. Fy-Yong van de Tongelreep, whelped in 1954, photographed at the age of 3 years. Bred by L.G.M. v.d. Broek.

great bone and a big, very typical head. She caused a sensation when shown for the first time, and she gained her title easily. The Countess de Changy's daughter, seeing her as an adult, remarked that she had never seen any Chow so similar to Ch. Rochow Adjutant She was mated to Kitty's Ch. Ki-Dong King, and this mating resulted in the fine bitches Ch. Mouch-Ka van Mongolie (Mr. van de Broek) and Ch. Shao-Ying-Tjio van Mongolie (van de Wouw). Mated to Ch. Ki-Dong Cheng Wong, she produced the German Ch. Wing-Wa van Mongolie and German Ch. Wau-Kwong van Mongolie, both owned by Mr. Erich Buchner from Berlin.

Henk and Kitty married in 1949 and their dogs came together in van Mongolie. They owned six Chows altogether, four of them full champions. There was, for example, Ch. Ki-Dong King. This dog had a successful show career. He gained nine Dutch championship certificates, holding the present record. King was the only dog to beat his half-brother, Int. Ch. Chang-Shi U-Kwong, in Holland, as happened in Utrecht when he was four years old. He was last shown at the age of eleven at the Dutch Chow Chow Club Specialty, under Mr. A.O. Grindey, an authority on the breed.

Ch. Man-Chu van Mongolie, born 1956, bred and owned by Henk van de Wouw. Sire was King van Mongolie ex Ch. Woolly van Majodo. Photograph taken when Man-Chu was 2½ years old.

Ch. Tsjomoloengma Aki Mi Ta, born in 1957, was bred and owned by Mrs. A. van de Saag. Sired by Hwang Ti Chao Chun ex Anjalina. Photographed at two years of age.

Fifty Chows were entered and quality was high, and King won Best in Show. Mr. Grindey wrote in *Our Dogs* of December 27, 1957:

> "My best of champions, an eleven-year-old dog, Ch. Ki-Dong King, was a real beauty such as I would like to see in Britain. In my opinion he is as good or better than any dog we have here today. I wished King had been entered in the National Dog Show in Birmingham the week before (approx. 3,500 entries), as he would, in my opinion, have won Best in Show all breeds there."

King proved his value as a sire. His name can be found in many important pedigrees all over the world. He is the grandsire of the famous Ch. Ghat de la Moulaine. From his progeny the best-known are Ch. Shao-Ying Tjio van Mongolie, Ch. Mouch-Ka van Mongolie and Ch. It. Perla van Mongolie, owned by Professor Guisanni, Italy. Dam of those three was Ch. Chang-Shi Up To Date. Others include: Dutch and Int. Ch. Pei-Whang's Yang Moi (dam: Luchow Panja), American and Mexican Ch. Ychouchanna van Mongolie (dam: Ch. Woolly van Majodo), owned by Mr. R. Hassenforder, France, and later by Clif and Vivian Shryock of

Ch. Ki-Dong King, born in 1946 and photographed here at 11 years of age. Bred and owned by Kitty van Donge. By Chang-Shi Noch-Ka *ex* Adinda van de Doorwerth.

California. The latter was the dam of the legendary Ghat.

Dutch and Int. Ch. Pei Whangs's Yang Moi, bred by W. Taale, was a great show bitch. She liked the show ring and showed herself, dancing through the ring as if she knew how beautiful she was. She holds the present record for Dutch championships, and Henk doubts any bitch will ever take it from her. She won no fewer than eleven Championship Certificates and many Bests in Group as well. Her last Championship Certificate was won when she was over ten years old at the big Rotterdam Ahoy Show, beating Int. Ch. Wamchow Che-Foo for Best of Breed and on the same day winning Best in Group again. It was a tragedy that from all the van der Wouw champion bitches she was one of the two that never produced. Ch. Shao-Ying Tjio was a big self-red bitch with great bone and a beautiful body. Once shown in the Hague under Mrs. Amice Pitt (on that historic day when this judge initiated the plans for sending to England Int. Ch. Chang-Shi U-Kwong), Shao won the bitch Championship Certificate, beating two of the Countess de Changy's champion bitches. It was a great thrill for her owners. Mrs. Pitt said on the occasion: "That bitch has no legs; she has real pillars." Mated to Int.

Kwan-Ti van de Tongelreep, red dog whelped in 1958 and pictured here at 2 years of age. He was sired by Int. Ch. Emperor van de Tongelreep *ex* Ch. Mouch-Ka van Mongolie. Bred and owned by L.G.M. v.d. Broek of Holland.

Ch. Kou-Ling Xolsky, she is the dam of King van Mongolie, a famous dog pet-named Prinsje. He was only shown on one occasion and won indeed, but he unfortunately had a small patch on his tongue, and his owners did not like him to become a subject of argument. Some specialist judges, however, thought it wrong to stress that point so severely, since he could not be faulted otherwise. He had huge bone, the heaviest I ever saw in a Chow, a beautiful body and a magnificent head. Prinsje's imperfection no doubt was lucky for his competitors. Mr. Grindey wrote: "A magnificent creature which must be worth his weight in gold as a stud force. He has Chang-Shi Noch-Ka on both his sire's and dam's side."

The Countess de Changy thought him the best Chow she had ever seen, and Paul Odenkirchen wrote in *The American Chow Chow*, October, 1964: "Such a dog is the incomparable King van Mongolie (Prinsje) who is regarded by many breeders the world over, including ourselves, as coming closer to the ideal specimen than any Chow to date. If I had to choose it would therefore be Prinsje." Among his progeny were dogs like the very famous Dutch and Int. Ch. Emperor van de Tongelreep and his brothers Int. Ch. Fy-Yong van de Tongelreep, Ch. Man-Chu van Mongolie. Another dog that has been of importance was Prins Again van Mongolie (out of Ch. Chang-Shi Up To Date). Ch. Man-Chu van Mongolie was a self-red, very short-coupled dog with great bone, a fine deep body and a magnificent head. He had a brilliant show career, being the only Chow dog on the Continent ever put over Int. Ch. Astom. This happened at the Hofstad Show in the Hague under Mr. van de Broek, just after Astom's return from England. Mrs. Vivian Shryock put him up Best in Show at the Dutch Chow Club Specialty when she judged in 1959 and said she

King van Mongolie, born 1950. Bred and owned by Henk van de Wouw of Holland. By Int. Ch. Kou-Ling Xolsky *ex* Ch. Shao Ying Tjio van Mongolie. Photographed at 2 years of age.

would have liked to own him. Man-Chu was the son of another inmate of the kennel, the beautiful red bitch Ch. Wooly van Majodo (Prins Again van Mongolie X U Kawa van Majodo), a middle-sized bitch with heavy bone and a beautiful head and expression. She won under the Countess de Changy at the World Championship Show in Dortmund, West Germany, in 1956.

At the height of success in showing as well as breeding, with six full Dutch champions in the kennel, times changed into what can be called "the dark years of Mongolie." An infection was brought into the kennel and the famous stud dogs were not able to impregnate bitches, so they no longer produced, a real tragedy with such valuable stock. From 1956 until 1961 one litter of one single puppy was bred. The van Mongolie owners had to make up their minds: either stop completely or get new blood and continue. Meantime they moved to their present address. The black bitch Ming Lee of Silverway was imported from Mrs. M.L. Bird in England. She was by Ch. Illustrious Lad of U'Kwong X Blue Bella of Silverway. She was not a show bitch, but her pedigree was beautiful, and she was one of the foundations of the "second van Mongolie period" in breeding. She was bred to Dutch, German and Int. Ch. Wamchow Che-Foo and whelped two black bitches, Ch. Anoz van Mongolie and the famous Dutch and Int. Ch. Sirikit van Mongolie, as well as Ch. Tschiang Kai-Chek van Mongolie, titled by many Chow experts as the best black dog they ever saw. He is a big, heavy, upstanding dog with great bone and a magnificent head. Ch. Sirikit and Tschiang Kai-Chek are big winners and greatly admired by many Chow fanciers all over the world.

After the Winners Show of 1964 in Amsterdam, the judge, Mr. A.O. Grindey, wrote in *Our Dogs* of December 18, 1965: "In bitches there was never a moment's hesitation. Sirikit van Monglie came into the ring and she was truly 'out of this world.' I don't think I have ever seen a more magnificent black bitch in all the many years I have been interested in Chows." Mrs. Ethel Downsborough of the Wongtung Kennels, after her visit to the Dutch Chow Club Specialty in 1967, wrote in *Our Dogs* of March 10, 1967: "Best in Show Dutch and Int. Ch. Wamchow Che-Foo, best bitch the black Ch. Sirikit van Mongolie. Either of these two exhibits could hold their own in the big ring at any championship show in England with a good chance for Best in Show." Ch. Tschiang Kai-Chek was three times Best in Show at the Dutch Chow Club Specialty with sixty to eighty Chows entered. He and his sister got the same high praise from all the judges.

From that time the new, successful period continued. In order to get new blood in time, then to breed back to the old strain again afterwards, two English dogs were imported. One was the red Andrew of Adel and the other a black, Ch. Alexis of Adel. They were bought from Miss Buckley's Kennel after she passed away. Andrew died after a year but was a fine, heavy-boned, perfectly balanced dog. Fortunately he left some good progeny. Ch. Alexis mated to Ch. Sirikit van Mongolie produced the biggest dog in the kennel, Ch. Mongo van Mongolie, a shaded light red with a heavy, deep body and an excellent movement. He is a well-known winner. He was Best in Show at the Dutch Chow Club Specialty 1972 with 82 dogs entered; Mr. Joe Braddon judged and was the fourth well-known British judge putting him up. The others giving him the championship certificate were Mrs. Fryer (Chungking), the Rev. D. Ford (Davlen) and Mr. A.O. Grindey, at big shows in Holland. Another well-known Dutch champion sired by Ch. Alexis of Adel was Mrs. J. Mimpen's home-bred Dutch and Int. Ch. Amarilla Kwei-Jang.

Other inmates of the Mongolie Kennel being full champions are the shaded red bitch Ch. Diotima van de Falkenweg (Tsun van Mongolie X Chang-Shi Haloti, a litter-sister to Int. Ch. Chang-Shi Hung Kwong), a light-shaded red bitch with real dignity. She won best bitch in show at the Dutch Chow Club Specialty 1970, at the age of ten. Another fine bitch is Ch. Renee

Go-Chow Blue Bing, blue dog born in 1969. Bred and owned by G. Oswald. Sired by Int. Ch. Wamchow Goe Neng *ex* Ti-Nah van Mongolie.

Int. and Dutch Ch. Sirikit van Mongolie, born 1963. Bred and owned by Henk van de Wouw of Holland. Pictured here at 3 years of age, she was sired by Int. Ch. Wamchow Che Foo *ex* Black Ming Lee of Silverway.

Int. and Dutch Ch. Wamchow Goe-Neng, born in 1965 and pictured at 4 years of age. Bred by Mrs. W. Lamerus and sold to Henk van de Wouw of Holland. Sire was Za-Chou van Majodo *ex* Wamchow Biyanka.

van Mongolie (Dutch and Int. Ch. Wamchow Goe-Neng X Ch. Anoz van Mongolie), a big shaded red, being 21 inches at shoulder, perfectly balanced, plenty of body, heavy bone, with perfect front and magnificent head. She got her title easily and was several times best of breed. Her sire is a well-known winner, Dutch and Int. Ch. Wamchow Goe-Neng, a shaded red dog, short coupled, with heavy bone, a gorgeous head full of expression and the presence and dignity so characteristic for a Chow. His show career has been very successful; he has been defeated only once. The van Mongolie Kennel usually has about twenty dogs, old ones included, as they have never sold an adult dog. At present the kennel has six of the ten full Dutch champions in the country, plus some others who need just one more certificate to finish their title. The kennel has owned all together 14 full Dutch champions and bred until now at least 16 full champions. Most have already been mentioned. Others are Ch. Wau-Kwong van Mongolie (Germany), Ch. Gai-Yuk van Mongolie (Italy); the bitches are Ch. Wing-Wa van Mongolie (Germany), Ch. Perla van Mongolie (Italy), Ch. Begum van Mongolie (Canada), and American and Mexican Ch. Ychouchanna van Mongolie (U.S.A.).

Mr. A.O. Grindey, who has also judged in the U.S.A. wrote in *Our Dogs* of October 2, 1970, after he had judged the German Chow Club Specialty:

"Returning to Holland with Mr.

L.G.M. van de Broek (President of the Dutch Chow Chow Club) I had the pleasure of seeing once again Mrs. Kitty and Mr. Henk van de Wouw's magnificent kennel of Chows just outside Amsterdam. A truly wonderful collection of blacks and reds."

Mrs. Mabel Fryer (formerly Cliff), who had judged in Holland at Barneveld on a previous Sunday, had also visited the kennel and had been most impressed:

"When you realize that here they have used Chang-Shi, Silverway and Adel breeding, material available to British Chowists for so long, to achieve what I can only describe—after all my 'globe-trotting' this year and last—as some of the finest Chows I have seen anywhere, it makes you think."

The van de Wouws, both judges for the breed for more than 25 years, have judged in many countries, including seven times in Great Britain. A great honor for Henk was judging the Golden State Chow Chow Club Specialty in California in 1969, where he drew an entry of 85 dogs, including a specials class of 22 American champions. In recent years they imported a Ch. Pandee's Jubilee son named Pandee's New World Ambassador, bred by Dr. Imogene Earle, a fine mahogany red dog, which proved to suit many Dutch and German bloodlines remarkably well. He has already produced successful winning stock. At the big Winners Show in Amsterdam in 1972 with an entry of 32 Chows, both champion titles for dogs in red and black were won by two of his sons, at thirteen and fifteen months of age. The red one also was Best of Breed. This is Dutch-American breeding that seems to be very successful.

Closely related to the Mongolie is the kennel bearing the name Van de Tongelreep, owned by Mr. L.G.M. van de Broek, who has been in Chows since 1939. His first bitch was Natascha van de Hornestad ('T Kell-Sie Pfaffikon X Nea Mai-Lo). He mated her to good dogs, more or less breeding the 'T Kell-Sie and Kou-Ling lines together with the van de Doorwerth strain. One of the best Chow Chows he bred was Dempsey van de Tongelreep, a nice deep-red dog. After the war however, he switched to another strain, purchasing the bitch Ch. Mouch-Ka van Mongolie (Ch. Ki-Dong King X Ch. Chang-Shi Up To Date). He bred her to King van Mongo-

Pandee's New World Ambassador, born 1970 and bred by Dr. Imogene P. Earle of the American Pandee Kennels. Exported to Holland and owned by Henk van de Wouw. His sire was Ch. Pandee's Jubilee ex Pandee's Zip Orah.

lie (Prinsje), a nephew-aunt breeding with a sensational result. This breeding was repeated five times, and it produced a number of high-quality Chows. Many were sold abroad and are found in many pedigrees in Europe and elsewhere.

From the first litter of this Prins X Mouch-Ka breeding came the famous and magnificent dog Dutch and Int. Ch. Emperor van de Tongelreep, regarded as one of the finest Chows ever bred. He was a deep self-red upstanding dog with best of legs, sturdily built body and a big, glorious head full of expression and dignity. In the prime of his life he was very hard to beat by any dog anywhere in the world, although there was some argument whether or not he had too much loose skin over his eyes. At the World Championship Show in Dortmund, West Germany in 1956 the Countess de Changy gave him the dog certificate over a large entry, thus giving him an honor he deserved.

Another specimen from the same breeding, a sister to Emperor, but from another litter, was the well-known bitch I'Ming van de Tongelreep. She was first owned by the Countess de Changy and

Int. Ch. Amarilla Kwei Jang, black bitch born in 1968. Bred and owned by J. Mimpen and photographed at 4½ years of age. Sire was Ch. Alexis of Adel *ex* Tjenpota.

The Professor, owned by Kitty van de Wouw of Holland. The Professor's complete name is Koeblai-Khan Tiong Bwa. This world champion dog was whelped in January, 1971.

Ch. Woolly van Majodo, red bitch pictured with her son, Ch. Man-Chu van Mongolie, one year old. Owned by Henk van de Wouw of Holland.

Ch. Mongo van Mongolie, red male, born in 1967, bred and owned by Henk van de Wouw of Holland. By Ch. Alexis of Adel *ex* Int. Ch. Sirikit van Mongolie.

Ch. Renee van Mongolie, born 1968. Bred and owned by Henk van de Wouw of Holland. She is 11 months old in this photo. Sire was Int. Ch. Wamchow Goe-Neng ex Ch. Anoz van Mongolie.

Int. and Dutch Ch. Wamchow Goe-Neng, born in 1965. Bred by Mrs. W. Lamerus and owned by Henk van de Wouw of Holland. Sired by Za-Chou van Majodo ex Wamchow Biyanka.

Andrew of Adel, born in 1963, was bred by Miss . E. Buckley. Owned by Henk van de Wouw of Holland. By Adel Dominic of Chey-Chow ex Ruby of Adel.

later went to the Odenkirchens in Canada, where she contributed to the Mi-Pao Kennel progeny. Another bitch from the same breeding, named Gy-Yang van de Tongelreep, was kept in the kennel while the dog Ch. Fy-Yang went to Germany and earned his champion title there. Mr. van de Broek then mated Ch. Mouch-Ka van Mongolie to her son Ch. Emperor van de Tongelreep, and from this litter (a very close inbreeding, of course) he got Kwan-Ti van de Tongelreep, a nice self-red dog but one that stayed in the shadow of his famous sire. His name, however, is in many well-known pedigrees through his daughter Canadian Champion Tiga and his son Canadian Champion Djimat van de Martinhoeve, both owned by the Mi-Pao Kennels in Canada. Another inmate of the kennel whose named is printed in many pedigrees was the dog Da-Lai van Mongolie (Ch. Emperor van de Tongelreep X Ch. Shao-Ying-Tjio van Mongolie). He was mated with Gy-Yang van de Tongelreep, and that mating resulted in Ch. Tiger van de Tongelreep (John and Ora Woodard,

USA) and the beautiful bitch American Ch. Bridget van de Tongelreep (Clif and Vivian Shryock, USA). Tongelreep was always a small kennel, mostly owning five to seven Chows. They were not very active in showing, nor did they breed a large number of Chows. But that great dog Dutch and Int. Ch. Emperor van de Tongelreep will be remembered by everyone who saw him even once. Mr. van de Broek has been a judge for the breed for many years and served as such in several European countries, including East Germany, Poland and England.

Two more Dutch kennels must be mentioned, not because of the number of champions they have bred (since they have been in the breed for only five to seven years) but because they belong to the more prominent kennels in the 1970's. In a small country such as Holland, where quality is rather high, it is easier for young breeders to build up a quality kennel within a few years. They can start with stock that others have bred after years of effort and experience, and if they do it the right way they can go forward very quickly.

One of these newer kennels is Kwei-Jang, owned by Mr. and Mrs. Mimpen. Starting with a Chow as a pet, they soon got interested in breeding and started buying good stock from the best bloodlines, which were the progeny of several champions. They bred their first litter in 1966 from a bitch called Sim Hiang Yinetao, based on King van Mongolie line on one side and Int. Ch. Kai-Men-Ti Liweng on the other side. She was mated to Mr. van de Broek's Roy-Bah-Ching van de Tongelreep, son of Int. Ch. Wamchow Che Foo, and a bitch named Tjenpota. She was mated to Henk van de Wouw's Ch. Alexis of Adel and produced the home-bred Dutch and Int. Ch. Amarilla Kwei-Jang, a small but nicely balanced black bitch, heavy boned, with a beautiful head and excellent movement. The Mimpens have several fine dogs and have made a good start.

Int. Ch. A-Tung van de Hagenbrink, born in 1964 and bred by Mrs. Dekker-Maris. Owned by Mrs. Ullmann. Sire was Int. Ch. Kai-Men-Ti Liweng ex Cha Tsin of Liang Ming Keou.

Go-Chow Bazooka, red dog born in 1969. Bred and owned by G. Oswald. Sired by Int. Ch. Wamchow Goe Neng ex Ti-Nah van Mongolie.

Another well-known present-day kennel is Go-Chow, owned by Mr. and Mrs. G. Oswald. They built up this kennel on the Mongolie bloodline. The basis of their kennel is the beautiful black bitch Ti-Nah van Mongolie, sister to Dutch and Int. Ch. Sirikit van Mongolie, Ch. Anoz van Mongolie and Ch. Tschiang Kai Tchek van Mongolie, and of equal high quality. As a puppy Ti-Nah was sold but came back in the Mongolie Kennels later on. As Mr. Oswald admired the bitch so much and the van de Wouw's owned her two sisters, Mr. Oswald obtained her and used her as the foundation of the Go-Chow kennel. She could have been a champion by now but was seldom shown and is now waiting to gain her last certificate. Mated to van de Wouw's Dutch and Int. Ch. Wamchow Goe-Neng, she produced amongst others two beautiful dogs, Go-Chow Bazooka and the magnificent blue dog Go-Chow Blue Bing, a very

Tse-Ho Kwei Jang, born in 1970, bred and owned by J. Mimpen of Holland. Sire was Int. Ch. Wamchow Goe-Neng ex Sim Hiang Yinetao.

Kwai Pao of Liang Ming Keou, born in 1970 and bred by H. Steegmans. Owned by J. Mimpen and sired by Henk v d Falkenweg ex Mhie Jou v d Rodeza. Pao was three year old when this photo was taken in Europe.

heavily-built blue dog with heavy bone and a big magnificent head, one of the best blues ever seen. Together with other high-quality Chows they represent a fine foundation for the future development of this kennel.

We can not finish the story about Chows in Holland, about whose quality the Dutch are so proud, without making special mention of the smooth Chow Chow. This variety of the breed, unknown in many countries, has found an enthusiastic fancier in Holland in Miss C.J. Veldhuis. Her parents already had smooth Chows during her childhood while living in the Dutch East Indies. The smooth Chow has remained her favorite ever since. It is indeed beautiful and has nothing to hide by an abundant coat, so it has to be really sound. It shows the characteristic stilted Chow gait more obviously than the long-haired variety, and if it is not a perfect mover the imperfection is seen at once.

Danny van Mongolie, born 1965, is pictured at 4 years of age. Bred by Henk v.d. Wouw of Holland and sold to J. Schenk. Sire was Int. Ch. Chang-Shi Hong Kwong ex Chu Ty van Majodo.

Ch. Alexis of Adel, born in 1962. Bred by Miss E. Buckley and owned by Henk van de Wouw of Holland. By Adel Dominic of Chey-Chow ex Ruby of Adel.

Wamchow Fabian, born in 1962. Bred by Mrs. W. Lamerus and owned by Mrs. M. Reyenga. By Heyville's Honey Boy ex Wamchow Biyanka.

Escort, whelped in 1968. Bred by R. Carlson and owned by Niels Hartmann. By Int. Ch. Hai-Min-Ki ex Carmencita.

Ch. You-Two's His Highness, born in 1966. Bred by Miss Martha Visser of Holland. Owner, Mrs. Karin Loven Grytte. Sire was Int. Ch. Mi-Pao's Piwa Rangan ex Mi-Pao's Poetri.

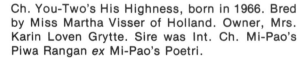

Int. Ch. Sumi of Junggwaw, black bitch born in 1958. This photograph was taken when she was eight years old. Bred by Stan Smedley and owned by Mrs. U. Leyden. Sired by Ch. Enrico of Junggwaw ex Chloe of Junggwaw.

Ti-Nah van Mongolie, born in 1964, was bred by Henk van de Wouw and owned by G. Oswald. By Int. Ch. Wamchow Che Foo ex Black Ming Lee of Silverway.

Int. and Dutch Ch. Kuang Wu of Liang Ming Keou, shown here at the age of 3 years, was born in 1961 and bred and owned by H. Steegmans. By Mi-Ka-Lo van de Loumi Hoeve.

Ch. Zoto's Emperor of Liang Ming Keou, whelped in 1961 and bred by H. Steegmans. Owner: Mrs. Aase Wandrup. The sire was Mi-Ka-Lo v d Loumi Hoeve ex Joengkai v d Loumi Hoeve.

Koeblai Khan Tiong Bwa, born 1971 and photographed at 8 months of age. He was bred by J. den Braber and is owned by Henk v.d. Wouw of Holland. Sire was Pandee's New World Ambassador *ex* Cinderella v.d. Burghardt.

Xdan van Mongolie, born 1970. This lovely two-year-old black was bred by Henk van de Wouw. He is owned by Mrs. Aase Wandrup. Sire was Ch. Tschang Kai Tchek van Mongolie *ex* Quite Peggy van Mongolie.

Zoto's Danehof, born 1971, bred by Mrs. Aase Wandrup, photographed at 1½ years of age. The owner is Bill Rasmussen. The sire was Int. Ch. Wamchow Goe-Neng *ex* Zoto's Mishja.

Miss Veldhuis bought her first smooth from Mr. and Mrs. Burroughs' Penhow Kennels, the greatest smooth Chow breeders Britain has ever known, although Mrs. D. Martin had some fine specimens as well at the time.

The first smooth imported to Holland was a fine bitch, Chu-Ping of Penhow, which unfortunately was killed in an accident before she could produce a litter. After that Miss Veldhuis bought Ch. Lung Hao of Penhow (by the long-haired Ch. Wong Tung Chang of Canton X smooth Chao of Penhow), a really fine, anatomically beautiful Chow. He is a full Dutch champion and as far as is known the only smooth full champion in the world. There are other smooth Chow fanciers in Holland, where there are about seven smooth Chows, both blacks as well as reds, and there are a few smooth Chow fanciers in Germany and Switzerland, where fanciers have become interested in this variety and have started breeding. However, the basis for breeding them pure is too small. In England only the U'Kwong Kennels of

Afternoon rest period in the Van Mongolie Kennels in Holland. This picture was taken in September, 1971.

The World Champion bitch Woolly van Majodo, photographed at 3½ years of age. She is owned by Henk v d Wouw of Holland. This bitch is the grandmother of one of America's most famous dogs, Ch. Ghat de la Moulaine, owned by Clif and Vivian Shryock of California.

Eric and Joan Egerton are breeding them. Good news is that Mrs. Burroughs, who stopped activities after her husband passed away, is making a new start in breeding the smooth Chows. But as the smooth is dominant in Chow breeding, the foundation has to be widened by using long-haired specimens. These efforts by a handful of enthusiastic fanciers of this nice old smooth variety will hopefully prevent it from disappearing.

THE CHOW IN LUXEMBOURG

Another small country whose name has become famous in the world of Chow Chows is Luxembourg. Being so close to Belgium and linked with that country in so many ways, this small country understandably has had some famous breeders. One of the oldest is Mrs. Hanff of the Hang-Fung Kennels. She built up her breeding with pure Chang-Shi and Kou-Ling bloodlines and some Dutch blood through her Ch. Fao-Tseou Dit Browny de la Moulaine, bred by Rene Hassenforder in France and by Prins Again van Mongolie X Vantschi van Majodo. Mrs. Hanff was the owner of the bitch Chang-Shi Sout-Chy (Ch. Kou-Ling Youki X Chang-Shi Victory). A well-known bitch from her breeding named Hang-Fung Scarlett went to the de la Moulaine Kennel in France.

The Hang-Fung Kennels, not really big, contributed its share to the breed in the area of the Continent referred to as the French-speaking part. The most famous and most important kennel in Luxembourg, however, started in the early 1950's: Palmiro and Irene Cottafavi's Mong-Fu Kennel. Their breeding is famous all over the Continent. The kennel keeps mainly twelve to fourteen Chows, and quality is very high. The Cottafavis are breeding regularly and exhibiting at nearly all the big shows in France, Belgium, Switzerland and Germany, but seldom in Holland. They started with de la Moulaine blood and thus indirectly with Chang-Shi, Kou-Ling and van Mongolie. One of their first bitches was Womya de la Moulaine by Int. Ch. Kou-Ling Rex out of Chang-Shi Doodle (Int. Ch. Chang-Shi Neron X Chang-Shi Tamky, both sired by Ch. Rochow Adjudant).

The only smooth Chow Chow champion in the world! Ch. Lung Chao of Penhow was the winner in Amsterdam, Holland in 1965 at 9½ years of age. He is by Ch. Wongtung Chang of Canton *ex* Chou Mei of Penhow. Breeders were Mr. and Mrs. Burrows and the owner Miss C.A. Veldhuis, Anhem, Holland.

That this bitch was a fantastic foundation to build upon needs no repeating. One of her sons, Chi-Chi Bu Mong-Fu, was a well-known show dog during 1954 and 1955. The first of many Mong-Fu champions following was the dog Int. Ch. Daley Mong-Fu, bred in 1954 (Baikal de la Moulaine X Biantse de la Moulaine). He gained his title in 1957. The year before the kennel purchased the bitch Int. Ch. Gwally de la Moulaine (Duang Lai de la Moulaine X Ychouchanna van Mongolie). She was the litter sister to the famous Ch. Ghat de la Moulaine.

In the meantime some Dutch blood had been imported: the bitch Ch. Kai-Men-Ti-Tai-Yun (Int. Ch. Kai-Men-Ti Liweng X Int. Ch. Beauty, a Liweng daughter). Bred to Ch. Daley Mong-Fu, she produced Ch. Indo Mong-Fu, a very nice dog. Another kennel mate was Fiang-Tse de la Moulaine (Prins Again van Mongolie X Vantschi van Majodo), a genuine Dutch bloodline. He was a brother to Mrs. Hanff's champion dog. But the great fame for the Mong-Fus was made by their well-known home-bred self-red dog French, Luxembourg, Swiss, Belgian and German Champion Jalu Mong-Fu (Int. Ch. Daley Mong-Fu X Int. Ch. Gwally de la Moulaine). He was one of the most famous dogs on the Continent and won twenty-one C.A.C.I.B.'s. He was also one of the top sires in France, Switzerland and especially in Germany. He did a tremendous lot of winning and was Best Dog at the big Berlin Show in 1967 under the English judge Mr. A.O. Grindey. He was a big upstanding dog with heavy bone and a beautiful body, and he had a nice head. He was a fine Chow Chow and a great champion; the only point to his disadvantage was his ear placement, which was not quite forward enough over his eyes. He was bred to numerous bitches, sired many successful winners and has ten full champions to his credit, including Int. French and Belgian Champion Mantsuko Mong-Fu (owner-breeder), Int. and French Champion Luang-Tai Mong-Fu (Mme. Coraboeuf, France), Int. and French Champion Ling Mong-Fu (Miss Peroz, France) and Int.

Champion Otomo Mong-Fu (Mrs. Fontignies, Belgium). The bitches are Int. Champion Laika Mong-Fu, Int. Champion Michiko Mong-Fu and Int. Champion Pu-Peh Mong-Fu, all owned by the breeder. Some other famous dogs from this kennel are Int. and German Champion Okito Mong-Fu (Germany), Int. and Luxembourg Champion Pu-Chi-Kat Mong-Fu (France) and Int. and German Champion Quin-Pao Mong-Fu (Germany).

This is quite a list and certainly is not complete. Jalu died in 1972, but his name will live on for many years in the pedigrees of hundreds of his progeny in Switzerland, France, Belgium, Italy and especially in Germany. This medium-size kennel, in this very small country, has contributed very much to the progress of the breed in many other Continental countries and is still breeding successfully. Both Cottafavis have been judges for the breed for some years and have judged in several Continental countries. They also judged the breed in Britain on one occasion.

CHOW CHOWS IN FRANCE

In France and Italy we learn that Chows were introduced there in the 1890's and were usually owned by members of "high society." A bit later they became popular with the better class of dog fanciers such as the Baronesse de Rothschild, Miss Patou, Oscar Strauss and Mrs. Watel-Dehayin. There were some good specimens at that time which walked with their owners in the Bois de Boulogne and on the boulevards in Paris.

One of the first enthusiastic breeders was Mr. Waldeck Rousseau. In 1892 he gave a black dog of his breeding as a present to Miss Ella Casella in England, where it was very successful in the show ring. But it was not until the early 1920's that the breed became more popular and admired by dog breeders. One of the first fanciers of that period was Mrs. Marechal of Paris, who became a well-known judge for the breed. She was the only French Chow judge who ever judged in Britain. This was in 1935 at the L.K.A. Show, where she put up Ch. Choonam Hung Kwong and Ch. Choonam Moonbeam. She was the first

International Ch. Gwally de la Moulaine, owned by Madame Cottafavi of Luxembourg. This beautiful bitch is a litter sister to the famous Ghat and is nine years old in this photograph.

Int. Ch. Laika Mong-Fu, red bitch born in 1962. Bred and owned by Mrs. Irene Cottafavi. Sired by Int. Ch. Jalu Mong-Fu *ex* Honga de la Moulaine. Pictured at three years of age.

Int. Ch. Dalai Mong-Fu, red dog born in 1957. Bred and owned by Mrs. Irene Cottafavi. By Baikal de la Moulaine *ex* Biantse de la Moulaine.

Int. Ch. Jalu Mong-Fu, born in 1960, and his daughter Int. Ch. Laika Mong-Fu, born in 1962. Bred and owned by Mrs. Irene Cottafavi.

Int. Ch. Mantsuko Mong-Fu, born in 1963, bred and owned by Mrs. Irene Cottafavi. He is by Int. Ch. Dalai Mong-Fu *ex* Juang-Thai Mong-Fu.

president of the French Chow Chow Club, which was founded in 1926. In 1927 a show was held in the Tuileries Gardens, where 36 Chow Chows were entered under the English judge Mrs. Fullerton. Amongst the exhibitors were Mrs. Marechal, the Baron Eugene de Rothschild showing Choonam Brillance, Mrs. Watel-Dehayin and Miss H.B. Ely exhibiting Black Kim (son of Blue Kim), Blue Moon of Amwell and Lee Wu (the sire of the famous Ch. Akbar).

Miss Ely was a British lady living outside Paris. She bought Lee Wu from Lady Faudel Philips after his win at Crufts in 1926. He was bred by Mrs. Sackville Golden by Ch. Lenning out of Ch. Susan of the East. Miss Ely's Wigwam Kennels were famous and among the leading Continental breeders at the time. Even the Belgian countesses and Mr. Bechet had their bitches mated by Wigwam dogs or bought puppies from this kennel. Some well-known Chows bred by Miss Ely were Ch. Wigwam T'So Lin, owned by Mr. MacMonnies in the United States; the beautiful Ho-Ho, owned by Miss Stillmann in the United States; and the famous dog Wigwam Wu-Wang (bred from two Amwells), owned by Lady Faudel Philips in Britain. He was a magnificent dog. The first time he was shown he was put over Ch. Rochow Dragoon, which caused quite a sensation. Unfortunately, he did not like the show ring, and although he did more winning and got some Reserve C.C.'s, he never finished his title. But the name of this famous French-bred dog gave value to many pedigrees at the time, like that of many other Wigwams spread out all over the world.

Mrs. Marechal was in Chows for many years and owned and bred some well-known first class Chow Chows. One of the best-known dogs from her breeding was Int. Ch. K'Foo Yen (Ch. Rochow Brigadier X Wigwam Yo-Yo). Another one was Int. Ch. Yvati, owned by the Countess de Changy. Mrs. Marechal was also the owner of the bitch Kou-Ling Mazurka. Another old time Chowist is Mrs. Diot, who has been in the breed for over forty years and was a president of the French Chow Chow Club for many years. Her first Chow was

Int. Ch. Pu-Shi-Kat Mong-Fu, red dog born in 1966. Bred by Mrs. Irene Cottafavi and owned by Mrs. M. Bertellin. By Nan-Chu Mong-Fu ex Int. Ch. Laika Mong-Fu. Pictured at four years of age.

Shuka. Later she owned Ch. Chang-Shi Spitfire (Chang-Shi Nochka X Chang-Shi RAF), a beautiful red dog, very well-known also outside France. Another Chow breeder who gave fame to the French Chow Chow not only in many Continental countries but also on the other side of the Atlantic was Rene Hassenforder, one of the greatest French Chow breeders. His decision to give up the breed is still regretted. He started his Kennel de la Moulaine in the early 1940's with mainly Chang-Shi and Kou-Ling blood. Rene bought the bitch that was worth her weight in gold for breeding: Chang-Shi Doodle (Ch. Rochow Adjutant son Ch. Chang-Shi Neron X a Rochow Adjutant daughter Chang-Shi Tamky). No wonder that she proved to be the best basis for a very high-quality breeding. He had her mated to Int. Ch. Kou-Ling Rex and got the well-known Wou-Ling de la Moulaine, Womiya de la Mou-

Uang-Kai de Black Dragoon, red bitch whelped in 1971. Bred by Mrs. Coraboeuf and owned by Mrs. Simone Nayrolles of France. Her sire was Sou-Chang des Fonds de l'Aulnaye *ex* Romy Thai Mong-Fu.

laine, Wally de la Moulaine, all well-known names in many pedigrees of winning stock. The kennel consisted mainly of twenty dogs, amongst which Hang-Fung Scarlett (an Int. Ch. Chang-Shi U'Kwong daughter), Yen (an Int. Ch. Chang-Shi Chaga Tippo daughter) and Ch. Chang-Shi Vanguard, a very nice dog bred from Liwu-Koo-Chi X Int. Ch. Chang-Shi Rolly Polly, a bitch that later went to the Sterlings in the United States.

The de la Moulaine dogs were very successful in the show ring, bred fine stock and were on top in France until a catastrophe in the form of a bad infection hit the kennel; Rene Hassenforder, this fine Chow lover, lost about eighteen of his beautiful Chows within a fortnight, including Wally de la Moulaine, in whelp to Ch. Ki-Dong King. He somehow found the courage to make a new start with a few dogs which survived the illness, and he bought some good puppies in Holland. He purchased two sisters, Vantschi and Vicky van Majodo (Hasja van Majodo X U'Kwa van Majodo). A bit later he got Ychouchanna van Mongolie (Ch. Ki-Dong King X Ch. Wooly van Majodo) and the adult dog Prins Again van Mongolie (King van Mongolie X Ch. Chang-Shi Up To Date), owned by Mr. Doll. Bad luck struck the kennel again when Vicky died very young. But Hassenforder, being a dedicated breeder who knew what he was after, secured some fine stock once again and in a rather short time. He bred the dog Duang-Lai de la Moulaine (Assam de la Moulaine X Hang-Fung Scarlett), a beautiful shaded red with heavy bone and a really magnificent head. Assam was later sold to Switzerland, when ill health caused a reduction of the number of dogs in the kennel. But from Duang-Lai

French Ch. Ri-Tung du Sama Khada, red dog born in 1968, was bred by Mr. Meyer. Owned by Mrs. Berger, and pictured at four years of age.

X Ychouchanna van Mongolie Hassenforder bred a very fine litter, bringing him, among others, the famous champion Int. Ch. Gwally de la Moulaine, owned by the Cottafavis in Luxembourg and the legendary American Champion Ghat de la Moulaine. As his health declined, Rene Hassenforder was forced to give up his Chow activities, and with much sadness his last Chows, American and Mexican Champion Ychouchanna van Mongolie and American and Mexican Champion Ghat de la Moulaine were sold to Clif and Vivian Shryock from California, who came at exactly the right moment to take them to the new world, where Ghat especially caused a great sensation. He became a top show dog and sire in his new homeland and passed on his great qualities to numerous progeny. No doubt he was the most famous French Chow ever bred.

When the Shryocks got Rene Hassenforder's permission to use his de la Moulaine kennel affix, the name of this prominent French Chow breed lived on in other parts of the world. May it continue to be as successful as it was before!

Other well-known French breeders and champions at the time were Chin-Chow breedings of Mrs. Dessaigne, who had quality dogs, including Chang-Shi

Kou-Ling Tcheou at seven months of age. Bred and owned by Rene Bechet. Born in 1945.

U'Shan (Chang-Shi Noch-Ka X Chang-Shi Tamky) and R'Shang-Hai bred by Mrs. Marechal. Then there were the Penhap Kennels of Mr. M. Fouchet and Mrs. Gilbert's de Claudinets, owner of Chang-Shi Typhoon, Wendri de la Moulaine and Chang-Shi UChing. Another kennel, de Hope of Mr. N. Letourneur, owned Utwang de la Moulaine and Wohama de la Moulaine. Other enthusiastic Chow lovers were the ladies Urruty and Ravel, thanks to the English imports Grest Westwood Roi Rouge and Great Westwood Larousse.

One of the oldest breeders, who is still active, is Miss S. Claudel from the well-known Ouah-Ouah Kennels near Paris. She is a very serious breeder, always on the lookout for quality. She imported a German dog, Ch. Long-Keu Siang (bred by Mrs. Janssen), and was the owner of Ming Tai, a fine bitch that did a lot of winning and bred, for instance, Int. and French Ch. Rex de Ouah-Ouah, owned by Mrs. Casparotti of Monaco. Miss Claudel recently imported two Dutch dogs, Ah-Colonel van Mongolie and the beautiful shaded red bitch Hope, both from the best Dutch bloodlines and very successful in the show ring. Another enthusiastic Chowist is Mrs. Descamps. She is a member of the French Chow Chow Club Committee and was the owner of, among others, Chang-Shi Foo Shima and Ch. Nun Ming de Pi Po Sin Tchang. Additional well-known French Chowists include Mrs. Coraboeuf of de Black Dragoon, breeder of Uang Kai de Black Dragoon, Onyx Thai de Black Dra-

Wally de la Moulaine, red bitch born in 1948. Bred and owned by Rene Hassenforder. Pictured at four years of age. By Int. Ch. Kou-Ling Rex ex Chang-Shi Doodle.

Ch. Kou-Ling Mouchka, bitch born in 1938. Bred by Rene Bechet of France. Her owner was Mrs. E. de Wilde. by Ch. K'Foo Yen ex Kou-Ling Ipao Mi. Photographed at 1½ years of age.

Int. Ch. Gwally de la Moulaine, red bitch born in 1957, was bred by Rene Hassenforder. Owned by Mrs. Irene Cottafavi. By Duang Lai de la Moulaine ex Ch. Ychouchanna van Mongolie. Pictured at three years of age. Gwally is a full sister to Ch. Ghat de la Moulaine, so well known in the U.S.

goo and Oursonne de Black Dragoon, and owner of Ch. Lungtai Mong-Fu. The biggest kennel by way of the number of dogs is owned by Mrs. Lambert-Klein, the du Penchateau Chow Chows, who bred several champions including Int. Ch. Plasco du Penchateau (Germany), a deep self-red dog, and owns Int. and French Ch. Brovin vom Melbtal.

Some French champions are Ch. Ri-Tung du Sama Khada, bred by Mr. Meyer from Lyon and owned by Mrs. Berger; Int. and French Ch. Ling Mong-Fu, owned by Miss Peroz, and Mrs. Bertellin's Int. and Luxembourg Ch. Pu-Chi-Kat Mong-Fu. Another excellent breeding is du Sytka from Mrs. Hamel, also a well-known breeder and exhibitor. One of her best-known dogs is the home-bred shaded red Int. and French Ch. Kwong du Sytka. In France Chow breeding is mostly in the

Assam de la Moulaine, red dog born in 1951. Bred and owned by Rene Hassenforder and pictured at two years of age. By Wou-King de la Moulaine ex Yen.

Int. Ch. Fao Tseou dit Browny de la Moulaine, a red dog born in 1956, was bred by Rene Hassenforder. Owned by Mrs. F. Hanff. By Prins Again van Mongolie ex Vantschi van Majodo. Four years of age in this photograph.

hands of small breeders and, apart from some English and Dutch importations, based largely on Belgian and Luxembourg bloodlines.

Int. Ch. Kou-Ling Xolsky, born in 1948, pictured with a few of his trophies at two years of age. Bred by Rene Bechet of France. Owned by Lou Nuyen.

Duang-Lai de la Moulaine, red dog born in 1954, was bred and owned by Rene Hassenforder. By Assam de la Moulaine *ex* Hang Fung Scarlet. Photographed at three years of age. Duang-Lai is the sire of Ch. Ghat de la Moulaine, top U.S. sire for record number of Chow champions.

Chang-Shi Doodle, red bitch born in 1943, was bred by the Countess de Changy. Owner was Rene Hassenforder. By Chang-Shi Neron *ex* Chang-Shi Tamky. Photographed at five years of age.

Kou-Ling Umatsu, born in 1946, bred by Rene Bechet. Owner, P. Luckhardt. By Kou-Ling Tcheou *ex* Kou-Ling Saida.

Int. Ch. Rex de Ouah-Ouah, red dog born in 1968. Breeder was Miss Claudel of Monaco, who co-owns the dog with Mrs. Gasparotti. Pictured at one year of age.

Int. Ch. Kou-Ling Imano, by Int. Ch. Rochow Brigadier *ex* Yang-Li. Born in 1935, Imano was bred by Rene Bechet. This photo was taken in 1938.

CHOW CHOWS IN ITALY

In Italy there is no official Chow Chow Club. Most Chow fanciers own one or more dogs and there are no large Chow Chow kennels. Perhaps the climate is not suitable for Chows. There are, however, a handful of Chow fanciers whose dogs are mainly imported from neighboring countries. One of them was for some time professor Bruno Giussani of the Kennel Taiwan. He tried to build up a kennel on first class bloodlines, traveling around to make himself acquainted with the stock on the Continent. He wrote an interesting pamphlet about Chow Chows in Italy but unfortunately gave up Chow activities after a few years.

The first C.A.C. in Italy was given in 1924, and the first Chow to get the title (in 1931) was Mr. Lello Lioce's home-bred, Black Jane. It took until 1938 before there was a second champion Chow. That was Wuncha Bleu di Val D'Adige, bred by the Duke d'Aosta, a well-known Chow lover at the time. Wuncha was the first Italian-bred champion. Her sire was T'Kell Sie Bonzo and her dam Beauty Della Toretta. But most Italian champion titles were gained by importations such as Ch. Kou-Ling Xarai and Ch. Kou-Ling Berina (Kou-Ling Xang-Tse X Kou-Ling Ivette), both owned by Mefalda Cassanella. Then there was Ch. Envoy of U'Kwong, bred by the English Mrs. Egerton, owned by Dr. A. Tessieri, and Ch. Perla van Mongolie (Ch. Ki-Dong King X Ch. Chang-Shi Up To Date) and Ch. Tagore van de Loumi Hoeve (Han-Tie Bambus X Azora van de Loemi Hoeve), both owned by Professor Giussani. Later on Dr. Codice imported the beautiful dog Ch. Gay-Yu van Mongolie (Sing-Foo van Mongolie X Wamchow Chan-Ny), while Mimma Fontana acquired Ch. Liany van de Tongelreep (Hwang-Ti Chao-Chun X Gy-Yang van de Tongelreep). Many other dogs from first-class bloodlines were imported, but a really prominent breeding program was not established. There are still some breeders and several Chow lovers, but Italy certainly is not of great prominence in the breed from an international point of view.

THE CHOW CHOW IN DENMARK

Denmark, in contrast to other Scandinavian countries, has no national "Spitzhound" in the way Finland has its Finnish Spitz and Norway the Norwegian Buhond and Elkhound, that is, apart from Danish interest in sledge dogs such as Siberian Huskies and Samoyeds. Sweden was the first Scandinavian country into which Chow Chows were introduced. Before World War II there were just a few Chows in Denmark and no interest in Chow breeding. In 1946 Mr. Poul Hansen and a friend, the veterinarian Dalborg Johansen, had a couple of Chows imported from England. Mr. Hansen remained interested in Chows all these years and still owns a bitch from Zoto (Wandrup) and Liang Ming Keou (Steegmans, Holland) blood. In Denmark, Chow breeding is in the hands of only a few breeders. Most specimens are in the possession of individual Chow fanciers, but the popularity of the breed has increased a great deal during the 1960's and early 1970's.

One of the largest and most prominent kennels in Denmark is Zoto, owned by Helge and Aase Wandrup, serious and enthusiastic Chow breeders and exhibitors, who based their kennel on Swedish stock at the start. Their first Chows were purchased from Miss Betty Berg, a famous breeder of Newfoundlands who kept and showed Chows as well. The first inmates of the Zoto kennel were the bitches Woo-Li-Shee Av Helluland, bought as a puppy, and Ming-Peng, bought as an adult bitch in whelp to Ch. Cho-San Peter av Helluland. She produced a litter of eight; one puppy, a bitch called Zoto Chu-Chu-Ming, was kept in the kennel. In 1955 the Zoto Kennel imported from England a beautiful 2½-year-old dog named Puki of Kantuki, bred by Mrs. Ansell. He was a fine cream of a good type and contributed much to the improvement of the Zoto stock. He caused a sensation when shown for the first time at the big Copenhagen Show and got his title in four successive shows. In 1959, the Danish Kennel Club became a member of the F.C.I., and Ch. Puki of Kantuki was the first Chow Chow to gain a C.A.C.I.B.

in Denmark. Woo-Li-Shee Av Helluland was the first bitch mated to Puki, and the one cream puppy she whelped was Ch. Zoto's Tai-Yang, the first home-bred Zoto champion. From the next litter two creams and two reds were born. The best-known of the four was Zoto's Esau, which was shown only once, as his owner did not like showing. On that one occasion he won the C.C. and was Best of Breed and Best of the Utility Group. It caused quite a sensation, since second to him was an imported Afghan Hound.

In 1957 another English dog was imported, Int. Ch. Hussar of U'Kwong, bred by Eric and Joan Egerton (Countess de Changy's Int. Ch. Astom X Nu-Huang Mopsa of Amwell). Hussar was a beautifully balanced upstanding dog with heavy bone and a nice head and expression. He is one of the most famous Chows ever in Denmark, and his name has given value to many pedigrees. He became Danish champion in 1960, Swedish champion in 1960 and Norwegian champion in 1961. He was only defeated once, at a show in Rotterdam, Holland, where he got the reserve championship. Five times he won Best of Group; in 1961, in Oslo, he was Best in Show all breeds, shown to perfection as usual by Mr. Helge Wandrup. The reason that he did not sire any champions was not that there were no Chows worth the title among his progeny but that the owners of these Chows were unfortunately not dog-show inclined at the time. The Wandrups can be considered the great pioneers of the breed in Denmark. They love the type of Chow the Dutch and most American breeders admire, but they had to fight to come through with that type of Chow Chow in the Scandinavian countries, which were more used to the old fashioned type.

But the Wandrups knew what they were after and went their own way. Int. Ch. Hussar of U'Kwong was bred to his daughter Dominique, and a bitch from that litter did quite well in the show ring, winning three C.A.C.I.B.'s, including one in Sweden. She was Zoto's Shi-Ang. In 1961 the Wandrups, who visited Holland several times, imported Ch. Zoto Emperor

Zoto's Zan Tippo, red bitch born in 1968. Bred and owned by Mrs. Aase Wandrup. Sire was Swe-Danes Shagga Tippo ex Zoto's Misjha.

Ch. Pu-Ki of Kantuki, cream dog whelped in 1952, was bred by Mrs. Ansell. Owner is Mrs. Aase Wandrup. Sired by Ch. Bbormot Yung-Li ex Lung-Yen of Kinlo.

Mr. Arthur Pedersen, Howi Kennels, Jonstrup, Denmark, with one of his dogs purchased from a kennel near Copenhagen.

of Liang Ming Keou (Mi-Ka-Lo van de Loumi Hoeve X Joengkai van de Loumi-Hoeve), bred by Mr. Steegmans. Emmer, as he was called, had a beautiful head and a fine disposition. Once a judge in Sweden wrote in his report that he was "too friendly." He was not very fond of the show ring but nevertheless won his title as a Danish Champion. From Hussar X Dominique, a bitch named Zoto's Gillie went to Mr. Arthur Pedersen, another Danish breeder, while her sister, Zoto's Mopsa, was kept in the kennel. Mopsa, bred to Zoto's Wung T'Sun, produced three bitches; one of them, Zoto's Flossie, is living with her owner, Mr. Nielsen, in New York. From the breeding of Ch. Zoto Emperor of Liang Ming Keou, a bitch named Mitsouko went to Mr. Bertrand in Brussels. She was shown only once and was Reserve Champion and "Chow Chow of the Year" in Belgium in 1967. Ch. Zoto Emperor of Liang Ming Keou sired many good Chows and appears in a lot of Danish pedigrees. Bred to his granddaughter Lingvu, he produced the Danish champion Zoto's Tai-Pan, a beautiful dog, dignified and with great presence.

No trouble is too great for the Wandrups to obtain the best results! Mr. Wandrup went all the way to Holland to have the bitch Zoto's Mishja (Ch. Emperor of Liang Ming Keou X Zoto's Vinnie Peng) bred to Henk van de Wouw's National and International Ch. Wamchow Goe-Neng. This litter was beautiful and produced, among others, a dog named Zoto's Danehof, a magnificent shaded light red, perfectly balanced and with a grand head, owned by the president of the Danish Chow Chow Club, Mr. Bill Rasmussen. Some others from this breeding were kept in the kennel. In the meantime, the Wandrups bought another Dutch dog, the black X'Dan van Mongolie (Ch. Tschiang-Kai-Tchek van Mongolie X Quite Peggy van Mongolie), a fine well-balanced heavy-boned black with a beautiful head and good action. He has already bred many bitches, and one of his puppies has been exported to Norway. Mishja was bred to him and produced a very promising litter.

Several other Dutch dogs were imported by other Danish Chow fanciers, such as Mrs. Arentsen of Copenhagen, who bought Joe-Tsche van de Hagenbrink (Rodeza's Tao X Wong-Ti van de Hagenbrink), bred by Mrs. Dekker-Maris. Cho-Weng and Ching-Ching van de Burghardt, a red dog and bitch, bred by Mr. Duppen from Lorenz van de Falkenweg X Mouchkana, was purchased by Aase Wandrup. Mr. Bill Rasmussen bought two blacks: the dog Mah-Jong and the bitch Chin-Chella of Liang-Ming-Keou (by Ch. Popoff van Sebastopol X Vivianne van Mongolie), bred by Mr. Steegmans. Denmark is the first of the Scandinavian countries to found a Chow Chow club. This came about in March, 1972; the club already has 175 members. The club's first show winners were the dog Zoto's Danehof and the bitch Danehof van de Cortenaer, another import also owned by Mr. Bill Rasmussen. She was bred by Ch. Popoff van Sebastopol X Li-Li van de Cortenaer by Mrs. Beekman in Holland.

The interest in exhibiting continues to grow. Some years ago usually three to five dogs were entered for a show, but in the 1970's twelve to eighteen Chows entered is not unusual. There are three breeders in the club: Mr. Jorgensen in Jylland and his Vallerbek Kennels; Mr. Bill Rasmussen, Danehof Kennels; and Aase Wandrup of the Zoto Kennels, the pioneer kennel in this country. All the other members own only one or just a few Chows, but Chows are much more popular in Denmark now and with the good bloodlines they have, the Danish Chow fanciers are building up a good breeding program.

CHOW CHOWS IN SWITZERLAND

In Switzerland the Chow Chow never reached great popularity either, although the climate there can be considered more favorable for the breed. One of the very first breeders was the Marchioness Del Mayno around 1907. She bred and even exhibited Chows. It took more than twenty years before Chows were entered in the stud-book, and those were mostly imported from well-known bloodlines in England, such as Amwell, Rochow, Choonam and the like. Even an American Chow Chow was imported, Olvida de Lamar. Among the earliest breeders were Mrs. von Erlach, a well-known judge for many years, and Mr. Wals of the Wakouwa Kennels. Not until the late 1930's were the first Chows of Swiss breeding entered into the stud book, and most of them were Wakouwas. In 1944 the Swiss Chow Chow Club was founded; the first president was Mr. Hans Wirz, an enthusiastic Chow lover with a vast knowledge of the breed. He was the breeder of the beautiful dog Ch. Yu Foo Han Fo Chu (out of Chang-Shi Taff X Lang-Shan Ursa), one of the finest Chows bred on the Continent. Chu was a beautiful shaded red with a big, magnificent head, very dignified and with great expression. For years he stood alone as the king of Chow Chows in Switzerland and was a dog that could have won anywhere. It is a pity that there are no progeny from this beautiful dog.

At the same time Miss Martha Bernegger had her big beautiful dog Ch. Yu Tang van Heidenkeller, another one with a great head. This dog died tragically of colic in 1952 on the second day of a show in Stuttgart, Germany, where he had won the certificate the day before. But in Switzerland also, during the first post-war years, it was mostly imports from Holland, Belgium and France that influenced the quality level of breed. Mr. Hans Wirz wrote in an article for *Schweizer Hundesport* in 1959 that all Swiss champion titles were won by foreign dogs. Many importations from the best bloodlines still do a lot of winning. There are a number of Dutch, Luxembourg, French and German dogs imported, and interest seems to be growing. A Dutch lady, Miss Hilleris Lambers, who is living in Switzerland, bred some very nice dogs and brought a black smooth to Switzerland, where there seems to be interest in this variety as well. Miss Lambers' young home-bred dog, Karya's Brandal, is widely admired in Switzerland. He is a beautiful well-balanced deep self-red with good legs and body and a nice head, sired by the American import dog of Henk van de Wouw, Holland, named Pandee's New World Ambassador X Panda, a Dutch-

Int. Ch. Chang-Shi Kitty Hawks. This lovely bitch was born in 1942 and was bred and owned by Countess de Changy. Photo taken in 1948.

Chang-Shi Noch-Ka, born in 1945. One year old in this photograph. Bred and owned by the Countess de Changy.

Czambo z Szelzga nad Wartq, lovely black dog owned by Szymandera of Poland.

Chang-Shi Snaff, bred and owned by the Countess de Changy. Born in 1944, he was sired by Ch. Kou-Ling Youki *ex* Chang-Shi Victory. This photo was taken in 1947.

bred bitch. Brandal was Best of Breed at the Dutch Chow-Chow Club Specialty in 1973 with 82 dogs entered.

Some of the many first class dogs imported in Switzerland are Tsjomoloengma Dschingis Khan (Hwang-Ti Chao Chun X Anjelina), bred by Mrs. van de Saag and owned by Mr. Andrea, who later owned Dschingis Khan van Kamtsjatka, a son of Int. Ch. Kai-Men-Ti Liweng, whose other son, Radya van Kamtsjatka, was the property of Mrs. Walter. Another well-known importation, also a son of Int. Ch. Kai-Men-Ti Liweng, was Int. Ch. Pascha van Sinkiang, a beautiful red dog who had a great reputation. He was owned by Mrs. Kofer. There were several descendants of Liweng in Switzerland and at least as many of another well-known dog, Int. Ch. Jalu Mong-Fu. They include Tai-Ping O Blue Tongue, owned by Mrs. B. Meyer; Int. Ch. Odine Mong-Fu, owned by the Countess

Yu-Foo Han Fu Chu, red dog born in 1948, bred and owned by Hans Wirz. The sire was Chang-Shi Taf ex Lang Shan Ursa.

von Halwyl in Geneva; Int. Ch. Pao-Kwai-Chu, owned by Mr. Schapper; and Tinga Mong-Fu, owned by Mr. Benitez. But there are also dogs from Dutch, French and German breeding to be found in Switzerland. Mr. Glattli, a member of the Swiss Chow Chow Club Committee and a well-known judge for the breed, owns a beautiful red dog, Ku-Chia Fung-Feng. There were also several Dutch dogs sent to Switzerland. The good bloodlines were imported, but mostly by individual Chow fanciers, and no really important breeding or big kennel is based on them.

CHOW CHOWS IN GERMANY

Germany, one of the biggest countries on the Continent, has its own very popular breeds, such as the Boxers and German Shepherds. Chow Chows were not very popular until well after the second World War. But even today, at shows where entries of 700 German Shepherds, and 500 Boxers are quite normal, the Chow Chow entry is usually between 25 and 40. The sport of dogs in Germany is different from that in the countries we have mentioned so far. There are many titles to be won, bound to certain shows and club shows. For instance, Clubsieger 19.., Bundessieger 19. . These are regarded as the best dog of every breed at the big show the German

Kennel Club holds every year. Then there is the German Kennel Club Champion and of course the National and International Champion, which are the normal titles given everywhere else on the Continent. But because the clubs and certain shows give titles which are added to the dog's name, there are numerous German dogs with several of those titles which are recognized only in Germany. If Holland or England had these titles, there would be dogs who would need half a page to write their names and include all the titles! So we restrict ourselves to the common titles of Champion and International Champion.

Although Germany is a big country, there are no prominent Chow Chow kennels. Mostly they consist of ten to fifteen dogs. In Germany the first Chow Chow was entered into the stud book in 1929. It was an English-bred bitch named Lwo of Quarry Hall (bred by Mrs. Stohn-Speyer and owned by Mrs. Schmidt-Fellner of Frankfurt). In 1930 the German Chow Chow Club was founded. The first president was Dr. Henninger and the secretary was Mrs. H. Heubner, who was also the first specialist Chow judge in Germany. She did a lot to stimulate interest in the breed and helped make it better known. Another of the earliest Chow fanciers and breeders was Mrs. Lotte Lewin. Following her were Mrs. Margot Huber (Kennel v. Elberwerder), the Countess Nina von Plauen (Kennel NingPao), Mrs. Margot von Opel of the automobile company (Kennel vom Engadin), who bought Int. Ch. Hussar of Chunking from the Belgian Countess de Changy. This Chow had great influence on Chow breeding in those early days. Mrs. Lotte Lewin owned Kennel Mongol, which she started in 1930. She is still alive, 80 years old now, and still follows Chow activities with great interest. Chow breeding in those early days was mostly founded on English bloodlines and importations from Kennels such as Niclos, Syrron and the like, going back to the well-known Rochows and Choonams. About 1934 one of the breeders who regularly imported good stock and whose breeding contributed to the progress of the breed was

Dog show in Lucerne, Switzerland in 1951. Open class for dogs with Henk van de Wouw judging in background. From left to right, Countess de Changy with her Int. Ch. Schild's Xabu I, Mrs. Stucki, candidate-judge in background, Mrs. Wirz with Yu-Fu Han-Fu-Tschu II, and Miss Bernegger with Int. Ch. Yutang von Heiden-keller III.

Feng Yu Hsiang Han Fu Chu, born 1938, shown here at 6 years of age. Bred and owned by Hans Wirz of Switzerland. Sire was Changson of Wakouwa ex Drago Ming Sulamith.

Int. Ch. Kwong de Sytka, red dog born in 1961, bred and owned by Mrs. Hamel. Pictured here at four years of age. A champion in France as well as a champion in Switzerland in 1964.

Mr. Julius Rauth of the Peking Kennels. In 1938 the best-known Chow Chow Kennel in Germany was founded by Mr. Willi Elbers with his El-Do-San breeding. This kennel usually kept about forty Chow Chows and imported many first-class dogs during the war, such as T' Kell Sie Brigand and many Chang-Shis. Among others were Chang-Shi Ducky (Ch. Chang-Shi Neron X Int. Ch. June Jubilee), Chang-Shi Cocktail (Ch. Choonam Chiang Tang X Chang-Shi Titch), Chang-Shi Mister Brown (Ch. Chang-Shi Neron X Chang-Shi Tamky) and the bitches Chang-Shi Marina (Ch. Chang-Shi Neron X 'T Kell Sie Mouse), Chang-Shi Neronne (Ch. Chang-Shi Neron X Chang-Shi NitChi), thereby obtaining the best Belgian bloodlines. Because of his personal situation during the war, Mr. Elbers had the opportunity to travel around and moreover could help the Countess de Changy get food for her dogs. As there was hardly any food for the people in those war years, it will be clear that it was worse where dog food was concerned and almost impossible to run a kennel like that of the Countess. Instead of money Mr. Elbers requested some puppies to pay for the dog food, thus building up his kennel on this prominent Belgian breeding.

One of the most famous dogs he bred was El-Do-San Oleander (Syrron Herbert X El-Do-San Frieda), a dog with huge bone and a magnificent head, one of the finest, if not the finest, specimen ever bred in Germany. On the other hand many insiders wondered whether the El-Do-San breeding was quite reliable as, apart from the beautiful Chang-Shis, the kennel owned several dogs of lesser quality, and many of the progeny could hardly stand up to their pedigrees. Before the war several Chows were also purchased from the Kou-Ling Kennels, such as Kou-Ling Tabou (Ch. Lucky Chang X Yang-Li), Kou-Ling Chink and the bitches Kou-Ling Otawa (Kou-Ling Loupi X Kou-Ling Nhi), Kou-Ling Mambia (Choonam Ming-Ti a Yang-Li) and so on. Moreover, there was a Russian lady, Madame Samsonow (Kennel Now-So-Sam), who had come to Germany after the Russian Revolution. She owned

Ch. Matjan, born in the 1940's and sired by Pucka Sahibv Blucherheim ex Magna von Blucherheim. Bred by Mr. Vennegoor of Germany and owned by P. Luckhardt.

some very fine specimens from first-class English bloodlines, bought from her friend the Countess de Changy in Belgium. She bred some well-known Chows such as Now-So-Sam Quick Fly, Now-So-Sam Quitouse, Now-So-Sam Quality, all by Choonam Tschiang-Tang X Choonam Blu-Ee. She owned Chang-Shi Tamky at the time but gave this bitch back to the Countess after the Chang-Shi Kennels were destroyed during the war to use this Ch. Rochow Adjutant daughter for the rebuilding of her kennel. There were some importations from Austria, as there was a well-known kennel at the time, named Of Chinese Dream, owned by Mrs. Johanna Ita from Vienna. Several dogs from that kennel which bred from good English bloodlines came to Germany. The best-known dog was Lan-Wang Of Chinese Dream, a fine, upstanding blue dog, owned by Mrs. Margarete Meurer.

Champion Sedora's Luvchow Honeybunch is pictured winning a first in Showmanship at the Kenilworth Kennel Club show, July 5, 1974, in Durham, Connecticut. Honeybunch is sired by Ch. Eastward Liontamer of Elster out of Canorwell Primrose Path.

Mi-Tu's Han-Su Shang is being awarded Best of Winners under Mrs. Mary Nelson Stephenson, Phoenix, Arizona, at the Club VI Specialty in Toronto, 1973. The handler is Herb Williams, who co-owns Shang with John C. Frederick Peddie. Shang not only finished his Canadian championship but also won his American title.

El-Do San Billa, red bitch born in 1944. Bred by W. Elbers and owned by M. Holthaus of Germany. By Chang-Shi Mister Brown ex Choonam Kouemdi. This picture was taken when she was five years old.

The last war years and the first post-war years were a very bad time for Germany. The country had been destroyed by the non-stop bombing and everything was dislocated. Of course the situation with the dogs was very bad. A virtually new start had to be made. Communication was bad, documentation was practically lost and there were very few dogs left to start any rebuilding. Regarding the situation after the war we quote Mr. Erich Buchner, the president of the Breeding and Judging Committee of the German Chow Chow Club and a well-known breeder and judge who had also judged abroad many times, including shows in England. In his articles on German Chow history published in the Chow Chow Club newspaper in September 1968 and in 1970, he wrote:

"When the war was over in 1945, the situation in the dog sport was the same for all different breeds. Many groupings had come up and at least two different Chow clubs existed along with the original German Chow Chow Club, having their own stud books and pedigrees. Dog-business and dog-trade prospered and in some cases breeders just made their own pedigrees for their puppies. The breeding of reliable pedigree Chows was done great harm this way and quality had declined. There were some excellent specimens in our country in the late thirties and early forties, but generally speaking our Chows showed many faults and lacked quality. Many showed light eyes, bad hindquarters, lack of bone and not enough substance. In 1945 the German Kennel Club certified the original German Chow Chow Club as the only one registered. The bona fide Chowists came together and organized themselves in one club which was called the Allgemeiner Chow-Chow Club. In 1950 Germany became a member of the F.C.I. again and the A.C.C.C. has been the certified Chow club for Germany ever since. In the same year the first big championship show was held. Until then there had been no contact with other Continental countries, apart from a few individual breeders who had made themselves familiar with the level of Chow breeding abroad. The A.C.C.C. coupled its specialty with the German Kennel Club Championship Show in Munich, in October 1950. The well-known, much-esteemed judge, Mr. Henk van de Wouw from Holland was invited to judge, being the first foreign judge for the breed in Germany since the war. Every one well-known in Chows was present at this event. Looking back, the judging caused great disappointment except to the very few people who knew how bad the breed had become. From the 52 exhibits only three got the qualification "Excellent," a few more "Very Good," but the majority was only qualified as "Good." In a resume of his judging Mr. van de Wouw remarked: 'On the whole the exhibits do not show serious faults, but there is a lack of high quality and type. When I speak of type, I do not only mean the type of head, though I think that very important, but with a typical Chow I mean a specimen showing the peculiar points of the breed, a dog that is typical in his whole general appearance. In many of the Chows shown to me the heads are too small and too plain, muzzles too pointed, eyes too big and too round. Nearly all the exhibits are too flat-sided and lack bone, hindlegs are not straight enough and fail in one of the most peculiar points of our breed, being the unique stilted gait. If, however, Chow fanciers would be able to import new blood from pure-bred first class bloodlines, I think the standard of Chow breeding will soon rise'."

The earlier-quoted Mr. Buchner continued:

"This day can be considered a revolution in Chow breeding in Germany. From there on, Chows were on the up-grade, slowly but surely, because of

Ch. Chang Wong v Erfttal, black dog born in 1948. Breeder, J. Stocksiefen of Germany; owner, Hans Better. By Lan-Wang of Chinese Dream ex El-Do-San Aruna Kwy. Pictured here at five years of age.

Lan Wang of Chinese Dream, born in 1940. This lovely blue dog, photographed at six years of age, was bred by Miss Johanna Ita of Vienna. By Sg. Lord ex Sgn. Choonam Blue Wonder. Owned by Miss Meurer.

Ch. Wau-Kwong van Mongolie, born in 1954. Bred by Henk van de Wouw and owned by Erich Buchner of Berlin, Germany. By Ch. Ki-Dong Cheng-Wong ex Ch. Chang-Shi Up To Date.

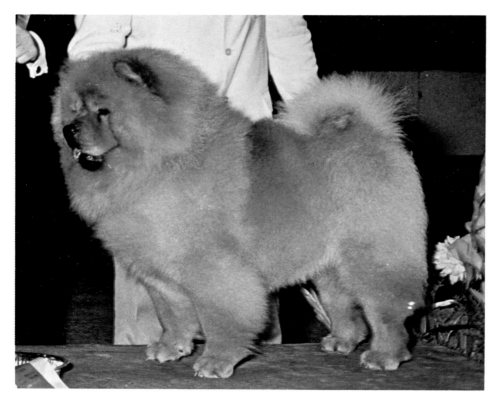

Canadian and American Champion Foo H'Sing's Mister Linn Wu was awarded group first at the Greenwood Kennel Club, August, 1971 by L.E. Piper. Mister Linn Wu, called "Buda," is co-owned by Mr. and Mrs. Herb Williams and Mr. John C. Frederick Peddie, Bu Dynasty Kennels, Toronto, Canada.

Pandee's Victoria is shown at the Old Dominion Kennel Club of Northern Virginia in 1972 going Winners Bitch and Best Opposite Sex under Ed Bracey, judge. Her sire is Titus Pandee van Mongolie, Dutch import, and her mother is Pandee's Katanga. Victoria, who finished her championship later on, was bred by Dr. Imogene P. Earle, Pandee Kennels, and is co-owned by her and Dr. JoAnne O'Brien, who is handling here.

Ch. Audrich Cassandra, shown here at 10 months of age winning at a 1970 dog show. The first time shown in Specials she was Best of Breed and third in the Non-Sporting Group. She was whelped in August, 1971 and was sired by Ch. Plainacre's Charman Fella *ex* Gotschall's Chada.

Ch. Autumn Sun Michael Bear finished in 13 shows and is pictured here winning Best of Breed under judge Mary Stephenson in 1972. Bear was bred by Carol Patton and Dr. Samuel Draper. His sire was Ch. Dre-Don Sun King of Craiglinden; dam was Liontamer Happiness is.

serious selection and importation from the best bloodlines from Holland and later from England as well. We owe a great deal of gratitude to our Dutch sporting-friends, especially to the Kennels Van Mongolie, Ki-Dong, van de Tongelreep, van Majodo, van de Loumi Hoeve and Kai-Men-Ti, for sending such first class stock to Germany. Looking at our present-day Chows as a whole, our Chows are really nice dogs, able to compete on an international level."

To Mr. Buchner's story we add that at that show mentioned, Best of Breed was a red dog named Ch. Dschingu of Meh-Thue (El-Do-San Pascha X Alfa von Bennelsheim), bred by Mr. Buchner and owned by Mrs. M. Strauss. When Kitty van de Wouw judged in Berlin in 1954 he got the certificate as well and was as far as is known the first post-war German full champion Chow Chow. From Mr. Buchner's explanation it will be clear that by far most of the present-day German Chows go back to Dutch bloodlines and some English stock, but during the last ten years the Mong-Fus, owned by the Cottafavis of Luxembourg, have been of considerable interest to the German Chow breeding as well. Mr. Buchner himself was one of the very first to import some Dutch Chows, such as Ch. Wau-Kwong van Mongolie and his sister Wing-Wa van Mongolie (Ch. Ki-Dong Cheng Wong X Ch. Chang-Shi Up To Date). He built up a good strain and bred among others his National and International Ch. King-Jumbo von Meh-Thue, a beautiful dog with heavy bone and a beautiful head.

As was mentioned before, many Chows were imported from the well-known Dutch kennels, while others were purchased in England. One of these was the bitch Int. Ch. Sumi of Junggwaw (Ch. Enrico of Junggwaw X Chloe of Junggwaw), bred by Mr. S. Smedley and owned by Mrs. U. Leyden from Cologne. This bitch has been of interest to the breed and can be found in many post-war pedigrees in East Germany as well. It may be interesting to see of how much influence the post-war importations,

mostly Dutch, have been. In 1955, at the A.C.C.C. Specialty held in Frankfurt, there was an entry of 62 dogs of which 25% were imports, and 9 had an imported dog as one of their parents. Fifteen years later at the A.C.C.C. Specialty in Wurzburg there was an entry of 100 Chows, of which 7 were imported and 26 were bred from one or two imported parents. This points out the progress German Chow breeding has made.

As there are no really big and prominent German Chow kennels, the building was done by small kennels. They had bitches bred in Holland and Luxembourg and occasionally imported puppies from these countries, a practice they are continuing to the present day. As the winning dogs are mostly owned by private Chow fanciers and smaller breeders spread all over Germany, it is impossible to name them all. Some of the best-known who have been of interest to the progress of breeding are the imports Nat. and Int. Ch. Wamchow Che-Foo (dog bred by Mrs. W. Lamerus, Holland, owned by Mrs. C. Hoffmann-Rooseboom, Munsten); Nat. and Int. Ch. Kai-Men-Ti Wuniang (bitch bred by Mrs. H. Wachholtz, Holland, owned by Mr. A. Metzger, Schriessheim); Cheng van Mongolie (dog bred by Henk van de Wouw, Holland, owned by Mr. G. Konrad, near Frankfurt), a dog that is in many pedigrees of winning stock; Int. Ch. A-Tung van de Hagenbrink (an Int. Ch. Kai-Men-Ti Liweng son, bred by Mrs. J. Dekker-Maris, Holland, owned by Mrs. W. Ullman, Kennel Na-Shan, who is also the proud owner of Int. Ch. Tao-Yeu-Chino, a beautiful shaded red bitch; and Int. Ch. Hsiung van de Hagenbrink (breeder Mrs. Dekker-Maris, Holland, owner Mrs. W. Ullman). Well-known German-breds are Int. Ch. Kama Lakschmi Ay-Wong-Ti (bred and owned by Mr. Adolf Metzger), a very big dog, bred from his sire's and dam's side back to Int. Ch. Kai-Men-Ti Liweng.

The 1970 A.C.C.C. Specialty drew a record entry for the Continent. Three foreign judges were invited: Mr. A.O. Grindey (England, red bitches), Mr. Henk van de Wouw (Holland, red dogs), Mr. Walter Glattli (Switzerland, all the blacks, both

Tai vom Kempken and his dam, Han-Pi-Wu Dewi-Danoe. Owner Mrs. C. Hoffmann-Rooseboom. Photograph taken in 1959.

sexes). While in 1950 three out of the 62 entries, or less than 6 per cent, got "Excellent," in 1970 the three judges gave 23½ per cent of the exhibits "Excellent" and nearly 50 per cent "Very Good." These figures say enough for the progress made in German Chow breeding. Most of the winning German stock was exhibited at that show, and many of the present-day German champions competed. One was Nat. and Int. Ch. Dschingis Khan U Milo (Int. Ch. Jalu Mong-Fu X Dschingis Khan Lyu),

owned by Mr. Kuhnel from Berlin and bred by Mr. Rudolf Bergner, who had started in the early 1950's with Chula Mong-Fu (a daughter of Womiya de la Moulaine), breeding from the best stock, mating his bitches to famous foreign stud dogs and purchasing puppies from the best bloodlines, including Me-Thue and Lou-mi-Hoeve.

Another important dog is Nat. and Int. Ch. Lung-Keu Siang Kin-Wong (Nat. and Int. Ch. Lung-Keu Siang Asow X Shi-

Int. Ch. Beauty, born in 1955 and bred by J. Rozeboom. Owner is Mrs. Wachholtz. By Int. Ch. Kai-Menti Liweng ex Gonja van Nunatak.

Ch. Tai Yang Yuan Bel-Liweng, bred and owned by Erika Baumann of Merseburg, East Germany. The sire was Int. Ch. Kai-Men-Ti Liweng ex Rai Fai vom Liebenlehn.

Ch. Mi-Pao's Tarate. This lovely bitch was sired by Int. Ch. Chang-Shi Hong-Kwong *ex* Ch. Meran v d Loumi-Hoeue. Owned by F. P.A. Odenkirchen, Waterdown, Ontario, Canada.

Ch. Eastward Liontamer of Elster pictured winning the Non-Sporting Group at the Hunterdon Hills Kennel Club show under Judge Raymond Beale. Louie is co-owned by Dr. Samuel Draper and the Robert Hetheringtons of Franklin Lakes, New Jersey.

Ch. Mi-Pao's Oehara, sired by Int. Ch. Chang-Shi Hong-Kwong *ex* J'Ming van de Tongelreep. Photographed in 1970, the dog is owned by F. P.A. Odenkirchen, Mi-Pao Kennels, Waterdown, Ontario, Canada.

Precious puppy!...Warlord's Matahara, owned and bred by Mr. and Mrs. Clarence H. Moss of the Clar-El-Mo Kennels in San Antonio, Texas.

Xitah Meisje van Mongolie, red bitch bred by Henk v d Wouw in 1970 and owned by Berno Ehrhardt of Germany. Sire was Ch. Tschiang Kai Tchek van Mongolie ex Quite Peggy.

Int. Ch. King-Jumbo von Meh-Thue, born in 1958. Bred and owned by Erich Buchner of Berlin, Germany. Sire was Ch. Wau-Kwong van Mongolie ex Ien-Ju Yeh von Meh-Thue. Photographed at 4 years of age.

Mao-Tse Bacco, red dog born in 1968 and bred by L. Klopfer. Owner is W.H. Meyer of Wurzburg, Germany. He was sired by Ch. Shiang Lo Entancelin ex Hou-Shan-San Donka.

Shiang-Lo Foo-Yang, born 1965, and bred by S. Lommatzsch. Owned by Freifrau von Holtzapfel of Germany. Sire was Int. Ch. Wamchow Che-Foo ex Lee-Shiu. Photographed when the dog was 21 months of age.

ang-Lo Alinda), bred and owned by Mrs. El Janssen, a beautifully balanced, sound dog whose name can be found in many pedigrees in Germany, France and Switzerland. Then there is Ch. Shiang-Lo Entancelin (Che-Kwong X Chinam V. Sinkiang), owned by Mr. W. Meyer, Wurzburg and bred by Mr. S. Lommzatsch, Hamburg. Mr. Lommzatsch is a well-known breeder who founded his breeding on Int. Ch. Kai-Men-Ti Liweng and other fine Dutch bloodlines. Another breeder is Mr. W. Meyer of Kennel Huo-Shang, who built up his breeding on Entancelin lines and with a black bitch, Mong-To Liang, bred by Mrs. U. Leyden. He is a judge for the breed as well and a breeder choosing good bloodlines. A very well-known champion, successful in the show ring in Germany and abroad, is the fine shaded red heavy-boned dog with a magnificent head named Nat. and Int. Ch. Quirit von Melbtal, owned by Mrs. M. Huhle and bred by Mrs. A. Ernst of Bonn, a very productive breeder who founded her breeding on the English Junggwaw line, Dutch (mostly Loumi-Hoeve) and Luxembourg bloodlines. Another of her breeding is Nat. and Int. Ch. Bi-Son-Ka von Melbtal (Int. Ch. Mantsuko Mong-Fu X Mong-To Isa). Mrs. Meyer-Wildeman, Bonn, a very serious Chow lover, owns and bred Int. Ch. Tung-Jen-Ay-Ching (Han-Ti Hwang-Feng X Nja-Na von Melbtal). From the winning blacks we must mention Ch. Veit von Palatinat (Lion von Meh-Thue X Noggi von Palatinat), owned by Mrs. Bures of Berlin and bred by Mrs. Gertrude Hoffmann, Willstett. She is one of the oldest and most productive Chow breeders in her country and is well-known abroad as well. One of her best-known champions is Ch. Filou von Palatinat (Chutong von Palatinat X Wally von Palatinat). This kennel was based on good bloodlines. One of her best-known dogs was Ki-Dong Chutong, a brother to Ch. Ki-Dong Cheng Wong, bred by Kitty van de Wouw of Holland. Then we have Ch. Anat Chiriqui (Ch. Veit von Palatinat X Princess Blue Gem Chiriqui), bred by Mrs. G. Playford, near Braunschweig, the German widow of an Englishman. She lived in

Ch. Shiang-Lo Entancelin, red dog born in 1964. The breeder was S. Lommatzsch and he is owned by W.H. Meyer of Wurzburg, Germany. Sire Che-Kwong *ex* Chinam van Sinkiang. He is photographed here at four years of age.

Int. Ch. Quirit von Melbtal, red dog born in 1961, was bred by Mrs. A. Ernst. Owner, Fritz Huhle. Sire was Int. Ch. Kai-Men-Ti Liweng *ex* Dabala von Melbtal.

Tag-El's Big Stink goes Winners Bitch for a 3-point major at her very first show in December, 1973. Handled by Evelyn Carter of McLoud, Oklahoma, at this Arkansas Kennel Club Show. Owned by Thomas and Evelyn Carter.

Opposite, upper photo:
Ch. Starcrest Spy of Poppyland, owned by Mr. and Mrs. Howard Kendall of Sepulveda, California.

Opposite, lower photo:
Yoko of Liang Ming Keou, beautiful European red bitch born in 1970. Bred by Mr. H. Steegmans and owned by Miss R. Steenmeijer. The sire was Henk von dom Falkenweg *ex* Mhie-Jou von dom Rodeza.

You-Two's Echo Emperor, born 1965. Bred and owned by Miss Martha G. Visser of Germany. By Int. Ch. Mi-Pao's Piwa Rangan *ex* Mi-Pao's Poetri. This photograph was taken when he was 4 years old.

Britain for some years after the war and kept some Chows there. She based her small breeding program on mainly English stock. A very fine black bitch, doing very well in the show ring all over the Continent, is Int. Ch. Chin-Chin O Bara (Int. Ch. Mantsuko Mong-Fu X Xantippe von Palatinat). She was bred by Dr. H. Schlick, Frankfurt, also one of the older breeders who looked for good bloodlines and bred a fine type of Chow Chow. She is owned by Mrs. B. Haussner, the wife of the A.C.C.C.'s secretary, living in Eschringen. She is a very successful exhibitor and one of the younger breeders who use excellent bloodlines. One of her best-known Chows is the black bitch Ch. Ku-Chia Chi-Chi.

There are quite a number of fine Chows spread over all parts of Germany. Those who followed the development of the German Chow breeding from the end of the war up to now have to admit that the Germans can be proud of the results.

CHOWS IN OTHER EUROPEAN COUNTRIES

The other F.C.I. member-states, such as Austria, Poland, Hungary and Czechoslovakia, have never been prominent in Chow Chow breeding, nor has there been any great interest. There are Chow breeders and lovers of the breed in those countries, but there is hardly any contact with outsiders, because it is almost impossible to visit without a special visa. Those countries have mainly bred from all strains and kennels that we have mentioned previously. There are at times big dog shows and sometimes foreign judges are invited, but really prominent kennels do not exist. In East Germany, virtually isolated since erection of the "Wall," there are many Chow fanciers, often people who were in the breed before World War II. They have some good bloodlines, mostly from West Germany, and there is Mong-Fu and Ki-Dong blood. Several Kai-Men-Ti Liweng descendants were born before the wall was erected, such as Ch. Tai Yang Yuan Bel Liweng, Ch. Tai-Yary-Yuan Din-Koh, and Ch. Tschang-Tschara Rhani, a black bitch. There are still some good specimens

Int. Ch. Mi-Pao's Piwa Rangan, born in 1963, bred by Paul Odenkirchen in Canada. Now owned by Martha Visser. Sired by Int. Ch. Chang-Shi Hong Kwong ex Ch. Tiga.

Fee von Ching-Cheng, red bitch and Fu-Kwey von Eschnapur, a black dog owned by Mrs. M. Laske of East Berlin, Germany.

in those countries. In Poland Mr. Szymandera owns some good Chow Chows, while in East Germany one of the best-known breeders is Mrs. Laske in East Berlin. As we have said, contacts with the countries mentioned is rare, and there are no competitions with dogs from western countries, so it is impossible to get an idea about the breeding Standard.

Ch. Starcrest Dandy Lion, bred by Joel Marston and owned by Don Foster and Jim Pierson of the Justamere Kennels in Monrovia, California. Photo by Missy.

Ch. Dre-Don's Bold Arrow winning Best of Breed under judge Samuel Draper at the 1971 dog show at Rochester, New York. Owned and handled by Donald Drennan, Dre-Don Kennels, Getzville, New York. A Stephen Klein photo.

Mongol Feng-Ying and his dam, Niclos Ruby, owned by Mrs. Lotte Lewin of Berlin, Germany. Photograph taken in 1939.

Chessie vom Haus Herth, a smooth black bitch whelped in 1962 and photographed at 5 months of age. This Dutch girl was bred by Herth and is owned by Miss H. Hille Ris Lambers of Switzerland. Sire was Chutong von Palatinat *ex* Ukwong Kai Lung.

Ch. Mong-To Lexi, born in 1965, bred by Mrs. U. Leyden of Germany. Sire was Eduard van de Falkenweg *ex* Int. Ch. Sumi of Junggwaw.

Ch. Dschingu von Meh-Thue, red dog born in 1949. Bred by Erich Buchner of Berlin, Germany. Owner, Mrs. Strauss. By El-Do-San Pascha *ex* Alfa von Bennelsheim. Two years of age in this photograph.

World Championship show in Dortmund, Germany in May, 1956. . . the judge is the Countess de Changy. Mr. Lou Nuyen with Int. Ch. Chin-Yu of Hanoi II, and Mrs. Kitty van de Wouw with Ch. Woolly van Majodo I. The Countess de Changy was one of the great Chow breeders of all time.

CHOW CHOWS IN NORWAY AND SWEDEN

Going up to the north, to the Scandinavian countries, we are happy to see that interest in Chows is growing considerably. There have always been Chow fanciers in those countries, but for years there was hardly any contact with them. Until some years ago Chow breeding was mainly based on English import stock, if you can speak about Chow breeding at all. It is remarkable that Chows were not more popular in the Scandinavian countries, because the character of the people as well as the climate are so suitable for the breed. Quoting from the Chow history of Denmark, Norway and Sweden as given by Mrs. Aase Wandrup of Zoto Kennels, Mrs. Selbach of the Tsing-Fu Kennels and Boo Lundstrom of the Kansus Kennels, we thank them very much for their contributions to this chapter.

Norway and Sweden are more or less separated from the other Continental countries not only because of their geographic location but also because of their quarantine requirements. Denmark does not have strict quarantine requirements, so cooperation with the other European countries is easier than with the fellow Scandinavian countries.

In Norway, the first Chows were allegedly imported about 1890, but there is no record of the very early Norwegian Chows. The development went very slowly. Chows were rarely seen and mostly owned by individuals. After World War II the breed became better known in Norway. One of the very first kennels was the Aagerd Kennel, owned by Mr. and Mrs. Aarsen, who can be considered the pioneers for the breed in their country. Their work and efforts contributed a great deal to the growing number of Chow fanciers in Norway. The earliest specimens were English importations as well as some Swedish ones. Later on Dutch stock was imported also. Those and the later imports from these countries are the basis of the present-day Chow breeding in Norway.

One of the most important kennels to contribute considerably to the progress of the breed is no doubt Mr. and Mrs. Messel's Af Manchu, a kennel based on the most successful combination of Swedish and Dutch bloodlines. Kennel Manchu imported several Chows, such as Int. and Nord. Ch. Red Princess III of Liang-Ming-Keou (Tzar of Junggwaw X Achmed of Liang-Ming-Keou), bred by Mr. Steegmans, thus getting together prominent English and Dutch bloodlines going back to Chang-Shi and Loumi Hoeve stock. He bred Red Princess to Nord. Ch. Mongols Red Prince, bred by Mrs. Adner from Sweden by her Dutch import King van de Tongelreep X Nallebo-Daniella. Mrs. Messel got another prominent Dutch bloodline this way. One of the results was Ch. Sun Yat-Sen of Manchu, owned by Mona Selbach, of the kennel Tsing-Fu. He is a full brother to Temujin of Manchu, the only Norwegian-bred Best in Show Chow.

At present there are about 300 Chows and a few other serious kennels in Norway. It is difficult to give the exact figure because of imports that have not been registered with the Club. There is no special Chow Chow Club in Norway. The Chows are joining the Norsk Polarhund Klubb (the Norwegian Polardog Club) together with the other Spitzhounds such as Alaskan Malamutes, Huskies and Samoyeds.

In Sweden there is an increasing interest in the breed as well. The first Chow Chows arrived in the 1920's. Some of the pioneers of the breed were, first, Miss Betty Berg of Kennel Helluland, who was one of the prominent breeders for years. Some of her best-known dogs were Swedish and Danish Ch. Sho-Sen Peter av Helluland and Ch. Itt San-Fru av Helluland, a bitch that is in many pedigrees and was famous at the time. There is Mr. Rune Jonson (Kennel Torshojden), who started in the breed in the mid-1940's. He imported Ch. Bbormot Dan Ul (bred by the English Mr. W. Robb) which became a Swedish champion as well.

In the early 1960's he purchased several English Chows. In 1963 he got Ch. Black Roi of Silverway (Ch. Minhow Edward of Junggwaw X Blue Bella of Silverway), bred by Mrs. M.L. Bird. Both Helluland and Torshojden gave up Chow breeding after many years of work in the best interests of the breed.

A few years after these pioneers, some new breeders came along. Among them was the late Gerda Adner of Kennel Mongol. Her name was, and is, still held in high esteem. She imported several English dogs from first class bloodlines like the Minhows (Mr. Frank Watkinson) including Ch. Minhow Malarctic, along with some other dogs from well-known Dutch kennels. In 1958 she bought King van de Tongelreep, bred by Mr. van de Broek, by Nat. and Int. Ch. Emperor van de Tongelreep X Ch. Mouchka v. Mongolie. In 1961 she purchased Nord. Ch. Kai-Men-Ti Yuan (Nat. and Int. Ch. Kai-Men-Ti Liweng X Int. Ch. Beauty), bred by Mrs. H. Wacholz. Other Chowists came into the breed and imported several good specimens with valuable pedigrees, such as Ch. Li-Wenky v. Kamtsjatka (Nat. and Int. Ch. Kai-Men-Ti Liweng X Petty v. Kamtsjatka), owned by the Kennel Matte of Erik Matson, another prominent Swedish kennel. Li-Wenky was the dam of the well-known Ch. Mattes H.M. Himself, while Ch. Kai-Men-Ti Yuan is the sire of Int. Ch. Hai-Mi-Ki.

A very valuable importation in the late 1950's was Mr. Matson's Int. and Nord. Ch. Emperor of U'Kwong, an Int. Ch. Astom son, bred by Joan and Eric Egerton. He certainly proved his influence on Swedish Chow-breeding. Another great name in Swedish Chow-breeding is Mrs. Karin Loven-Grytte of the Kashis Kennels. She bred many champions. She still is the most prominent breeder and has contributed very much to the progress of the breed. Her kennel consists mainly of fifteen to twenty Chows of the best English bloodlines. Some of the best-known English importations are Int. and Nord. Ch. Supersonic of Kaioko, bred by Mrs. M. Crompton, by Ch. Wong-Tung's Chang of Canton X Roberta of Kaioko (this dog did a lot of winning in the Scandinavian pedigrees); also there was the well-known Junggwaw's, bred by Mr. and Mrs. S. Smedley from Bredbury, as well as Int. Ch. Tensing of Junggwaw and Int. Ch. Dusky Maid of Junggwaw. In 1966 Mrs. Loven-Grytte imported a Dutch dog named Ch. You-Two's His Highness, bred by Miss Martha Visser, (from Int. Ch. Mi-Pao's Piwa Rangan X Mi-Pao's Poetri), both imported into Holland from the well-known Canadian Mi-Pao Kennels. The background of those two first-class Chows goes back to Chang-Shi and van de Tongelreep. Another Junggwaw champion was imported and is now in the hands of Mrs. Inge Hansen, a young breeder.

Sweden cannot be compared with countries like England and Holland, where the number of Chows or progress in the quality level is considerable. At the beginning of the 1970's there were about ten kennels as well as several private people keeping one or more Chows. Early in 1970 some new blood was imported from Eng-

Ch. Sun Yat-Sen II of Manchu, red dog born in 1964, bred by M. and H.F. Messell. He is owned by Mona K. Selbach of Norway. Sire was Ch. Mongols Red Prince *ex* Int. Ch. Red Princess III of Lian-Ming-Keou.

land and Holland, which is expected to contribute to the Chow breeding program in the country.

It may be interesting to know that Sweden exported a Chow to Holland; Miss Martha Visser imported the bitch Kashis Natalie (Int. Ch. You-Two's His Highness X Swedish Ch. Kashis Honey II). One of the older breeders is Boo Lindstrom (Mrs. Britt Lindstrom) who has been in Chows for over twenty years and is the owner of the Kansus Chow Kennels. She is carefully breeding for health and soundness. The kennel is built mainly on English bloodlines, particularly on Int. and Nord. Ch. Black Roi of Silverway, who was taken over from Kennel Torshojden at the time. The kennel also owns the well-known bitch Int. and Nord. Ch. Skansabrons Queen Beauti, bred by Professor Polanski from Int. and Nord. Ch. Supersonic of Kaioko X Nord. Ch. Kashis Galina Pani (Ch. Emperor of U'Kwong X Kashis Lucinda). Other importations from this kennel are Swedish Ch. Jason of Junggwaw (Count of Junggwaw X Fi-Fi of Junggwaw, a Ch. Fairwood Fu Simba daughter), and Lu-Lu of Junggwaw (Hanz of Junggwaw X Ranee of Junggwaw).

One of the last interesting purchases Mrs. Britt Lindstrom made was the dog

Jowtrix Jaducator, bred by Mr. J. Trick of England. He is by Shou Mong-Fu (the black Pongo Mong-Fu X Int. Ch. Pu-Peh Mong-Fu), a dog bred by the Mong-Fu Kennel in Luxembourg and imported to England by Mr. Trick. No doubt all those imports from the best English and Continental stock will be of value to the Swedish Chow breeding efforts. It is also interesting to note that Mrs. Britt Lindstrom, as a hobby, uses her Chows as sledge-dogs in winter when there is much snow all over Sweden. She has also used them for elk-hunting with considerable success. As a kennel always has to renew itself, according to Mrs. Lindstrom, she continues bringing new blood into her breeding from time to time.

The reason why Sweden has not organized a Chow Chow Club as yet may be that going to dog shows means traveling great distances. The biggest and most important show is the Stockholm International Dog Show, held every autumn, where the best dogs in the country usually compete and judges from all parts of the world are invited to officiate.

At the end of this chapter on the Continental Chow, it becomes evident that the heart of the Continental Chow breeding was, and still is, in the smaller countries.

Norwegian and Swedish Ch. Temjin of Manchu, red dog born in 1964, bred by M. and H.F. Messell. Owner is Frank Stene of Norway. The sire was Ch. Mongols Red Prince ex Int. Ch. Red Princess III of Liang-Ming-Keou.

The most famous kennels, such as Wigwam, T'Kell'Sie, Chang-Shi as the greatest of the great, Kou-Ling, van Mongolie and Mong-Fu, together with smaller serious breeders have contributed a great deal to international Chow breeding all over the world, working toward the creation of the beautiful, present-day Chow Chow, the only dog in the world for the real Chow lover!

Ch. Monkay Doung, red dog born in 1963, is owned by Mrs. Billet. Photograph taken in 1970.

Ch. Mattes H.M. Himself, red dog born in 1963 and bred and owned by Eric Mattsson of Sweden. Sire was Int. Ch. Emperor of Ukwong ex Ch. Li-Wenky van Kamtsjatka.

Ch. Gotschall's Van Van, owned by Donald L. Drennan and Valetta Gotschall of Getzville, New York. The sire was Ch. Loy-Jean's Chi-Yan Kid *ex* Gotschall's Dusty. Van Van was one of the great Best in Show Chows in the 1960's.

5. THE CHOW CHOW IN THE UNITED STATES — The Beginning

According to American Kennel Club records, the first Chow Chow was exhibited in the United States at Westminster in 1890, thirteen years after the first Westminster event. The dog's name was Takya, and he was entered by Miss A.C. Derby, his owner, in the breed "Chinese Chow Chow Dog." This breed name perhaps suggests why the Chow Chow has been referred to occasionally as The Chow Dog, particularly by the public, rather than as The Chow Chow.

Two pioneers of the breed in America must be mentioned first: Dr. and Mrs. Henry Jarrett, who established the first Chow Chow kennel in Philadelphia. They owned Yen How, who was the first winner of note, in 1902 and in the years following. The Jarretts remained active all of their lives, and Dr. Jarrett served as secretary of The Chow Chow Club, Inc. from its beginning for 35 years.

According to Will Judy, one of the breed's most eminent authorities, the year 1905 represents the most important date in the early history of the breed in the United States, for in that year Mrs. Charles E. Proctor founded her Blue Dragon Kennels and imported Chinese Chum, who in June of 1905 became the first Chow Chow to finish his American championship. Siring both Black Cloud and Night of Asia, Chinese Chum was the first American champion to sire a champion. Night of Asia finished his title in September, 1905. Chinese Chum went Best of Breed at Westminster in 1906 with several Chows competing. Old-timers consider Chinese Chum the father of the breed in the United States. Chinese Chum, one recalls, was sired by the English Champion Shylock, who thus becomes the grandfather of the Chow in America.

In those early years Mrs. E.K. Lincoln established her Greenacre Kennel, Fairfield, Connecticut, and imported many English Chows. Eastern Star was one of their famous champions and won Best of Breed at Westminster in 1914. The Lincolns owned about fifty champions and continued actively in the breed through the 1930's. Another famous breeder was Mr. Franklin Hutton of Winsum Kennels, Long Island, N.Y.

In the early 1920's, Claire Knapp, who became Mrs. W.O. Penny, established her Clairedale Kennels and remained active for many years. Her Champion Clairedale Son Too was perhaps her greatest Chow as both a winner and a sire. His father was the great Champion Winsum

Ch. Greenacre Tsu Sima, Chow bitch, was owned by Mrs. E.K. Lincoln of Greenacre Kennels, Fairfield, Connecticut.

Champion Chia Linnchow is shown here in 1934. Her mother was Madame Queen of Na-Poo and her father, Ch. Chia-Wan's Blue Monarch. Chia was heavily line-bred to the great Ch. Choonam Brilliantine.

Greenacre Kennels were the owners of Champion Su T'Sun of Five Ash who was handled to a Best in Show, all breeds, in 1927 in Denver, Colorado. He was handled by James Deignan who managed Mrs. Lincoln's Greenacre Kennels from 1915 until 1935. Mrs. Lincoln was Ada Olive Proctor, socialite-heiress, part of whose family is still active in pure-bred dogs today. Su T'Sun won many Specialties and was Best of Breed at Westminster in 1928.

Greenacre Felicity's Triumph was owned by Mrs. E.K. Lincoln of Fairfield, Connecticut, one of the most important breeders and exhibitors of Chows from 1906 until 1935. According to Ormond Deignan, whose father James Deignan managed the Greenacre ChowChows from 1915 until 1935, Mrs. Lincoln usually owned about 60 adult dogs and was a prolific breeder of great quality.

A 1937 photograph of Mrs. H. Page's trio of Chow Chow puppies, known as the Pagemoor Chows.

The Greenacres Chow shown here is unidentified except for his owner, Mrs. E.K. Lincoln whose world-famous Greenacre Kennels in Fairfield, Connecticut was one of the most influential Chow kennels of the early period of Chow history in the United States beginning in 1906 and continuing well into the 1930's.

Here is a Clairedale Chow Chow from the important Clairedale Kennels who were very active in the 1920's and 1930's. Miss Claire Knapp, who became Mrs. W.O. Penney, was the owner of this kennel and a breeder of note. This Chow is thought to be Ch. Clairedale Son Too, born December 13, 1927, a famous show dog and sire. However, no documentary proof does exist that this Chow is Son Too.

A Tauskey photograph of the Tally-Ho Kennels' famous Tally-Ho Black Image of Storm, photographed as a young dog in 1936.

A former Vice President of the Chow Chow Club of America and owner of the Car Mae Kennels poses with a Chow Chow puppy.

Ch. Greenacre Ah Ling, born August 29, 1924, was Best of Breed at Westminster in 1929 over an entry of 66 other Chows. Bred by Mrs. E.K. Lincoln, Greenacre Kennels, Fairfield, Connecticut, Ah Ling was owned by Ormond Deignan whose father, James Deignan, managed Mrs. Lincoln's kennels for many years. Ah Ling was a Group winner, one of the most famous Chows of the day.

Ch. Bar Maid of Tally-Ho, owned by the late Mrs. L.W. Bonney of Oyster Bay, Long Island, New York. A Tauskey photograph.

Ch. Blue Periwinkle of Kang Shi, shown here, is one of the most celebrated Chow bitches in the history of the breed in America. Blue Periwinkle was imported from England along with Blue Winkle, a male, by Mrs. E.K. Lincoln of Greenacre Kennels, Fairfield, Connecticut. Many historical Chow records mention that Blue Periwinkle won a Best in Show in the early days of Chows—the 1930's—but no one specifies exactly where Blue Periwinkle won that supreme honor. Ralph Hellum, manager of Ledgeland's Kennels, believes she won the Best in Show in California, but that opinion has not been authenticated.

A bevy of Ledgelands' Chow Chows owned by Mrs. David Wagstaff of Tuxedo Park, N.Y., shown here with their devoted kennel manager for more than 35 years, Mr. Ralph Hellum.

Min T'Sing, bred by Franklin Hutton. Son Too was the father of Champion Farland Thundergust, who in turn was the sire of Champion Far Land Thunderstorm, owned by Mrs. L.W. Bonney.

In 1911 Mrs. Bonney began her famous Tally-Ho Kennels of Dalmatians, then later added Chow Chows. She acquired her first Chow puppies from Mrs. Penney in 1924. The male was Soom of Clairedale, and the bitch was called Tally-Ho Sultan's Ana. In 1932 Mrs. Bonney bought Far Land Thunderstorm from Mr. and Mrs. William MacFarland of Camden, New Jersey. In 1936 Thunderstorm was bred to Champion Tyra of Wauchow, whom Mrs. Bonney had acquired from Mr. W.R. Crawford. One puppy lived. He was Tally-Ho Black Image of Storm, who became a three-time Best in Show winner as well as a fine sire. He died in 1951. Mrs. Bonney's companion and partner, Miss Kathleen Staples, owned Champion Jimmee Boy, also sired by Champion Black Image of Storm, who was a prominent winner. Be-

Ch. Tally-Ho Image of Storm, shown by Mrs. Bonney, pictured winning Best in Show at Cedarhurst, Long Island in 1937. The judge was O.C. Harriman. This Chow was one of the all-time greats.

A Chow Chow from days gone by. . . Ch. Jimmee Boy, owned by Miss Kathleen Staples, a partner of the late Mrs. Flora Bonney of the Tally-Ho Kennels, Oyster Bay, Long Island, New York.

Ledgelands' Kassie, owned by Mrs. David Wagstaff of the Ledgelands Kennels in Tuxedo Park, New York.

Ledgelands' Boy Blue II, owned by Mrs. David Wagstaff of Ledgelands Kennels, Tuxedo Park, New York.

sides being important breeders and judges, Mrs. Bonney and Miss Staples also made a fine contribution to the Chow Chow Club, Inc., the parent organization, which had been founded in 1906; Mrs. Bonney first became President in 1936 and served many terms in that office. When she died in 1967, she was First Vice-President.

The El-Cher Kennels of Mrs. Hugo Prinz, the Clairedale Kennels, the kennels of Wallace MacMonnier, and Mrs. William Fitzgerald had built their strains on the Winsum bloodlines. Their originator is Champion Winsum Min T'Sing, bred by Franklin Hutton and born in 1911. Sired by English Champion Ackum out of Boni, Winsum Min T'Sing must be singled out as the progenitor of the greatest number of winners in early American chowdom. R.W. Tauskey, a distinguished photographer of Chow Chows as well as other pure-bred dogs for more than fifty years, recalls that Champion Winsum Min T'Sing was the most important Chow in the early days. Mrs. Georgia King, editor of *The American Chow Chow* for many years and a leading authority on the breed today, concurs that Min T'Sing was the greatest Chow of the early period. Mr. and Mrs. E.C. Waller bought Winsum Min T'Sing from Mr. Hutton in 1915. Min T'Sing sired Champion Sum Sultan, who in turn sired many champions. Champion Ledgeland's Sancho is a Sum Sulton son. Sancho is the sire of Champion Ledgeland's Solo Chink and Mrs. Prinz's Champion Yuan Chu of El-Cher.

Mr. Ralph Hellum, kennel manager for the Ledgeland Kennels of Mr. and Mrs. David Wagstaff, agrees with other authorities that Champion Winsum Min T'Sing is the most important sire in the early period. Mr. Hellum also recalls that Mrs. Lincoln imported from England Blue Winkle, a male, and Blue Periwinkle, a female; both did considerable winning in the early days.

The exact year remains unknown in which Mrs. Wagstaff acquired her first Chow, Black Dragon, a male; it was perhaps sometime in 1917 or 1918. Black Dragon was bred by and purchased from the Green Dragon Kennel of Mr. and Mrs.

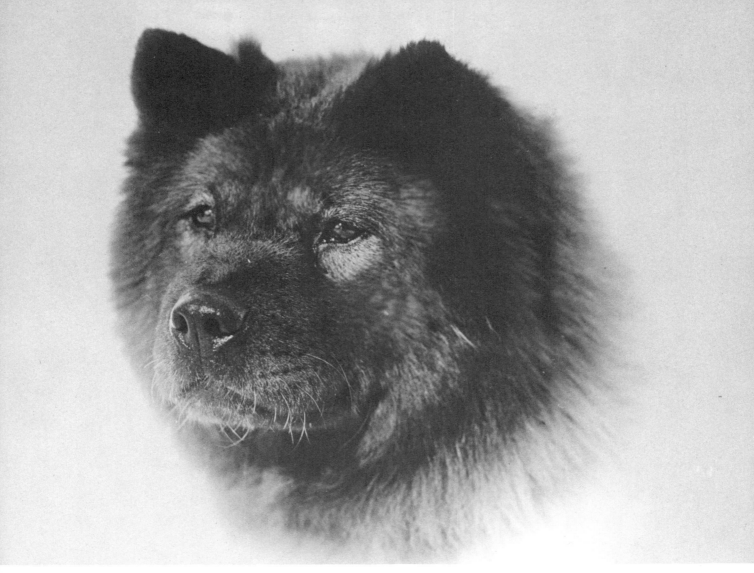

Ch. Greenacre Eastern Star won Best of Breed at Westminster in 1914 over an entry of 52. Eastern Star was born in the U.S. in 1907 according to Westminster records; however, some Chow records indicate that Mrs. E.K. Lincoln, owner of the Greenacre Kennels, imported Eastern Star.

This Specialty Show win for Ch. Wupei Nagyur Tut came in June, 1956 at the Chow Chow Club, Inc. Specialty Show held at Greenwich, Connecticut. Mr. H. Foster Howell was the judge, and Ralph Hellum handled for owner Mrs. David Wagstaff.

Trophy inspection at the Ledgelands Kennels by two of their Chow winners in 1924 show competition. Ledgelands is owned by Mrs. David Wagstaff, Tuxedo Park, New York.

Proctor. A partnership was agreed upon by Harry Peters of the well-known Windholme Kennels and Mrs. Wagstaff, and many of their first Chows were housed at the Peters' kennels in Islip, Long Island. Later on the partnership was dissolved, and Mrs. Wagstaff's Chows lived at Ledgelands in Tuxedo Park, N.Y.

Mrs. Wagstaff acquired a young bitch named Kiyodai in 1920. Kiyodai was sired by English Champion Chelsea Pensioner and became the mother of one of Mrs. Wagstaff's favorite bitches, Busy Issy, sired by the famous Champion Winsum Min T'Sing. Busy Issy was bred in 1923 to Bergsusa, one of the big-star names of the day, owned by T.E.W. Downs.

Champion Ledgelands' Sancho was one of the first champions bred by Mrs. Wagstaff; he was a red dog, sired by Champion Sum Sultan out of Kiyodai.

Opposite—

Mrs. David Wagstaff, owner of the famous Ledgelands Chow Chow Kennels in Tuxedo Park, New York. The Chow Chow never had a better friend than this great lady whom Chowists will always cherish.

Ledgelands' Black Coat Susie, photographed in 1943 by Percy T. Jones. Owner was Mrs. David Wagstaff of Tuxedo Park, New York.

Ledgelands' Lao Sun, Winners Dog, and Black Myster II, Reserve Dog at the May, 1953 Parent Club Specialty Show. Lao Sun was handled by Ralph Hellum for owner, Mrs. David Wagstaff.

Ch. Ledgelands' Chiao-Son, an early Chow Chow owned by Mrs. David Wagstaff of Tuxedo Park, New York.

Ch. Ledgeland's Zu-Zan from the April, 1937 championship list. Owners were Mr. and Mrs. David Wagstaff of Tuxedo Park, New York.

The 14th annual dog show of the Leash Club held at Ledgelands, the David Wagstaff estate in Tuxedo Park, New York, on April 26, 1941 shows the Best In Show Chow Chow, Ledgelands' Blueberry. Percy T. Jones, photographer.

One of the Ledgelands' Kennels Chow Chows which was campaigned in 1937. . . Ch. Ledgeland's Ba San. The Ledgeland Kennels were owned by Mr. and Mrs. David Wagstaff, Tuxedo Park, New York. A Walter Levick photo.

Ledgeland's Candy, owned and shown by Mrs. David Wagstaff of Tuxedo Park, New York, is pictured winning the Non-Sporting Group at the 1949 Framingham District Kennel Club show. Mrs. Wagstaff is the handler.

Ch. Wupei Nagyur Tut, a winning Chow Chow at the 1955 Crufts Show in England was imported by Mrs. David Wagstaff for her Ledgelands Kennel in Tuxedo Park, New York. Tut was Best of Breed at Westminster in 1956.

Mrs. David Wagstaff of Tuxedo Park, New York with four Chow Chow puppies photographed by Percy T. Jones in May, 1944.

Sing Too, an early Chow owned by Robert W. Wren of Easton, Pennsylvania. Photo by Felker's Studio.

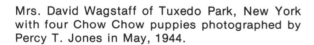

Mrs. Wagstaff imported Ledgelands' Ula of Sheen, by Mrs. Faudel Phillips' famous English Chow Pusa of Amwell, out of Champion Pickles, a well-known English bitch who, it has been often said, was never beaten in the show ring.

During the 1930's and 1940's, and until Mrs. Wagstaff's death in 1957, Ralph Hellum, who was Mrs. Wagstaff's kennel man for more than thirty-five years, finished many champions, including Champion Ledgelands' Chiao-Son, Champion Ledgelands' Tuff-fei, Champion Ledgelands' Hung Wu, Champion Pagemoor's Boy Blue (purchased from Mrs. Frederick R. Humpage's Pagemoor Kennels as a young class dog) and many others.

Perhaps most memorable of all the Ledgelands' Chows was Champion Wupei Nagyur Tut, whom Mrs. Wagstaff imported from Joseph H. Baileff of England in

1955; the dog had been Best of Breed at Cruft's that year. In 1956 he was Best of Breed at Westminster and won the Southern Chow Chow Specialty show, the New England Chow Chow Club Specialty show, the parent club specialty held at Greenwich, and the all-breed Twin Brooks Kennel Club show of April 15, 1956 under the Honorable Katharine St. George, who represented New York's 27th District in Congress from 1947 to 1965. At the present time Mrs. St. George's daughter, Mrs. Priscilla St. George Ryan of famed Prune's Own Kennels, Tuxedo Park, N.Y. is campaigning a Chow Chow.

Dr. and Mrs. A.V. Hallowell of Philadelphia had a small kennel in the 1930's. H. Kenneth Stine, who worked for the Hallowells, recalls that their Champion Black Monarch of Far East was outstanding. In February, 1940 their Champion Lle Wol

Whoopee for Wupei! A Best in Show win under the Honorable Congresswoman Katharine St. George at the 1956 Twin Brooks Kennel Club show in New Jersey for Ch. Wupei Nagyur Tut. Owner, Mrs. David Wagstaff, Ledgelands Kennels, Tuxedo Park, New York. Ralph Hellum handling.

Ledgelands' Hung-Wu, winner of the Non-Sporting Group at the 1950 Greenwich Kennel Club show. Ralph Hellum handling for owner Mrs. David Wagstaff, Ledgelands Kennels, Tuxedo Park, New York.

Ledgelands' Kodamo, Best of Opposite Sex at the 1956 Westminster Kennel Club show. Ralph Hellum handles this bitch for owner Mrs. David Wagstaff of the Ledgelands Kennels, Tuxedo Park, New York. Miss Adele Colgate, a famous dog woman, is the judge.

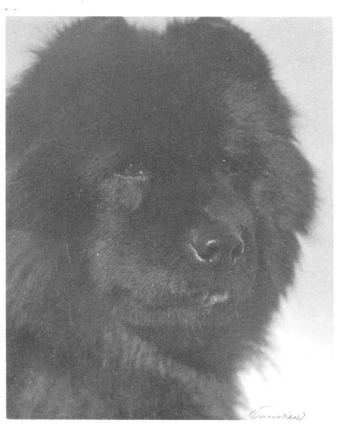

Wendi Loo Sunlegh, owned by George L. Ratcliffe of South Portland, Maine, photographed many years ago.

A headstudy of a black Chow Chow owned by the E.H. Goodwins of Plainfield, New Jersey photographed by Tauskey several years ago.

Ch. Ledgelands' Tuff-Fet, Best of Breed at the Chow Chow Club of America's Specialty Show on November 11, 1935. Owned by Mrs. David Wagstaff of Tuxedo Park, New York.

Mrs. David Wagstaff and some of her Ledgelands Chow Chows and their friend, a Labrador, all of Tuxedo Park, N.Y.

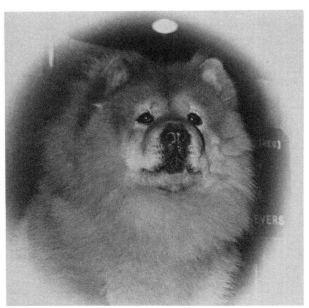

Ch. Lin-Wing of Adel, photographed in 1951. Owner was Mrs. David Wagstaff of the Ledgelands Kennels in Tuxedo Park, New York.

Lah Son, by Champion Far Land Thundergust, won the non-sporting group at Westminster under Judge Lindsey. According to Stine, now an A.K.C. non-sporting judge, Lle Wol Lah Son placed second in the Westminster group in 1938, 1939 and 1941. No other Chow would win the group at the Garden until 1969, when Champion Gotschall's Van Van, owned by Donald Drennan and Violetta Gotschall, accomplished the honor under Alva Rosenberg.

Certainly the most outstanding Chow of the 1930's was Champion Yang Fu Tang (Oct. 10, 1929-July 12, 1936), bred by the Hoffmans of Yang Fu Kennels, Milwaukee, Wisconsin. Sired by Champion Yang Fu King X Yang Fu Queenie, Yang Fu Tang was a fine sire and the long-time record holder of the breed with 22 Best in Shows, all breeds. He held the top show record for the breed for 28 years.

In April, 1964 Yang Fu Tang's record was broken by Champion Ah Sid the Dilet-tante when he won his 23rd Best in Show, all breeds. (The Dilettante's complete record can be found in the chapter "Kennels of Today.")

At the time of Yang Fu Tang's death he belonged to Mrs. Louise Seamer, who had owned him most of his adult life. He was the grandson of the great International Champion Choonam Brilliantine of Manchoover. Tang was the result of a mating of father and daughter and was produced by the combination of Brilliantine and Win Sum Min T'Sing bloodlines.

The English import of the period that had the most influence on the breed was the grandfather of Yang Fu Tang, English and American Champion Choonam Brilliantine of Manchoover, bred by Mrs. Manooch and shown in England until he gained his title there at the age of sixteen months. Purchased by Mrs. Earl Hoover for $9,800, Brilliantine became the sire of many champions, including Champion Yang Fu King, who in turn produced the great winning Champion Yang Fu Tang. Mrs. Hoover also had the honor of importing and owning Ch. Blue Stocking of Manchoover, the first Chow bitch to win a Best in Show, all-breeds, in the U.S.; it was at the Illinois State Fair, Springfield, on Aug. 22-24, 1929. The second Chow bitch so honored with a Best in Show was Ch. Pandee's Red

Ch. Lle Wol Lah Son, Best of Breed at Westminster in 1938 and 1939 and again in 1940 when he went on to Group First at the Garden. No other Chow Chow was to win a Group at the Westminster Kennel Club show until 1969, when Ch. Gotschall's Van Van won a Non-Sporting Group First under the late judge Alva Rosenberg. Ch. Lle Wol Lah Son was bred and owned by Dr. and Mrs. A.V. Hallowell of Delphi, Pennsylvania.

A handsome trio of Ledgelands Chow Chows—Kassie, Yumi and Boy Blue II. All owned by Mrs. David Wagstaff of Tuxedo Park, New York.

Noted judge and Chow breeder Mrs. Gless Beamer gives top award to Mrs. Harold E. Lee's Ch. Cheng Lee's Dar Kee. She has 7 Bests of Breed, a Group First, and several Group placings to her credit. This lovely home-bred was photographed by Joan Ludwig.

Mrs. George A. Hyder's Chow Chow photographed many years ago.

Shanghai Chief, owned by the Shang-Hi Kennels of Mrs. B.J. Houston of Cincinnati, Ohio, photographed many years ago.

Ch. Ming Loo Sing was a well-known winner and sire in the 1930's. He was the father of Champion Pitchu Wu Linnchow, one of the best bitches of this period. He was owned by the Linnchow Kennels in Tinley Park, Illinois.

Ad-A-Kan's Trojan of Linnchow, sire of Flagg's Ch. Chubby Chinaman. Trojan's photo was a part of the Chow collection of Ralph Hellum who managed Mrs. David Wagstaff's Ledgelands Kennels.

Fan Tan of Glenmont, photographed many years ago.

A 1930 photo of Wyndcrest Donnie, owned by Miss K.J. Kandra of Asbury Park, New Jersey.

Ch. Pagemoor's Boy Blue wins Best of Breed at the May 13, 1944 Plainfield Kennel Club show with Ralph Hellum handling for Mrs. David Wagstaff, owner of the Ledgelands Kennels in Tuxedo Park, New York.

Ch. Yang Fu Tang, from the 1930's—lived from October 10, 1929 until July 12, 1936. Although bred by the famous Hoffman brothers of Milwaukee, he was owned most of his adult life by Mrs. Louise Beamer. Yang Fu Tang held the Best in Show record for Chow Chows until it was broken by Ch. Ah Sid the Dilettante.

Pomfreto Gorgeous Smut, owned by Mrs. W.W. MacDonald of San Francisco, pictured at a Los Angeles Kennel Club Show many years ago.

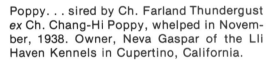

Poppy. . . sired by Ch. Farland Thundergust ex Ch. Chang-Hi Poppy, whelped in November, 1938. Owner, Neva Gaspar of the Lli Haven Kennels in Cupertino, California.

Ch. Hong Kong Kings Red Boy, photographed many years ago.

Born in April, 1938, Ch. Chun Kee of East, owned by Mr. and Mrs. Chester H. Lawrence, and Chun Kee's son, Chun Kee Jo, owned by Mr. and Mrs. Frank Alexander. This photograph was taken in 1944. Chun Kee's father was Ch. West's Sun of East, a famous Chow of his day.

Sing, owned by Dr. Imogene P. Earle, in 1961.

One of Champion Choonam Brilliantine's most striking sons was International Champion Chia Wan's Blue Monarch, owned by Mr. and Mrs. Ralph W. Spike of Port Huron, Michigan. He was a Best in Show winner and the sire of several champions.

Of importance on the West Coast in the late 1930's was Champion West's Sun

of East, owned by O.H. West of California. His sire was Champion East is West, and Sun of East himself was the sire of several champions, including the great Jo Jo Hanson, owned by Mr. and Mrs. Walter Hanson, a Best in Show winner and important sire. Many notable Chows in California during the 1940's were sired by Champion Jo Jo Hanson: Champion Me-Li Loy Wong, Champion Richow Poppy Jo, Champion Peep Bo of Broadhurst and

This elegant lady, Mrs. Walter Hanson, is shown with her Ch. Jo Jo Hanson, an important winner and sire in the 1940's in California; Jo Jo was a Best in Show winner. His sire was Ch. West's Sun of East owned by O.H. West of southern California.

A litter of Chow Chow puppies, circa 1930, owned by M. Girard of the Changworth Kennels in Westbury, Long Island.

Two famous ladies in the Chow Chow world and a well-known Chow, Ch. Hanson's Hooper Du are pictured here at the Chow Chow Club's National Specialty, Harbor Cities Kennel Club, Long Beach, California, in June 1949. Mrs. Walter Hanson is handling her black home-bred to Best of Breed over an entry of 208 Chows. This is said to be the largest group of Chows ever assembled at any show in the United States. An important Chow breeder, Mrs. John G. (Agrippina) Anderson, Washington, D.C., judged on this record-breaking occasion sponsored by the Parent Club.

This gorgeous black bitch, Ch. Hagen's Cindy Von Trott, finished her championship in 75 days. She was bred by Norma Hagen and her immediate ancestors carried the original Five Ash blood. She was purchased from Norma Hagen by Mrs. Florence Wilson Graham, shown handling above, who campaigned her to her title. Later Cindy was sold to the James Handleys of Texas.

these three Best in Show winners: Champion Li Ching's Chang of Ferg-Sun, Champion Miltenberger Toffee Sun of Jo and Champion Five Ash Jo Jo. Mr. and Mrs. Leroy King's Champion Kinghai Jill should be mentioned as an important bitch of this period.

Ernest Shook, owner of Fu San Chows in Burlington, Wisconsin, bought his first Chow Chow in 1934 as a pet for the children. They and the late Mrs. Shook were charmed by their remarkable resemblance to teddy bears, and once they made the dog a member of the family they were devoted to the breed from then on. As a matter of fact, Ernest Shook owes his life to this first Chow. He was charged and trampled by a bull, and when he regained consciousness the dog was keeping the bull at bay until help came. The accident resulted in a permanent disability, but Ernest Shook realizes that he would not be alive if the Chow hadn't acted out of his sense of protectiveness.

When this first Chow died, the Shooks

purchased another from the Lu Tang Kennels. First a bitch was purchased, and then they bought a dog. They raised two or three litters from this pair; when the bitch died at 14 years of age, they decided they would like to breed and show Chows in earnest. It was about this time that they met Sophie Schroetter and asked her help in finding a good brood bitch to start them off. A succession of good Chows resulted which kept their interest in the breed going.

When Mrs. Shook died, Ernest Shook quit showing as much as he would like, but with a few promising youngsters around the house, he is going to make every effrot to get back to the show ring.

Poppyland, one of the important Chow kennels of the middle period belonged to Mr. and Mrs. Howard Kendall, Wilmington, California. Pete and Howard Kendall acquired their first Chow, The Pagoda King, a male, in the 1930's and sometime later a bitch, Ching, from Mrs. Bee Burton. Their first show Chow was Champion Tonkee Brilliantine, who finished her championship before a year of age. She was sired by Mr. and Mrs. Cecil Mybock's famous Champion Wulee Brilliantine, whom the Mybocks bred, and was a sister of Champion Sing Fu Brilliantine, owned by Mr. and Mrs. D.C. Dillingham of Sing Fu Kennels. Mrs. Dillingham today is Mrs. Hazel A. Gray; she no longer breeds Chows but occasionally judges a Chow sweepstakes. She has owned and bred several Chows of note.

Shortly after the Kendalls acquired Tonkee, they bought Champion Impee Brilliantine, Tonkee's full brother. About this time Mrs. Palmer Boustead of San Francisco, an ardent Chowist and Chow handler, suggested that the Kendalls adopt Poppyland as a kennel name, for it had both oriental and California connotations.

The Kendalls' first homebred to succeed in the show ring was Champion Honee of Poppyland, sired by Champion Chia Wan's Blue Bedouin out of a litter sister of Champion Impee Brilliantine. Honee made her first big win as a young bitch, going Best of Breed over several

Ch. Greenacre Ah Ling, owned by Mrs. E.K. Lincoln, whose Greenacre Kennels in Fairfield, Connecticut were handled by James Deignan who managed Mrs. Lincoln's celebrated kennels for about 30 years.

Ch. Hanson's Triple Jo. Owner Mrs. Walter Hanson handling. Bred by Rado Schultze, the sire was Me-Li San Dee ex Kinghai Bo-Peep.

Ch. Tonkee Brilliantine, the first champion owned by the Howard Kendalls of Sepulveda, California, owners of the Poppyland Kennels.

champions and placing first in the non-sporting group. Impee sired the well-known Champion Chen Lee's Wah Gee of Poppyland who, in his short lifetime, sired twenty-five champions and won many groups. Some of the Kendalls' other winners include Champion Jon-Nee Linnchow of Poppyland, Champion Blue Blazes of Poppyland (a Best in Show winner) and Champion Trojan of Poppyland. Poppyland's most famous Chow is undoubtedly Champion Starcrest Spy of Poppyland, bred by Joel Marston out of his Poppyland Choo Choo by the famous imported sire Champion Ghat de la Moulaine, owned by Mr. and Mrs. Clifton Shryock. Spy, a multiple group winner, became the sire of many champions, including Champion Eastward Liontamer of Elster. Spy won a Best in Show in Mexico and won the parent club specialties in 1962 in Seattle and again in 1964 in Cleveland as well as many regional specialties. Champion The Coach of Poppyland is now the Kendalls' leading stud.

Ch. Cheng Lee Wahgee of Poppyland, an early Chow Chow belonging to the Howard Kendalls of California.

Ch. Trojan of Poppyland, a winning Chow shown extensively in the 1950's, owner-handled by Mrs. Howard Kendall. Photograph by Joan Ludwig.

Ch. Starcrest Spy of Poppyland in a beautiful outdoor setting. This great Chow Chow is owned by the Howard Kendalls, Poppyland Kennels, Sepulveda, California.

Another California kennel of this period that should be mentioned is Ferg Sun of Mrs. Madaline L. and L. Perry Ferguson, who started breeding Chows in 1942 and continued to do so through the 1950's and early 1960's. Her two outstanding show dogs were American and Canadian Champion Li Ching's Chang of Ferg Sun and Champion Ching Run of Ferg Sun, whom this writer remembers well as Fergie, a magnificent specimen who won many admirers for the breed. He was a multiple-group winner. In November, 1948 Champion Li Ching's Chang of Ferg Sun won

Best in Show at the Sun Maid Kennel Club in Fresno, California under Mrs. Beatrice Godsol, a well-known all-breed judge. Chang won two other Best in Shows, all breeds, in Canada.

One of the most active and lively kennels in the country during the 1940's was Linnchow, owned by Mr. and Mrs. H.P. Schmidt of Tinley Park, Illinois, and their daughter, JoAnne Schmidt O'Brien, who later became a Doctor of Veterinary Medicine and an associate of Dr. Imogene P. Earle of Pandee Kennels, Laurel, Maryland.

Two Chow Chow puppies owned by the Howard Kendalls of California investigate their new Christmas toys.

Ch. Starcrest Spy of Poppyland and his stuffed toy dogs. Owned by the Howard Kendalls of California.

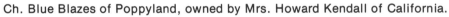

Ch. Blue Blazes of Poppyland, owned by Mrs. Howard Kendall of California.

Ch. The Coach of Poppyland, owned by the Howard Kendalls of Sepulveda, California. His sire was the famous Ch. Starcrest Spy of Poppyland.

Ch. Willmar's Westy Brilliantine and his handler, Palmer Boustead, win Best In Show at the Beverly Riviera Kennel Club show in Santa Monica in September, 1951. Colonel E.E. Ferguson was the judge. Brilliantine is owned by Mr. and Mrs. William T. Bonsor of San Francisco. A Joan Ludwig photograph.

Ch. Ching Run of Ferg Sun, a beautiful Chow Chow owned by the Fergusons, pictured in 1969.

Movie star Marilyn Maxwell, a great Chow admirer, with Howard Kendall of the Poppyland Kennels. Marilyn was a close friend of Joel Marston and all of the Starcrest Chows.

American and Mexican Ch. Starcrest Spy of Poppyland, owned by Mr. and Mrs. Howard Kendall. Spy is the sire of many champions, including Ch. Eastward Liontamer of Elster.

Ch. Ink Spot of Ferg Sun pictured winning Best of Opposite Sex under judge Mrs. Ann Ross at the Golden State Chow Chow Specialty Show. Ink Spot is owned and shown by Clif and Vivian Shryock of Hawaiian Gardens, California. Ink Spot was bred by Madaline Ferguson of Long Beach, California. Photo by Joan Ludwig.

Ch. Ching Run of Ferg Sun as a puppy, sired by American and Canadian Ch. Li Ching's Chang of Ferg Sun was whelped in 1951 out of Chi Chi of Ferg Sun. Owned by L. Perry Ferguson and Madaline L. Ferguson, handler, of Long Beach, California. The judge is the late all-rounder, Eva Hill.

Linnchow puppies in the 1940's. Their mother was the well-known Champion Pitchi Wu Linnchow, dam of six champions. The little girl was a visitor to Linnchow Kennels but not a part of the Schmidt family.

American and Canadian Ch. Li Ching's Chang of Ferg Sun, born in June, 1944. Owned by L. Perry and Madaline Ferguson of Long Beach, California. His sire was Ch. Jo Jo Hansen ex Li Ching of Ferg Sun.

Ch. Linnchow Yu Huso, owned by Logan Patton, was born August 25, 1945. He was Best of Breed at Westminster in 1949 and 1950 over an entry of 13 and 21, respectively. His breeder was the well-known Linnchow Kennels, Tinley Park, Illinois. Mr. Patton is presently a judge of Chows and a few other breeds and lives in Sharon, Pennsylvania.

Miss JoAnne Schmidt proudly shows off her Linnchow dogs, owned by her parents, Mr. and Mrs. H.P. Schmidt of Tinley Park, Illinois. JoAnne was an excellent junior handler and recalls that this photo was made in 1938 or 1939. Later on after her parents' death she continued to breed Chows from the Linnchow line. After becoming a Doctor of Veterinary Medicine and marrying, Dr. JoAnne O'Brien became associated with Dr. Imogene P. Earle of the Pandee Kennels in Laurel, Maryland.

Ch. Linnchow Chu Fu II (who died in 1952) was one of the top winners of Mr. and Mrs. H.P. Schmidt's Linnchow Kennels. His sire was Ch. Tohio Sontang and his dam Nu Nui Linnchow, C.D. Chu Fu II retired the Chow Chow Club's Challenge Trophy with seven legs on it; he won over 50 Bests of Breed and many Group Firsts during the 1940's.

In the 1940's Linnchow Kennels were very proud of Ch. Pitchi Wu Linnchow, a fine winner and excellent producer.

Two illustrious ladies in American Chowdom! Mrs. Lauretta Schmidt of Linnchow Kennels, Tinley Park, Illinois is shown handling Ch. Linnchow Chan Yie who finished his championship undefeated. The lady wearing the judge's badge is Mrs. L.W. Bonney of the Tally-Ho Kennels in Long Island, New York, a breeder and judge of international repute. Chan Yie was sired by Ch. Linnchow Chu Fu II, the well-known sire, and his dam was Ch. Sheng Lian Linnchow, both owned by the Schmidts.

Ch. Linnchow Li Fu, sired by Ch. Linnchow Chu Fu II out of Ch. Sheng Li An Linnchow, was a well-known son of a well-known father. Both were owned by Linnchow Kennels which were owned by Mr. and Mrs. H.P. Schmidt of Tinley Park, Illinois.

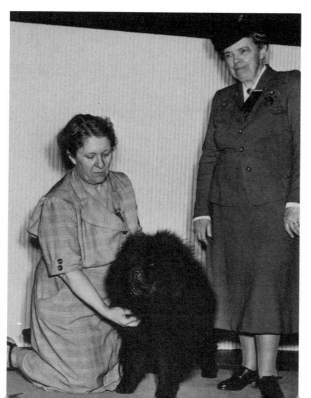

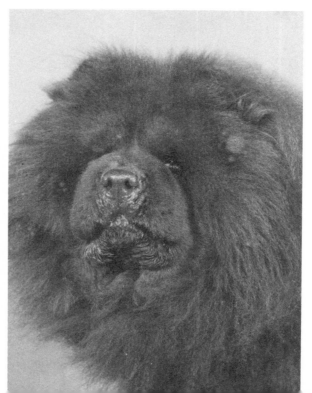

Ch. Linnchow Chu Sen, shown here with his owner and breeder, Mrs. Lauretta Schmidt, whose Linnchow Kennels were very prominent during the 1930's and 1940's. Chu Sen was sired by Mrs. Schmidt's famous Ch. Linnchow Chu Fu II out of Ch. Cheng Lian Linnchow, a well-known bitch of the period.

One of the Schmidts most celebrated Chows was Champion Linnchow Chu Fu II, who won several groups and over fifty Best of Breeds. He sired sixteen champions. His ancestors were Champion Moosilauke Pao Tang and Champion Crimson Pao on his sire's side and Champion Yang Fu Tang and Clairedale lines on his dam's side. Chu Fu II retired the Chow Chow Club's Challenge Trophy. He died in 1952.

Another important Chow of the Schmidts was Champion Pitchi Wu Linnchow, an outstanding brood bitch who produced six champions. Her sire was Champion Ming Loo Sin and her dam Loh Moh Linnchow; she had a combination of Clairedale, Blue Monarch and Yang Fu Tang bloodlines.

Other important exhibitors of Linnchow dogs were Mr. and Mrs. George Curzon of Champaign, Illinois; Chows they exhibited included Champion Linnchow Mi Cho Boi, Champion Linnchow Mi Chee Sonn Gee and Champion Mi Chee Mi Mei Linnchow. Later on the Curzons bred Chows under their Martonge kennel name.

An important sire of the 1940's was Champion Chinaman's Chance, owned by Mrs. Viola deVoy of Gary, Indiana, and two Best in Show winners during this period were Champion Ah Jim's Barbaric Emperor, owned and bred by Abby Jane Betschowas, and Champion Blue Blazes of Poppyland, owned by Mr. and Mrs. L. Howard Kendall.

Mrs. Naomi Humphries of Kentucky bred several important Chows during the 1940's and 1950's, namely Champion Chum Yong Fu Fun, a Best in Show winner, Champion Lakeview's Stormcloud, Champion Toi Woo, Champion Lake-

Yes, there was Junior Showmanship in 1940! Paul Schmidt won the boys division with Madam Queen of Na Poo, 7 years old, a foundation bitch of Linnchow Kennels, Tinley Park, Illinois owned by Paul Schmidt's parents, Mr. and Mrs. H.P. Schmidt. Paul's sister, Dr. JoAnne S. O'Brien, is also well known in the breed today. The black Chow shown by Barbara Osborne, winner of the girls first prize was called Ebony but nothing is recalled about her genealogy. However, Dr. O'Brien remembers that Madam Queen was strongly line-bred to Ch. Choonam Brilliantine, an import who figured strongly in American Chowdom.

Ch. Linnchow Sheik Too was a winner in the early 1940's for his owners, Mr. and Mrs. H.P. Schmidt who owned the Linnchow Kennels in Tinley Park, Illinois.

Non-Sporting Group First over an entry of 51 Chows at a Contra Costa Kennel Club several years ago was Ch. Linnchow Ming Loo Yet, being shown by his owner, Mrs. William D. Ross. The judge was Paul Schmidt.

Linnchow Chan is being awarded Winners Dog by Howard Kendall, well-known Chow breeder of the Poppyland Kennels in Wilmington, California, at the St. Louis Chow Chow Specialty in the mid-1940's. Paul Schmidt, son of Mr. and Mrs. H.P. Schmidt, owners of Linnchow Kennels in Tinley Park, Illinois, was handler.

This lovely Chow Bitch, Ch. Fluji Linnchow, won Best of Breed over male specials at the St. Louis Chow Chow Club's Specialty in 1941. Fluji, sired by Ch. Linnchow Ho Chow is related through her dam to Nu Nui Linnchow, C.D., and to Ch. Clairedale Son Too, and Ch. Yang Fu Tang, two great early Chows. Fluji was bred and owned by Mr. and Mrs. H.P. Schmidt, Linnchow Kennels, Tinley Park, Illinois.

Here is JoAnne Schmidt at the International Kennel Club in Chicago in 1938 with Champion Chia Linnchow. JoAnne was a top junior handler as a youngster and later on became a Doctor of Veterinary Medicine, president of the Chow Chow Club, Inc., National Parent Organization, and an associate of Dr. Imogene Earle of the Pandee Kennels in Laurel, Maryland.

Eight beautiful Linnchow Chow Chows relax under a summer Illinois sun with their delightful handler, Miss JoAnne Schmidt in 1943. All these Chows were owned by JoAnne's parents, Mr. and Mrs. H.P. Schmidt, whose Linnchow Kennels in Tinley Park, Illinois, were known from coast to coast.

view's Chum Fun and Champion Tim's Charley Woo.

For many years Mrs. Bessie Van Dusen has bred some outstanding winners in her Nor-Ton Kennels in North Tonawanda, N.Y.; her Champion Nor-Ton's Silver Moon produced many champions during the 1950's. One of his sons, Champion Nor-Ton's Kim Sing, owned by Mrs. Fanny B. Smith of Charlotte, North Carolina, was widely shown in the South and was a Best in Show winner.

One should not forget Mr. and Mrs. John G. Anderson of Silver Spring, Md., who through the years had produced some fine specimens. Their Champion Dai Fu King of Glenmont was a multiple group and Best in Show winner in the 1940's.

Another outstanding winner during the 1940's was Champion Wu Chan Tu, owned by Mr. and Mrs. Roland L. Smith, Belmont, Mass. and bred by Lola Thompson, who was active for many years in the breed. Wu Chan Tu had won many non-sporting groups, including Boston in 1943, and was Best of Breed in 1940 and 1941 at the New England Chow Chow Club specialty shows.

During the 1930's and 1940's Mr. and Mrs. George Armitage were active and produced several fine Chows, among them Champion Ge-ni's Han Yu. Another breeder of note was Mrs. Frederic P. Humpage of North Wilbraham, Mass., whose Pagemoor Kennels were active for some twenty-five years. Champion Kway of

Linnchow show dogs pictured in 1944 against a Chinese silk backdrop, a bench decoration typical of the 1930's and 40's but seldom seen today. From left to right are Tippi Tin Linnchow, the black bitch; Ch. Sheng Li An Linnchow; Ch. Maka Lee Linnchow, and the only male on the extreme left, Ch. Linnchow Chu Sen, a full brother to the well-known Ch. Linnchow Li Fu. Ch. Sheng Li An Linnchow bred to Ch. Linnchow Chu Fu II produced Ch. Linnchow Li Fu. All of these dogs were owned by Mr. and Mrs. H.P. Schmidt, Tinley Park, Illinois.

Pagemoor was Best of Winners at Morris and Essex in 1949. Champion Pagemoor's Chita was another winner.

And, of course, one cannot overlook Mrs. Valetta Gotschall whose Gotschall Kennels, Carrollton, Ohio, had turned out some fine Chows. In the forties she owned Champion Charmar Ching's Sun Tu, and Champion Nor-Ton's Black Onyx, and Champion Nor-Ton's Ching Li Fu.

In the forties and fifties Mr. and Mrs. S.E. Luckey of Seattle were very active.

One recalls vividly their magnificent Ch. Beeson's Thunderstorm and their Luck-ee Model Pao Tang and Luck-ee Model Pusa.

Mr. and Mrs. Frank Beeson, Spokane, Washington began breeding Chows in the 1930's and continued well into the 1960's. They owned Champion Major's Bomba-dier, Champion Beeson's Tor-Chee and they bred Champion Beeson's Thunder-storm and later on in the sixties Char-Lee Beeson de la Moulaine.

Ch. Linnchow Ming Loo Yet, born in 1946, is being awarded Best in Show at the San Francisco Dog Fanciers, Inc. Combined Specialties show, July 30, 1949. The owner-handler of Ming Loo Yet is Mrs. William D. Ross; the judge is Edward Goodwin, breeder-judge of New Jersey. Mrs. Will Judy, wife of the owner and publisher of *Dog World*, presents the trophy. Mr. Judy was the author of the principal book on the Chow published in the 1930's. Ming Loo Yet was Best of Breed at the Westminster Kennel Club show in 1951 under William L. Kendrick.

May, 1941 at the Carolina Kennel Club Show in Greensboro, North Carolina, saw judge Joseph W. Burrell give Best In Show to Ch. Lao Tang of Chung-Kuo, owned by W.A. McIlwaine of Washington, D.C. Club president W.S. Corsbie presents the trophy.

Another Best In Show Chow Chow from the 1940 era, Ch. Ah Jim's Barbaric Emperor, pictured here taking the top award at the Marin North Bay Kennel Club Show. Judge, A.W. Brockway.

The late Ch. Kinghai Sparkle, pictured placing Best of Opposite Sex at a Chow Chow Specialty some years ago at the Harbor Cities Kennel Club show in California. The judge was the late Mrs. Grace Bonney. C. LeRoy King handling. Mrs. C. LeRoy and Mrs. Georgia King are co-owners.

Ch. Tsang Po's General Fu, owned by the Tsang Po Kennels, wins the Non-Sporting Group at a Lawton-Ft. Sill show under judge Rees L. Davies. Trophy presented by Mrs. K.J. Goodell for the Lawton Veterinary Hospital.

Ch. Sing Fu Brilliantine photographed at the age of three on May 1, 1941 by R. Noble Estey at Laguna Beach, California. Sired by Ch. Wulee Brilliantine *ex* Fluffee Brilliantine, Brilliantine was owned by Hazel A. Crag of Nevada City, California.

Chow Chow Specials Class at the Chow Chow Club's Specialty Show at the Harbor Cities Kennel Club, June 1949, Long Beach, California, judged by noted breeder-judge Mrs. John G. (Agrippina) Anderson, Washington, D.C. There were 208 Chow Chows in this June event, said to be the largest entry of the breed ever assembled in the U.S. Best of Breed was awarded to the black home-bred, Ch. Hanson's Hooper Du owned by Mr. and Mrs. Walter Hanson, important California breeders.

Robert and Norma Taynton do not have a kennel per se. . . they have four Chow Chows that they say "live in, around and surrounding" their home and ballet studios in Detroit, Michigan. Each of the dogs has its own 8 x 16 run outdoors to the side of their studio-theatre, and one of the Chow Chows is always free, night or day, in the enclosed yard surrounding their property.

The Tayntons first fell in love with the breed during Prohibition when they lived over a speakeasy in New York. The owner of the speakeasy raised a litter of Chows in the backyard of the brownstone, and Robert and Norma fell in love with them as they watched them grow up, back in 1931. They bought one of the males, named San Toy, and have had a love affair with Chows ever since.

From then on they were never without a Chow, but they could not show, since

Several years ago the winner of a Non-Sporting Group at the San Mateo Kennel Club was Mr. and Mrs. William D. Ross's Ch. Pago Pago's Tong King. Mrs. Ross handled under judge Anton Rost.

The late Ch. Winkee of Kinghai, bred and owned by Mr. and Mrs. C. LeRoy King (Mrs. King handling) is pictured winning under judge Gaston Valcourt. The late Mr. Valcourt was owner of the Mandarin Kennels and noted for his blue Best in Show Chow Chow, Ch. Chia-Wan's Blue Bedouin.

Ch. Tao Tang of Chung Luo wins a Non-Sporting Group. Owner, W.A. McIlwaine of Vienna, Virginia.

they were never sure where their dance company would be playing. The Chows traveled with ease and soon became theatre-oriented and appeared with the dance company appearing in their doll shop and gypsy ballets. This also enabled them to be declared "working dogs" when they traveled outside the United States.

The Tayntons have done much to publicize the Chow Chow by showing and winning with a magnificent team of matched red Chows which attract the attention of judges and spectators alike.

Mrs. Agrippina Anderson, a famous lady in Chow Chows, is pictured here with Ch. Dai Fu King of Glenmont, a top winner and sire. Mrs. Anderson not only was a well-known breeder and Chow judge but also the president of the National Capital Kennel Club for many years. Mrs. Anderson was responsible for the late Sidney Joan Wellborn's interest in Chows. Mrs. Anderson died in 1973.

Chow fancier John T. Anderson and his Ch. Honey Boy of Glenmont, photographed at a dog show several years ago.

Ch. Dai Fu King of Glenmont is shown with his owner, John G. Anderson. His wife Agrippina was known all over the U.S. as a lover of Chows, an excellent breeder, and a reputable judge. The Andersons were responsible for the late Sidney Joan Wellborn's devotion to Chows. Miss Wellborn bred some notable Chows at her Ah Sid Kennels in Clinton, Maryland.

Ch. Glenmont's Ting-Ah-Ling, bred by Agrippina Anderson and owned by the Gerald Sterlings. This superb champion sired six champions and won three Group Firsts the same year Mrs. Wagstaff's English import "Wupei Nagur Tut" won three Group Firsts. These two top males were tied for top honors at the time. The sire was Cyclone of Procyon ex Nor-Ton's Jet Moon.

Ch. Pandee's Pooh Bah was one of Pandee's foundation sires. His father was Ch. Dai Fu King of Glenmont owned by John and Agrippina Anderson of Washington, D.C. Pooh Bah sired Dr. Imogene Earle's famous Ch. Pandee's Red Rufus I and Ch. Pandee's Simple Simon.

At the 13th annual dog show of the Monmouth County Kennel Club show held in New Jersey in June, 1941, judge Mrs. Milton Erlanger awarded Best in the Non-Sporting Group to the Chow Chow Ch. Jimmee Boy, owned by Miss Kathleen Staples and handled by Donald Sutherland. Percy T. Jones photo.

Ch. Kway's China Doll finished at seven months and twelve days old, making her one of the youngest Chow Chows to win the championship title. Bred and owned by Brockway Crouch. Her sire was Ch. Kway Fire Flame ex Kway Fire Belle. China Doll was born in 1962.

Rilling's Lotus Bud, or "Sugar," owned and shown by Douglas and Florence Broadhurst of Redwood City, California, is pictured winning at the Del Monte show several years ago under judge L. Howard Kendall. A Joan Ludwig photograph.

Best In Show at the Atlanta Kennel Club's 57th Annual all-breed dog show in 1959 was Ch. Nor-Ton's Kim Sing, owned by Fanny B. Smith of Charlotte, North Carolina. Kim was handled by B.H. Luallen under judge William Kendrick. Mrs. Almand Carroll, first vice president of the club, and Mr. Roy L. Ayers, president of the club, present the awards.

An adorable four-month-old Chow Chow puppy bred and owned by the late Florence Broadhurst of Redwood City, California.

Ch. Kway Fire Flame winning Best of Breed at the 1965 Chicago Specialty Show under judge Haskell Schuffman. Flame was bred and owned by Brockway Crouch. The sire is Ch. Kway Ball of Fire *ex* Sinn Dee Kway WX. Flame was whelped in 1958.

Best of Breed at the Southern Chow Chow Club Specialty Show held in Pikesville, Maryland on April 6, 1957 was Elsie Frederick's Ch. Dawn of Hi-Clear. Miss Kathleen Staples was the judge, Evelyn Shafer photographer. Dawn was owner-handled.

Nor-Ton's Terry Toy photographed at 11 weeks of age in 1948. Bred by Bessie Volkstadt of North Tonawanda, New York, whose Nor-Ton Kennels are very well known.

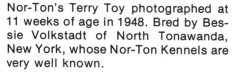

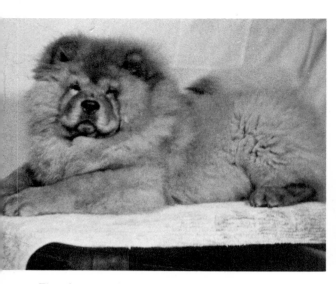

The famous International Ch. Nor-Ton's Silver Moon at five months of age. Bred and owned by Bessie Van Dusen Volkstadt of North Tonawanda, New York. Silver Moon was the sire of many champions.

A Best In Show in 1951. The show at Marion, Ohio, on January 28 of that year saw Ch. Al-Edi's Supreme take the "supreme" win for owners Mr. and Mrs. Albert G. Todter of Greenville, Ohio. The judge was Carey Lindsay.

The shiny black Chow Chow Ch. Al-Edi's Magic, owned by Florence Stanton of Chagrin Falls, Ohio, was Best of Breed winner at the Greater St. Louis Chow Chow Club show in April, 1952. A Frasie Studio photo.

FRASIE

Best In Show at the 1952 Kern County Kennel Club show was the handsome Chow Chow Ch. Burton's Wong Dai, handled by Mrs. Howard Kendall for Mrs. Bee Burton! Judge Edwin Pickhardt made the coveted award. Photograph by Joan Ludwig.

Ch. Win Soon Typhoon of Mt-Air, pictured at two years of age in 1956. She is described by owner Mrs. Jacqueline Capelle of Gresham, Oregon as being blonde with white trim.

A Non-Sporting Group winner at the National Capital Kennel Club show was Rollies Chubby Boy owned by Joseph A. and Bernice Rohleder. Mrs. Milton Erlanger was the judge, and Mr. Rohleder handled. Mrs. Marguerite S. Tyson presented the trophy. A William Brown photograph.

Mrs. Agrippina Anderson, left, with Ch. Lilbern's Tan King, who was Best of Breed at the New England Chow Chow Specialty, June 6, 1954. Tan King was a son of Mrs. Anderson's famous Ch. Dai Fu King of Glenmont. The bitch on the right, Pagemoor's Chita, is Best of Opposite Sex. Bred and owned by Mr. and Mrs. Frederic R. Humpage of North Wilbraham, Mass. of Pagemoor Kennels. Chita is handled here by the manager of the Humpages's kennels. The judge is unidentified.

The best Non-Sporting Group Brace under judge George Beckett several years ago was owned by Mr. and Mrs. C.H. Evans of Grand Rapids, Michigan. Mrs. Evans is shown handling. A Frasie Studio photograph.

Ch. Chang-Shi Lotus Blossom, whelped in December, 1957. Her sire was Ch. Chang-Shi Zygoto *ex* Ch. Chang-Shi Zip's Golden Glory. Owners, Lucile and Jerry Sterling, Nashville, Tennessee.

The Southern Chow Chow Club's Specialty Show in 1953 was won by Ch. Owhyo Wag-Gee, owner-handled by Stephen Gillich of Rahway, New Jersey. Judge at this event was Arthur Stanton, Jr. Mr. Stanton was a leading breeder of Chow Chows for years, and a former past president of the parent club, the Chow Chow Club, Inc. Note the lovely Chow Chow necktie worn especially for the occasion by Mr. Gillich. Evelyn Shafer photo.

The Non-Sporting Group at the Garden in February, 1957 with Mary T. MacEachern gaiting her International Champion Ky-Lin's Midas down the mat for the judge. Midas is an American and Bermudian champion, the only Chow Chow to have a Bermuda title to date. Mrs. MacEachern's Wu San Kennels are in Sodus, New York.

Fu San Geisha Kai, photographed at seven months of age by owner Ernest L. Shook of Burlington, Wisconsin. Sire was Ch. Tiaga Ti of Fu San *ex* China of Fu San.

Ch. Martonge Jo-Jo of Peke Chow winning Best of Breed under judge Ramona Van Court at the 1968 Mattoon Kennel Club show. Jo-Jo was sired by the famous Ch. Ghat de la Moulaine out of T-Sang-Po's Empress Choi Hu and was whelped May 22, 1961. Owners: the George Curzons of White Heath, Illinois. Photo by Ritter.

The 1951 Non-Sporting Group winner at the Harbor Cities Kennel Club show in California. Palmer Boustead shows Mr. and Mrs. William Bonsor's Ch. Willmar's Westie Brilliantine to this win under judge Mrs. Hayes Blake Hoyt. Alyce Lewis presents the trophy in this Joan Ludwig photograph.

Ch. Dre-Don's Kimi Kai, owned by Ed and Florence Volk of Tonawanda, New York, is pictured winning at the 1966 Onondaga Kennel Club show with his handler Ronald Wanzer. His parents were Ch. Loy-Jean's Chi-Yan Kid and Ch. Loy-Jean's Sassi Lassi. His litter brother is Ch. Dre-Don's Sun-King of Craglinden, owned by Dr. Samuel Draper.

224

The lovely red bitch Ch. Peep Bo of Broadhurst, whelped in July, 1948. She won her title in eight shows and was never below a reserve winner. One of her biggest victories was at the 1950 Harbor Cities Kennel Club show, where she went Winners Bitch for a major over thirty-five bitches. Owned and bred by Florence and Douglas Broadhurst of Redwood City, California.

Eldon McCormack's Loy-Jean's Beau Monty, pictured as a young dog winning under judge Vincent Perry. A Roberts photo.

A Non-Sporting Group winner at the Harbor Cities Kennel Club show several years ago was Ch. Winchow Chu Fu Son Too. The judge was Earl Lounsbury, with Alice Scott, dog columnist, presenting the trophy. Dog handled by Clif Shryock.

Two famous lady Chowists, Mrs. Agrippina Anderson (the judge), left, awards Winners Bitch to Linnchow Kitty Bear at the Baltimore County Kennel Club show in 1966. Kitty Bear's breeder and owner-handler is Dr. JoAnne Schmidt O'Brien, a Chow breeder of long standing and former president of the Chow Chow Club, Inc., the Parent Organization. Mrs. Anderson was a prominent Chow breeder and judge who died in 1973. Kitty Bear, who finished her championship later on, now resides with Dr. O'Brien in Washington, D.C.

Ch. Chum Yong Fu Fun, owner-handled by Mrs. Earl F. Humphries, wins Best In Show at the Tennessee Valley Kennel Club Show in April, 1962 under judge Col. Edward D. McQuown. Club president Mr. R.B. Wood, Jr. presented the trophy.

First in the Non-Sporting Group Brace Class at the 1952 Westminster Kennel Club show was Mrs. David Wagstaff's Ledgelands' Wei Wang and Ledgelands' Kaszuie. Mrs. Wagstaff and her kennel manager, Ralph Hellum, handling.

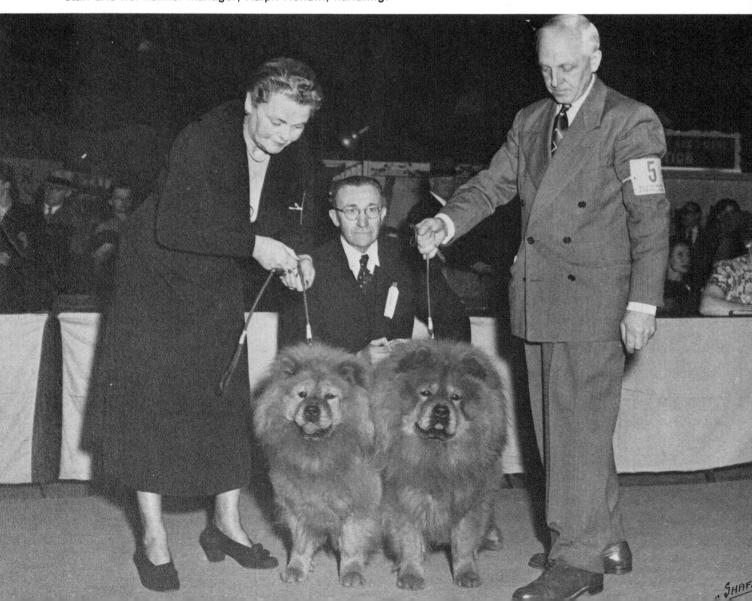

Little Robert Bell with famous Chowist Brockway Crouch and Ch. Jean's Kway, bred by Jean Ferguson. The sire was Ch. Ghat de la Moulaine *ex* Ming Wo Ti. Photographed in 1962. Mr. Crouch was a very important breeder, exhibitor, and judge.

Pandee's Alpha Sing won Winners Dog at the Southern Chow Chow Specialty, April 9, 1960, under the well-known English breeder-judge, Miss C.E. Collett who also wrote a book on the Chow. Dr. Imogene P. Earle bred Alpha Sing and owned him at the time of this photo, but he was sold later to Joel Marston of Starcrest Kennels, Sun Valley, California. Dr. JoAnne O'Brien is the handler.

Ch. Tiaga Ti of Fu San, whelped in November, 1966, at the kennels of owner Ernest L. Shook which are located in Burlington, Wisconsin.

The late great judge and Chow Chow breeder and enthusiast Mrs. L.W. Bonney awarded an important win to Ch. Ah Sid the Avant Garde at the Kennel Club of Northern New Jersey in 1965. Robert Forsyth handling for owner Dr. Samuel Draper.

American and Canadian Ch. Loy-Jean's China Boi was whelped September 28, 1955 and died August 5, 1968. Winner of seven All Breed Best in Show Awards and 11 Specialties, he was Best of Breed at Westminster twice and had many Group placings to his credit. He was the sire of ten champions. Owned by Floyd and Jeanne Messer of Lake Havasu City, Arizona. China Boi was one of the all-time greats.

Kay Medford, the droll comedienne on the Dean Martin television show, presented the Best in Show trophy to Elsworth Howell's choice for this award at the Bronx County Kennel Club in New York in March, 1969. The lucky winner, Ch. Five Ash Vicki Jo, owned by Ah Sid and Pennyworth Kennels, was handled by Jeanne Millett. Captain Arthur J. Haggerty, president of the club, looks on. Vicki Jo was bred by Florence Wilson Graham who has been breeding Chows for more than 50 years.

Ch. Starcrest Kway, sired by American and Mexican Ch. Ghat de la Moulaine ex Poppyland Choo Choo. Whelped in February, 1961; the breeder was Joel Marston, the owner Brockway Crouch.

The late Brockway Crouch, an old-time breeder, pictured with Jet Starcrest Kway, black bitch, and with Ch. Kway Fire Flame. Mr. Crouch was also a fine judge of Chow Chows.

Mrs. Agrippina Anderson, famous Chow breeder and judge, awards Winners Bitch to Pu Si Ma Wong, who is owned and handled by Kay Wheeler, wife of Mr. Clayton E. Wheeler, Chow breeder and judge.

Ch. Pandee's Jubilee was a leading show dog and stud at the Pandee Kennels of Dr. Imogene P. Earle in Laurel, Maryland for several years. Although bred by Dr. Earle, he was co-owned by Dr. Earle and Dr. JoAnne O'Brien who handled him to all his wins, including Best in Show, all breeds, at the Valley Forge Kennel Club show in Pennsylvania, September, 1969.

Mi-Tu's Heh Tzi, male whelped in December, 1969. Bred by the Robbs of the Mi-Tu Kennels, he was sired by Chi-Sing's Shu-Heh-Sambo ex Chi-Kwang's Han Su Mei. Owned by Mr. and Mrs. J. Berne, Toronto, Canada.

Sharbo Pocha, owned and bred by the Robert Gilbs of Round Lake, Illinois. Pocha, sired by Charmar Chorister *ex* Sharbo Tai-Sha is pictured winning Best of Breed at a recent show in this Graham photograph.

Ch. Nor-Ton's Beau Sing pictured winning at 18 months of age at a Beaumont, Texas Kennel Club show with handler Anne Goodwin. Beau finished his championship in 1968. Owned by Fanny B. Smith of Charlotte, North Carolina.

Ch. Plain Acre's Charman Fella, photograph by Creszentia Allen. Fella was originally owned by Joan Wicks Ott and Samuel Draper and was later sold to Mr. and Mrs. Richard Meaney of Connecticut.

Ch. Cherokee's Red Feather, born May, 1964, wa sired by Gin-Ling's Liza of Cherokee ex Bob Bet Wan Sun. Owned by Mr. and Mrs. Oral E. Cris who own the Cherokee Kennels in Cathlame Washington.

American and Canadian Ch. Nor-Ton's Yim-Lee, American and Canadian C.D., whelped in July, 1952, poses for the camera. Breeder is Mrs. Bessie Van Dusen Volkstadt; owner is Betty-Mae Sewards.

Ch. Chang-Shi Xabu finishing for a championship title at a Reston, Virginia Kennel Club show. Born in September of 1965, the sire was Chang-Shi Ki-Foo (the Belgian import) *ex* Ch. Chang-Shi Poppy Western Style. Shown here under judge Mildred Heald to Best of Winners. Handler is co-owner Gerald Sterling.

Jon Ell's Mei Ling, mother of show quality Chow Chow puppies at Maxine Joner's Chow Chow Kennels in Vancouver, Washington. Sire was Golden Eagle *ex* Nanking Loi Idol of Budda.

Ch. Ah Sid's the Avant Garde pictured winning the Non-Sporting Group at the Penn Treaty Kennel Club show in May, 1966, with Mrs. Jane Forsyth handling for owner Dr. William Fritz of Carleton, Michigan. Mr. Tom Lee is the judge.

Ch. Palm's Lucy of Chia Hsi, bred by Harold and Adie Toudt and owned by Earl and Mae Palm, pictured winning at a recent show. Photo by Ritter.

Ch. Starcrest Mr. Christopher, bred, owned and handled by Joel Marston, Starcrest Kennels, Sun Valley, California. The judge here is Mrs. Cecil Lee, well-known Chow breeder-exhibitor.

Three-year-old Cody Morgan and his pal Rusty, 4½ months of age. Cody is the son of Mr. and Mrs. James Morgan of the Eastward Kennels, Las Vegas, Nevada.

Ch. Fa-Ci Chinkapin, photographed in 1972. His sire was Carlee's I'm the Won Pandee ex Fa-Ci Cineraria, and he was whelped in November, 1969. The beautiful red dog was Best of Winners on the way to his championship at the 1971 National Chow Chow Specialty Show and the 1972 Westminster Kennel Club Show. Owner, James R. Facciolli, Jr., of Downingtown, Pennsylvania. Photograph by Bob Pastor.

Ch. Dre-Don Sun-King of Craglinden, at 5 months of age, wins Best Puppy in the Non-Sporting Group at the 1966 Union County Kennel Club Match show under judge Isabel Bernfeld. Owner-handled by Dr. Samuel Draper. A Michael Loconte photograph.

Ch. Scotchow Liontamer Sayso, owned and shown by Joan M. Hannephin and sired by Ch. Eastward Liontamer of Elster ex Ch. Scotchow Witching Hour. Co-breeders were Dr. Samuel Draper and Joan Hannephin.

237

Tsang Po's So-Pai Cher, sired by Ch. Sanglo's Tishimingo ex Ch. Tsang Po's Ming Lee. Owned by Dr. and Mrs. Edward North.

Ch. Ah Sid Liontamer Jamboree, young son of the famous Liontamer, owned by Desmond Murphy and Dr. Samuel Draper of Monroe, New York. Jamboree was #6 Chow Chow in the Top Ten Chow Chows in the nation in 1973.

The lovely red Liontamer Ah-Tum Hetherchow, owned by Merilyn Morgan. Ah-Tum was whelped in July, 1967, as part of the Liontamer "A" litter.

Farresdale's Moulaine Chan Ce photographed at 10 months of age. The sire was Liontamer Firecracker ex Ch. Kway Star's Moulaine Ha Chin Na. Bred and owned by Mrs. Pearl E. Farres, Farresdale Chows, Charlotte, North Carolina.

Ch. Pandee's Tillitha, black Chow Chow owned by Harold and Adie Toudt of the Chia Hsi Kennels in Dousman, Wisconsin.

Ch. Starcrest Spy of Poppyland, Group and Specialty winner and sire of many champions, including Ch. Eastward Liontamer of Elster. Spy is owned by Mr. and Mrs. Howard Kendall.

A magnificent headstudy of Ch. Scotchow Liontamer Leo as a young dog. Leo is a litter brother of Ch. Scotchow Liontamer Louise and Ch. Scotchow Liontamer Leone. Bred by his owner, Miss Joan Hannephin of Wheeling, West Virginia

Ch. Scotchow Home By Dark, photographed in 1963 winning at a show with handler Dr. Nancy Lenfestey. Bred and owned by Joan M. Hannephin, the sire was Ch. Scotchow Liontamer Leo *ex* Ch. Scotchow Madam Queen.

This beautiful cinnamon Chow bitch, Chere's Chablis O'Prophet, shown at 9 months of age, is pictured being handled by Rick Donnelly, who is the owner of Chablis's sire, Ch. Don-Lee's Prophet. Her mother is Don-Lee's Luxury Lace and her breeder-owner Sherrie Harper of Huntington Beach, California.

Starcrest's Fros-Tee, bred by Joel Marston and owned by Earl and Mae Palm. This cinnamon Chow, whelped in 1972, was sired by Ch. Don-Lee Prophet *ex* Ch. Starcrest Bewitched of Ho-San and is pictured winning under judge Dr. Erica Huggins.

Ch. Scotchow Sum Wun of Lakeview, bred by Mrs. Earl F. Humphries and owned by Joan M. Hannephin of Wheeling, West Virginia.

The only Chow Chows being shown in the United States as a team are these littermates, all males, owned and shown by Robert and Norma Taynton of Detroit, Michigan. These magnificent dogs are pictured winning Best Team in Show at a Hoosier Kennel Club show under judge Haworth Hoch. Left to right are Ch. Dre-Don's Van Ace's Lao Yang Tze, Ch. Taynton's San Toy II, Gotschall's Lin Ch'e and Ch. Taynton's P'an Hu.

Tag-El's Little Rock, pictured winning under judge English at the 1972 Hutchinson, Kansas show. He finished with 5 majors and 18 points. Owner and handler is Evelyn E. Carter, Tag-El Chow Chow Ranch in McLoud, Oklahoma.

Ch. Tsang Po's Kwai Chu, bred and owned by the Hal Allens, is pictured winning her championship at 7 months of age at the Panhandle Kennel Club in 1973 by winning the Non-Sporting Group.

Jade's Cisco Kid, shown taking Best of Winners at the 1972 Chico Dog Fanciers Association Show under judge Janis Hampton. Cisco Kid was bred and is owned by Nelson and Diane Tardy, Union City, California.

Ch. Carlee's Emperor Chu winning another Non-Sporting Group, this time at the Trumbull County Kennel Club show under the expert piloting of handler Jane Kay. The regal Emperor is owned by Carole R. Whitlock, of Culpepper, Virginia, a leading breeder for many years.

Ch. Gotschall's Top Brass (the black) and his sire, Ch. Gotschall's Chang Kou Chian, 4 times Best in Show dog, owned and handled by Thomas Cassidy. Top Brass is owned by Mrs. Valetta Gotschall of Ohio. The judge is Mrs. Mildred M. Heald.

The magnificent Chow Chow male Ch. Liontamer Mardi Gras pictured winning Best of Breed at the 1972 Fort Collins Kennel Club show under judge Helen James. Mardi is handled by Dolores Maltz for owner Mary Alice Elliott of Denver, Colorado.

A great moment for the Chow puppy Liontamer Charlie Chan as he is awarded Best Puppy in the Non-Sporting Group at the Monticello N.Y. Kennel Club Match, March 16, 1975 in Monticello, N.Y. "Charlie," owned by Dr. and Mrs. Maurice Fox, Spring Valley, N.Y., was handled by Desmond Murphy. Later in the day, "Charlie" went Best Puppy in Match over more than 400 puppies of all breeds.

Ch. Lakeview's Han-Sum, one of the country's top Chows, owned by Mr. and Mrs. Joseph Gregory, winning the breed under judge Dr. Samuel Draper at the Atlantic Kennel Club show in October, 1970. Mrs. Robert F. Black, Jr. presents the trophy. Photo by Earl Graham.

Ch. Audrich Most Happy Fella is pictured winning Best of Breed at the 1973 Northwestern Connecticut Dog Club show under judge Ramona Van Court. This dog finished his championship in just 9 shows with one 5-point major and two 3-point majors. His sire was Ch. Plain Acres Charman Fella *ex* Audrich Raggedy Ann. Bred and owned by Audrey and Richard Meaney, Audrich Kennels, Northfield, Connecticut.

Balthazar Liontamer Yum-Yum, winning a Group at a 1971 match show. Yum-Yum is owner-handled by Robert Borsuch.

Tsang-Po's Christy, pictured going Best of Opposite Sex at the Buck Horn Kennel Club in September, 1972. Christy is shown handled by Wayne Quigley for owner Mary Alice Elliott, with whom he co-owns Christy.

Ch. Liontamer Kudos shown winning the Group at the 1973 International Kennel Club of Chicago under judge Maxwell Riddle. Sired by Ch. Eastward Liontamer of Elster ex Ch. Hetherchow Liontamer Daz-zel, Kudos is owned by Mrs. Priscilla St. George Ryan, Prune's Own Kennels, Tuxedo Park, New York.

Best Junior Puppy at the 1971 Ramapo Kennel Club Match Show was Liontamer Kudos, handled by Jeanne Brock for owner Jean Hetherington. The judge was Alexander C. Schwartz, Jr. Kudos was later sold to Mrs. Priscilla St. George Ryan.

Ch. Shamrocks Golden Nugget, owned and shown by her breeders, Larry and Carol Kelly of El Cajon, California.

6. THE CHOW CHOW IN THE UNITED STATES—Kennels of Today

As this book goes to press in the mid-1970's, we look to the future of the Chow Chow with growing interest and great assurance. There has been an unquestionable surge of interest in our breed over the past few decades, caused largely by some very exceptional dogs and dedicated breeders who continue to bring the Chow Chow to the attention of the dog fancy.

We have just been over the rich heredity the Chow Chow brought with it from China and the steady establishment and growth of the breed in Britain, on the Continent, and in America.

With this background in mind, we present in this chapter an alphabetical review of some of today's top Chow Chow kennels and a little bit about their activities and future plans for the breed. We are sure you will agree that while the successes of today's—and yesterday's—great dogs are recorded in show catalogues, stud files, and American Kennel Club records, it is good to keep up with what their owners and breeders are doing to make these great wins and show records possible.

AH SID

The late Sidney Joan Wellborn, Clinton, Maryland, had known Chows since she was a young girl when she became a close friend of Agrippina Anderson and her husband John, whose Glenmont Kennels in Washington, D.C. were well known. Although Joan had helped Agrippina show her Chows, she herself did not become active in the breed until the 1950's. One of Joan's first Chows was Ch. Pagemoor's Son of Wag-gee, whom she called Junior. He was bred by Mrs. Catherine Humpage. Junior's qualities were very important in es-

tablishing the Ah Sid line, for Joan once told Sam Draper, "The gods must have been smiling on me when Mrs. Humpage let me have Junior. His balance, cobbiness, coat and style were passed on to all his heirs."

Junior became the sire of Ch. Ah Sid's Jem when he was bred to Joan's bitch, Ah Sid's Shar-Lu. Jem produced Ah Sid The Dilettante when she was bred to Ch. Pandee's Silver Mug, whom Joan and Jack Davis had purchased from Dr. Earle. At that time Jack Davis became a partner with Joan in their kennel, which they registered as Ah Sid; it remained so until her death in 1971. He continues to breed Chows.

There were two outstanding bitches that The Dilettante produced which should be mentioned, Ch. Joere de Noir and Ch. Ah Sid's Mon Caprice. Joere was called "Ally-B" and was bred to Ch. Ky-Lin's Quintus to produce what Joan and Jack considered the greatest Chow they bred, Ch. Ah Sid The Avant Garde, a black male purchased in 1965 by Sam Draper, one of his first Chows. The Avant Garde won 17 Groups and the parent club Specialty in 1966 under Florence Broadhurst at the Anapolis show.

In July, 1963 The Dilettante, called "Buddy," tied the Best in Show record of 22 Bests in Show held by Ch. Yang Fu Tang set in the 1930's. Immediately after this win Joan and Jack and Buddy's handler, Jane Kamp Forsyth, decided that 25 BIS's would be the goal—then retirement.

Shortly afterward Buddy suffered a setback which was to cause him to miss almost all the 1963 fall season. It was not until March, 1964 that he was again in form—the greatest form of his magnificent career. In April, 1964 he won Best in Show number 23 to break Yang Fu Tang's record. In May he won his 24th BIS, and in July Buddy won his 25th Best in Show, this one at the beginning of the New England circuit. He was six years and three months old at the time. His handler decided to continue showing him until the end of the circuit even though their goal of 25 Bests in Show had been achieved.

Buddy continued his winning streak. At Carroll County he won Best in Show number 26, followed by two Groups at Lakes Region and Rockingham County. Then on July 17, 1964 he was flown back to Maryland and the saga was ended. Total wins: 26 Bests in Show, over 90 Group Firsts, and more than 200 Bests of Breed. A truly great record.

In the late 1960's Joan became associated with Mrs. Margaret Newcombe of Pennyworth Kennels in New Hampshire, a well-known Whippet breeder and exhibitor. Together Joan and Peggy bought Ch. Five Ash Vicki Jo from Florence Wilson Graham of the Five Ash Kennels in California, one of the oldest Chow breeders in the country. Vicki Jo was handled by Jeanne Millett to many Group and Bests in Show. Vicki Jo was an outstanding Chow with a magnificent personality that made him memorable in the ring.

When Joan died after a short illness, the Chow world was shocked and bereaved. Jack Davis and Joan's family asked Sam Draper to write an *In Memoriam* tribute to her for *Kennel Review* magazine. The final two paragraphs of that tribute aptly sum up her contribution to the breed and are repeated herewith:

"Joan's judging proceeded splendidly. She enjoyed going over the Chows, an enterprise that demanded and received affection and concentration — and hearty applause after each class. One could see that Joan's devotion to the Chows was a permanent love and not just a short-lived liaison. As she selected the winners, she looked longingly at the losers. As the sun played on the trees and water, and on the shining Chows, it enveloped us in the all-suffusing brightness and joy of knowing Joan, of loving Chows, and of remembering the perfect day."

Ch. Ah Sid's the Dilettante, pictured winning the Group at the Devon dog show in October, 1959, handled by the late Joan Wellborn of the famous Ah Sid Kennels. The renowned judge Alva Rosenberg awards the trophies and rosette in this Evelyn Shafer photograph.

Joan is still missed by her friends, for she was unique and memorable. She was worthy of praise and admiration. Her partner, Jack Davis, continued to breed and exhibit Chows on a limited basis in memory of Joan. Long may Ah Sid reign!

AUDRICH

In 1965 Audrey and Richard Meaney decided to establish a Chow Chow kennel in Northfield, Connecticut.

While their kennel has been in existence a relatively short number of years, they have done extremely well, having owned and bred several champion Chow Chows. Among their championship dogs are Ch. Audrich Black Orpheus, Ch. Audrich Cassandra, Audrich Most Happy Fella, Ch. Plain Acres Charman Fella, Gotschall's Chada and Audrich Raggedy Ann.

AUTUMN-SUN

While Autumn-Sun is relatively new in the breed, starting around the early 1970's, the owners, Jeanne and Harry Brock, are not new to the dog show and breeding world.

Ch. Audrich Black Orpheus, sired by Ch. Ah Sid the Avant Garde *ex* Ky-Lin's Quickstep. He is the foundation stud of Audrey and Richard Meaney's Audrich Kennels in Northfield, Connecticut, who are his breeders as well as his owners.

Group First at the 1972 Golden Gate Kennel Club show under judge Joseph Gregory were the blue litter mates Cricket and Audrich Vida Blue of Tamarin. Vida Blue is owned by Audrey and Richard Meaney of the Audrich Kennels in Northfield, Connecticut.

In the middle 1960's they raised and exhibited Toy Poodles. Though they loved the dogs, they were not quite satisfied with the toy dog temperament and felt they had not yet found their favorite breed. In 1971 they sold out all their Poodles and acquired what they knew to be their first love, a Chow Chow.

The first year of showing their little bitch was a good one. She completed her championship and they have a major on another bitch.

The Brocks are situated in Chester, New York and are seen at many of our Eastern shows with their lovely dogs.

BETMAR

Betty and Mark Schellenberg first fell in love with Chow Chows with their first one. Their Ching was a faithful guard dog and companion for over thirteen years.

After their marriage in 1959, the Schellenbergs bought many wonderful Chows, hoping to combine the Nor-Ton, Mi-Pao and Ghat de la Moulaine blood-

Audrich Angus MacTavish, born October, 1972, was sired by Ch. Audrich Black Orpheus ex Audrich Raggedy Ann. He is shown here at six months of age winning Best of Winners and Best of Breed from the Bred by Exhibitor class under judge Cyril Bernfeld. Bred and owned by Audrey and Richard Meaney of the Audrich Kennels in Northfield, Connecticut.

lines, which they believed to be the very best available. The plan was spoiled by Ghat's death at an early age and the subsequent deaths of their Mi-Pao male at the age of two. Uterine cancer claimed the lives of their two champion bitches, Leesa and Zaida, also at the age of two.

However, they did have one especially outstanding litter from a mating of Ch. Ghat de la Moulaine and Heidi de la Moulaine, who was Ghat's half-sister on his dam's side and his granddaughter on her sire's side. Three of the four puppies from this litter achieved their championships and the fourth, though never shown, grew up to be quite a replica of his famous uncle, Ch. Starcrest Spy of Poppyland.

By 1973 the Schellenbergs had acquired another fine young Mi-Pao male and expect a top Nor-Ton bitch to commence their original breeding plans once again.

Canorwell Bamboo wins Best of Winners and Best of Opposite Sex for a three-point major her first time shown. This lovely bitch is owned by Jeanne and Harry Brock of Autumn-Sun Chow Chows, Chester, New York and handled by Mrs. Brock.

Other dogs owned by the Schellenbergs and Beck and Thelma Bechtol are American and Mexican Ch. Betmar's Zeus de la Moulaine, American and Mexican Ch. Mi-Pao's Hidji Ti Sarewoe, Ch. Betmar's Leesa of Shang-Lo, Mongo Moulaine of Betmar, Heidi de la Moulaine, Chang-Shi Rebel Redhead, Miki de la Moulaine and Nor-Ton's Sugar Moon.

CARCHOW

Bill and Dorothy Carr established Carchow Kennels in 1967 and are quick to tell you that their kennel is large in size but small in the number of dogs they maintain in it. The kennel consists of two females and one male, and they have no plans for more than these three for some time to come. The Chows are their hobby and they want to keep it their hobby and a pleasure and not let it get to be work.

The Carrs are striving to produce the very best Chow Chows they possibly can and naturally have the betterment of the breed foremost in their minds. They enjoy the people they have met in the breed and enjoy the shows. Bill Carr does all the handling and enjoys working and training the dogs.

Their love for the breed began in 1950, but they didn't start to become interested in the show ring until 1967, when they decided to establish a kennel with the Carchow name. They purchased Ch. Carchow Gudi Tu Shuz from the Poppyland Kennels, and they now also have Ch. Carchow Gudi Tu Tu, which they bred out of Ch. Tsang Po's Betara. Ch. Tsang Po's Travlin Man Carchow was acquired from Dr. and Mrs. Edward R. North, Jr. They are also the proud possessors of Ch. Carr's Hop-You-Lik-Me.

CARLEE

Carole Whitlock's Carlee Kennels, Culpepper, Virginia, one of the most beautiful Chow kennels in the United States, has been active for many years in our breed.

Carole received national recognition in September, 1964 when her great Ch.

Mexican and American Ch. Betmar's Zeus de la Moulaine, owned by Clif and Vivian Shryock, pictured winning B.O.B. under Langdon Skarda at the 1967 Fort Worth Kennel Club show. Zeus was the first champion from the "Z" litter bred by Betty Schellenberg and Vivian Shryock.

A darling Chow Chow puppy owned by the William Carrs of Alexandria, Louisiana.

Lilbern's Chinese Red Robin won five groups and two Bests in Show in a three-week period between Sept. 4 and Sept. 27, when Red Robin was eight years old. He was handled by Jane Kay. The two Bests in Show were at the Raleigh Kennel Club and at the Old Dominion Kennel Club. He had won a total of three Bests in Show, nine group firsts and 35 Bests of Breed, all accomplished with limited campaigning.

Another important Chow at Carlee is Ch. Carlee's Sabu of Barwick, a handsome black male that won Best of Breed over an entry of 21 under Kenneth Given at the Talbot Kennel Club, Easton, Maryland, on August 20, 1966. He also placed third in the group.

Carole's Ch. Kway Star Topaz of Carlee, which finished her championship in July, 1966 with four majors and two Bests of Breed and two group placements, must be singled out as an outstanding Chow bitch. Several other Chows of this period include Ch. Carlee's Fancy Dan, Ch. Loy-Jean's Hey Boy, Ch. Golden Boy of Geddesburg, Carlee's Ginger Blossom and Carlee's Double Trouble.

In 1968 Mrs. Whitlock acquired Fa-Ci Black Iris, a gorgeous black bitch, from her breeder, James Faccioli, Jr., and finished her championship.

In 1968 Jane Kay, who handled most of the Carlee Chows, showed Carlee's Emperor Chu to his championship in three weekends from the puppy class with six Bests of Breed, one group and three group placings. Emperor Chu was among the 22 champions sired by Don Drennan's great Chow, Ch. Loy-Jean's Chi Yan Kid. When Chu was just a year old, first time out as a special, he won Best of Breed and group second at the Shawnee Kennel Club under Mrs. Erica Huggins. The next day at the Old Dominion show he was Best of Breed under Mrs. Mildred Heald and won the group under Raymond Beale. Chu's untimely death was a tragedy for Carole, for Chu's potential was enormous, and his outgoing, friendly personality endeared him to many admirers. One felt that Carole cherished Chu as much as she had cherished Red Robin, and she grieved particularly at Chu's passing.

In 1973 Ch. Carlee's General Fa-Ci had several Bests of Breed and group placements. In 1973 Ch. Dre-Don's Van Ace, co-owned at that time by Mrs. Valetta Gotschall and Carole Whitlock, was shown occasionally with success.

Carole Whitlock has had several kennels in Virginia, but the present one in Culpepper is magnificent, from all reports. Anyone fortunate enough to visit Carlee Kennels has always reported that its facilities are beautifully planned, tastefully executed and immaculately maintained. The landscaping of flowers, lawn, lakes and trees is a picturesque setting for Carole's beautiful Chow Chows, for which there is nothing too good. One hopes that Carole Whitlock will continue to breed Chows in the future, for she has contributed a great deal in the past.

Ch. Chang-Shi Zygoto, Belgian import, whelped in August, 1950 (died March, 1964), bred by the late Countess de Changy. Zygoto was the top champion producing sire in the Chow Chow breed. He produced 16 champions between 1952 and 1964. This is a world record for a Chow sire. Zygoto's sire was Int. Ch. Chang-Shi T'Chao *ex* Mei-Yu-Chee of Adlung. Owned by Gerald and Lucile Sterling of Nashville, Tennessee.

Two Belgian-bred future champions imported by the Gerald Sterlings of Walnut Grove, Nashville, Tennessee. The sire was Ch. Chang-Shi Zygoto, and their breeder was the late Countess R. de Changy.

Ch. Chang-Shi Rock and Roll, Bamboo Loo, So Yung Jo, Ki-Foo and Kan-Zi with Jerry and Lucile Sterling in front of their kennel at Walnut Grove, Nashville, Tennessee. The modern kennel is equipped to handle up to forty Chows.

Littermates with their owner, the late Lucile Sterling. . . Chang-Shi Mr. Boss Man and Chang-Shi Xabu.

A 1960 Christmas card photo of the Gerald Sterlings with a line-up of half a dozen of their top-winning Chow Chows.

Ch. Chang-Shi Oh Boy Ahmon Joy pictured winning Best of Breed at a recent Nashville, Tennessee Kennel Club show under judge Virgil Johnson. Sire was Ch. Glenmont's Ting-Ah-Ling ex Ch. Chang-Shi Zip. Owned and handled by Lucile Sterling.

The Gerald Sterlings with Chang-Shi Xabu, Chang-Shi A-Go-Go, Chang-Shi Poppy Western Style, Chang-Shi Mr. Boss Man, and Milgene's Gay Debutant at their home in Walnut Grove, Nashville, Tennessee.

254

Gerald Sterling with Chang-Shi Ki-Foo, at their Nashville, Tennessee home and kennel.

Ch. Chang-Shi Choonam Kwong sired by Ch. Chang-Shi Zygoto *ex* Ch. Fireball's Black Angel. Whelped January 4, 1956. Owners are Lucile and Jerry Sterling of Nashville, Tennessee.

The Gerald Sterling's Poppy Western Style "at home" in Nashville, Tennessee.

Chang-Shi Mr. Boss Man, home-bred male whelped in September, 1965. The sire was Chang-Shi Ki-Foo, the Belgian import, and Ch. Chang-Shi Poppy Western Style. Owners are Mr. and Mrs. Gerald Sterling of Walnut Grove, Nashville, Tennessee.

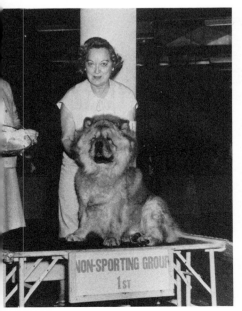

Hanoi Angel Face, bred in England by Dulcie Smith and imported by Jerry and Lucile Sterling of Nashville, Tennessee. The sire was the renowned U'Kwong Attaboy *ex* Fancy Pants of Kalamunda.

Chang-Shi Hop T. Lee of Don-Lee, bred by Rick and Reba Donnelly is pictured winning at the 1972 Memphis, Tennessee Kennel Club show with Lucile Sterling handling. The sire was Ch. Starcrest Matinee Idol *ex* Elster's Fortune Koo-Kee.

Chang-Shi Phoebe, home-bred bitch which made her contribution to the breed via the whelping box. Her sire was Ch. Chang-Shi Shanghai Jester *ex* Ch. Chang-Shi Taffy Sweet Stuff. Owned by Lucile and Jerry Sterling, Walnut Grove, Nashville, Tennessee.

Ch. Chang-Shi Rock and Roll at home in Nashville, Tennessee with owners Lucile and Jerry Sterling. Whelped in 1956, Rock and Roll won a Group First when he was just 10 months old. His sire was Ch. Chang-Shi Zygoto ex Ch. Fireball's Black Angel.

The foundation stud at the Chang-Shi Kennels. . . Ch. Chang-Shi Zygoto (August 2, 1950-March 18, 1964). He was bred by the Countess R. de Changy of Brussels, Belgium. Zygoto established a record for the Chow breed by having sired 16 champions, making him top stud throughout his lifetime. To owners Lucile and Jerry Sterling this Chow Chow was the ultimate. . . possessing all of the requisites and attributes demanded by the Chow Chow breed Standard.

10-week-old puppy and future champion Chang-Shi Rock and Roll. Rock and Roll won a Group First at 10 months of age. Owned by the Gerald Sterlings, Walnut Grove, Nashville, Tennessee.

Chang-Shi Zesha, imported from Belgium by the Gerald Sterlings of Nashville, Tennessee. Bred by the Countess de Changy, the sire was Ch. Tchang-Chaga Tippo ex Chang-Shi Y-Zam-Bah.

Champion Charmar Chatterbox, one of the top stud and show dogs and Mr. and Mrs. Charles Evans' Charmar Kennels in Grand Rapids, Michigan. Chatterbox was bred by Betty Mae Sewards and was sired by Charmar Chit Chat out of Ky-Lin's Honey-Lee.

CHANG-SHI

In 1946, Jerry and Lucile Sterling purchased a pair of black Chow Chows in Nuremberg, Germany. Two years later they added a pair of red Chows purchased from the Comtesse Robert de Changy in Belgium, and the Chang-Shi Kennel in Nashville, Tennessee, founded on the Choonam and Rochow bloodlines from the Chang-Shi Kennel in Belgium, was established in this country.

The kennel now consists of some 40 Chows with the record of 28 Chow champions, 22 of them home-breds, with 19 finished since 1957. Several others are well on their way to titles. The Sterlings started to breed Chows in 1951 and entered the show ring the following year.

Some of the home-breds which won their championships are Chang-Shi Choonam Kwong, Chang-Shi Shanghai-Jester, Taffy Sweet Stuff, and Chang-Shi Carless Coquette. Imports have included Ch. Chang-Shi Zygoto, Quad. International Ch. Rolly Polly, and Quad. International Ch. Schild's Xanda. The Chows which the Sterlings consider to be nearest to their ideal are Quad. Int. Ch. Schild's Xanda in bitches and Ch. Rochow Adjutant and Ch. Sabu in males.

In 1957 Chang-Shi established a world's record in the breed. They campaigned five home-breds to championship, all from the same litter, and all earning their titles at 10 months of age, two of the males winning Group Firsts. In 1958 they repeated this achievement when they campaigned another five home-breds to championship. The in 1959 they broke their own record by finishing titles on six home-breds. This is a record that has not been equalled or surpassed to the present date either in this country, England or Continental Europe!

The Sterlings are members of the Chow Chow Club, Inc., the Southern Chow Chow Club and the Nashville Kennel Club. Jerry Sterling holds offices in the C.C.C., is a licensed professional handler and is eligible to judge at Chow Chow Specialty shows not held in conjunction with all-breed shows. For relaxation he likes golf and water sports. Lucile, when not at the dog shows or getting ready for them, enjoys her garden club, playing bridge and painting. She also designs the Chow Chow calendar they send out each year at Christmas to their Chow friends. They are referred to as "the calendar couple."

In 1971, Lucile was elected President of the Chinese Chow Chow Club of London, England, an honor that had never before been bestowed on an American. In 1973, Colonel Sterling was elected president of The Chow Chow Club, Inc., and was later re-elected to a second term. Presently, the Sterlings are limiting the exhibiting of their Chows to Specialties, thereby reducing their activities to a minimum. They do hope the various responsibilities which have made this necessary will change enough to allow them to resume a more active campaigning of the Chang-Shi Chows in the near future.

CHARMAR

Mrs. Charles (Marjorie) Evans' Charmar Kennels were established in 1939. It is known for the success of its linebreeding program based on the breeding of Charmar Ching, C.D., a prepotent sire, to ten excellent daughters and granddaughters of the leading champions of the 1930's and 1940's. Top bloodlines were thereby combined and a careful selection of Chows retained for the breeding of recessives. This produced an excellent predictable linebred strain which has had a considerable impact on the breed in the United States.

By the beginning of 1973, over 47 linebred home-bred champions had been finished at Charmar, while many additional champions from Charmar stock had also made their mark in the breed and trace at least a portion of their ancestry back to the Charmar linebred Chows.

Although linebreeding has been the predominant theme at Charmar, some outside stock has been added from time to time to strengthen the line. However, all of this stock has been at least 50% Charmar linebred.

Marjorie Evans believes her Chows to be especially noteworthy for their appealing and equable dispositions, heavy and sound structure, and reliability of type. She and her husband, the late Charles Evans, established the kennel in Grand Rapids, Michigan.

CHEROKEE

The Cherokee Chow Chow Kennels are owned by Mr. and Mrs. E. Crisp of Cathlamet, Washington; they originated in 1957.

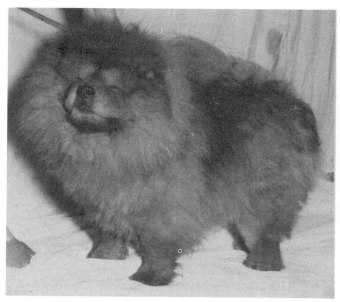

Ch. Cherokee's Tom Tom, a black stud force at the Cherokee Kennels of Mr. and Mrs. Oral E. Crisp of Cathlamet, Washington.

Champion Charmar Golden Belle, owned and bred by Marjorie and Charles Evans of the Charmar Kennels, Grand Rapids, Michigan. Belle is sired by Ch. Charmar Town Talk out of Ch. Charmar Chop Chop.

Cherokee's Sootie, a winning black from the kennels of Mr. and Mrs. Oral E. Crisp of Cathlamet, Washington.

260

As children both of the Crisps had Chows in their family, and after they married several other breeds were introduced into the family. None had the appeal of the Chow Chow which they purchased in 1957. His name was Salle's Golden Pal, and he was their first show Chow.

Before moving to Oregon from Southern California they had several Chow Chows and were given two Chow Chows bred in Tangiers which could not be registered with the American Kennel Club.

In 1959 they moved to Oregon and purchased Gin-Ling's Liza of Cherokee. Liza produced Ch. Cherokee's Tom Tom, Ch. Cherokee's Red Feather, Ch. Cherokee's Nik-Nak and Cherokee's Sootie. In her one and only time shown, Sootie won a 5-point major. She was then sold to James Facciolli and has since produced champion get.

Tom Tom and Red Feather have had many Group Placements, and Nik-Nak has one Best in Show. He was listed among the Top Ten Chow Chows in 1968 and was retired at five years of age. However, he was brought out of retirement at the age of 7 and won the Pacific Northwest Chow Chow Club specialty show over several other champions. He still loves the shows and is once again winning in the breed and taking Group Placements.

CHIA HSI

In 1967 Harold and Adie Toudt of Dousman, Wisconsin got started in Chow Chows. Their kennel name originated with their first home-bred Chow, named Yu Tu's Pry Den Joy. *Chia Hsi* means joy in Chinese, and this was exactly what their dog represented to them. They purchased three dogs of show quality in the 1960's and finished all of them; Ch. Shanglo's Jill of Chia Hsi was their first consistent Breed winner. Ch. Elster's Gee Nee of Chia Hsi was a show winner and then established herself as their valued brood bitch. She was also the first Chow Chow to be certified by the OFA, and she has a list of certified offspring as well.

Ch. Pandee's Tillitha is the Toudts' pride and joy in the early 1970's. She is jet

Adie and Harold Toudt's Don-Lee's Umbo of Chia Hsi. Sire was Ch. Don Lee's Prophet ex Livin' Doll of Poppyland.

Cherokee's Happy, owned by the Oral Crisps of Cathlamet, Washington.

261

black and is called Tina. The Toudts' Ch. Wah-Hu's Image of Buddha finished his championship in under one year of age and is valued as a stud force at their kennel.

The Chia Hsi kennels will house up to 20 Chow Chows and is located on the edge of the lovely Kettle Moraine State Forest; the Toudts consider it perfect for the breeding, raising and showing of their prized dogs. Mrs. Toudt is the OFA representative from the parent organization, The Chow Chow Club, Inc. and has been widely praised for her work in this connection.

CHENG LEE

The House of Cheng Lee was established in 1940 by Mr. and Mrs. Harold E. Lee of Arroyo Grande, California. It began when a dear friend lost his Chow Chow. It was the first one they had ever seen and when their dog was killed by a truck, they immediately purchased a new puppy. The Lees went to the same breeder and bought their first Chow Chow. He was a six-week-old male puppy named Cheng Yat Sic II.

While everyone loved Cheng, the yard fences couldn't hold him and the Lees worried that he might get killed on the road. They thought it best to sell him before he met the same terrible fate their neighbor's Chow Chow had met. They attended the Pasadena Kennel Club Show and talked with some of the breeders about buying their dog. It was suggested that they enter him at a show and offer him for sale. Selling dogs at the shows was permissible in those days.

The day of the show the entire family went along and when Cheng won his class and a lovely trophy they couldn't pull the "for sale" sign down quick enough! Within the month they had decided to buy a red bitch; soon after that they had a litter of six puppies by an outside well-known stud. The Lees were deeply into a brand new hobby, one they have always enjoyed. . .

That first litter produced their first home-bred champion, Cheng Lee's Sunnee. When the Lees lost their lovely Bamboo, they vowed once again that was *it*! They decided that their Ch. Cheng Lee's

262

Seven-week-old Playin' Jane of Chia Hsi, owned by Harold and Adie Toudt

Ch. Playin' Jane of Chia Hsi, bred by Harold and Adie Toudt and co-owned with them by Maynard and Joyce Hellbusch of Janesville, Wisconsin. Lloyd Olsen photo.

This magnificent Joan Ludwig photograph of Ch. Cheng Lee Jung Lung of Five Ash typifies the true Chow Chow. Owned by Mr. and Mrs. Harold E. Lee of Arroyo Grande, California, Jung Lung is a Group winner and has 15 Bests of Breed. During his show career he has been left out of the Group only three times and has defeated some of the West Coast's top Chow Chows.

Ch. Cheng Lee Jung Lung of Five Ash, Best of Breed winner at a Santa Barbara Kennel Club show; owned by Mr. and Mrs. Harold E. Lee of Arroyo Grande, California. Cheng is a Group winner and has many Group Placings to his credit.

Judge Dorothy Nickles awards Winners ribbons to Ellen Moss and her Ch. Warlord's Counter Spy at the 1971 Tulsa, Oklahoma dog show.

Almoh Sno Moonman would be their last Chow Chow. That was almost two years ago, and as this book goes to press, the Lees are crazy about a new red bitch puppy, and it looks as if history may repeat itself!

CLAR-ELL-MO

When Clarence and Ellen Moss moved into their new home in San Antonio, Texas in 1936 they realized they needed a watchdog. The region was relatively sparsely settled at that time, and when they called Boston Terrier friends the friends recommended a Chow Chow. So they purchased their first Chow Chow bitch, Fooey Man-Chuey. They soon learned that the breed was affectionate as well as protective and from that day they have always had a Chow Chow as a pet and a guard dog.

In 1967 the Mosses retired from the business world and turned their interests toward breeding and showing Chows. Even as a hobby it has kept them both busy. They have finished three Chows and are working on an international championship for their Ch. Warlord's Counter Spy. Their kennel consists of two champions and a male and a few females and their occasional puppies. The Mosses are proud to state that they believe at least half of the lovely Chows Chows in San Antonio are out of their kennel or at least related to it. They both derive a great deal of pleasure from the dogs and are in Chow for the betterment of the breed.

DON-LEE

Soon after Rick and Reba Donnelly were married they purchased their first Chow Chow puppy. When they went to pick her up they saw a picture of the famous Ch. Ghat de la Moulaine in a magazine and decided immediately to pay a visit to the Shryocks to see the dog in the flesh. When they saw him they realized right away that they had purchased a pet Chow rather than a show prospect.

The help and encouragement given by the Shryocks got them into the showing and breeding of Chows. With additional help from Howard and Pete Kendall and Le Roy and Georgia King, they were "in the breed." They leased Starcrest Gina of Poppyland from the Robert Porters and ordered a bitch puppy from Bessie Volkstadt and purchased Porter's Playboy. They also purchased Don-Lee's Petunia of Elster, who finished her championship as a puppy. They kept Don-Lee's Amy of Porter from their first breeding in 1965, and with Amy, Petunia and Playboy they had the foundation of the Don-Lee Kennels. But in 1967, with both bitches in whelp, tragedy struck. Amy died from gastric torsion and Petunia died after a Caesarean section. Their sadness was almost unbearable.

Howard and Pete Kendall offered them Livin' Doll of Poppyland, a litter sister to Petunia to help them get started again, and Doll and Elster's Fortune Koo Kee became their brood bitches. These bitches, bred to the proper studs, brought them many excellent Chows; Livin' Doll, bred to Ch. Beamer's Chummy Chinaman, produced the outstanding Ch. Don-Lee's Prophet.

Prophet finished his championship at a Specialty at the age of 6 months and 26 days. Only a youngster himself, he has sired many youngsters which are among the top winners in the 1970's, with many more moving up.

The very first home-bred Chow Chow at the Clarence Moss' Clar-Ell-Mo Kennels in San Antonio, Texas. Yang Fu Tang Fu Manchu was his name, and 1937 was the year. His sire was Yang Fu Tang's Son Too.

Ch. C. Candy Porter, bred by Rick and Reba Donnelly in 1967. Owner is Jane Porter Tracy. Candy's sire was Ch. Porter's Playboy and her dam was Ch. Don-Lee's Petunia of Elster.

Magnificent headstudy of Ch. Don-Lee's Prophet at two years of age. He was whelped in August, 1970; his breeder-owners are Rick and Reba Donnelly of Westminster, California. The sire was Ch. Beamer's Chummy Chinaman *ex* Ch. Don-Lee's Jewel of Ho-San.

wo champions and two proud owners. . . Ch. Warlord's Counter Spy (left) and Ch. Chu Fu Mein with Mr. and rs. Clarence H. Moss of the Clar-Ell-Mo Kennels in San Antonio, Texas.

Ch. Don-Lee's Petunia of Elster, bred by Bill and Florence Elster and owned by Rick and Reba Donnelly of the Don-Lee Kennels. Whelped in November, 1964, she is a litter sister to the famous Ch. Eastward Liontamer of Elster. The sire was Ch. Starcrest Spy of Poppyland *ex* Ken-Wan's Tahg-Along.

Chin Lee of Pa-Tin-J with his blue playmate, Patti Chew Mi Ko, photographed in 1971. Owned by the Clar-Ell-Mo Kennels of Mr. and Mrs. Clarence Moss of San Antonio, Texas.

The Donnellys are particularly proud of their breeding and are happy to say all their dogs are OFA certified clear. They are also particularly proud of the tribute paid to their foundation bitch, Petunia, by Georgia King in the December, 1967 issue of *The American Chow Chow Magazine*, which read as follows: "We know that lovable, beautiful Petunia will be a remembered symbol to Rick and Reba. Her memory will be the firm foundation upon which they will build her lasting tribute—more and more Don-Lee home-breds modeled in her image, exhibited in honor and pride and bred to keep forever alive her quality and temperament."

Ch. Don-Lee's Bomber photographed winning Best of Breed under judge Irene Khatoonian at the 1968 Bakersfield Kennel Club show in California. He is owned and handled by Darlene Randall.

Don-Lee's Quit Ur-Bit-Chin, Chow Chow bitch puppy at just three months of age. Her sire was Ch. Starcrest Mr. Christopher *ex* Livin' Doll of Poppyland. She was born in January, 1971 and is owned by Carol Kelly, El Cajon, California.

Ch. Donnelly's Q-Tee de Krikett, photographed at 2½ years of age. Whelped in 1971 and sired by Ch. Starcrest Mr. Christopher *ex* Livin' Doll of Poppyland, her breeder-owners are Rick and Reba Donnelly of the Don-Lee Chow Chow Kennels in Westminster, California.

In magnificent full bloom. . . Ch. Don-Lee's Prophet at 2½ years of age. Bred and owned by Rick and Reba Donnelly of Westminster, California, Prophet finished his championship title in March, 1971. A major stud force at the Donnelly Don-Lee Kennels.

Don-Lee's Amy of Porter, just four weeks old and posing for the show ring! Whelped in 1965, her sire was Ch. Betmar's Zeus de la Moulaine *ex* Starcrest Gina of Poppyland. Bred and owned by the Don-Lee Kennels of Westminster, California.

Ch. Porter's Playboy, Best of Winners and Best of Breed at the 1966 Imperial Valley Kennel Club show under judge Major Godsol. Sired by Ch. Ghat de la Moulaine *ex* Starcrest Gina of Poppyland, he was bred by Bob and Jane Porter and owned and handled by Rick Donnelly, Don-Lee Chow Chow Kennels, Westminster, California.

Fifteen-year-old future champion Don-Lee's Petunia of Elster, whelped in 1964. One of the brood bitches at Rick and Reba Donnelly's Don-Lee Kennels in Westminster, California.

Don-Lee's Prophet at 3½ months of age with Susie Donnelly at 4½ years of age. Prophet was whelped in April, 1966 and is owned by Rick and Reba Donnelly of the Don-Lee Kennels, Westminster, California.

Ch. Don-Lee's Jewel of Ho-San at four years of age. Whelped in 1969, she was bred by Rick and Reba Donnelly of the Don-Lee Kennels and is the dam of Ch. Don-Lee's Prophet. Her sire was Ch. Starcrest Mr. Christopher and her dam Livin' Doll of Poppyland.

Six-week-old puppies whelped in 1962 at the Don-Lee Kennels of Rick and Reba Donnelly in Westminster, California. Sired by the great Ch. Ghat de la Moulaine *ex* Starcrest Gina of Poppyland, they grew up to be Ch. Porter's Playboy and Ch. Porter's Primadonna.

Ch. Don-Lee Petunia of Elster photographed at 1½ years of age. Whelped in November, 1964, she is owned by the Don-Lee Chow Chow kennels.

Don-Lee's Calico of Tien Hsia photographed at 1½ years of age. Whelped in 1967, she is owned by Rick and Reba Donnelly of Westminster, California.

Champion Charmar Sing Song, owned and handled by Mrs. Marjorie Evans of Grand Rapids, Michigan, pictured winning in this photo by Ritter. Sing Song is sired by Ch. Charmar Chatterbox *ex* Charmar Grand Duchess.

Ch. Mi-Pao's Assoe, by Int. Ch. Chang-Shi Hong-Kwong *ex* Mi-Pao's Berbuka. Owned by F. P.A. Odenkirchen, Mi-Pao Kennels, Waterdown, Ontario, Canada.

Ch. Dre-Don Sun-King of Craglinden pictured as a puppy at the Sackets Harbor, New York dog show in September, 1966. Owner, Samuel Draper.

Joan Brearley and her 12-week-old Chow Chow puppy, Ho Tai, bred by Dre-Don Kennels.

DON-RAY

The Don-Ray Chow Chow Kennels of Mrs. Bertha Smith in Cincinnati, Ohio have been in existence since 1936. Mrs. Smith says it started almost as an accident, since her husband disapproved of any kind of activity in the sport of dogs. Their son wanted a Chow Chow, and a red bitch was purchased for him for his birthday. Later they purchased a black male, much against her husband's wishes, of course, and only promises of keeping the two dogs from breeding together made him relent. However, "accidents" do happen, and when the first litter arrived, a further promise was made to him to sell all the puppies; they did, but it nearly broke their hearts.

Later on through the years other breeding "accidents" occurred, and about this time Mr. Smith began to take an interest. Eventually he was helping to groom the Chows and taking them to the shows, and Don-Ray was in operation!

The Smiths showed their first Chow in 1942 and registered their kennel name in 1948. But they have done little breeding or showing since Mr. Smith's illness and since the time of his passing. But their love for the Chow Chow continues. . .

DRE-DON

Dre-Don's Chow Chow Kennel was established in 1962 strictly as a hobby, with the main goal being quality, not quantity. It was to be a kennel of all show stock to be used for breeding purposes, with each dog receiving personal attention at all times.

The Dre-Don foundation stock was purchased from the old Loy-Jean Kennels and was combined with the Ghat de la Moulaine bloodlines. Every breeding is carefully selected to combine the best of the individual dogs and their lineage in hopes that their get will make a genuine contribution to the breed. With this in mind also, all their stock is X-rayed normal for hip dysplasia. The Dre-Don Chow Chows are not only bred to be champions themselves but also are the producers of champions.

Donald L. Drennan, who established his kennel in Getzville, New York, states

Don-Ray's Blackout winning a 5-point major as Winners Dog at the 1963 Southern Chow Chow Club show under the late judge Mrs. Florence Broadhurst. Owner-handler is Mrs. Bertha Smith of the Don-Ray Kennels in Cincinnati, Ohio.

Left:
Ch. Starcrest Mr. Christopher, born February 10, 1968, and owned by Joel Marston of Sun Valley, California.

Below:
Balthazar Liontamer Yum-Yum winning Best in Match at the Kenilworth Kennel Club show in 1971. Mr. Paul Silvernail, judge, and Mrs. Edith Ventimiglia, presenting the trophy. Yum-Yum was shown by Robert Borsuch, her owner, in this Charles Mintzer photograph.

Above: The glorious Ch. Scotchow Liontamer of Frankee, owned by Joan M. Hannephin, pictured winning the Non-Sporting Group at the 1968 Rubber City Kennel Club Show under judge Ray Beale, Jerry Rigden handling for owner. Frankee was bred by co-author Samuel Draper and Jeanette Hetherington and was sired by Ch. Eastward Liontamer of Elster *ex* Ch. Scotchow Samantha. Norton of Kent photograph. **Below:** Ien-Ju-Yeh v. Meh-Thue, born in 1957. Bred and owned by Erich Buchner of Berlin, Germany. Sire was Weng-Yin van Majodo *ex* Wing-Wa van Mongolie.

that he realized Chow Chows are as individualistic as people. . . and because of the variety of Chow Chow personalities he does his best to match the right people with the right puppies. He also believes that there is no short cut when it comes to breeding consistent winners. His doctrine of complete honesty and sincerity has brought great personal satisfaction as well as many new friends throughout the country who enjoy the company of Dre-Don Chow Chows.

Don has bred and owned several great Chows, including Ch. Gotschall's Van Van (co-owned with Valetta Gotschall), a multiple Best in Show winner which won the Group at the Westminster Show at Madison Square Garden in 1969 under the late judge Alva Rosenberg. Another Dre-Don Chow should be mentioned, Ch. Loy-Jean's Chi Yan Kid, the sire of 22 champions when he died in 1974.

Don's hope for the future is Dre-Don Diamond Drop, an outstanding black male by Ch. Fa-Ci Chinapin X Ch. Dre-Don Dinah Dee.

EASTWARD

Mrs. Merilyn J. Morgan of Las Vegas, Nevada established her Eastward Kennels in 1967, though in her own mind she says it actually started in 1951 with the purchase of a lovely Afghan Hound! This began her interest in exhibiting at dog shows, although college and a job kept her from participating in the fancy as much as she would have liked.

For as long as she can remember Merilyn had been fascinated by the Chow Chow. Even as a youngster she can remember a Chow Chow which ran loose in the California town where she grew up, and she has always been intrigued by this fascinating Oriental dog! It wasn't until No-

Don-Ray's Abigail, bred by Bertha Smith of the Don-Ray Chow Chow kennels in Cincinnati, Ohio.

Ch. Starcrest Eastward Roman pictured with his owner, Mrs. Merilyn J. Morgan of Falls Church, Virginia.

278

A thrill of a lifetime!. . . Ch. Gotschall's Van Van wins the Non-Sporting Group at the Garden in 1969. Handling for owner Donald Drennan of Getzville, New York is Bud Moser under judge Alva Rosenberg. Van Van is only the third Chow Chow to win a Group at the Westminster Kennel Club event. William P. Gilbert photograph.

vember, 1964 that Merilyn found herself in a position to start looking for a Chow Chow to purchase after years of studying show entries and bloodlines of top dogs.

Finally she called Vivian Shryock to ask about available puppies. It was Vivian who informed her that the William Elsters of Long Beach, California had a new litter. Merilyn purchased one and he turned out

to be the sensational Ch. Eastward Liontamer of Elster! Her first Chow was later to become one of the top-winning Chow Chows in the history of the breed after he was sold to Dr. Samuel Draper and Mr. and Mrs. Robert A. Hetherington, Jr.

Merilyn now owns Ch. Starcrest Eastward Roman, Liontamer Ah-Tum Hetherchow and Eastward Liontamer Lucy.

Ku-Chia von Meh-Thue, red bitch born 1958. Bred by Erich Buchner of Berlin, Germany. By Ch. Wau-wong van Mongolie *ex* Ien-J-Yeh von Meh-Thue. Pictured at 2 years of age.

Ch. Five Ash Kissing George winning Best of Breed at the Redwood Empire Kennel Club show in May, 1972. Al Lemar handles for owner and breeder Florence W. Graham.

Ch. San Kee Papa's Sweet Stuff, her owner is Dorothea Rademaker of Teaneck, New Jersey, owner of the San Kee Kennels. The sire was San Kee Majongg Shen of Mount Air *ex* Ch. Chang Shi Dixie Debutante.

Dre-Don Van Jarrett, owned by Donald Drennan of the Dre-Don Kennels, Getzville, New York was featured on one of Mr. Drennan's Christmas cards.

Opposite:

Ch. Liontamer Juno, owner-handled by Mrs. Robert A. Hetherington, Jr., at a Tri-State Chow Chow Match Show in July, 1971 under judge Donald Drennan.

Ch. Nor-Ton's Royal Moon, bred and owned by Bessie Volkstadt, Nor-Ton Kennels, North Tonawanda, New York.

Nor-Ton's Chindu Chan, sire of the famous Ch. Loy-Jean's China Boi, bred and owned by Bessie Volkstadt, Nor-Ton Kennels, North Tonawanda, New York.

Pandee's Uranus, pictured going Winners Dog, Best of Winners, and Best of Breed under Mrs. Erica Dixon Huggins, a former Chow breeder, at the National Capital Kennel Club show in March, 1973, has since become a champion. Uranus is owned by Dr. Imogene Earle of famed Pandee Kennels in Maryland. Sired by the Dutch import Titus Pandee van Mongolie, Uranus' mother is Pandee's Chu Lyn Cin of Ka-Je.

Don-Lee's Jubilee, shown here at the Ventura, California Summer show in 1974 with her owner, Mrs. Larry Kelley, El Cajon, California, is awarded Winners Bitch for a major by Dr. Samuel Draper, Monroe, New York.

Schotchow Georgii, owned by Mr. and Mrs. J.B. Finale of Castle Shannon, Pennsylvania. Bred by Joan M. Hannephin, the sire was Ch. Scotchow Home by Dark *ex* Schotchow Red Ching Ching.

Ch. Eastward Liontamer of Elster, pictured as a young dog, being handled by his early owner, Merilyn Morgan, to a Non-Sporting Group win under judge Haywood Hartley at the Kennel Club of Beverly Hills in 1967. Ramona Van Court presents the trophy to "Louie," who was sold to Dr. Samuel Draper and Mr. and Mrs. R.A. Hetherington, Jr., of Mahwah, New Jersey. Photo by Joan Ludwig.

Ch. Farresdale Gam Chee Moon Too, Ch. Farresdale Hsiao Kwang T'Sing and Ch. Farresdale Wei Wong T'Sing. Mother is in the center, with her daughter on the left and her son on the right. Sire of the September, 1945 litter was Ch. Shoh Dee T'Sing of Farresdale. Breeder was Mrs. Pearl E. Farres, Farresdale Chows, Charlotte, North Carolina.

Ch. Farresdale Fergmo T'Sing, photographed in October, 1947, with his breeder-owner, Mrs. Pearl E. Farres, Farresdale Chows, Charlotte, North Carolina. The sire was Ch. Shoh Dee T'Sing of Farresdale ex Far Land Nancy.

Ch. Eastward Liontamer of Elster, photographed at eight months of age at the Santa Barbara Kennel Club show in August, 1965 winning a four-point major under judge Vivian Shryock; this was the fourth time he had ever been shown. He is pictured with his owner at the time, Merilyn Bowden. Liontamer is now the property of Mr. and Mrs. Robert A. Hetherington, Jr., and Dr. Samuel Draper, who campaigned "Louie" to his position of being one of the top Chow Chows of all time.

Farresdale's Moulaine Chan Ce at four months of age. Bred and owned by Mrs. Pearl E. Farres of the Farresdale Chow Chows in Charlotte, North Carolina. Sire was Liontamer Firecracker ex Ch. Kway Star's Moulaine Ha Chin Nu.

Ch. Liontamer Love and Kisses. Impy was never defeated by any other bitch while completing her championship. She is co-owned by Mr. and Mrs. Rick Donnelly and Dr. Sam Draper.

Karya's Brandal, a red dog born in 1971.

Ch. Don-Lee's Bomber, whelped in 1965, is owned by Darlene Randall Wood. Bomber is shown winning under judge William Pym at the 1969 Imperial Valley Kennel Club show. Bred by Rick and Reba Donnelly of the Don-Lee Chow Chow kennels. Bomber's sire was Ch. Porter's Playboy ex Ch. Don-Lee's Petunia of Elster.

Fa-Ci Cineraria, a beautiful red bitch, pictured going Winner's Bitch at the 1972 Trenton Kennel Club show under judge H. Kenneth Stine. She was whelped in October of 1968 and her sire was Ch. Pagemoor's Tedi Lee II *ex* Dre-Don's Tara Lure. She is handled by her owner's wife, Mrs. James Facciolli, Jr. of Downingtown, Pennsylvania. Mr. Stine is a well-respected Chow judge and a former breeder.

ELLWANGER

Fred and Eleanor Ellwanger do not use a kennel name, though they have been in Chow Chows since the early 1930's. They do very little breeding but have maintained an active kennel since the 1930's with two or three Chows on the premises at all times.

Their love for the breed is manifested through their enjoyment of showing good Chows in the show ring, and they have been successful in this respect.

One of their excellent show dogs was Ch. Wan Ho Rocket. He was of the Chiawan bloodlines on the sire's side and the Ho Han Chu Glo lines on the dam's side. He was a red dog and was shown during the 1950's.

Kway's Barbarian, purchased directly from Brockway Crouch, was another notable dog shown during the 1950's. Ginger, as she was called, was a lovely red and was 11 years old at the time of her death.

During the 1960's the Ellwangers

Ch. Five Ash Viki Jo wins Best of Breed at the Westchester Kennel Club Show in September, 1967 under judge Anna Katherine Nicholas. Viki Jo is owned by Joan Wellborn and Margaret Newcombe. Jeanne Millet is the handler. Photo by Evelyn Shafer.

showed Ch. Loy-Jean's Princess Mauri, purchased from the Messers of Loy-Jean fame. She was sired by the famous Ch. Loy-Jean's China Boi out of Ch. Princess of Hia-Nan.

Their latest acquisition is a British import, Ch. Fahsondu Black Xpo, purchased from Mrs. Hudson in August, 1969. Xpo and Mauri are now the mainstays of their small kennel. Xpo has at least one Best in Show, all breeds, and several groups to his credit.

FA-CI

James R. Facciolli, Jr. of Downingtown, Pennsylvania is the owner of the Fa-Ci Chow Chow Kennels, which he established in 1964. He started with a red bitch, Dre-Don's Tara Lure. She was out of Ch. Loy-Jeans Chi-Yan Kid and Ch. Miss Muffet de la Moulaine. She was bred twice to Ch. Pagemoor's Tedi Lee II, with both breedings producing champion get. From the first litter there was Ch. Fa-Ci Tamarack, and from the second breeding came Ch. Ki Do's Jp She Ming.

Mr. Facciolli then purchased a black bitch, Cherokee's Sootie, and she was bred to Ch. Fa-Ci Tamarack twice. Two champions were produced from this combination: Ch. Fa-Ci Black Iris and Ch. Fa-Ci Anniversary. And so it went with subsequent breedings and more champion Chow Chows.

Another Chow Chow at Fa-Ci Kennels is Ch. Fa-Ci Chinkapin. The Facciollis are devoted to the Chow and have produced some excellent specimens, with many more good ones to come.

FARRESDALE

Pearl E. Farres' Kennel, in Charlotte, North Carolina, was established in 1935. Pearl Farres believed that the market for really top Chow Chows was limited and has always kept her kennel and breeding program on a small scale, breeding for disposition and quality rather than quantity.

Pearl and her late husband lived in Washington, D.C. when they bought their first Chow Chow. The puppy was only a little over three months old, and they knew

Farresdale's Wun Dol Mongolie winning a 5-point major her first time shown under judge Dr. Samuel Draper at the 1970 Atlanta, Georgia, Kennel Club show. Bred and owned by Mrs. Pearl E. Farres of the Farresdale Chows, Charlotte, North Carolina. Sire was Ch. Star Kway *ex* Shia-Ken. Graham photo.

nothing about pedigrees or an organization called the A.K.C. But Manchees Oang Bing opened the door to another world for them. Bing, bred to a Min T Sing bitch, produced a litter of two champions, one a male who continued the Farresdale line of champions for several generations.

Pearl Farres claims she owes her success to four women who started her off on the right foot. They are Mrs. Thacker Walker, who taught her how to read a pedigree; Mrs. William Baer, who taught her the importance of balance in a dog; Mrs. Claire Perry, who taught her how to breed to bring out the best in a line; and Mrs. Robert Hackman, who advised her to keep the important records of breedings, whelpings, feeding, etc., for comparisons. These bits of advice, along with her carefully chosen dogs, have been the basis of her kennel since the first litter was whelped in 1936.

FIVE ASH

Florence Wilson Graham of Five Ash Kennels in Redondo Beach, California has been breeding and exhibiting Chows for more than fifty years, making her the Chowist of longest standing in our country.

Mrs. Graham first owned dogs in the early 1920's. She used to walk in a park near her home, and during her walks she frequently saw a mahogany Chow in an apartment window. This Chow attracted her immediately to the point that she always looked forward to seeing it on her walks. When she finally realized that she was making the trips to the park really to see the Chow, she decided that she must own one.

Mrs. Graham got in touch with Wallace MacMonnies of the Maxown Kennels in New York. He bred Maxown Punch and owned briefly Ch. Mah Jong Min T'sin and Ch. Hong Kong King, which reportedly had cost the highest price ever paid for an American Chow before the huge price paid later on for Ch. Choonam Brilliantine.

Mrs. Graham (in those days she was Mrs. A.O. Wilson) bought a daughter of Ch. Maxown Punch, called Snoo Kee II, from Mr. MacMonnies. Mrs. Graham learned that Mrs. E.K. Lincoln, one of the most important early Chow breeders, whose Greenacre Kennels are legendary, had just imported Su T'Sun of Five Ash from England. Mrs. Graham shipped Snoo Kee II to the East Coast to be bred to Ch. Su T'Sun of Five Ash, and she remained there with Mrs. Lincoln until she was four weeks in whelp.

Four puppies were born from this breeding, among them Su T'Sun of Five Ash II, who later became a famous champion. When Mrs. Lincoln finally saw the son, she is reported to have said that he was a better Chow than his father. Ch. Su T'Sun of Five Ash II was the first Five Ash United States champion and became the foundation sire of Mrs. Graham's kennel.

According to Mrs. Georgia King, founder and editor for many years of *The American Chow Chow*, "Mrs. Graham's years in the breed make her America's oldest active breeder and exhibitor. She was fortunate in getting a correct start from Mr. MacMonnies and Mrs. Lincoln. Down through the years, she has carried one pre-

Mrs. Florence Wilson Graham, owner of the Five Ash Kennels in Redondo Beach, California, has been breeding Chows for more than 50 years and has truly made an outstanding contribution to the breed.

Mrs. Florence Wilson Graham, one of America's most distinguished Chow breeders, is pictured here with Ch. Wood's Pago Pago whose sire was Ch. Five Ash Victory. Pago Pago was the sire of many champions and was later sold to Viola De-Voy.

dominating thought, top bloodlines with emphasis on top quality brood matrons. From the days of Ch. Su T'Sun II, Five Ash has figured prominently in California Chow history. She never hesitated to either buy or breed to a good Chow when it was available, and she kept her original bloodlines alive by following this practice."

Mrs. Graham acquired Ch. Five Ash Jo Jo as a puppy as the result of her cooperation in the breeding of one of her home-bred bitches, Five Ash Gloming to Ch. Jo Jo Hamson, one of the great Chows in California, a Best in Show winner and important sire owned by Mr. and Mrs. Walter Hanson. Ch. Jo Jo Hanson was sired by O.H. West's Ch. West's Sun of East. Jo Jo also was a Best in Show winner and can be seen in the pedigrees of most of the present-day Fish Ash stock. Another important link to the present was Ch. Five Ash Black Magic, a home-bred, also sired by Ch. Jo Jo Hanson out of the home-bred bitch Ch. Five Ash Black Coo-Kee.

Although Mrs. Graham's original stock was red, she also loved black Chow Chows and bred some very fine blacks. It was mostly through Mrs. Graham's efforts that excellent blacks began appearing in the Southern California showring. "Ch. Five Ash Black Magic," wrote Mrs. King, "was one of the soundest Chows of his day, with beautiful feet, legs, and a true Chow gait. His showmanship was the envy of his competitors and something we see too rarely in the showring. With his head held high, he paraded about the ring as if to say, 'I am the King of Dogdom,' and he usually was, when shown."

In checking the pedigree of Ch. Starcrest Spy of Poppyland on his dam's side (Poppyland Choo Choo), one notices the concentration of Ch. Five Ash Jo Jo. The Kendalls bred Choo Choo in order to preserve the qualities of one of California's finest home-breds, Ch. Five Ash Jo Jo. Choo Choo produced many fine Chows.

Ch. Five Ash Jo Jo sired another important home-bred, Ch. Five Ash Victory, a very beautiful Chow Chow with a head comparable to that of any import. He was the sire of numerous winners of the

1960's; although not campaigned heavily, he had Group credits.

Ch. Five Ash Victory was the sire of Ch. Five Ash Vicki Jo, whom Mrs. Graham sold to the Ah Sid Kennels and the Pennyworth Kennels in the late 1960's. Vicki Jo was an outstanding Chow with several Bests in Show, all breeds, and many Group wins to his credit. Vicki Jo won Best of Breed and Group three at Westminster in 1968 under R.J. Schulte and Henry Stoecker, respectively. Vicki Jo's untimely death was a sad event for Mrs. Graham and his eastern owners. Mrs. Graham's philosophy in breeding Chow Chows was to produce dogs that were structurally correct. She began her career with Chows which had beautiful feet, legs and gait, and these qualities have stayed in the Five Ash line ever since.

In 1972 Mrs. Graham's Ch. Five Ash Kissing George, a home-bred (by Ch. Five Ash Hi Jet X Five Ash Tai Tai) was Best of Breed at the Chow Chow Club's National Parent Club Specialty in Santa Ana, California under Derek Rayne, the all-rounder.

She is currently showing Five Ash Hong Kong (Ch. Five Ash Hi Jet X Fish Ash Chin Chin), which in a very limited number of shows placed high on the list of 1973 top winners.

Mrs. Graham has forgotten the number of Chow Chow champions she has bred and finished through the years, though it would be safe to say that she is undoubtedly responsible for the greatest number of champions among all breeders. New fanciers can be inspired by Mrs. Florence Wilson Graham who, after more than fifty years of active participation in the Chow Chow breed says, "Thanks for the many wonderful hours Chow Chows have given me and the engrossing interest they have added to my life."

GOTSCHALL

The Gotschall Kennels were established in 1933 and have consistently bred top-quality show and breeding stock since then. Believing that "like produces like," they consistently bred only the best to the best to achieve success. The Gotschall line goes back to the Ch. Yang Fu Tang breeding in the 1930's, and in the 1940's they owned and showed Ch. Ah Lee Hi Tiger Joe, the dog that figured prominently among the top-winning Chows of that era.

The Gotschall dogs were bred to the Ghat de la Moulaine bloodlines in the 1960's, and their two Best in Show dogs, Ch. Gotschall's Van Van and Ch. Gotschall's Chang Kou Chian, were a direct result of this breeding program. Part of their breeding program involves the feeding of natural food products carried through the normal diet used to maintain their show dogs. Good food and care and plenty of exercise keep their dogs in top-winning condition.

Gotschall Kennels have owned or bred 17 champions through 1972, and it doesn't stop there. Many more winners are on their way up. Mrs. Valetta E. Gotschall is particularly proud of the show record of Ch Dre-Don's Van Ace. As of 1972 he had 55 Bests of Breed, 3 Group Firsts, many Group Placements and was #4 Chow Chow in the Top Ten in the nation for 1970. By mid-1970 Chian had won 5 all-breed Bests in Show handled by his owner-handler Thomas A. Cassidy.

Jon Ell's KaLee, sired by Pearl Crestson Black Flash *ex* Silverstone's Sadee. Shown by Maxine Joner, Vancouver, Washington.

Ch. Gotschall's Gay Blade, whelped in June, 1970, attained championship at the Lima, Ohio Kennel Club Show under judge Mrs. Carl B. Cass, in May, 1972. The handler is Thomas A. Cassidy for owner Mrs. Valetta E. Gotschall of Carrollton, Ohio. Martin Booth photograph.

A famous Chow Chow from several years ago, Ch. Ah Lee Hi Tiger Joe, a dark red, sired by Ch. Stormcloud of Shanghi *ex* Ch. Ah Lee Hi Wan Lee, and owned by Mrs. Valetta E. Gotschall of Carrollton, Ohio. Mrs. Gotschall is a well-known breeder.

Ch. Dre-Don's Van Ace, born in September, 1966, is pictured here winning the Non-Sporting Group at the 1970 Trumbull County Kennel Club show. The judge was Louis Murr and the handler Thomas A. Cassidy. Ace's show record up to 1973 was 55 Bests of Breed, 3 Non-Sporting Group Firsts, 4 Seconds, 11 Thirds, and 6 Fourths. Owner was Mrs. Valetta E. Gotschall of the Gotschall Kennels in Carrollton, Ohio.

JON-ELL

Muriel Maxine Joner, owner of the Jon-Ell Kennels in Vancouver, Washington, has owned Chow Chows for over 20 years. When her 14-year-old Chow died, she vowed to replace it with a purebred registered one. But instead, she bought two. Jon-Ells Mei Ling came first, and then Maxine went back to the breeder and bought her sister, Jon-Ell's Nikki Loo. This was the start of the Jon-Ell kennel.

Maxine, when the time came, sent Mei Ling to be bred to the famous Ch. Ghat de la Moulaine. The mating produced a litter of four, and Maxine kept them all. The breeding was repeated, and

Maxine also kept two of the five males from the second litter. These Ghat puppies have been the strength in her Jon-Ell breeding and showing stock.

Maxine has been secretary and Treasurer of the Pacific Northwest Chow Club and a member for years. She is also a past president and member of the Vancouver Kennel Club and a member of the local humane society; she was instrumental in getting a shelter constructed in the area. She has two sons who have kept her busy for the past decade and have managed to get her active in their 4-H activities.

While Maxine also keeps busy with her work with stray and abandoned animals, she manages to keep six Chows in her kennels. With their five acres of land, Maxine hopes to start raising Chow Chows again in the future on a larger scale. In the meantime, she devotes her attention to Mei Ling, Gigi Moulaine, Golden Penny, Kim van Majodo and Mogee San.

Jon Ell's Mo-Gee-San, whelped in August of 1962. The sire was Ch. Ghat de la Moulaine *ex* Jon Ell's Mei Ling. This photo was taken at 9 months of age. Owner, Maxine Joner, Vancouver, Washington.

Ch. Jon Ell's Gigi Moulaine. Owner-handler is Maxine Joner of the Jon Ell Kennels in Vancouver, Washington.

Jon Ell's Nikki Loo pictured winning Best of Opposite Sex at a recent show. Shown and owned by Maxine Joner of Vancouver, Washington.

Mrs. Valetta E. Gotschall of Carrollton, Ohio, with some of her top-winning Chow Chows. Highest here is Ch. Miss Muffet de la Moulaine; center, Ch. Dre-Don's Van Ace; and lowest, Ch. Gotschall's Gay Garnet. Also photographed is handler Thomas Cassidy.

A Chow Chow with his socks on. . . and ready for a rabbit hunt on the desert with his owner, Roy A. Keesaman of Arroyo Grande, California. Ch. Kee-Zee Keesaman of Cheng Lee is the Non-Sporting dog about to be used for sport!

Ch. Kee-Zee Keesaman of Cheng Lee, just back from a Honda ride with a friend. His owner is Roy A. Keesaman of Arroyo Grande, California. Who says a Chow Chow is a Non-Sporting dog?

298

Ch. Gotschall's Chang Kou Chian, a multiple Best in Show Chow Chow, was shown extensively by his owner, Thomas A. Cassidy. His breeder, Valetta Gotschall, is one of the top Chow Chow breeders in the country. Chang was sired by Ch. Dre-Don's Van Ace out of Ch. Gotschall's Gay Garnett and was born November 15, 1969.

Ch. Kee-Zee Keesaman of Cheng Lee, pictured winning under judge Charles W. Marck at the 1972 Santa Maria Kennel Club show. Born October 18, 1966, his sire was Ch. Starcrest Spy of Poppyland *ex* Ch. Cheng Lee's Bamboo of Porter. Owned by Mr. and Mrs. Roy A. Keesaman of Arroyo Grande, California.

KEESAMAN

The Roy A. Keesamans of Arroyo Grande, California do not have a kennel but live with two Chow Chows which they believe are extra special. Mrs. Keesaman has loved Chows since 1930, and she obtained her first one in 1931. Since that time she has always had at least one—and sometimes as many as three—Chows which have been house dogs.

Her first show quality Chow Chow was purchased from the Otho Wests. He was a son of their beautiful Ch. West's Sun of East and a grandson of the famous Ch. East is West. From that time there were many other Chow Chows of pet type until they got their American and Mexican Ch. Kee-Zee Keesaman of Cheng Lee. Mrs. Keesaman says he is the most delightful Chow Chow she has ever had the pleasure of owning.

He was bred for them by their friends, the Harold Lees. They had the pick of the litter and first showed him at the age of two years. They had planned to show him sooner but a raccoon got into their garage and almost killed him when he was four months old. But by September, 1968 he was ready for the show ring and within 28 days finished for his championship with a total of 18 points. He was shown in Mexico in the spring and fall of 1970 and on September 13, 1970 finished for his Mexican title.

While shown on in September, October and November of 1970 he earned the rating of #9 Chow Chow in the United States, with 11 Bests of Breed in 12 times shown and placed in the Group 8 times, including a Group First. He is a proven sire with several champion offspring and others pointed. Mrs. Keesaman was formerly Mrs. Chester H. Lawrence, and Chun Kee of East, their other Chow at present, was owned under that name.

KY-LIN

Ky-Lin began as a dream back in 1936, in Scotland, when Betty-Mae Sewards was a child and saw her first Chow Chow. She was raised with Fox Terriers and Labradors and never in her life has been without a dog. But the Chow was her goal for breeding, and owning them became her dream and ambition.

In 1949 she purchased her first Chow, and in 1952 she bought the foundation dog for her kennel. . . Nor-Ton's Yim-Lee, purchased from Bessie Volkstadt. He was a successful show dog, winning his American and Canadian championship titles and going Best of Breed at a Westminster Show. To the best of her knowledge, he is also the only Chow Chow to have earned both an American and Canadian C.D. obedience degree. He was a powerful stud and is behind every Chow Chow she owns, through her selective line-breeding and cautious out-breeding.

Betty-Mae's theory is to "make haste slowly," so she is proud of the fact that in 24 years she has bred 38 champions.

The Ky-Lin kennels maintain approximately 75 adult dogs and are situated in Spencerville, Indiana, where Betty-Mae Sewards is pleased to find that the Chows have the same love of the land that she does and blend well with the horses, cows, cats and domestic animals there. Ky-Lin plans to introduce further generations of quality Chow Chows to the dog fancy in the future.

A marvelous head study of a Ky-Lin Kennels Chow Chow owned by Betty Mae Sewards of Spencerville, Indiana.

Ch. Ky-Lin's Black Witch finished with 5 majors and 2 reserves in 7 weeks. Whelped in August of 1960, her sire was American and Canadian Ch. Ky-Lin's Magnus *ex* Ky-Lin's Baybee Doe. The breeder was Betty-Mae Sewards. Owner is Elaine Johnson of Evanston, Illinois. Photo by Elaine.

A darling puppy from the Sewards' Ky-Lin Chow Chow Kennels in Spencerville, Indiana.

American and Canadian Ch. Ky-Lin's Magnus, whelped in September, 1958. Breeder-owner Betty-Mae Sewards of Ky-Lin Farms, Spencerville, Indiana, who has been in Chow Chows for a quarter of a century.

Mrs. Naomi Humphries and her Best In Show winning Fu Fun pictured winning during 1959. Photo by Evelyn Shafer.

Another of Betty-Mae Sewards' important Chows from the 1950's, Ch. Ky-Lin's Circus, whelped in November, 1959. Ky-Lin Farms are in Spencerville, Indiana. Circus was sired by Ch. Nor-Ton's Half Moon ex Canadian Ch. Ky-Lin's Yin.

Ch. Ky-Lin's Cutty Sark, pictured finishing his championship under judge A. Treen at the Muskegon Kennel Club show in May, 1972. Cutty Sark (whelped in August, 1970) is owned, shown and trained by James D. Sewards of Ky-Lin Kennels, Spencerville, Indiana. Earl Graham photo.

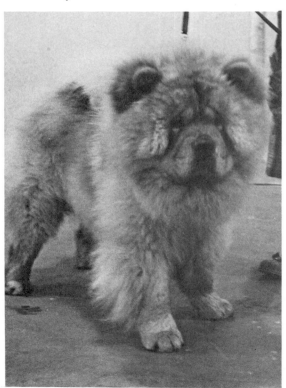

Mamie R. Gregory's magnificent Ch. Lakeview's Han Sum, pictured here in a classic Evelyn Shafer photograph taken in 1965. Han Sum is one of the breed's all-time top-winning Chow Chows.

LAKEVIEW KENNELS

One of the most important Chow breeders of long standing in our country is Naomi Humphries Scott of Lakeview Kennels, Louisville, Kentucky. Always in the forefront of American Chowists, Naomi is an expert handler who, through the years, has finished many champions. Energetic and hardworking, Naomi is to be admired for her years of devotion to our breed.

In the 1950's Naomi showed several Chows to their championship; included were Ch. Chum Yong Fu Fun, which won several groups and a Best in Show, all breeds, as well as Ch. Lakeview's Chum Fun and Ch. Lakeview's Stormcloud and Ch. Tim's Charley Woo. Ch. Chum Yong

Fu Fun, an important sire and winner, died in 1963.

In 1957 Naomi Humphries showed her Chow Ch. Lakeview's Typhoon to Winners Dog at the Southern Chow Chow Specialty, winning the first leg on the $800.00 sterling silver Challenge Trophy under breeder-judge Kathleen Staples.

Naomi's next leg on this important trophy was won in 1958 by her Chum Yong Fu Fun as Winners Dog at the Southern Chow Chow Specialty under Howard C. Bogue. Fu Fun finished his championship later on.

The third and final leg on this Challenge Trophy was won in 1964 by Naomi's Lakeview's Chum of Waulee, who finished

Here is Mrs. Naomi Humphries Scott handling her Ch. Lakeview's Jo Jo to First in the Group at the Badger Kennel Club, Madison, Wisconsin in July, 1972. Jo Jo had won the Badger Kennel Club Specialty Show earlier that day. Jo Jo is co-owned by Naomi Scott, David Reynolds, and Don Aull who make up the Lakeview Kennels today.

Another Best In Show Chow Chow, this time winning the Heart of the Plains Kennel Club show under judge Mrs. Flora Bonney. Ch. Chum Yong Fu Fun is handled by his owner, Mrs. Naomi Humphries Scott. Photo by Tepe.

his championship that day under Mrs. Ann Beamer, breeder-judge, and retired the magnificent sterling trophy permanently.

Another impressive cup valued at $500 was retired in 1962 when Mrs. Humphries' Chow Ch. Chum Yong Fu Fun took Best of Breed for the third time in the Southern Chow Chow Specialty show, thus winning outright this expensive trophy.

In 1964 Naomi bred one of the most famous litters in American Chow history, a litter whelped July 5, 1964 by Ch. Lakeview's Chum of Waulee out of Lakeview's Yum Yum. This litter contained six future champions, including the multiple Best in Show winner Ch. Lakeview's Han Sum and the group winner and important sire Ch. Scotchow Sum Wun, owned by Joan Hannephin of Wheeling, West Virginia.

Han Sum finished his championship at eleven months of age. He had a Best of Breed win from the classes at the St. Louis Specialty in 1965 under well-known breeder-judge Hal Allen of Lubbock, Texas. Han Sum won the Puppy Sweepstakes at the North Texas Chow Chow Specialty and at The Chow Chow Club, Inc. National Specialty at Forth Worth. He is a combination of three Best in Show bloodlines — Ch. Chum Yong Fu Fun, Ch. Ghat de la Moulaine, and Ch. Loy-Jean's China Boi. Han Sum's dam, Lakeview's Yum Yum, dam of four champions to finish in 1965, is a granddaughter of Ch. Chum Yong Fu Fun, one of Naomi's great sires.

Han Sum was sold after the St. Louis Specialty to Mrs. Mamie Reynolds Chinetti, who was to marry Joe Gregory, and together they would campaign Han Sum to one of the top Chows in the nation.

In the early 1970's Naomi Humphries Scott formed a partnership with David S. Reynolds of Lewisport, Kentucky and Don Aull of Owensboro, Kentucky. It was in this new partnership that Lakeview continued the winning ways established for many years by Mrs. Scott.

Throughout the early 1970's, David Reynolds represented the Lakeview team by showing Ch. Lakeview's Mr. Lu-Kee, sired by Ch. Beamer's Chummy Chinaman out of Plain Acre's Belle Chien, bred by

Lii Haven Bombadier, sired by Pag Chow's Wonderbar ex My Lucky Star. Owned by Neva Gaspar of Cupertino, California.

Manota Stertz and Chuck Williams. A multiple group and Best in Show winner, Mr. Lu-Kee was awarded the Supreme Chow Chow Award for 1973 by the parent organization, The Chow Chow Club, Inc. David and Naomi also showed Ch. Lakeview's Jo Jo to several important wins; he was sired by Naomi's stud, Ch. Lakeview's Chum of Waulee out of Ch. Charman's Fancy of Plain Acre. Jo Jo was Best of Breed at the Badger Kennel Club Specialty Show as well as group first. He also won the group at the Mid-Kentucky Kennel Club show in 1974 under Mrs. Mildred Heald. The Lakeview team also showed Ch. Lakeview's Joi to her championship, her father being Ch. Lakeview's Jo Jo and her mother Ch. Lakeview's Go Go Girl, a sister of Ch. Lakeview's Han Sum.

With years of experience of breeding many fine champions and with the upcoming prominent young stock at Lakeview, plus the youth and enthusiasm of her two new partners as well as. her own, Naomi's future and that of David and Don is predictably happy. One has not heard the last of Lakeview... and that is as it should be.

Mr. and Mrs. Robert A. Hetherington, Jr., pose by the lake at their Liontamer Kennels in Mahwah, New Jersey, with their two favorite breeds. Ch. Liontamer is with Mrs. Hetherington, and the Bulldog Ch. Hetherbull's Arrogance is with Mr. Hetherington. A Michael Loconte photograph.

LLI HAVEN

Neva Gaspar has championed Chow Chows since 1936, when her Lli Haven kennel name became known in the show ring. Neva Gaspar operates her kennel in Cupertino, California.

Over the years many top winning Chows have been associated with her kennels; among them are Pag Chows Wonder-bar, Ch. Starcrest Richard the Lion, Pandee's Buccaneer, Ch. Jean's Len Mi Yen, Shang-Hi Tang and Lli Haven's The Lions Cub.

Neva was on the Board of Directors of The Chow Chow Club, Inc. for several years and still maintains an active interest in breeding and in all matters pertaining to the Chow.

LIONTAMER

Samuel Draper had owned a few Chows before he met Mr. and Mrs. Robert A. Hetherington, Jr., of Mahwah, New Jersey. Once acquainted, Dr. Draper and the Hetheringtons brought Ch. Eastward Liontamer of Elster from Merilyn Bowden Morgan in May, 1967, thus forming a partnership which has led to great success in Chows.

During the summer of 1967 Bob, Jean and Sam also bought a fine young bitch from Bessie Volkstadt, which they registered as Arrogant Melody of Nor-Ton, and a bitch from Paul Odenkirchen in Canada, which they called Mi-Pao Arrogant Decoration. At first they called their Chow Chow kennel Arrogant, since the Hetheringtons had their Arrogant Bulldogs. However, that name gave way to Hetherchow, and when a good friend, Kay Finch of the Crown Crest Kennels, came to visit and was so impressed with Liontamer she suggested, "Your kennels should be called 'Liontamer'—the perfect name." It has remained so ever since.

Arrogant Melody of Nor-Ton, called "Bess," was bred to Liontamer and produced for the new partners their first litter, born in August, 1967. They called this the "A" litter; it consisted of Liontamer All-American, Al-My-Tee and Ah Tum Hetherchow. All-American made his championship as a puppy.

In 1968 Scotchow Sum Dai Dream was purchased from Joan Hannephin's Scotchow Kennels. Bred to Liontamer, she produced the "D" litter of three champions whelped August, 1968. The three bitches, Daz-zee, Doll-ee and Heatherchow Liontamer Dai-Zi, each has in turn produced at least one champion to date. Doll-ee is co-owned by Mr. and Mrs. Robert Borsuch of Connecticut and Dr. Draper. Doll-ee was bred to Ch. Pandee's Jubilee and in September, 1970 produced two outstanding bitches, Balthazar Liontamer Amie and Balthazar Liontamer Avril, both owned by the Bernard Kennedys of Wallingford, Connecticut; both became champions very young.

The "F" litter should be mentioned as outstanding also. In December, 1968 two males and a female were born to Ch. Scotchow Samantha. The black bitch, Scotchow Liontamer Foggy Dew, and Scotchow Liontamer Frankee were sold to Joan Hannephin, who finished their championships early, Frankee with several Groups and Foggy Dew with Group placements. The second male, Liontamer Funny Face, was sold to Mr. and Mrs. Claudio Alonso of Puerto Rico; he also is a Group winner.

Another notable son, whelped in January, 1968, was sired by Liontamer out of Gotschall's Velvet Nite, a litter sister of Ch. Gotschall's Van Van. The son was Ch. Liontamer Mardi Gras, owned by Mary

Liontamer Firecracker and Liontamer Mardi Gras pictured at eight weeks of age with Jean Hetherington holding the two little armfuls. Firecracker is owned by Marion Grissom and Mardi Gras by Mary Alice Elliott. Breeder was Carolyn Lou Kipp. Sire was Ch. Eastward Liontamer of Elster *ex* Gotschall's Velvet Nite, a litter sister to the famous Ch. Gotschall's Velvet Nite, a litter sister to the famous Ch. Gotschall's Van Van.

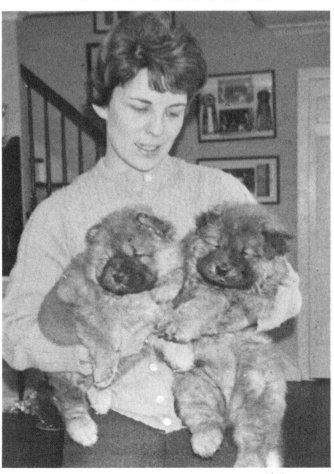

Alice Elliot of Denver, and a fourth generation Best in Show winner which began with Ch. Ghat de la Moulaine, Ch. Starcrest Spy of Poppyland, Ch. Eastward Liontamer of Elster, all Best in Show winners.

Ch. Samantha whelped another litter in October, 1970; this litter included other top show winners, including Ch. Ah Sid Liontamer Jamboree, Juno and Juggernaut and a female, Ju-Ju Bees, owned by Jack Davis of Ah Sid Kennels. Jamboree is co-owned by Sam Draper and Desmond Murphy, who handled Jamboree to the number six position in the Top Ten Chow Chows in the U.S. in 1973, 1974 and 1975.

The Bernard Kennedys bred Daz-Zel to Liontamer to produce a top male, named Liontamer Kudos, which is now owned by Mrs. Priscilla St. George Ryan, "Prune's Own" Kennel, Tuxedo Park, New York. Kudos won the Group at Chicago International in the spring of 1973, handled by Ted Young, Jr. Mrs. Ryan owned a Chow as a child and grew up as a neighbor to Ledgelands, Mrs. Wagstaff's famous kennel.

While now retired from the show ring, Liontamer's show record demonstrates that he has been in the Top Ten Chows in the nation since 1966; in 1967 he was top Chow, but not Supreme Chow, as he had not yet won any Bests in Show; in 1968 he was number four Chow Chow. In 1969, 1970, and 1971 he was Supreme Chow Chow based on the parent club rating system. He was shown sparingly in 1972 and 1973 and was again among the ten best Chows. Liontamer has won 10 Bests in Show, all breeds, 52 Non-Sporting Groups, and over 300 Bests of Breed. He won the Chow Chow Club's national parent club Specialty in 1968, 1969, 1970, 1971 and 1973, under five different judges, both all-rounders and breeders. This is a record for parent club Specialties. As of the beginning of 1974 Liontamer had sired 20 champions, including 6 Group winners and a Best in Show winning son. This is an enviable record, indeed, and his present owners, former owner and breeders are justifiably proud. Liontamer will live forever in the annals of Chow Chow history.

Mrs. Robert A. Hetherington, Jr. of Franklin Lakes, New Jersey, who co-owns Ch. Eastward Liontamer of Elster with her husand and Dr. Samuel Draper, puts on a demonstration in the ring at the Manhattan Savings Bank annual dog exhibit, held each year in the lobby of the branch at Madison Avenue and 47th Street in New York City. This public exhibition does much to introduce purebred dogs to the public and has been a regular feature of the bank each year for about 15 years; it tells the visitors to the bank exactly what goes on at a dog show.

The adorable 1970 Christmas card of the Robert Hetheringtons of New Jersey. The fabulous top-winning Chow Chow Ch. Eastward Liontamer of Elster shares the spotlight with the children and his top-winning Bulldog friend, Ch. Hetherbull Arrogance in front of the fireplace in their trophy room.

Our favorite tossed salad. . . Hetherchow Liontamer Eclair with her Bulldog friend Hetherbull Arrogant Fury, owned by the Robert Hetheringtons and Dr. Samuel Draper and photographed so ingeniously by Albert E. and Creszentia Allen of New Jersey. This famous duo appeared in the same photograph on very popular note paper.

He lives in retirement with the Hetheringtons along with three Brussells Griffons, a Bulldog or two and an Airedale bitch. His superb temperament serves him well with Danny and Trish Hetherington, but the Siamese cat drives him crazy!

Since Dr. Draper moved from New Jersey to Monroe, New York, he has established an annex to Liontamer Kennels where, among others, liver Ch. Dre-Don Sun-King of Craglinden, Ch. Westfield Liontamer Athena, Liontamer Le Lio of Chia Hsi, Starcrest Liontamer Memoire, co-owned with the Hetheringtons, Ch. Ah Sid Liontamer Jamboree and Liontamer Bounce, all owned by Sam and Desmond Murphy, who shows most of the Chows. Desmond and Sam are the breeders of Ch. Liontamer Love and Kisses, who was never defeated by another bitch during the entire time she was competing for her championship. She is co-owned by Sam and Mr. and Mrs. Rick Donnelly.

A favorite photograph of Ch. Eastward Liontamer of Elster, taken by Evelyn Shafer for owners Dr. Samuel Draper and Mr. and Mrs. Robert A. Hetherington, Jr.

Ch. Eastward Liontamer of Elster is shown above winning his fifth Best In Show—all breeds—under Major Godsol at the Baltimore County Kennel Club on April 19, 1970. On this occasion he won Best of Breed at the Southern Chow Chow Specialty Show under breeder-judge H. Kenneth Stine over an entry of 55 Chows. He went on to win the Group under Maxwell Riddle and then went on to a triumphant Best In Show. At this time it brought his record up to over 100 Bests of Breed and 35 Group Firsts. He was also Top Sire in the country at this time and was #1 Chow Chow in *Popular Dogs* Phillips System as a top-winning show dog. "Louie" is owned by the Robert A. Hetheringtons and Dr. Samuel Draper and handled by Ted Young, Jr. A William P. Gilbert photograph.

American and Canadian Ch. Luck-ee Mimi Soong, a daughter of Ch. Luck-ee U'Kwong Royalist *ex* Baby San Sukoshi. Bred by Mr. and Mrs. Howard Higbee and shown here with owner Grace Luckey. The judge at this show was Mrs. Erica Huggins. Roberts photo.

LUCK-EE

The Luck-ee Kennels of Grace Luckey in Seattle, Washington, were established in 1946 when the Luckeys bought their first show dog. While they had owned Chows as pets for many years, their first show prospect was a five-month-old dark red male purchased from the Yangtze Kennels in Los Angeles. The dog was followed by a young bitch from the same Yangtze kennels; they became Ch. Yangtze's Model Son and Yangtze's Debutante. These two Chow Chows and another dog and bitch from the Chung Kuo Kennels in Virginia were to become the nucleus of Luck-ee.

Grace has always kept her kennel on a small scale, since the dogs are pets first and then show dogs. Over the years she has owned and bred and shown 23 Chows to their championships, and four have earned C.D. obedience degrees.

American and Canadian Ch. Yangtze's Model Son and his son, American and Canadian Ch. Luck-ee Model Lao Tang, as well as Ch. Yangtze's Debutante, Ch. Beeson's Thunderstorm and Ch. Sun Beau of Staphorst (bred by Grace and owned by Kathryn Moser) have all been Group winners. One of her bitches, Ch. Luck-ee U'Kwong Rose, may have set some sort of record recently when she finished her championship at ten years and four months of age! Rose, born in April, 1963, won two majors at the shows in August, 1973, to complete her championship. . . proof positive that a good dog gets better with age!

Ch. Luck-ee Champagne Lady pictured with her owner-breeder-handler, Grace Luckey of Seattle, Washington, winning the Best of Winners award under judge Winifred Heckmann at a Pacific Northwest Chow Chow Specialty show. The sire was Ch. Luck-ee U'Kwong Royalist ex Luck-ee Bubbling Over, C.D. Bennett Associates photograph.

A 1973 champion, Luck-ee U'Kwong Prunella, bred by Grace Luckey of Seattle, Washington. She is shown here with her owner and handler winning under judge Virginia Sivori at the 1973 Olympic Kennel Club Show in Renton, Washington. The sire was Ch. Bob-Bet's Chan ex Ch. U'Kwong Red Rose. Prunella's litter sister, owned by the Robert Wrights, also finished her championship title in 1973.

MAGI

A dream was born in 1939 when a Chow Chow puppy came into the home of Elaine Johnson. This dream accreted more substance in the early 1960's with the naming of the Magi Chow Chows, a small primarily show kennel.

Ch. Ky-Lin's Black Witch finished for her title in seven weeks with five majors and two reserves. Ch. Cin Dee's Carousel of

Magi had the distinction of winning majors at both Westminster and the International Kennel Clubs within the same year. As far as Elaine can ascertain, Carousel is the only bitch to do this. Ch. Ky-Lin's Black Mug earned his title undefeated in Open Dog Black Classes with five major wins, the only black male Chow Chow to accomplish this record in over twenty years, as far as Elaine can determine.

Since 1939 and the arrival of the very first Chow Chow, there have been only six weeks without at least one Chow Chow in the Johnson household! Their owner, Elaine Johnson, was for a long time a Chow Chow columnist for *Popular Dogs* magazine and for many years served as Historian for the Chow Chow Club, Inc., the parent organization.

Ch. Ky-Lin's Black Mug is pictured going Best of Breed at the International Kennel Club of Chicago under judge William Kendrick at the 1971 show. Black Mug was whelped in November 1968, his sire being Ah Sid Silver Chalice *ex* Ky-Lin's Crinoline. The breeder was Betty-Mae Sewards. Black Mug is owned and handled by Elaine Johnson of Evanston, Illinois. Photograph by Ritter.

Ch. Cin-Dee's Carousel of Magi, winner of major points at both the Westminster and International Kennel Club of Chicago Kennel Club shows. Bred by Mr. and Mrs. B.R. D'Amico, Magi is owned by Elaine Johnson of Evanston, Illinois. Whelped in October, 1962, his sire was Ch. Ky-Lin's Circus ex Ky-Lin's Cindy Lu. Photo by Elaine.

Fantastic headstudy of the typical wrinkled face of the Chow Chow! The lovely Ch. Liontamer Mardi Gras, owned by Mary Alice Elliott of Denver Colorado, is a Best in Show, All Breeds winner.

Ch. Starcrest Fancy Me, owner-handled to Best of Breed at the Golden State Chow Chow Specialty Show in May, 1971 by Mary Alice Elliott of Denver, Colorado. Fancy was just 16 months of age at the time. The judge was Hazel Gray.

While Mary Alice Elliott has had Chows for over 30 years, her kennel has been in existence only since the early 1970's. The Mardi Me Chow Chows, located in Denver, Colorado, boast not only show dogs but also dogs which work in obedience as well. Snooks, or Cho Co's Gee Gee, has her Companion Dog degree, while Cho Co's Kee Jo, Liontamer Mardi Gras and Starcrest Fancy Me all have their AKC championships.

Mary Alice Elliott is an exhibitor of Chow Chows and one of the breed's staunchest promoters. She can always be counted on to give help and advice to beginners in the Chow breed and to help others train for the show or obedience ring. She also helped to establish a local Chow Chow club in the Denver area in the late 1960's, and it is still going strong.

Ch. Liontamer Mardi Gras is a top-winning Chow Chow and has a remarkable show record which has done much to endear the Chow Chow to the fancy. Mary Alice has been active in The Chow Chow Club, Inc., for many years and has served several terms as Treasurer.

Cho Co's Gee Gee, C.D., a daughter of Ghat is Denver's first C.D. Chow Chow. Owned by Mary Alice Elliott of Denver, Colorado.

Homer Tepe captures Ch. Linnchow Mi Chee Sonn Gee winning at a show. Sonn Gee was owned by Mr. and Mrs. George Curzon of White Heath, Illinois and was whelped March 29, 1951.

The George Curzons' Sassie-Jo of Martonge wins under judge Louis Murr at the 1965 Sandemac Kennel Club show. E.H. Frank photograph.

A handsome headstudy of a winning Chow Chow from the 1940's. . . Ch. Linnchow Mi Cho Boi, whelped in May, 1948 and owned by the George Curzons of White Heath, Illinois.

MARTONGE

Right after World War II the George J. Curzons of White Heath, Illinois, started raising Chow Chows. They called their kennel Martonge. Their first dogs, or breeding stock, was purchased from the Linnchow Kennels.

Their first really big show winner was Ch. Mi Chee Mi Mei Linnchow, who in 1953 won the parent club award for being the top-winning bitch in the United States. Their first noteworthy brood bitch was Fan Tan, the dam of their Ch. Linnchow Mi Cho Boi, and also their first home-bred champion. Ch. Sassie-Jo of Martonge was finished to championship from the 6-to-9-month Puppy Classes.

Other Chows of note were Ch. Linnchow Mi Chee Sonn Gee, Ch. Tsang-Po's Fan Tan Dude, Ch. Martonge Jo-Jo of Peke Chow, Chee La Linnchow and Fan Tan Su Ki Linnchow, to name a few.

Martonge is a combination of the four family names. . . Margaret, George, and the two children, since the Curzons consider their children to have been an integral part of their kennel operation until they married and left home.

For many years the Curzons have maintained their interest in the local kennel club, the parent club, and in the Pekingese breed as well as in the Chow Chows. They have only recently curtailed their breeding program somewhat, preferring to help the young people in the area get started in the breed.

Above Right:

Ch. Tsang-Po's Fan Tan Dude wins Group Fourth at the September, 1963 Heart of the Plains Kennel Club show. The Dude is owned by the George Curzons of White Heath, Illinois, although Hal Allen is pictured handling.

Right:

Ch. Mi Chee Mi Mei Linnchow wins Best of Breed at the St. Louis Chow Chow Specialty Show in 1953 under judge Leroy King. Mi Mei was sired by Ch. Linnchow Mi Cho Boi *ex* Chee La Linnchow and owned by the George Curzons of White Heath, Illinois.

DE LA MOULAINE

This world-famous kennel name now belongs to Clif and Vivian Shryock of Hawaiian Gardens, California. Their first show Chow was purchased from the Marhal Kennels in 1946. Marhal's Yang Tang was his name, and he distinguished himself by earning a C.D. degree before he had reached the age of one year, but this lovely show prospect died before ever reaching his full potential in the show ring. The Shryocks then purchased a two-year-old male from the Marhal and Sing-Fu Kennels. This dog, named Wo-Hu, finished his championship by winning two Non-Sporting Groups and went on to become the first Chow in the history of the breed to win a group and a C.D. degree. While being shown in the obedience ring, Wu-Ho was always top-scoring champion all breeds.

The Shryocks' most famous dog, of course, was the magnificent Ch. Ghat de la Moulaine, bred in France. Ghat stood 19 inches at the shoulder and weighed 68 pounds. Ghat is known, among other things, for bringing good heads and expression back to America, and certainly for focusing attention on the breed in the show ring. Purchased in 1959, when he was 20 months old, from the de la Moulaine kennels of Rene Hassenforder, Ghat won Best of Breed and Group Third at his first show in this country.

His second show was another matter or, as Clif Shryock puts it, "proof that you can't win them all." Ghat was not in the ribbons and the next day was just reserve at the N.T.C.C. Specialty. But this was to be the last time he was defeated in the classes. The next two days he was Best of Breed and Group Third and the next (at the Fort Worth Show) he went all the way to Best in Show under judge Lou Starkey. This heralded the beginning of an illustrious show career! Ghat finished his championship by winning another Non-Sporting Group and added more Groups and Bests in Show in

One of the greatest Chow Chows of all times. . . the French import Ch. Ghat de la Moulaine, owned by Clif and Vivian Shryock of Hawaiian Gardens, California. Ghat is pictured winning the Non-Sporting Group at an Imperial Valley Kennel Club Show under judge Vincent Perry, handled by his owner, Clif Shryock. A Joan Ludwig photo.

short order. He was also the first Chow Chow to win a Best in Show in Mexico.

During the time he was racking up his impressive show record, this great dog was also proving himself as an important sire. He set an all-time record of siring 36 American champions and one Canadian champion. Over 100 of his grandchildren are doing well all over the country today.

Ghat was top-winning Chow Chow in America in 1960 and fifth ranking dog of all breeds. In 1961 he was the top Non-Sporting Group Stud Dog.

Since Ghat's accidental death in November, 1963, his sons and daughters have continued to be on the top ten lists, and now the next generation is following this same tradition. Nearly every important breeding kennel in the United States has Ghat's bloodlines and is proud that he is still rated the top sire of Chow Chows. Immediately following Ghat's demise, the Shryocks became active in club activities and concentrated on judging for awhile.

Opposite:

Ch. Ghat de la Moulaine winning Best in Show at Fort Worth, Texas. Co-owned by Clif and Vivian Shryock, Hawaiian Gardens, California.

Ch. Lyle's Age of Aquarius, owned by Clif and
Vivian Shryock of Hawaiian Gardens, California.

Dogs from the last litter sired by Ghat. . . the Z litter. Left to right, Mexican and American Ch. Zeus
de la Moulaine, Ch. Zaida de la Moulaine and
American and Mexican Ch. Zip de la Moulaine.
Bred by Betty Schellenberger of Texas.

English and American Ch. U-Kwong Fleur is
awarded Best of Opposite Sex by Dr. Samuel
Draper at the Ventura County Dog Fanciers Association, July, 1974, in Ventura, California. Fleur
was imported from England by Mr. and Mrs. Clif
Shryock of Hawaiian Gardens, California. Mr.
Shryock is shown handling here.

Ch. Mark's Missi Lee, a lovely Chow Chow bitch
owned by Clif and Vivian Shryock of California.

A 1960 Best in Show win at Salinas, California, for the fabulous Ch. Ghat de la Moulaine, owned and shown by Clif and Vivian Shryock of Hawaiian Gardens, California. Judge is Derek Rayne.

Ch. Wo-Hu, C.D., pictured with judge George M. Affleck winning at a show in 1948. Wo-Hu was owned and shown by Clif and Vivian Shryock of Hawaiian Gardens, California.

Ch. Winchow Chu Fu Son Too, owned by Clif and Vivian Shryock of California.

American and Mexican Ch. Ychouchanna van Mongolie, imported from Holland and owned and shown by Clif and Vivian Shryock of Hawaiian Gardens, California. Ychouchanna is the dam of the great Ghat de la Moulaine.

Ch. Ming Fu Ling of Soutee pictured winning Third in the Group at the 1949 San Angelo Kennel Club in Texas under judge Alfred Mitchell. Ming always placed in the Group when he won Best of Breed. Owners were Clif and Vivian Shryock of Hawaiian Gardens, California.

In 1972 Lyles Age of Aquarius was imported; the "Blu Dog" was an immediate success, quickly finishing his championship. His first time shown as a champion he won the Group at the Golden Gate Kennel Club show. It was the first time a blue Chow had won a Group in the United States in over 20 years. Blu had a fabulous disposition and "sold the breed" wherever he went, but tragedy struck when he died of botulism poisoning while attending four international championship shows in Mexico City on December 1, 1972.

In 1972, on one of the Shryocks' many trips to Europe to attend dog shows, they purchased English Ch. U-Kwong Fleur from Joan and Eric Egerton of the famous U-Kwong Kennels. Time will tell whether this lovely bitch will enjoy as successful a career in this country as she did in her native England.

Vivian also judges in Europe. She was the first American to judge the breed in Western Germany after World War II. She was invited to judge a specialty show in Hamburg in 1958. Shortly after that she judged in Strasbourg, France, and in 1959 she was the first American ever to judge Chow Chows in Holland. In the United States she has judged the Chow Chow Club Specialty show twice, first in 1962 in Seattle and later in Cleveland, Ohio.

Some of the Shryock's other top Chows were Ch. Ming Fu Ling of Soutee, Ch. Marks' Missi Lee, Ch. Ink Spot of Ferg Sun, Ch. Winchow Chu Fu Son Too, American and Mexican Ch. Bridget v.d. Tongelreep, American and Mexican Ch. Ychouchanna v Mongolie, Fluffy Chinese Princess, Ch. Betmar's Zeus de la Moulaine and Ch. Betmar's Zip de la Moulaine.

The latest acquisition of de la Moulaine is a magnificent young English dog, U-Kwong Mr. President, whose father is the great C.C. record holder of all breeds, Ch. U-Kwong King Solomon.

American and Mexican Ch. Betmar's Zeus de la Moulaine, owned and shown by Clif and Vivian Shryock of California.

American and Mexican Ch. Bridget v d Tongelreep, imported from Holland by Clif and Vivian Shryock of Hawaiian Gardens, California. Bridget is photographed winning under Beatrice Godsol in 1965.

American and Mexican Ch. Betmar's Zip de la Moulaine pictured winning Best of Breed at just 6 months and 2 days of age! Owned and shown by Clif and Vivian Shryock of Hawaiian Gardens, California. Charles Hamilton, judge; Mrs. Shryock, handler.

American and Mexican Ch. Betmar's Zeus de la Moulaine, bred by Betty Schellenberg and Vivian Shryock. Zeus, sired by the famous import Ch. Ghat de la Moulaine, is part of the well-known "Z" litter.

The Great Ghat! Another Best In Show win for Ch. Ghat de la Moulaine, the magnificent French import owned by Clif and Vivian Shryock. This time the judge was Thelma Von Thaden, and Club President Edith Izant presents the trophy at this September, 1963 event. A Lippincott photograph.

Heidi de la Moulaine, bred by Clif and Vivian Shryock and owned by Betty Schellenberg of Fort Worth, Texas. Heidi is the dam of the Shryocks' world-famous "Z" litter.

Chow time at a Chow kennel! Heidi de la Moulaine and her "Z" litter sired by Ch. Ghat de la Moulaine in November, 1963. From left to right: Zaida, Heidi, Zorro, Ch. Zip and Ch. Zeus. Bred by Betty Schellenberg and Vivian Shryock.

Ch. Ghat de la Moulaine, imported and owned by Clif and Vivian Shryock of Hawaiian Gardens, California on the left, and on the right Poppyland Choo Choo, bred by Mr. and Mrs. L. Howard Kendell and whelped on May 1, 1958. Choo Choo was owned by Joel Marston of Sun Valley, California.

Ch. Nor-Ton's Madonna Moon, bred and owned by the Nor-Ton Kennels of Bessie Volkstadt of North Tonawanda, New York.

Bessie Van Dusen Volkstadt's Nor-Ton Kennels have been one of the most respected and well-known establishments of Chows for several decades. To date Nor-Ton has produced over one hundred champion Chow Chows, 24 of which are also Canadian champions.

As a dedicated breeder, Bessie Volkstadt has always believed in and has purchased the very best stock available to maintain her kennel's reputation. Buying from only the best bloodlines in the United States has proved that the best begets the best. She has enjoyed winning from her own line breeding and has an enviable record of producing and exhibiting top quality Chow Chows.

Her Nor-Ton Chow Chow Kennels are located in North Tonawanda, New York, and we are pleased that so many of her famous dogs are represented in photographs throughout this book. After over thirty years of breeding, she is particularly proud of her Ch. Nor-Ton's Silver Moon, American and Canadian Champions Nor-Ton's Tin Sin, Half Moon, Farland Moon and Royal Moon; her bitches Ch. Arrogant Melody of Nor-Ton, Nor-Ton's Dona Lin and Nor-Ton's Sparkle of Moulaine are particularly treasured and valuable to her breeding program. She recently acquired a young male from Liontamer Kennels, Ch. Liontamer High and Mighty, whose mother, Ch. Arrogant Melody of Nor-Ton, was sold earlier to the Hetheringtons and Sam Draper. His father is Ch. Eastward Liontamer of Elster. High and Mighty will soon have some champion sons and daughters to his credit.

Nor-Ton and Bessie will be remembered for many years to come as very important names in Chow Chows!

Bessie Van Dusen Volkstadt and Nor-Ton's Sugar Moon, owned by Betty Schellenberg of Fort Worth, Texas. Mrs. Volkstadt has been a leading breeder for many years in her Nor-Ton Kennels.

(CH) Red Rufus

(CH) Simple Simon

(CH) Alpha Sing

Season's Greetings from the Pandee Champions and I. P. Earle

(CH) Red Sing
BIS Lancaster Pa. 1961

Four well-known Pandee champions grace this Christmas card which Dr. Imogene P. Earle of Laurel, Maryland, sent out a few years ago. Ch. Pandee's Red Rufus II is upper left; Ch. Pandee's Simple Simon, upper right; Ch. Pandee's Alpha Sing (a mutiple Best in Show winner on the west coast) stands in the center; below him on the right is the celebrated Chow bitch, Ch. Pandee's Red Sing, one of two Chow bitches ever to win a Best in Show, all breeds, the other being Ch. Blue Stocking of Manchoover owned by Mrs. Earl Hoover.

PANDEE

Pandee Kennels, owned by Dr. Imogene P. Earle of Laurel, Maryland, have been active in Chows since the 1940's and are well-known from coast to coast. Dr. Earle, a Ph.D in bio-chemistry, spent her professional career specializing in nutrition, knowledge of which has made a strong contribution to the success of the Pandee breeding and conditioning program.

One of Pandee's important early Chows was Pandee's Pooh Bah, who was sired by Agrippina Anderson's famous Ch. Dai Fu King of Glenmont. Pooh Bah sired Ch. Pandee's Red Rufus I and Ch. Pandee's Simple Simon. One of Pandee's best-known Chows, Ch. Pandee's Alpha Sing, was heavily linebred to Pooh Bah. Alpha Sing was sold to Joel Marston of Starcrest Kennels in California, where he won several Bests in Show, all breeds, in the 1960's. Three other famous Pandee Chows which should be singled out are Ch. Pandee's Simple Simon, Ch. Pandee's Red Sing, and Ch. Pandee's Red Rufus II, born in 1956, all used as a Christmas card by Dr.

Ch. Pandee's Jessica, a cinnamon, is part of the Pandee "J" litter bred and owned by Dr. Earle. Starcrest Jupiter of Pandee, now owned by Joel and June Marston of Sun Valley, California, also was one of the litter. The sire of the litter was Ch. Pandee's Jubilee and the dam Pandee's Zip Orah.

Earle, when they were photographed together at the height of their careers. Ch. Pandee's Red Rufus II became an important winner and sire. He was the sire of Ch. Pandee's Alpha Sing and was the grandsire Ah Sid the Dilettante and Ch. Pandee's Red Sing, one of the most famous Chow bitches in the history of the breed in the United States. She was one of two Chow bitches which had the honor of going Best in Show, all breeds, in our country. Red Sing won her Best in Show at the Lancaster Kennel Club Show in Pennsylvania in 1961 under the late judge George Hartman. Red Sing was sired by Pandee's Kiki Poo, and her mother was a Loy-Jean bitch.

Whenever Pandee comes to mind, one thinks not only of Dr. Earle but also of her associate and friend, Dr. JoAnne Schmidt O'Brien, who usually handles the Pandee Chows in the show ring. JoAnne's parents owned Linnchow Kennels in Tinley Park, Illinois in the 1930's and 40's, one of the most prominent and active kennels in the Mid-west. After successfully completing school to become a Doctor of Veterinary Medicine, Dr. O'Brien continued to show and breed the Linnchow line established by her parents. That the Linnchow line was successfully bred to the Pandee line can be seen in the breeding of Blu Cee Linnchow to three different Pandee males, including Pandee's Alpha Sing. These three different matings produced six champions. From the breeding with Alpha Sing, Blu Cee became the dam of Pandee's Cin Nee Linnchow, a truly outstanding brood bitch which was the dam of Ch. Pandee's Jubilee and Pandee's Zip Orah, another great brood bitch. Zip Orah became the dam of Ch. Pandee's Kinda Smart, Ch. Pandee's Kenya, Pandee's Katango, Starcrest Jupiter of Pandee, and Pandee's Katrina, C.D., the latter two owned by Joel Marston and Prudence Baxter, both of California.

Undoubtedly, Pandee's Cin Nee Linnchow's most celebrated progeny was Ch. Pandee's Jubilee, which won an all-breed Best in Show in 1969. Jubilee sired nine champions, including three Specialty Show point winners.

Champion Pandee's Lu Cee Pet was a part of Ch. Pandee's Red Sing's only litter. She was owned by Dr. Imogene Earle, Pandee Kennels.

Four-month-old Nor-Ton's California Moon, bred by Bessie Volkstadt of Nor-Ton Kennels in North Tonawanda, New York.

These puppies, owned and bred by Dr. Imogene P. Earle, are part of the only litter which Ch. Pandee's Red Sing, the Best in Show winner, ever produced. The father of these Chows was Ch. Pandee's Red Agate of Water's Gift.

Titus Pandee van Mongolie, bred by Henk and Kitty van de Wouw, Nederhorst den Berg, Holland, was imported by Dr. Imogene Earle and Dr. JoAnne O'Brien. Titus is 11 months of age in this photo. He is the sire of Ch. Pandee's Victoria and other winners, including Ch. Pandee's Uranus. Titus was sired by Int. Ch. Wanchow Goe Neng out of Jolly Drop van Mongolie.

Another bitch from this Blu Cee Linnchow by Alpha Sing litter, Ginny Tu Linnchow, produced Ch. Kitty Bear Linnchow (1964) and Ch. Scotchow Am I Blu, owned by Joan Hannephin, whose own Scotchow line is based in part on Pandee-Linnchow bloodlines through Pooh Bah, Red Rufus, Ch. Scotchow Sing Along and Ch. Pandee's Hi Sing, dam of Ch. Scotchow Samantha, mother of several champions from the Hetherington-Draper Liontamer Kennels. Ch. Kitty Bear Linnchow is the seventh generation direct descendant from Ch. Chia Linnchow (born in 1934); she is the first homebred Linnchow champion of Mr. and Mrs. H.P. Schmidt.

When Dr. O'Brien and Dr. Earle traveled to California to attend the Chow Chow Club's National Specialty in April, 1969, they met Henk van der Wouw of the Van Mongolie Kennels in Holland, who judged the Golden State Chow Chow Club's Regional Specialty the day before the parent event. Mr. van der Wouw awarded Pandee's Jubilee the male points to finish Jubilee's championship. At that time Dr. O'Brien and Mr. van der Wouw decided to exchange males; later on he sent them Titus Pandee van Mongolie. Titus has sired several American champions, including Ch. Pandee's Uranus and Ch. Pandee's Victoria. They sent Mr. van der Wouw Pandee's New World Ambassador, who has sired a van Mongolie champion called "The Professor."

Another outstanding male, Pandee's Meeko, shown by Dr. O'Brien, won Best of Winners at the parent club's National Specialty held in conjunction with the Santa Ana Valley Kennel Club Show in April, 1972, and has now finished his championship. Meeko's sire was Jubilee.

The future of Pandee augurs well, as Drs. Earle and O'Brien have several excel-

A senior citizen, Pandee's Pooh Bah, is shown at 11 years of age. The foundation sire of Pandee Kennels in Laurel, Maryland, Pooh Bah was sired by Agrippina Anderson's well-known Ch. Dai Fu King of Glenmont. Pooh Bah is the sire of Ch. Pandee's Red Rufus I and Ch. Pandee's Simple Simon, among others. Ch. Pandee's Alpha Sing is line bred heavily to Pooh Bah. Dr. Imogene P. Earle, owner of Pandee Kennels, started breeding Chows more than 25 years ago.

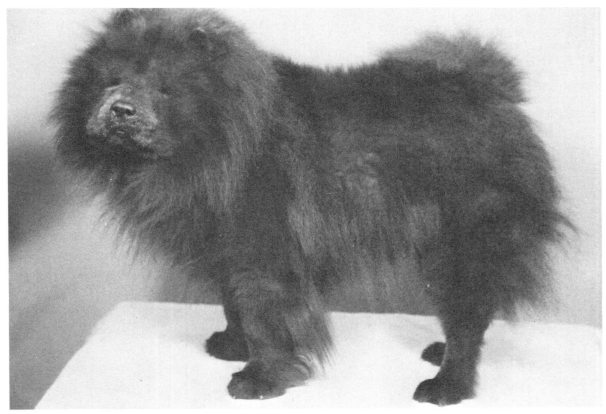

Ch. Pandee's Simple Simon, pictured here in 1961, was owned and bred by Dr. Imogene P. Earle. A brother of Ch. Pandee's Red Rufus I, Simple Simon was sired by Pandee's Pooh Bah out of Melissa of Barwick. Pooh Bah was one of the foundation sires of Pandee.

One of the most famous Chow bitches in the history of the breed, Ch. Pandee's Red Sing won a coveted Best in Show award at the Lancaster Kennel Club, Lancaster, Pennsylvania, in 1961. The late Harry Brunt gave her the Group, and the late George Hartman the BIS, all breeds. Red Sing, sired by Pandee's Kiki Pooh out of a Loy-Jean bitch, was bred by the late Louis Crabill and sold to Dr. Imogene Earle by Mr. Crabill for $35.00, as a puppy. Dr. Earle owned Red Sing the rest of her life. She was handled to her Group and Best in Show wins by Dr. JoAnne O'Brien.

Ch. Plain Acre's Charman Twiggy, whelped in 1969, is pictured with Manota Stertz winning Winners Bitch and Best of Opposite Sex on the way to her championship. The judge at this 1970 Lexington, Kentucky show was R.R. Schulte. Breeder is Manota M. Stertz of Cincinnati. Sire was Ch. Lakeview Chum of Wau Lee *ex* Ch. Charman's Fancy of Plain Acres.

BEST OF OPPOSITE SEX

Champion Pandee's Red Rufus II, owned by Dr. Imogene P. Earle, Pandee Kennels, Laurel, Maryland, was the father of Ch. Pandee's Silver Mug owned by the late Sidney Joan Wellborn of Ah Sid Kennels in Clinton, Maryland. Silver Mug in turn sired Ch. Ah Sid the Dilletante.

lent bitches and important studs. With the expert medical advice of Dr. O'Brien as well as her infinite knowledge of Chows, past and present, her integrity and expert handling, combined with Dr. Earle's experience, professional knowledge of nutrition in the feeding and development of puppies and her integrity and know-how as a breeder, they should continue to produce Pandee Chows to rank among the best in the country.

On November 22, 1970, judge Owen Grindey, English Chow breeder and judge, awarded Pandee's Kenya Winners Dog at the Maryland Kennel Club, Baltimore. Kenya, sired by Ch. Pandee's Jubilee out of Pandee's Zip Orah, later became a champion. He is owned by Dr. Imogene Earle and handled here by Dr. JoAnne O'Brien.

PLAINACRE

Manota Stertz met her first Chow Chow when she was 16 years of age. She had her first kennel of Chows when she was in her twenties, but after only a few years she had to give it up at the time of her husband's death. In the early 1960's she began again. The Plainacre Kennels were in business once more.

She began with one good bitch, and her first litter produced Ch. Plainacre's Hoodlum Prince. She was then able to get a good linebred bitch from her own breeding in Plainacre's Belle Chien, and she became the foundation of the kennel. Belle has produced at least one champion in every litter; one litter saw three finish to their championships. Most of her success, Manota tells us, is from her breeding of

Ch. Pandee's Jubilee, owned by Dr. Imogene P. Earle and Dr. JoAnn O'Brien. Jubilee is a Best In Show winner and sire of many champions. He is pictured here winning Best of Breed at the Wallkill Kennel Club show in July, 1971 under judge Dr. Samuel Draper. A William P. Gilbert photo.

334

Ch. Charman's Fancy of Plain Acre, whelped in August, 1966. Bred by Manota Stertz, the sire was Ch. Beamer's Chummy Chinaman ex Plain Acre's Belle Chien.

Plain Acres Pat-Tee Kate, whelped in 1971, and bred and owned by Manota M. Stertz of the Plain Acres Kennels in Cincinnati, Ohio. Sire was Ch. Lakeview's Chum of Waulee *ex* Plain Acres Belle Chien.

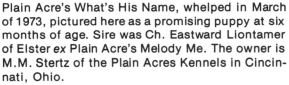

Ch. Shamrock's Klan-Cee, bred by Carol and Larry Kelly, and co-owned by Mary and Bob Weist and Manota Stertz. Whelped in September, 1972, the sire was Plain Acres Holy Smoke *ex* Don-Lee's Jubilee.

Headstudy of classic beauty features Plain Acre's Melody Me, bred by Manota M. Stertz of Cincinnati, Ohio. Melody was whelped in November, 1970.

Plain Acre's What's His Name, whelped in March of 1973, pictured here as a promising puppy at six months of age. Sire was Ch. Eastward Liontamer of Elster *ex* Plain Acre's Melody Me. The owner is M.M. Stertz of the Plain Acres Kennels in Cincinnati, Ohio.

#1 Chow Chow in the nation for 1973—Ch. Lakeview's Mr. Luc-Kee, bred by Manota M. Stertz. The sire was Ch. Beamer's Chummy Chinaman *ex* Plain Acre's Belle Chien. Luc-Kee has many Group and Best of Breed wins and three Bests in Show. Luc-Kee is pictured winning here under British judge Stanley Dangerfield. He was whelped in August, 1967. Co-owner and handler is David Reynolds.

Belle to Ch. Beamer's Chummy China-man. They both have the same sire, and their dams are litter sisters.

At Plainacre there are never more than seven Chows in the kennel at one time, and bitches are never bred more than once a year. They are now in the fifth generation of the quality breeding that Manota Stertz is proud of. Belle was retired from breeding with nine champions to her credit and many more on their way to their championships.

In the early 1970's Manota Stertz had two heart attacks and has been forced to curtail her breeding activities, but she was lucky enough to find Bob and Mary Wuest, right in Cincinnati, who have the same ideals as she has, and the latter are now co-owners of Plainacre Kennels and will carry on Manota Stertz's good work for many years to come.

RU-BIL

Ruby A. Van Over lists her kennel as Ru-bil Kennels, Home of Shang-Tai Chows, and it is situated in Highland, Michigan.

Plain Acres Holy Smoke, whelped in June, 1970 and photographed here at two years of age. Sired by Ch. Beamer's Chummy China-man ex Ch. Plain Acres Charman Twiggy. Owned by Carol Kelly, Shamrock Kennels, El Cajon, California.

Ruby acquired a Chow Chow of pet quality in 1955, and after that there never was another breed as far as she was concerned! When the original dog grew old, Ruby began to think about another Chow Chow to fill the gap once it was gone. At a dog show in Pontiac, Michigan, she met Betty-Mae Sewards, owner of the Ky-Lin kennels. It was Betty-Mae who captivated Ruby with the qualities of the breed and Ruby also got the "show bug!"

Shortly thereafter Ruby purchased two black bitches from Betty-Mae, Ky-Lyn's Snow Queen and Ky-Lin's Snow Flake, and finished Snow Queen. From this first champion Ruby has now finished 13 more! In 1968 she was presented with the Breeder of the Year Award.

By 1973, Ruby was maintaining a kennel of 15 bitches and 4 studs, three of which are champions. In her own words, Ruby claims that the kennel is operated with one factor in mind—to better the qualities of the Chow Chow!

Some of the top Chows since the kennel was originated in 1964 have been Ch. Rubilvan's Rebel of Ky-Lin, Ch. Shang-Tai's Sandy Prince, Ch. Shang-Tai's Silver and Gold, Ch. Shang-Tai's My Kind of Black, Ch. Shang-Tai's Ebony Empress and Ch. Shang-Tai's Frosty Linn.

SHANGLO

The Shanglo Kennels, located at Tigard, Oregon, came into being in 1933 when Wayne Summit and Mildred Fairchild decided to indulge their mutual interest in the Chow Chow breed.

Over the years there have been several Chow Chows with the Shanglo prefix, and to date they are most proud of Ch. Shanglo's Kodee, Shanglo's Choo-Choo, Shanglo's Jill and Shanglo's Prince. Two brood bitches are also particularly outstanding and something for them to be proud of. They are Shanglo's Black Magic and You Two's Bijou.

SAN KEE

Dorothea Rademaker has been a breeder and exhibitor of Chow Chows since 1930 and has finished several champions over the years. Her dogs are also well known for their marvelous dispositions.

Some of the top show dogs she has bred or owned over the years are Ch. InKee II, Ch. San Kee Xoodan Sensation, Ch. Chang Shi Dixie Debutante, and Ch. San Kee Papa's Sweet Stuff. Her top stud dogs which produced so well for the San Kee name were Yap Sam of Waving Willows and San Kee Majon GG Shen of Mount Air.

The San Kee Kennels are in Teaneck, New Jersey, where a large wooden sign featuring a Chow Chow identifies the home site of the lovely San Kee Chow Chows.

SHAMROCK

Larry and Carol Kelly of El Cajon, California both came from families where there have always been Chow Chows around. . . when they were married they finally acquired a Chow bitch of their own and were bitten by the "show bug." As Carol puts it, "Then we were bitten by the worst bug of all, the quest for the *perfect* Chow Chow through breeding."

In order to try to accomplish this they began a three-year study of the Chow Chows of the past. They studied pedigrees and genetics and set out to meet as many of the Chow Chow people as they could to broaden their knowledge of the breed. Their search included the physical health and problems in the breed as well. The Kellys state that if they had not made so many good friends in the breed during their research they might have fallen by the wayside, since the study was so vast and far-reaching.

Since the early 1970's they have managed to acquire the stock they desired for their breeding program, and their puppies are now beginning to reflect some of the characteristics they consider to be ideal. Their puppies show massive head and body type and a profusion of coat and good movement. They reaffirm their dedication to keep the breed free of hip dysplasia.

SOO-Z

Suzy Anderson is the owner of the Soo-Z Kennel in Santa Rosa, California. Suzy first saw a Chow Chow at the home of a friend and decided on the spot it was her dream dog. It was 1963 when she had the opportunity of getting a pick of the litter puppy from Lee McDermott and purchased Soo-Z's Wong Dai Ming. So loving and devoted was her Mr. Wong that she also acquired his litter brother for her sister, Laura Becker. It was Laura actually who got involved in dog training classes and also made her Shar-Li a champion as well.

These were followed by Shanglo's Soo-Z's Dar-Lin. She was the foundation bitch of the Soo-Z's Haven kennel, and a show dog as well. At 6 months and 17 days of age, she won a 5-point major from the puppy class under judge Ramona Van Court and was also Best Opposite Sex to her grandfather, Ch. Starcrest Spy of Poppyland. She has many Bests of Breed to her credit. She went on to win her championship in 1968, and was always owner-handled. She was bred to Ch. Plainacre's Wun Dae Dream, and two in this litter became champions. One of them, Ch. Wun Dae Dream's Kikko Jade, was #6 Chow Chow in the nation's Top Ten the first year he was shown by owner Marilyn King. Dar-Lin is

Ch. Shamrock's Golden Nugget as a three-month-old puppy. Owned and bred by the Larry Kellys of El Cajon, California. Whelped in November, 1971; the sire was Ch. Don-Lee's Prophet *ex* Kelly's Coco Chanel Pauska.

Ch. Plain Acres Hoodlum Prince, a magnificent winner out of Manota Stertz' first litter of Chow Chows and her first champion. The sire was Beamer's Lin Yu Tang ex Beamer's Scarlet Imp. The litter was whelped in 1964. The Plain Acre Kennels are in Cincinnati, Ohio.

still producing quality puppies to carry on the Soo-Z line of Chow Chows.

Suzy Anderson keeps her kennel small, with just three bitches, and is proud of the mark she is making in the breed. She keeps active in the breed as Recording Secretary of the Northern California Chow Chow Club and is also a member of the parent club. She also belongs to the Mensona All Breed Club.

SCOTCHOW

Joan M. Hannephin started her Scotchow Kennels in 1964; they are located at Wheeling, West Virginia. Over the years she has owned, bred and shown many magnificent Chow Chows and is extremely dedicated to the breed.

The first to come to mind are Ch. Scotchow Liontamer Louise, Ch. Scotchow Liontamer Frankee, Ch. Scotchow Sum Wun of Lakeview and Ch. Scotchow Liontamer Foggydew, all names which we know to be winners or among the top Chow Chows in the country.

Joan Hannephin is particularly proud of her stud force at the Scotchow Kennels. Ch. Scotchow Liontamer Leo and Ch. Scotchow Home By Dark are two which are reproducing themselves admirably. Her brood bitches, Ch. Scotchow Sing Along, Ch. Scotchow Madam Queen and Ch. Scotchow Samantha, are producing puppies which will keep Scotchow Chow Chows in the show ring and winning in the future.

Ch. Scotchow Sweet Sum Wun, whelped January, 1965, bred and owned by Joan M. Hannephin of Wheeling, West Virginia, is pictured here winning under judge Virgil Johnson.

The glorious Ch. Scotchow Liontamer Louise, owned by Joan Hannephin of the Scotchow Kennels and sired by the all-time great Chow Ch. Eastward Liontamer of Elster. Photographed by Tauskey.

Ch. Pandee's Alpha Sing with owner Joel Marston and judge Frances Holland at a California dog show.

A new-born litter of mixed colors at Starcrest Kennels in S Valley, California.

Ch. Scotchow Sunshine Boy, bred and owned by Joan M. Hannephin of Silver Ho Farm, Wheeling, West Virginia. The sire was Ch. Scotchow Home By Dark *ex* Scotchow Liontamer Butt-R-Cup. Samuel Draper is the breeder of Butt-R-Cup.

Ch. Scotchow Liontamer Foggy Dew is pictured winning under judge William Kendrick. Bred by Samuel Draper and Jean Hetherington. Foggy Dew is owned by Joan M. Hannephin of Wheeling, West Virginia.

Not yet eight months old at the time this photo was taken, Scotchow Prime Time wins a Non-Sporting Group under judge William Ackland. Peter Green handles this marvelous puppy for owner Joan M. Hannephin of Wheeling, West Virginia.

Joel Marston's Starcrest Sterling Silver, bred at his Starcrest Kennels in Sun Valley, California.

A Chow Chow youngster from Joel and June Marston's Starcrest Kennels in Sun Valley, California.

Ch. Starcrest Witch Away, bred by Gerald Fink and owned by Joel Marston of Sun Valley, California, whom she is pictured with here. Whelped in June, 1965, the sire was Ch. Starcrest Richard the Lion *ex* Ch. Indian Star's Yu Lui. The judge, Mrs. Elsie Frederick, well-known Chow breeder, awards Witch Away Best of Opposite Sex from the Novice Class in Santa Ana, April 30, 1967.

Handler Dr. Nancy Lenfestey poses Joan M. Hannephin's Ch. Scotchow Am I Blu. Bred by the Linnchow Kennels, Blu was sired by Ch. Pandee's Simmonson Linnchow *ex* Ginny Tu Linnchow and was whelped on November 5, 1964.

The glamorous movie star Marilyn Maxwell was on hand to present the Best in Show trophies to Joel Marston's black Chow Chow, Ch. Pandee's Alpha Sing, handled here by Frank Sabella.

The two Marston children with one of their favorite Chow Chow puppies from their parents' Starcrest Kennels in Sun Valley, California.

Ch. Starcrest Richard the Lion photographed at 6 months of age with owner Joel Marston and judge Palmer Boustead, a famous old-timer in Chows.

Mack the Black, photographed at ten weeks of age. Owners are the Starcrest Kennels of Joel Marston in Sun Valley, California.

Ch. Starcrest Mr. Christopher, fantastically coated Chow Chow owned by Joel Marston of Sun Valley, California. Mr. Christopher is a multiple Group winner and an important sire.

Ch. Starcrest Dandy Lion as a puppy; bred by Joel Marston and owned by James M. Pierson and G. Don Foster, Justamere Kennels.

Little live lion dogs line up with two figurine lions. Puppies bred by Joel Marston, Starcrest Kennels, Sun Valley, California.

Photographed in August, 1970, the two-month-old Wide Track Bummer and the one-year-old Tali with Lucia Hester of Fort Worth, Texas. Bred by the Tag-El Chow Chow Ranch in Oklahoma.

Ch. Starcrest Dandy Lion, born in 1970, was sired by Ch. Starcrest Mr. Christopher *ex* Starcrest Lemon Twist. He is co-owned by Don Foster and Jim Pierson of the Justamere Kennels, Monrovia, California.

A litter of five Chow Chows bred at the kennel of Joel and June Marston in Sun Valley, California.

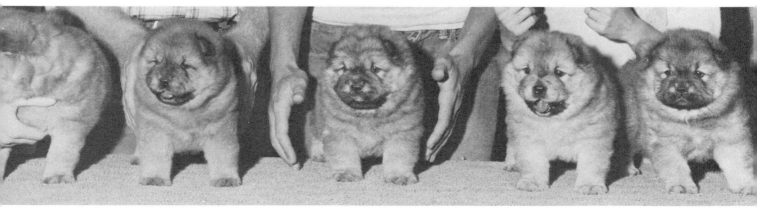

Starcrest Soo Ve-Ner pictured winning a 4-point major as Best of Winners at the
1973 Little Rock, Arkansas Kennel Club show under judge Mrs. Carl B. Cass. Bred
by June Marston, Soo Ve-Ner is sired by Ch. Starcrest Mr. Christopher *ex* Starcrest
Lemon Twist. Owned and handled by Evelyn E. Carter of the Tag-El Chow Chow
Ranch in McLoud, Oklahoma.

TAG-EL

Thomas and Evelyn Carter owned the Tag-El Chow Chow Ranch in McLoud, Oklahoma. The Carters had an unregistered Chow Chow bitch which they had raised along with their sons as their introduction to the breed. At about the same time the Chow had to be put to sleep, Tom Carter had to have serious surgery, and they decided another Chow Chow would be perfect as therapy for him. They purchased Keiki King Carter, a black Chow, through an ad in the newspapers. Shortly thereafter they purchased Princess Star Carter from W.R. Davis, and once they started showing they got interested in breeding as well.

A move to the country in the early 1970's found them building their own kennel a bit at a time, where each Chow has his own 15 x 25 foot run and his own house. A main kennel house is what they are planning next as their interest in breeding good Chows continues to grow.

Ch. Starcrest By Jupiter O'Sharbo, bred by Joel Marston and owned by Robert and Sharon Gilb of Round Lake, Illinois. The sire was Starcrest Jupiter of Pandee *ex* Starcrest Witch Away.

Judge Erica Huggins awards Best of Winners to Ch. Tag-El's Little Rock at the 1972 Oklahoma City Kennel Club show in March, 1972. Whelped in November, 1970, Little Rock was sired by Ch. Mi-Pao's Batoe Ketjil *ex* Ghat's Little Doll Caroline. Bred by James B. Murphy; the owner-handler is Evelyn E. Carter of McLoud, Oklahoma. Twomey photograph.

Typical Chow Chow puppy with personality-plus! It's the future Ch. Starcrest Autumn Haze Tiawin, a cinnamon bitch owned by A.J. Overturf of Dallas, Texas.

TAMARIN

The Tamarin Kennels, owned by Prudence Baxter in California, is located in Marin County, adjacent to San Francisco Bay. It is a small kennel in an area which allows access to many dog shows!

Prudence Baxter maintains about eight dogs; all but two are champions, and two have earned their obedience titles. Since 1968, however, she has finished six bench champions and five obedience titlists.

Prudence is particularly interested in the black and blue Chow Chows and will concentrate on these colors in her breeding program. Her lovely blue dog Ch. Starcrest Twilight Idol has many Bests of Breed and a Group Fourth to date. Her other Group winner is Ch. Tamarin Midnight Idol. Both of these are out of her foundation brood bitch, Ch. Pandee's Katrina, C.D.

Prudence declares she breeds for intelligence and alertness as well as conformation, since she is interested in providing the capability of the Chow Chow in obedience work. Her Ch. Hung Jai Lin Fa is a Canadian C.D. and the only U.D. Chow Chow in the history of the breed. Prudence Baxter hopes that her Tamarin name will be known and respected for having intelligent as well as beautiful Chow Chows, all of them owner-handled and trained.

As of the first half of 1974, her Ch. Tamarin Midnight Idol had won his first all-breed Best in Show, with 9 Bests of Breed, 1 Group First, 3 Group Seconds and two Group Thirds added to his show record. Midnight Idol became the top-winning Chow in the U.S. in 1974.

The authors are particularly grateful to her for having supplied us with so much pertinent information about Chow Chows in obedience.

Ch. Starcrest Black Sapphire, owned by Joel and June Marston of Sun Valley, California. Whelped in March, 1971, Sapphire is pictured here with Joel Marston winning at a show during the 1970's. Her sire is Ch. Starcrest Mr. Christopher and her dam Starcrest Lemon Twist.

Ch. Pandee's Katrina, C.D., shown finishing her title with owner-trainer-handler Prudence Baxter, Tamarin Kennels, San Anselmo, California. The sire was Ch. Pandee's Jubilee *ex* Pandee's Zip Orah.

Prudence Baxter of San Anselmo, California, owner of the Tamarin Kennels and two six-week-old blue Chow Chow puppies, Starcrest Twilight Idol and litter sister. Idol later became a champion.

Ch. Tsang-Po's Ah Fu photographed winning at a show in 1971. Bred and owned by the H. Allens, Lubbock, Texas. Judge is Dorothy Nickles.

Tsang-Po's Chia Pao pictured winning a four-point major at eight months of age under judge Edd Bivin at the North Texas Chow Chow Club. Pao is owned by Ed and Martha Henne of Jackson, Mississippi and was bred by the Ed Norths, also of Jackson.

TSANG-PO (The Allens)

Hal and Marie Allen (now of Lubbock, Texas) rented a house in 1942 and offered to take care of the Chow and the cat that lived there. The owner doubted whether the dog would take to the new tenants, but the Allens offered to give it a try and found the Chow was agreeable to their family life. The Allens tried to buy Teddy when they were transferred to another state, but the owners would not sell. As soon as they reached Texas, they set about trying to get themselves a Chow. They finally found a Chow, a little red bitch which they purchased for fifty dollars, which was a good price in 1942. Nikki arrived in an apple crate, and though they knew nothing about bloodlines, they later found out she was a granddaughter of the Best in Show Chow Jo Jo Hansen.

The following spring when Nikki was just six months old they went to their first show. They didn't win, of course, but their learning process had begun! After this first venture they never missed a dog show within a 500-mile radius. Nikki was bred to Ch. Miltonberger's Toffee Jo in 1945 and had one puppy. In 1946 she was bred again to her grandsire, Jo Jo Hansen, and puppies from this mating produced champions in America and Canada.

A heart attack meant a slowing down for the Tsang-Po kennel, but after a year of rest the kennel was sold and Hal opened a grooming shop. He also judged, did lots of showing, and continued to breed on a smaller scale, "for disposition and beauty." This had become their slogan. Over the years they have bred over 50 champions, though now they limit their breeding to just one litter a year, though the Allens' foster daughter, Mrs. Pat North, is carrying on the kennel name along with her husband, Dr. Edward North. The Allens' Ch. Tsang-Po's Kwai Chy was breed bitch of the year in 1969, and the Dan Fredericks own Tsang-Po's Pa-Li-Cho Li-Qu-Tu, a Best in Show winner and #10 of the top ten Chows in the nation in 1970.

Ch. Mi-Pao's Betara, owned by the Tsang-Po Kennels of Dr. and Mrs. Ed North, Jr., of Jackson, Mississippi. Judge is Maxwell Riddle. An Earl Graham photo.

On the way towards her championship, Ch. Tsang-Po's Ming Lee is shown winning at the Pensacola, Florida Kennel Club show in October, 1970. Ming is owned by Dr. and Mrs. Edward North of Jackson, Mississippi, and is being shown by Mrs. North.

Ch. Tsang-Po's Kwai Chy was Chow Chow brood bitch of the year in 1969 producing 11 champions out of 20 puppies. Bred by the Allen's at their Tsang-Po Kennels in Lubbock, Texas. "Lady" is a celebrity in the Chow fancy. Hal Allen is the owner-handler.

Dr. and Mrs. Ed North, Jr.'s Tsang-Po's Chu Hien Tsu, pictured winning at a show in 1951 under judge Anthony Stamm. Twomey photo.

Magnificent headstudy of Dr. and Mrs. Ed North's Ch. Tsang-Po's Chu Hien Tsu.

Kibitzer! Dr. Ed North gets a cold stare unless he shares the "chow"! This glorious red puppy grew up to be Tsang-Po's Ming Lee. She is three months old in this photo.

TSANG-PO (The Norths)

Tsang-Po was originally the kennel name of the Harold Allens, spanning 40 years in Chows. Since 1969 it has been used by Dr. and Mrs. Edward North of Jackson, Mississippi.

Pat North owned a Chow Chow as a child, back in the days when Chows were not very "popular," and, as a result, someone shot her "teddy bear." Her father had wanted to replace the dog, but there just weren't any Chows in the South at that time. In 1969, however, Pat did get another Chow Chow from the Hal Allens. Pat's husband "flipped" over their Ming Lee.

Shortly after the arrival of Ming Lee, Dr. Edward and Pat North received a call from Hal Allen, and he asked them if they would like to have a black male to play with Ming Lee. Two weeks later, Tsang-Po's Linn's FuYi arrived. This was the first black Chow Chow either of them had ever seen, and they loved it. This was the beginning of their serious endeavors in the breed, and the Chow Chow is now the only breed they own. At the time of the arrival of Ming Lee they had thirteen Great Danes and two Saint Bernards!

Since the early days in Chows the Norths have finished six champions, and many of those they have sold have also made their mark in the breed. Ming Lee produced many champions for them as their foundation brood bitch. Some of them are Ch. Tsang-Po's Chu Hien Tsu, Ch. Mi-Pao's Betara, Ch. Tsang-Po's So-Pai-Chee, Ch. Tsang-Po's Linn FuYi, Ch. Tsang-Po's Chu Fu Chu, Ch. Tsang-Po's Ai Tse of Starcrest, Ch. Tsang-Po's Lil Bit O' Starcrest, Ch. Tsang-Po's Chia Pao and Ch. Tsang-Po's Christy.

Ch. Tsang-Po's Lil Bit O'Starcrest, pictured at ten months of age. Breeder-owners are Dr. and Mrs. Ed North, Jr. of Jackson, Mississippi. Twomey photo.

Ch. Tsang-Po Yum Yum, bred and owned by the Hal Allens of the Tsang-Po Kennels in Lubbock, Texas.

A twelve-week-old Tsang-Po puppy with two visiting friends, at the home of Dr. and Mrs. Edward North, Jr.

Ch. Ghat's Canton Mandarin, bred by Hal Allen, Tsang-Po Kennels, Lubbock, Texas. This is a reproduction of an oil painting owned by the breeders. Sire was the great Ghat.

A real black beauty! Tsang-Po's Linn's Fuyi, owned by Dr. and Mrs. Edward North, Jr. of Jackson, Mississippi. Photo by Twomey.

Ch. Tsang-Po's So-Pai-Chee owned by Dr. and Mrs. Edward North, Jr. pictured winning at a recent show with Mrs. North handling. Charles Nelson is the judge. Twomey photo.

Tsang-Po's Autumn Nocturne, C.D., bred by the Allens and owned by Shirley Nelson. She was whelped in November, 1968.

Ch. Tsang Po's Travlin Man Carchow, bred by Dr. Edward R. North and owned by Bill and Dorothy Carr of Alexandria, Louisiana. The Travlin Man is pictured here winning the Breed, after which he went on to Non-Sporting Group Third at the 1973 Meri-Miss Kennel Club Show. Breed judge was Dorothy Nickles, pictured here. Group win was under judge Alfred Treen. This sensational win was made from the classes with a five-point major.

Ch. Peng Pei-Pi Li-Ku-Tu finished her championship at eight months of age from the puppy class and had a Best in Match win over 200 puppies at six months of age. Owned and handled by Mrs. Mariam Frederick of Baton Rouge, Louisiana. Breeders were Mr. Hal Allen and K.H. Harter.

WU SAN

Mary T. MacEachern and her late husband, Russell, have owned Chow Chows since 1938, but it wasn't until 1949 that they formed Wu San Kennels in Sodus, New York and began an active breeding program. When asked how the MacEacherns first got into Chows, Mary replied, "A man owed us money and the only collateral he had was a Chow puppy, which we took. We've loved the Chow ever since and have finished fourteen champions!"

Perhaps it was Mary's greatest thrill when in February, 1957 she handled her great Chow Bermudian and American Champion Ky-Lin's Midas in the Westminster Non-Sporting Group after he had won Best of Breed under Miss Kathleen Staples, noted breed authority. Midas had been handled in the breed by Ralph Hellum, kennel manager of Mrs. David Wagstaff's Ledgelands' Kennels in Tuxedo Park, New York, and in the group by Mrs. Mac-Eachern.

Born in 1955, Midas was acquired from Betty-Mae Seward's Ky-Lin Kennels in Indiana and became one of the country's top winning Chows.

Another fine show Chow at Wu San was Ch. Wan Ho Folly and Ch. Wu San's Velveteen. Wu San's best studs were Wu San's Mr. Thunder, a homebred, and Ch. Wu San's Frostee Sno'man. Wu San's Dark Pantomine and Wu San's Tinker Belle, daughter of Ch. Wu San's Me Wun Two Sun and granddaughter of Ch. Ky-Lin's Midas, were two outstanding brood bitches.

Recently Mary MacEachern purchased a beautiful young bitch of the Dre-Don, Liontamer, Fa-Ci bloodlines and believes she will turn out well for showing and breeding. Her friends hope so, since they all say, "No one loves the Chow Chow more than Mary."

Ch. Wu San's Frostee Sno'Man pictured going Best of Winners on the way to his championship under judge Mrs. Lynwood Walton at a 1973 North Country Kennel Club show. Handled by owner Mrs. Mary T. MacEachern of Sodus, New York. Klein photo.

Wu San's Ramo and Comet at Mary MacEachern's Wu San Kennels in Sodus, New York.

Ch. Scotchow Sing Along, an important bitch bred and owned by Joan M. Hannephin of Wheeling, West Virginia. Sing Along was whelped January 6, 1965. Dr. Nancy Lenfestey is the handler.

7. THE CHOW CHOW IN CANADA

As the dog world grows smaller, thanks to modern transportation, the possibilities of enlarging our dog show world grow bigger all the time. More and more Chow Chows are winning both their American and Canadian championships, more and more Chow Chows are being shipped far distances for stud service, and the communication between breeders has added immeasurably to better Chow Chows, all of which further endears the breed to the dog fancy.

Canadian Chow Chows have been setting records, and kennels are spreading across Canada as interest in the breed reaches across the country. We present here a cross-section of some of the leading Canadian kennels and their breeding and showing plans which insure the future of the breed in that country.

This beautiful headstudy is of Canadian and American Champion Foo H'Sing Mister Linn Wu, whom his owners call "Buda." He was the top-winning Chow in Canada in 1971, second top-winning Non-Sporting dog in 1971, and top-winning puppy, all breeds, in Canada in 1970. He is co-owned by Mr. and Mrs. Herb Williams and Mr. John C. Frederick Peddie, BuDynasty Kennels, Toronto, Canada.

BUDYNASTY

Joan and Herbert Williams and John C. Frederick Peddie of Toronto, Ontario have been raising Chows since 1963. Formerly their kennel was called "Lidice," but in 1973 the name was changed to BuDynasty, a combination of two of their well-known Chows, Canadian and American Ch. Foo H'Sing's Mr. Linn Wu (called "Buda") and Minhow Masquerade (called "Dyna").

Mr. Linn Wu was one of the top Chows in Canada in 1970 and 1971, winning many Bests of Breed and eleven Groups. He was Best in Show at the 9th Annual Chow Chow Fanciers of Canada Specialty on September 18, 1971 in Toron-

to under Dr. Samuel Draper. He also won two Bests in Show, all breeds, in Canada. Mr. Linn Wu's son Canadian and American Ch. Mi-Tu's Han-Su-Shang, bred by Pat Robb of Canada, has the distinction of winning Best of Breed at the Westminster Kennel Club in February, 1974 from the Open Dog class, defeating all the Specials!

One of the most honored and titled of present-day Canadian Chows is Canadian and American Ch. Lidice's Ko Ko, C.D.; he won five Groups in Canada and the National Canadian Chow Specialty Show under Mrs. Ann Beamer, noted breeder from the United States. Ko Ko is co-owned by Mr. and Mrs. Herb Williams and Mr. John C. Frederick Peddie, all of Toronto, Canada, where they co-own BuDynasty Kennels.

The judge was Joseph Faigel, and Shang's handler was his co-owner, Fred Peddie. By May, 1974 Shang had won 15 Non-Sporting Groups in Canada and four Bests in Show, all breeds, including the Sportsman's Show in Toronto, two Ottawa shows, and one at Chatham, Ontario. He is well on his way to becoming top Canadian dog (all breeds) for 1974. Shang also won a Best in Show, all breeds, in June, 1974 in Wisconsin after having gone B.O.B. at a Chow Specialty held with the all-breed event.

BuDynasty's top brood bitches are Minhow Masquerade and Mi-Tu's Han Su Linn.

The philosophy of Herb and Joan Williams and Fred Peddie is to show as much as possible in both the United States and Canada and to promote friendly relations between the American and Canadian

Ch. Mi-Tu's Han-Su Shang goes Best of Breed at the annual Chow Chow Fanciers of Canada Specialty Show in Toronto, September, 1973. The judge is Canadian all-rounder Thomas Joel. Shang is owned by Herbert Williams, handling, and John C. Frederick Peddie, both of Toronto.

Westminster 1972 is the setting for this photo of Lidice's Ki Ki, left, Winners Bitch; Lidice's Ko Ko, center, Winners Dog, and Canadian and American Ch. Foo H'Sing's Mister Linn Wu, Reserve Winner's Dog, all under judge Mrs. Florence Broadhurst of Woodside, California. Ki Ki and Ko Ko went on to win the Best Brace in the Non-Sporting Group under Heywood Hartley. All three Chows are co-owned by Mr. and Mrs. Herb Williams and Mr. John C. Frederick Peddie, BuDynasty Kennels, Toronto, Canada, who is kneeling on the right. Mrs. Broadhurst was a prominent Chow breeder and judge.

Starcrest Surmount at 15 months of age, pictured here winning Second in the Group at Portland under judge Maxwell Riddle. He is handled by Pat Tripp for owner Mrs. Barbara Kristoff, Champad Kennels, Toronto, Canada.

breeders. These three enthusiastic Chowists work tirelessly in the Chow Chow Fanciers of Canada in order to help put on annually one of the most beautiful shows anywhere.

BuDynasty strives in their breeding program for outstandingly friendly temperaments, Chow Chows that can be called "people dogs." From all indications our breed is indeed fortunate to have such ardent, loyal, hard-working partisans to promote Chow Chows in both the United States and Canada.

CHAMPAD

Champad is the kennel name representing the Chow Chows owned by Mrs. Barbara Kristoff, Toronto, Canada. Mrs. Kristoff got into Chows late in the 1960's. She is the owner of American and Canadian Champions Starcrest Peek-A-Boo of Ho-San and Starcrest Surmount, her stud dog. There are two other Chow Chows at Champad at present bearing the Champad prefix. They are Champad's Lam Sam Man Doy and Champad's Soo Li of Nahanni.

American Ch. Starcrest Peek-A-Blue of Ho-San, presently owned by Mrs. Barbara Kristoff of Toronto, Canada, owner of the Champad Kennels. Peek-A-Blue is pictured with her former owner-breeder, June Marston of the well-known Starcrest Kennels in Sun Valley, California. The judge is Mr. Harold Lee, a Chow breeder. Her sire was American Ch. Starcrest Matinee Idol *ex* American Ch. Starcrest Bewitched of Ho-San.

Champad's Lam Sam Man Doy, a six-month-old blue bitch puppy bred by Mrs. Barbara Kristoff and owned by her. Her sire was Ch. Sumi's Chimney Sweep *ex* Chu Chui Jen, both owned by Mrs. Kristoff of Toronto, Canada.

Ch. Chi-Kwang's Han Su-Chang, whelped in May of 1967, and owned by Karin H. Hammerich of Ontario, Canada. The sire was Foo H'Sing's Han Fei Tzu *ex* Chi-Kwang's Chinky-Ling-Su.

Champad's Soo Li of Nahanni, a seven-month-old black bitch bred by Mrs. Barbara Kristoff of Toronto, and owned by Mr. and Mrs. Graham Stalder. Her sire is American and Canadian Ch. Starcrest Surmount *ex* Champad's Lam Sam Man Doy.

· CHI-KWANG

The Chi-Kwang Kennels of Mrs. M.J. (Joey) Nattrass are located in Pickering, Ontario. They were established in 1946 and were originally in Toronto.

Chi-Kwang had the honor to breed, own and handle the first Chow Chow in Canada to win the award of Best Puppy in Show, all breeds.

Stud dogs at Chi-Kwang were Ch. Fum of Junggwaw and Ch. Foo H'Sing's Fu Ting, litter brother to Mrs. Wiesman's famous Fu Tu. The brood bitches were Chi-Kwang's Han Su-Mei and Ch. Gypsy of Junggwaw.

FOO H'SING

Mrs. Madge P. Wiesman's Foo H'Sing Kennels were established in 1957 in Vancouver, British Columbia.

In 1957 Mrs. Weisman acquired Canadian Ch. Chi-Kwang's Su-Ling from Mrs. Joey Nattrass. Soon after, a black Chow named Cheetah of Kinshan was imported from England. Unfortunately Cheetah died at two years of age, a bitter blow to Mrs. Wiesman's plans. In 1961 Mrs. Wiesman imported Minhow Miss Sadie Wu, and in April, 1963 Sadie Wu whelped six sons. One of these sons was Canadian Ch. Foo H'Sing's Fu Tu, who went on to estab-

Canadian Ch. Minhow Miss Sadie Wu, owned by Mrs. Madge P. Wiesman of Vancouver, British Columbia, Canada. This bitch had many honors as one of the outstanding Chows in Canada.

Ch. Foo H'Sing's Fu Tu, whelped in 1963. Owned by Mrs. P. Garwood of Canada. The sire was Ch. Norton's Half Moon ex Ch. Minhow Miss Sadie Wu.

Chi-Kwang's Han Su Mei, born in May of 1967 and sired by Foo H'Sing Han Fei Tzu ex Chi-Kwang's Chinky-Ling-Su. Her daughter, Mi-Tu's Gem-Sing, is seen in the background. Owners: Mr. and Mrs. R. Robb of the Mi-Tu Kennels in Aurora, Ontario, Canada.

Ch. Foo H'Sing's Fu Ting, whelped in April, 1963 and owned by Mrs. Madge P. Wiesman of Vancouver, British Columbia, Canada. The sire was Ch. Norton's Half Moon ex Ch. Minhow Miss Sadie Wu.

369

Hi-Bo's Adiraja, male Chow Chow sired by Rangan vom Kempken *ex* Mi-Tan's Istri-Ganti. Owned by F.P.A. Odenkirchen, Mi-Pao Kennels, Ontario, Canada.

Foo H'Sing's Mister Linn Wu at just six weeks of age. He was born in November, 1968 and was sired by Ch. Minnhow Mirza *ex* Ch. Minnhow Miss Sadie Wu. Owned by Mrs. Madge P. Wiesman, Foo H'Sing Kennels, Vancouver, B.C., Canada. Later on this Chow was sold to Mr. and Mrs. Herbert Williams of Toronto, Canada.

Mr. Herb Williams looks pleased as he accepts the ribbons and trophy signifying that his American and Canadian Ch. Foo H'Sing Mister Linn Wu has won the Group Specialty at the Club VI Non-Sporting Specialty under Jean Lepley in 1970. Mister Linn Wu is co-owned by Mr. and Mrs. Herbert Williams and Mr. John C. Frederick Peddie, BuDynasty Kennels, Toronto, Canada.

Ch. Foo H'Sing's Fu-Tu, a history-making Chow Chow in Canada, is photographed here at nine and a half years of age. He was whelped in April, 1963 and is owned by Mrs. P. Young, Caesarea, Ontario, Canada.

Hanchow's Tar-Baby, born October 31, 1965, was sired by Ch. Ting Hows Rum and Coke *ex* Brubara's Tien Rung. Owner, Mrs. Hanna Kallus-Kuester of the Hanchow Kennels in Kingston, Ontario, Canada.

Ch. Minnhow Miss Sadie Wu, the greatest Canadian Chow producer and show winner in the history of the breed in that country. Her sire was the British Champion Minnhow Edward of Junggwaw and her dam was British Champion Minnhow Gem of U'Kwong.

lish records for the breed. He was the top-winning Chow Chow from 1964 through 1967 and again in 1969. He was the first Chow Chow in Canada in twenty years to win a Best in Show. He won another Best in Show later in 1967.

From a more recent litter whelped by Sadie Wu another great Chow Chow, Canadian and American Ch. Foo H'Sing's Mr. Linn Wu, has attained success. He has since bettered Fu Tu's record by winning three Bests in Show in 1971.

In recognition of Sadie Wu's contribution to the breed through her excellent and successful progeny, the Chow Chow Fanciers of Canada dedicated their 9th Annual Specialty Show to the late Ch. Minhow Miss Sadie Wu. It was an unforgettable honor to both her and Mrs. Wiesman. The juge at this important event was Dr. Samuel Draper, co-author of this book. At the club dinner in 1969 Neil McEachern made the following statement in regard to Sadie Wu. He said in part:

"The Chow we honor tonight combines three characteristics: quality, quality in her descendants and personality. She is, unhappily, no longer with us, but I consider it a rare privilege to have known her well throughout most of her life. Ladies and gentlemen, the name which will appear on the President's Trophy for 1969 will be Ch. Minhow Miss Sadie Wu, a truly outstanding Chow. Before I call Joey Nattrass up here to accept the trophy on behalf of Gem's owner, Mrs. Madge Wiesman, I'd like to tell you about Gem's record.

"Gem herself appears on these trophies six times and her descendants 14 times. Between 1963 and 1968, Gem and her descendants captured 20 of our 36 awards. In 1963, Stan Whitmore judged our first Specialty Show and awarded Gem Best of Opposite Sex. We held our seventh Specialty Show last fall, and of the 14 top awards over these years, Best of Breed and Best of Opposite Sex, Gem and her descendants captured eleven.

"Since 1964, when the first of Gem's sons earned his Canadian championship, I have been able to count 50 titles awarded to Chows; 14 of these went to Gem's sons,

grandsons and granddaughters, and great-grandsons and great-granddaughters. I think it is truly remarkable that 28% of all Chows earning a conformation title in Canada since 1964 stem in one way or another from this splendid imported bitch.

"Looking around the room tonight, I see only one or two people who have not at one time owned one of Gem's puppies, or a more distant descendant. The rest of us, if we were lucky enough to know Gem herself, often recognize her endearing ways in our own dogs.

"Ladies and gentlemen, I salute Ch. Minhow Miss Sadie Wu, a truly outstanding Chow Chow, a Chow who will live in our memory for many, many years."

HANCHOW

In 1965 Mrs. Hanna Kallus Kuester established her Hanchow Kennels in Kingston, Ontario. It is a small kennel and at present the Chow Chows in residence are either too young or too old to be in the show ring. Mrs. Kuester will have to wait for a while before she returns.

Mrs. Kuester has had Chow Chows since 1943, when she purchased her first one from the Chang-Shi Kennels. Although World War II influenced Chow Chow breedings, Mrs. Kuester did manage to acquire this Adjutant offspring, from the Chang-Shi Kennels, while in Germany.

When she moved to Canada in 1951 she began to look around for a companion for her Chow, and bought Ting How's Rum and Coke. Rummy was followed by Brubara's Tien Rung. Soon afterwards Rummy's mother, Currie's Zapata, was looking for a home and ended up at Hanchow. From that moment on Hanna Kuester was entangled in the joys and sorrows of Chow breeding, showing and raising, as she puts it.

While professionally occupied as a language teacher, Hanna Kuester insists that the Chow Chows are still strictly a hobby, but they take up every moment of her free time.

Ch. Merah van de Loumi Hoeve, a Chow Chow bitched owned by the Mi-Pao Kennels in Ontario, Canada.

You-Two's Commander Black, sired by National and International Ch. Kwang-Wu of Liang-Ming-Keou *ex* Mi-Pao's Poetri. Owner, F.P.A. Odenkirchen, Mi-Pao Kennels, Waterdown, Ontario, Canada.

KEBA-YAN

While Mrs. Patricia Young and her husband have been interested in the breed for over a decade, they started becoming active in breeding Chow Chows only in 1973 with their first litter. Their Ch. Foo H'Sing's Fu Tu is one of their show dogs, and Mi-Tu's He-Shing is their brood bitch. Their male is called Yangtze, and the bitch is called Keba, and it is the combination of parts of their call names which form the Keba-Yan kennel prefix they intend to use in their breeding program.

Keba-Yan is located in Ontario.

374

MI-PAO

The Mi-Pao Kennels of F.P.A. Oden-kirchen are located in Waterdown, Ontario, and were established in the late 1950's.

The late Mrs. W.S.M. Kloos-Dixon started her Woe-Kau Kennels on December 11, 1939 and originated the present Dutch Chow Chow Club on October 26, 1941. As the grandmother of Minnie Odenkirchen-Kloos, she is indirectly responsible for the creation of the Mi-Pao Kennels. Based directly on Dutch and Belgian—and indirectly on English bloodlines—credit is given to the Chang-Shi, Kou-Ling, Mongolie, Tongelreep, Loumi-Hoeve and Majodo Kennels. First acquisitions were concentrated on descendants of National and International Ch. Kou-Ling Xolsky, Nat. and Int. Ch. Emperor van de Tongelreep, Ch. Ki-Dong King and Za-Chou van Majodo. The common ancestor to these dogs was Chang-Shi Noch-Ka, a dog linebred to Ch. Rochow Adjutant, who is unequaled in his influence in the breed, according to Mr. Odenkirchen.

With the acquisition in 1964 of Int. Ch. Chang-Shi Hong-Kwong and I'Ming van de Tongelreep, the Noch-Ka bloodline at Mi-Pao Kennels was completed.

Magnificent headstudy of a Mi-Pao Chow Chow, owned and bred by F.P.A. Odenkirchen of Ontario, Canada.

I'Ming van de Tongelreep, owned by the Mi-Pao Kennels in Waterdown, Ontario, Canada. Her sire was King van Mongolie *ex* Ch. Mouchka van Mongolie.

A typical Chow Chow puppy featured on the 1973 Christmas card for the Odenkirchen's Mi-Pao Kennels in Ontario, Canada.

International Champion Chang-Shi Hong-Kwong, a Chow that has made history, sired by Int. Ch. Astom *ex* Chang-Shi Fatima. Owned by the Mi-Pao Kennels, Waterdown, Ontario, Canada.

Ch. Djimat van de Martin-Hoeve, owned by F.P.A. Odenkirchen of the Mi-Pao Kennels in Waterdown, Ontario, Canada. The sire was Ch. Kwang-Ti van de Tongelreep ex Heliam.

Sinkiang's Brandy, pictured at 6 weeks of age. Born March 5, 1972, his sire was Ch. Foo H'Sing's Mister Linn Wu *ex* Ch. Kin-Chi's Ceecee. Owned by Neil and Rose McEachern of Ottawa, Canada.

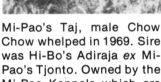

Mi-Pao's Taj, male Chow Chow whelped in 1969. Sire was Hi-Bo's Adiraja *ex* Mi-Pao's Tjonto. Owned by the Mi-Pao Kennels which are located in Ontario, Canada.

Since more than 50% of the Standard is devoted to the head, Mr. Odenkirchen believes that the head of the Chow requires the breeder's particular attention, since both the broad skull and short muzzle are recessive traits. He also believes, however, that exaggeration of any particular feature (for instance, the head, excessive coat, etc.) in preference to total balance has often hurt the breed and must be avoided. While the original Standard was based on Chow VIII, the lack of mathematical precision has provided breeders the opportunity to improve the breed far beyond its original model. If breeding is to be seen as a form of creative art, any fashionable additions to the Standard would restrict further development immensely. Kennels of the past which have contributed significantly to the development of the breed, such as Chang-Shi and Choonam, were only able to do so by being free to promote their specific interpretation of the Standard, thereby creating a variety within the variety. Consequently, Mr. Odenkirchen sees it as a fundamental necessity for the continued well-being of the breed that its fanciers be encouraged to form their own opinions even if they seem to differ from our present ideas. It is unavoidable, in his opinion, that Chows of tomorrow will look different and are, hopefully, an improvement over our present specimens.

Mr. Odenkirchen considers his Belgian import International Ch. Chang-Shi Hong-Kwong and Hi-Bo's Adiraja, his top stud dogs, and Ch. Tiga and Mi-Pao's Tjonto among his best brood bitches. Other top dogs at Mi-Pao are Canadian and American Ch. Mi-Pao's Timang, Int. Ch. Mi-Pao's Piwa Rangan, Ch. Djimat van de Martin-Hoeve and Ycu-Two's Commander Black.

The late Ch. Ting How's Rum and Coke, whelped in 1963. Owner was Hanna Kallus Kuester, Hanchow Kennels, Kingston, Ontario, Canada.

MI-TU

Mr. and Mrs. R.D. Robb have been in Chow Chows since 1965 with the purchase of a bitch from the Mi-Pao Kennels. She was followed by a male puppy from Mr. and Mrs. Copely which was from Mi-Pao stock also. When they decided to register a kennel name they combined parts of the names of each of their Chow Chows, and Mi-Tu Chow Chow Kennels was established at their Aurora, Ontario address.

The Robbs showed the male, Mi-Tan's Kwan-Ti-Chee-Foo, to his championship, which he finished at the age of two years. Unfortunately the bitch died and another was purchased from the Chi-Kwang Kennels. Her name was Chi-Kwang's Han Su Mei and she has produced many outstanding dogs. Among them was Canadian and American Ch. Mi-Tu's Mai Mai, Ch. Mi-Tu's Tien How (a Group-winning bitch) and her most recent, Ch. Mi-Tu's Han Su Shang, a Group winner in the United States at the age of eight months. Shang has gone on to many other spectacular wins.

While never bred to the same male twice, Han Su Mei has consistently produced fine puppies. Five of her sons and daughters have points towards their championships.

Mi-Tu is a very small kennel of just three or four dogs, and the Robbs find that the combined bloodlines of Chi-Kwang, Foo H'Sing, Kin-Chi and Minhow (England) are producing fine puppies they can be proud of!

SINKIANG

The Sinkiang Kennels of Mr. and Mrs. N.V. McEachern in Ottawa, Canada, were established in 1966. During this period they have bred or owned many champion Chow Chows, including the following: Ch. Sinkiang's Fum Tee Chee, Ch. Sinkiang's Wu Satu, Ch. Sinkiang's Wu Ying and Ch. Kin-Chi Ceecee.

SUYAN

Suyan is the kennel name of Mrs. Yan Paul in Ontario; it has been in existence since 1930. Mrs. Paul is a well-known

Mi-Tu's Han Fu Ting, male born in June, 1970. Sire was Ch. Foo H'Sing's Fu Ting ex Chi-Kwang's Han Su Mei. Owned by Mr. and Mrs. G. Katoen of Downsview, Ontario, Canada and bred by Mi-Tu Chow Chow Kennels, Canada.

Mi-Tu's Miss Cheeky, photographed at eight weeks of age, was whelped in July, 1973. Her sire was Ch. Kin Chi's Ku Sa and her dam Chi-Kwang's Han Su Mei. Bred by the Mi-Tu Kennels in Canada and owned by Lucille and Jerry Sterling of Nashville, Tennessee.

Mi-Tu's Gem-Sing, sired by Ch. Mi-Tan's Kwan Ti Che-Foo ex Chi-Kwang's Han Su Mei. Owners are Pat and Russ Robb who own the Mi-Tu Kennels in Ontario, Canada.

Sinkiang's Wu Satu, photographed at 8 months of age in October of 1968. She is pictured winning Best Canadian Bred Puppy in the Non-Sporting Group at a recent show. Owners are Rose and Neil McEachern of Ottawa, Canada.

Chow Chow fancier and a popular judge at the American dog shows as well as in Canada.

Some of the outstanding Chow Chows with which she has been associated are Ch.

Chia Wans Glamor Girl, Ch. Chia Wan's Ginger Snap, Ch. Suyan's Yang Tse and Ch. Suyan's Choo Che. In addition to Yang Tse, Ch. Farland Thundergust of Ku is a stud at Mrs. Paul's Suyan Kennels.

This striking headstudy of Ch. Pandee's Jubilee by William Gilbert shows the typical scowl of the Chow as well as the short muzzle and correct ear set. Jubilee, who died prematurely, sired many champions. He was co-owned by Dr. Imogene P. Earle and Dr. JoAnne O'Brien, a former president of the Chow Chow Club, Inc., the Parent Organization. Dr. O'Brien showed Jubilee to one Best in Show, all breeds, under Frank Landgraf, at the Valley Forge Kennel Club in September, 1969.

8. THE CHOW CHOW STANDARD

GENERAL APPEARANCE—A massive, cobby, powerful dog, active and alert, with strong, muscular development, and perfect balance. Body squares with height of leg at shoulder; head, broad and flat, with short, broad, and deep muzzle, accentuated by a ruff; the whole supported by straight, strong legs. Clothed in a shining, offstanding coat, the Chow is a masterpiece of beauty, dignity, and untouched naturalness.

HEAD—Large and massive in proportion to size of dog, with broad, flat skull; well filled under the eyes; moderate stop; and proudly carried. *Expression*—Essentially dignified, lordly, scowling, discerning, sober, and snobbish—one of independence. *Muzzle*—Short in comparison to length of skull; broad from eyes to end of nose, and of equal depth. The lips somewhat full and overhanging. *Teeth*—Strong and level, with a scissors bite; should neither be overshot, nor undershot. *Nose*—Large, broad, and black in color. Disqualification—nose spotted or distinctly other color than black, except in blue Chows, which may have solid blue or slate noses. *Tongue*—A blue-black. The tissues of the mouth should approximate black. Disqualification—tongue red, pink, or obviously spotted with red or pink. *Eyes*—Dark, deep-set, of moderate size, and almond-shaped. *Ears*—Small, slightly rounded at tip, stiffly carried. They should be placed wide apart, on top of the skull, and set with a slight forward tilt. Disqualification—drop ear or ears. A drop ear is one which is stiffly carried or stiffly erect, but which breaks over at any point from its base to its tip.

BODY—Short, compact, well-sprung ribs, and let down in the flank.

NECK—Strong, full, set well on the shoulders. *Shoulders*—Muscular, slightly sloping. *Chest*—Broad, deep, and muscular. A narrow chest is a serious fault.

BACK—Short, straight, and strong. *Loins*—Broad, deep, and powerful. *Tail*—Set well up and carried closely to the back, following line of spine at start.

FORELEGS—Perfectly straight, with heavy bone and upright pasterns. *Hind Legs*—Straight-hocked, muscular, and heavy boned. *Feet*—Compact, round, cat-like, with thick pads.

GAIT—Completely individual. Short and stilted because of straight hocks.

COAT—Abundant, dense, straight, and offstanding; rather coarse in texture with a soft, woolly undercoat. It may be any clear color, solid throughout, with lighter shadings on ruff, tail, and breechings.

The magnificent Ch. Liontamer Mardi Gras, pictured at 18 months of age, owned by Mary Alice Elliott of Denver, Colorado. A McLaughlin photo.

Ch. Ky-Lin's Red Buddha, sired by Ch. Ky-Lin's Circus *ex* Ky-Lin's Spring Dawn. Owned by the Wah-Hu Chow Chow Kennels in Glen Ellyn, Illinois.

Ch. Chang-Shi Sweet Stuff finished for her title in three consecutive shows, including a Specialty and the huge Harbor Cities show in California. Whelped in 1958, her sire was Ch. Chang-Shi Shanghai Jester *ex* Chang-Shi Joli Coeur. She is handled here by Gerald Sterling, who co-owns her with his wife Lucile Sterling, of Nashville, Tennessee. Judge is Vivian Shryock.

A Best in Show for a Canadian Chow!
American and Canadian Champion
Foo H'Sing Mister Linn Wu receives
the top prize at the Sault Sainte Marie
Kennel Club in May 1971. Mister Linn
Wu won eleven group firsts, two Chow
Specialties and one Group Specialty.
He is co-owned by Mr. Williams, his
wife Joan, and Mr. John C. Frederick
Peddie, Bu Dynasty Kennels, Toronto,
Canada.

Ch. Gotschall's Torando and Ch. Gotschall's Bow, owned by Belva Kennedy of Massena, New York, Stormy and Candy were photographed in October, 1969.

—Nose spotted or distinctly other color than black, except in blue Chows, which may have solid blue or slate noses. Tongue red, pink or obviously spotted with red or pink. Drop ear or ears.

Approved March 11, 1941

INTERPRETATION OF THE STANDARD

After having talked with the major breeders of Chows who have been active for more than ten years, this writer discovered the majority felt that the best source in the past and likewise today is Will Judy's *The Chow Chow* (1934), out of print for many years. His authority remains unchallenged, so that is why he is quoted from time to time.

The standard begins with "**General Appearance**," in which *massive* is the first word which means a large mass, or weighty; sometimes it suggests largeness and even boldness. It is difficult, somehow, to think of the word massive in reference to a small Chow, but the question of size does not enter here, for a Pekingese can be thought to be massive. And the correct Chow, large or small, does have mass or substance. *Cobby* needs some explanation. It means compact and short—coupled, that is, with ribs close together. *Powerful dog, active*

and alert with strong muscular development means exactly what it says and requires no special interpretation.

The next words to be commented on are: *perfect balance. Body squares with height of leg* (leg including upper arm and shoulder blade) *at shoulder.* This specifically means the length and height of the Chow makes a **square**, not a **rectangle**. One sees many Chows today whose length of body from the shoulder to the end of the body is much longer than the height of the dog, thus making a rectangle, giving the appearance that the Chow is too long to be well balanced. This lack of leg compared with the length of the Chow is one of the breed's most frequent and outstanding faults. A Chow with short legs (compared to his body length) looks as if he is standing in a hole, or even worse looks somewhat like a pig, pigs having long bodies and short legs. Both images are totally wrong, for the correct Chow's outline should make a nearly perfect **square**, not a rectangle.

Since the head is mentioned next as *broad and flat with short, broad, and deep muzzle,* it will be examined next. Then somewhat further on, the head is described as *large and massive in proportion to the size of the dog with broad, flat skull; well filled under the eyes; moderate stop; and proudly carried.*

A good portion of the Chow Standard is devoted to the Chow's head which is obviously extremely important. The head

Ch. Hetherchow Liontamer Dai-Zi, whelped August 29, 1968. Her sire is Ch. Eastward Liontamer of Elster, her mother Scotchow Sum Dai Dream. She is owned by Kay Thomas of Denver, Colorado.

Ch. Li-Lee's Wat-A-Boy, owned by the McElmurrays of the Li-Lee Kennels, reg., Lansing, Michigan.

should be large in proportion to the whole body, massive in relationship to the Chow's all-over appearance. The skull should be broad and flat (not perfectly flat, as the skull does have a certain curvature as the occipital ridge runs up through the middle of the skull). Under the eyes must be well-filled; there must be no sharp-pointed muzzle as in the Keeshond, for example. If the Chow face falls away considerably from the eyes, the Chow's face and muzzle look snipey or foxy, which is completely incorrect.

As far back as 1914 Lady Dunbar of Mochrum first published *The Chow Chow* (England) and stated, "A Chow Chow, to be really good according to regulation, must have a broad flat skull and be well filled out under the eyes, with muzzle moderate in length and broad from eyes to point." Another idea that is sometimes put forward in regard to the width of the muzzle is that the outer edges of the muzzle should be on a straight line with the outer edges of the eyes. Another way of seeing the muzzle is to visualize it as a perfectly square box; it should be as *wide* as *long* as *deep.*

Next, *accentuated by a ruff; the whole supported by straight, strong legs.* The ruff is of extreme importance, for it is this hair that surrounds the head which

American and Canadian Ch. Luck-ee U'Kwong Royalist pictured winning Best of Breed at seven years of age under judge Maurice Baker. Sired by Ch. Loy-Jean's Beau Monty *ex* Ch. U'Kwong Red Rose, he is shown, owned and bred by Mrs. Grace Luckey of Seattle, Washington.

Ch. Sharbo Talisman, bred and owned by the Robert Gilbs of Round Lake, Illinois. The sire was Ch. Charmar Red Dragon *ex* Ch. Royal-Rin's Licorice Candy.

Ch. Nor-Ton's Miss Moon, bred and owned by Bessie Van Dusen Volkstadt, Nor-Ton Kennels, North Tonawanda, New York.

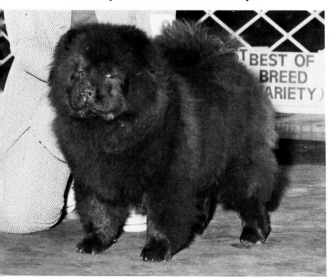

Practice session for the Taynton Chow Chow team, the only team of Chows being shown today. Robert and Norma Taynton of Detroit are the owners and trainers of, left to right, Lin Ch'e, Ch. P'an Hu, Ch. Lao Yang Tze and Ch. San Toy II.

Ch. Griffchow's Mar Ja's Show Ling is pictured winning the Group at the Columbia Kennel Club show in 1974 under judge Dr. Malcolm E. Phelps. In 1974 Mr. Buttons won three Group Firsts, 6 Group Seconds, 5 Group Thirds and 1 Group Fourth. His sire was Ch. Tung Wang of Nichow *ex* Tsang Po's Chu Mi Shu.

Below:
Two smooth Chow Chows. At right is Lung Chao of Penhow, a Dutch champion bred by Mr. and Mrs. E. Burrows that finished in 1965 at 9 years of age. At left is Ukwong Tiga, a smooth Chow Chow bitch puppy. Tiga was bred by Mrs. Roberts out of Ukwong Red Prince *ex* Ukwong Zazu. They are owned and photographed by Miss Chr. A. Veldhuis of Holland.

gives it the "lion-like" or true Chow expression. A Chow without a ruff is like a king without a crown.

Clothed in a shining, offstanding coat, the Chow is a masterpiece of beauty, dignity, and untouched naturalness. If a Chow is healthy and is brushed regularly, his coat will have a sheen to it; it should stand up because of its harsh texture and not lie flat on the body, which a soft coat would likely do. Later on in the Standard, the coat is described as *abundant, dense, straight* and once again as *offstanding*. Most Chow breeders believe that abundant means long as well as thick; perhaps so, but that the hair is dense and straight and offstanding appears more essential than the coat's length. However, in the show ring the Chow with the abundant, long coat usually has the advantage, providing, of course, that the dogs have some merit in addition to their long coats.

One knows that the Chow is a masterpiece of beauty, so that does not require further comment. And everyone recognizes that the Chow has an innate dignity which is part of his appeal. However, *untouched naturalness* might be gone into. This speci-

fic directive says that the Chow may **not** be scissored to make his coat the same length all over, which would give the dog a "teddy-bear" look, a stuffed quality which is natural in a puppy but not in a mature animal. The British do "tidy up" their Chows, actually removing the surplus hair on the neck, between the forelegs, on the tail, etc. This tidying up, plucking and/or trimming is *specifically forbidden by the American Standard*. The only place a bit of trimming is allowed is on the toenails, and on the feet to give them the *compact, round, cat-like* quality specified by the standard. Otherwise, the Chow should not be touched with a sharp-bladed knife or scissors.

After the general appearance, the next subtitle in the Standard is "**Head**" which has been delved into above. **Expression** follows: *essentially dignified, lordly, scowling, discerning, sober and snobbish— one of independence.* None of these adjectives needs particular clarification, but the term *scowling* should be emphasized. The scowl on a Chow comes from the loose skin around his eyes and on his forehead, a wrinkling of the skin in the center of the

Chang-Shi Party Doll, pictured winning at the 1961 Southern Chow Chow Specialty under judge Howard Bogue. She was Winners Bitch and Best of Opposite Sex for a 5-point major on the way to her championship. Handled by Jerry Sterling of Nashville, Tennessee.

Best of Breed at the Southern Chow Chow Club Specialty Show in April, 1958 was Ch. Hi Clear Black Bomber, owned and handled by Bertha Smith. Photo by Evelyn Shafer.

forehead and on the top horizontal line of the forehead. It is precisely the scowl that gives the Chow its unique expression of being somewhat abrasive-looking, or sharp, as well as sober and snobbish. A plain-faced or a plain-foreheaded Chow does not fit the Standard even though it may have a short, broad muzzle of sufficient depth as well as the typical almond eye. He must have a scowl to achieve that complete Chow expression. Of course the scowl can be overdone if there are too many wrinkles which tend to give the dog a Bloodhound or Bulldog look. A Chow head is not a Bloodhound head nor is it a foxy head; it resembles, perhaps, the lion more, but using the term lion-head is only metaphorical, not literal. Nevertheless, the Chow's scowl should not be that of the Bloodhound when his wrinkles are pulled up over his skull and foreface. With no scowl and a snipey muzzle, the Chow might look "foxy," which is also patently incorrect.

Since so many breeders do swear by Will Judy, he is quoted here. "The Chow can better afford to lose almost any other trait except that of his expression and necessary scowl."

Ch. Five Ash Victory, bred and owned by Florence Wilson Graham. Victory was sired by Ch. Five Ash Jo Jo *ex* Five Ash Inkee.

Ch. Plain Acre's Holy Smoke, bred by Manota M. Stertz and whelped in June, 1970. Sire was Ch. Beamer's Chummy Chinaman *ex* Ch. Plain Acre's Charman Twiggy. Pictured here winning Best of Winners on the way to championship.

An informal study of
Eastward Mona of Pandee.
This lovely bitch is owned by
Merilyn Bowden Morgan of
Falls Church, Va.

Below:
Vong-Shi Mong-Fu, a red dog
born in 1971, pictured here at
1½ years of age. Bred and
owned by Mrs. Irene
Cottafavi. By
Nan-Chu-Mong-Fu *ex* Int. Ch.
Pu-Peh Mong-Fu.

Pandee's Katanga is considered by Dr. Imogene P. Earle, Pandee Kennels, to be the kennel's most outstanding brood bitch. Dam of several champions, Katanga was sired by Ch. Pandee's Jubilee out of Pandee's Zip Orah.

Below:
Quito de Ouah Ouah, a red dog born in 1967 and shown here at 4 years of age, was bred and owned by Miss Claudel.

The muzzle which is referred to next has been analyzed above. The standard goes on to say that the lips should be somewhat *full and overhanging*. Tight lips or those that just barely stretch over the teeth are not correct or typical. As for the bite, the teeth are *strong and level* with a scissors bite; *should be neither overshot nor undershot*. It has been our experience that the majority of breeders who have bred an occasional Chow which was either overshot or undershot were very persistent in trying to eradicate this fault. No Chow that has a defective bite can win consistently in top group competition. Such a Chow might even finish his championship (provided he had other worthy characteristics) but not proceed much further with a show career.

The nose is large, broad, and black in color. (*Disqualification—nose spotted or distinctly other color than black, except in blue Chows which may have solid blue or slate noses.*) If the pigment of a Chow puppy is strongly black, it will turn black as early as three weeks of age although every Chow puppy is born with a pink tongue and sometimes with a lighter nose than black. If the pigment isn't strong, the nose and tongue may turn black as late as 10 months of age.

The tongue is a *blue-black. The tissues of the mouth should approximate black.* (*Disqualification—tongue red, pink or obviously spotted with red or pink.*) Of all the interesting characteristics of the Chow, the most fascinating and the most unique of all features is the blue-black tongue. Zoologists tell us that only the Chow has a blue-black tongue of all the canine family, and only certain bears have a tongue of a similar color in the entire animal world. In 1789, the Rev. Gilbert White wrote in *The Natural History of Selborne* (England) concerning the first pair of Chows to be seen in England; he makes a point of their tongues. "Their eyes are jet-black, small, and piercing; the insides of their lips and mouths are of the same colour, and their tongues blue."

Ch. Pandee's Cassanova goes Winners Dog at the Southern Chow Chow Specialty in April 1972 under judge Mrs. Margaret Shoemaker, a former Chow breeder. Cassanova, sired by Ch. Carlee's Fancy Dan whose sire was Ch. Pandee's Red Rufus II, is owned by Dr. Imogene P. Earle and shown by Dr. JoAnne O'Brien.

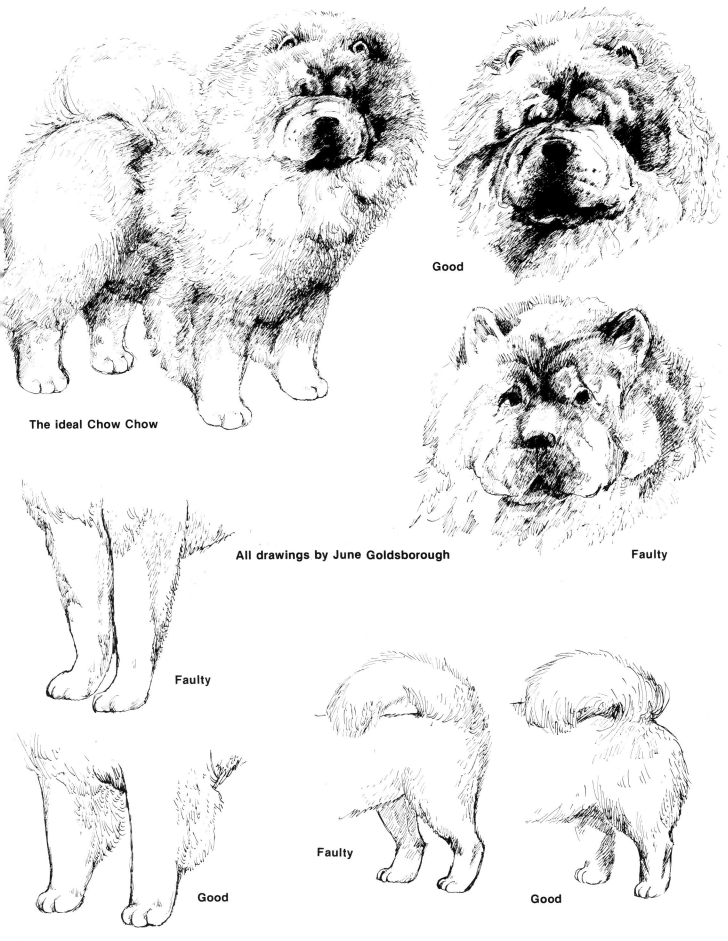

The ideal Chow Chow

Good

Faulty

All drawings by June Goldsborough

Faulty

Good

Faulty

Good

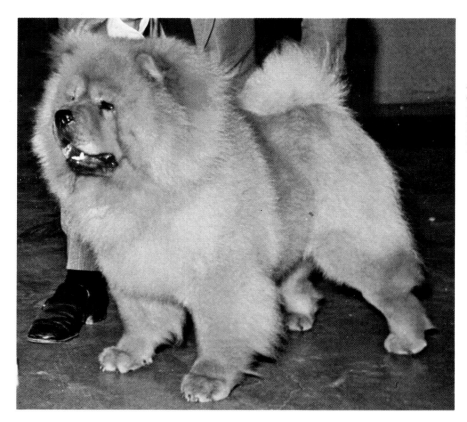

American and Canadian
Champion Foo H'Sing Mister
Linn Wu wins group first at the
London Canine Association,
London, Ontario, Canada in
1971.

Below:
Tsang Po's Kwan Yin, owned by
Mr. and Mrs. S.W. Burgess and
bred by the H.A. Allens of
Lubbock, Texas. Kwan Yin was
whelped June 25, 1972

Tsang Po's Kwan Yin, whelped in 1972 and bred by Hal Allen, Tsang Po Kennels, Lubbock, Texas; owned by Mr. and Mrs. S.W. Burgess. Sire was Ch. Starcrest Mr. Christopher *ex* Ch. Tsang Po's Kwai-Chy.

Below:
The adorable three-month-old Eastward Julian, another puppy from the Eastward Kennels of Merilyn Bowden Morgan.

Ch. Tsang-Po's Pa-Li-Cho Li-Kee-Tu wins Best in Show under judge Mrs. Sadie Edmiston at the 1966 McAllen, Texas show. Whelped in 1964, his sire was Ch. Jean's Wan Woo *ex* Ch. Tsang-Po's Miss Lu Shan Kway. Owned by Mr. and Mrs. Dan Frederick of Baton Rouge, Louisiana and handled by Mrs. Frederick.

Another Chow scholar has written, "No other species of animal, no other breed of dog, has this tongue color. It is one of the mysteries, let us say, one of a number of mysteries connected with the Chow. It may be that long generations, rather long centuries ago, there may have been an arctic wolf or there may have been a famous Chow in those early days when

there were not many Chows which with some strange quirk of heredity, possessed a blue tongue and transmitted it in all his get."

Eyes are dark, deep set, of moderate size, and almond-shaped, according to the Standard. Once again, one should refer to Will Judy, for his ideas on the Chow's eyes appear indispensable to one's understanding of this unique characteristic.

"Every dog, every breed, has a round or globular eye. Where the standard states that the eye should be small or triangular or almond shaped, it refers specifically to that portion of the eye which is seen by the observer. The shape of the eye, therefore, is determined by the outline of the eyelid and the position of the eyeball in the head." The Chow's eye must be dark, not necessarily black. No matter what the coat color of the Chow is, even very blonde or light cream, his eye must be dark. A light brown eye would be a fault, and it would mar the Chow's expression.

The Chow's eye should be deep set and placed far back into the head, not like those of a Pekingese, which protrude. The loose skin around the Chow's eyes helps to give this deep set eye its character. The eye should be of moderate size, not too small and not too prominent but in proportion to the size of the dog's head. A big bulging eye can be ruinous to the proper expression. Almond-shaped means what it says; the eye looks like an almond, somewhat narrow and triangular.

The ears are small, slightly rounded at tip, stiffly carried. They should be placed wide apart, on top of the skull, and set with a slight forward tilt. (Disqualification— Drop ear or ears. A drop ear is one which is not stiffly carried or stiffly erect, but which breaks over at any point from its base to its tip.)

One sees today many poor ears, too widely set on the side of the head, almost floppy, and ears that are too large and well-rounded, not slightly rounded at the tip as they should be. Remember the ears must tilt forward not to the left and right as a poorly placed ear would do.

The next subhead is **Body**, which was treated briefly above but will be looked at again here.

The best explanation of the words, *short, compact, with well-sprung ribs, and let down* is given by Will Judy in his book *The Chow Chow* referred to earlier.

As Judy says, "The phrase compact may be said to correspond to cobby. The phrase 'well ribbed up' does not refer to

Impressive head study of the blue male Starcrest Sterling Silver, bred by June Marston and owned by A.J. Overturf and Richard Inmon of Dallas, Texas.

Ch. Ah Sid The Aide De Kamp, owned by Dr. William Fritz of Carleton, Michigan, is pictured winning a Non-Sporting Group under renowned judge Anna Katherine Nicholas at the Windham County Kennel Club in Willimantic, Connecticut, in May, 1965. Jane Kamp is Rocky's handler.

Qui-Yang de Pipo Sun Tchang, bred and owned by Mr. Bujardet, Paris, France, was whelped in 1967. His sire was Int. Ch. Jalu Mong-Fu *ex* Ch. Nuhming de Pipo Sun Tchang. A champion in France in 1969, Luxembourg in 1970, Monaco in 1970 and Belgium in 1971.

A closeup of the quality of Tsang Po's Ho Toi, owned by Mr. and Mrs. Burgess and bred by Hal Allen, Tsang Po Kennels, Lubbock, Texas.

out-spreading ribs, that is, ribs which run horizontal some distance from the backbone, before turning downward but refers to the closeness of one rib to another. There should be little space between ribs.

"For a body to be let down in the flank means that the chest must be rounded. . . and that the last pair of ribs spread out well and are near to the rump. To be let down in the flank means that there cannot be any cut-up of loins and that the body is short."

The neck is strong, full, set well on the shoulders. A long neck, goose neck or horse neck is not permitted if the head is set well or prominently on the body. A correctly set neck and head make it hard to determine where one begins and the other ends. As one authority has put it, "It might be said that a good Chow has no great length of neck."

Ch. Plain Acre's Charman Fella, owned and shown by Mrs. Joan Wicks Ott, pictured winning under judge Melbourne Downing at the Riverhead Kennel Club show in July, 1969. Later Charman Fella was purchased by Audrey Meaney of Connecticut.

Shoulders are muscular and slightly sloping. Rather than stating that the shoulders are well laid back, the Standard says the shoulders are muscular and slightly sloping. Chow breeders do not seem to stress the Chow's shoulders and few, if any, comments are made or written concerning this part of the Chow's anatomy.

Chest is broad, deep, and muscular. A narrow chest is a serious fault. Broad means wide from left to right and the chest must be well let down from top to bottom. The deep chest, according to the most successful breeders must extend itself down to the middle of the elbows. One sees many narrow-chested Chows with shallow briskets. The indication in the Standard that a narrow chest is a serious fault was added to the Standard on March 11, 1941, according to *The Complete Dog Book*, the official publication of the American Kennel Club. Obviously, at that time, the majority of breeders believed there were too many narrow-chested Chows and proceeded to have the Standard modified to stress the narrow chest which is the only serious fault listed by the Standard.

Of the remaining subtitles, comments will be given on *tail, forelegs, hind legs,* and *gait.*

As for the tail, it is *set well up and carried closely to the back, following line of spine at start.* As long as the tail follows the line of the spine at the start of the tail, it can fall off the back to either side of the back. Of course if the tail is set up on the back (which is ideal) the tail would tend to stay directly on the spine and not curve to either side. There are even some Chows that have a curl or kink at the very end of the tail. As long as the tail follows the line of the spine, at least at the start, there is no harm in a curl at the end. In the normal standing or walking position, the Chow's tail remains close to the back, so there is no open space or air between the tail and its resting position on the dog's back. When the Chow is running and/or playing, the normal tail will move off the back into the air. That is to be expected, of course. This writer once observed a judge who did not place a Chow, one of the finest Chows be-

The ten month old black Chow Chow Ch. Ah Sid's the Avant Garde pictured with his owner, Dr. Samuel Draper. The Avant Garde was later sold to Dr. William Fritz of Michigan, who later campaigned the dog.

Ch. Mi Chee Mi Mia Linnchow was owned by Mr. and Mrs. George Curzon of White Heath, Illinois. This bitch was bred by Linnchow Kennels in Tinley Park, Illinois and was one of several Linnchow Chows owned and shown by the Curzons who later on bred Chows under their Martonge kennel name. Mr. and Mrs. Curzon have remained active in the breed for many years. He is currently the Chow columnist for the *AKC Gazette.*

ing shown, in a group that he should have won. When questioned diplomatically after the judging, the judge replied, "Well, how could I place that Chow? When he was making the last circle (at rather a fast trot) his tail left his back and went into the air!" A more experienced Chow judge or breeder judge would have realized that when a Chow walks fast or runs, his tail may lift slightly off his back; it is a natural occurrence, one not to be penalized severely.

The forelegs should be *perfectly straight, with heavy bone and upright pasterns.* Perfectly straight means just that. The bone in the forelegs should be heavy; likewise the hind legs. Often a Chow will have much heavier bone in his front legs than in his hind legs, giving an appearance that is somewhat out of balance and displeasing to the eye. Big legs in front and toothpick-like legs in the rear do not give a picture of symmetry or balance or of beauty.

The *pasterns should be upright,* of course; a dog up on his toes does make an image that is active and alert, part of the true Chow picture. The hind legs must be *straight-hocked, muscular and heavy boned.* A great deal has been written about the Chow's hind legs having a straight hock, but apparently not enough, for of the two unique characteristics of the Chow, his blue-black tongue and his straight hocks are often ignored if not misunderstood. The Chow judge seldom, if ever, fails to look at the exotic tongue and pigment of a Chow, yet how many judges ever run their hands over the straight hocks of a Chow? These straight hocks produce a strange gait which the Standard indicates is *completely individual. Short and stilted because of straight hocks.* When a Chow moves, it is as if he walks on stilts which tends to prevent his moving out with the smoothness associated with a sporting or working dog. A slight roll results, and the effect is one of short, choppy steps in the rear. Strangely the judges seem to like Chows that move more smoothly and evenly and often a Chow whose gait is more closely related to that of a Springer Spaniel than to that of "stilts" makes an impression in the group. This is a serious error on the part of the judge, who should reward the Chow whose rear action is different from that of any other breed. One eminent authority, Maxwell Riddle, is fascinated by the Chow and explains the origin of the straight hock as its natural evolution owing to the Chow's having had originally to move through quantities of snow with agility. On the other hand, some canine scholars have written that the straight hock provides a more edible piece of meat! Whatever the truth is concerning the origin of the Chow's peculiar hock, the explanation is lost in antiquity. One can only speculate about its origin; however, what is important is that the straight hock remains and should be bred for and honored as a distinguishing characteristic.

Head study of the beautiful Miki de la Moulaine, owned by Betty Schellenberg of Fort Worth, Texas. Sire was Ch. Ghat de la Moulaine; dam was Fluffy Chinese Princess.

Ch. Carlee's Emperor Chu, shown winning the Non-Sporting Group at the Old Dominion Kennel Club of Northern Virginia in April, 1969. Handled by Jane Kay for owner Carole R. Whitlock of Culpepper, Virginia. The judge is Ray Beale, the photographer, Evelyn Shafer.

Plain Acres Holy Smoke and Don-Lee's Jubilee, photographed in 1972. Owned by Larry and Carol Kelly of the Shamrock Kennels in El Cajon, California.

EUROPEAN STANDARDS

Now that we have discussed at length the accepted current American Standard for the Chow Chow, we record here the Standard of breed points drawn up by the British and the Germans. We think you will agree that the comparisons are interesting and worthy of comment, especially in a book that presents the history of the Chow Chow in Europe in such detail.

THE BRITISH STANDARD

CHARACTERISTICS—A well balanced dog, leonine in appearance, with proud dignified bearing; loyal yet aloof; unique in its stilted gait and bluish-black tongue.

GENERAL APPEARANCE—An active, compact, short-coupled and well balanced dog, well knit in frame, with tail carried well over the back.

HEAD AND SKULL—Skull flat and broad, with little slope, well filled out under the eyes. Muzzle moderate in length, broad from the eyes to the point (not pointed at the end like a fox). Nose black, large and wide in all cases (with the exception of cream and white in which case a light-colored nose); but in all colors a black nose is preferable.

EYES—Dark and small, preferably almond-shaped (in blue or fawn dog a light color is permissible).

EARS—Small, thick, slightly rounded at the tip, carried stiffly erect but placed well forward over the eyes and wide apart, which gives the dog the peculiar characteristic expression of the breed, viz. a scowl.

MOUTH—Teeth strong and level, giving scissor bite. Tongue bluish-black. Flews and roof of mouth black, gums preferably black.

NECK—Strong, full, set well on the shoulders and slightly arched.

FOREQUARTERS—Shoulders muscular and sloping. Forelegs perfectly straight, of moderate length and with good bone.

BODY—Chest broad and deep. Back short, straight and strong. Loins powerful.

HINDQUARTERS—Hind legs mucular and hocks well let down and perfectly straight which are essential in order to produce the Chow's characteristic stilted gait.

FEET—Small, round and cat-like, standing well on the toes.

TAIL—Set high and carried well over the back.

COAT—Abundant, dense, straight and stand-off. Outer coat rather coarse in texture and with a soft woolly undercoat. The Chow Chow is a profusely coated dog and balance should therefore be assessed when the coat is at its natural length.

COLOR—Whole colored black, red, blue, fawn, cream or white, frequently shaded but not in patches or parti-colored (the underpart of tail and back of thighs frequently of a light color).

WEIGHT AND SIZE—Minimum height for Chows to be 18 inches, but in every case balance should be the outstanding feature and height left to the discretion of the judges.

FAULTS—Drop ears, tongue splashed or patchy, tail not carried over the back, parti-colored, off-black noses except in the colors specified, viz. creams, whites, blues or fawns. Any artificial shortening of the coat which alters the natural outline or expression of the dog should be penalized. (The Standard of the smooth variety is identical with the above except that the coat is smooth.)

THE GERMAN STANDARD
Translated by Hanna K. Kuester

DISTINGUISHING MARKS—Well proportioned, leonine in appearance, with proud, dignified bearing; faithful, but reserved; unique in his stilted gait. Blue-black tongue.

GENERAL APPEARANCE—A lively, strong, compact and well proportioned dog, harmonic in structure. The tail is well carried over the back.

English and American Champion U'Kwong Fleur, bred by Mrs. Joan Egerton and owned and imported by Clif and Vivian Shryock of Hawaiian Gardens, California. The sire was English Ch. Fairwood Fu-Sim-Ba ex U'Kwong Harmony.

Int. Ch. Kama-Lakschmi-Ay Wong-Ti, born in 1961. Bred and owned by Adolf Metager of Germany. Sire was Int. Ch. Lung-Keu-Siang Asow ex Int. Ch. Kai-Men-Ti Wuniang.

HEAD AND SKULL—Skull flat and broad, with little stop; part under eyes well filled in. Muzzle moderately long, broad from eyes to tip (not pointed at the tip like a fox). Nose large and broad and in all cases black. On blue and cinnamon animals a nose of that same color. With all colors a black nose is to be preferred.

EYES—Dark and small, preferably almond-shaped. On blue and cinnamon animals a lighter color permitted.

EARS—Small, thick, lightly rounded at the tips, carried stiff upright, but directed well forward over the eyes and standing far apart, which lends the dog the characteristic surly expression of the breed (scowl).

MOUTH—Teeth strong and even, scissor bite. Tongue blue-black; lips and palate black. Gums preferably black.

NECK—Powerful and strong, well set up on the shoulders and lightly arched.

FOREHAND—Shoulders muscular and sloping. Forelegs perfectly straight, of moderate length, with heavy bone.

BODY—Chest broad and deep; back short, straight and strong; loins powerful.

HINDQUARTERS—Hind legs muscular; hocks positioned low and perfectly straight, which gives the Chow the peculiar, desired, characteristic stilted gait.

FEET—Small, round and cat-like. Standing well up on the toes.

TAIL—Set high and carried well over the back.

COAT—Abundant, dense, straight and offstanding. The outer coat rough to the touch, with coarse structure. Soft, woolly undercoat.

COLOR—Solid black, red, blue, cinnamon, cream or white. Frequently shaded, but not spotted or dappled. Lower parts of tail and breechings often of lighter color.

SIZE—Minimum height for Chows should be 18 inches (45.5 cm). In individual cases, however, good proportion should be the main mark and size left to the discretion of the judge.

FAULTS—Drop ears, speckled tongue, tail not carried over the back, dappled coat, non-black nose. (The Standard for the short haired variety is identical to the above, except that the coat is short.)

405

Joel Marston, a prominent figure in Chow Chows, is pictured back in the 1940's with three promising puppies from his Starcrest Kennels in California.

9. BUYING YOUR CHOW CHOW PUPPY

A typical quality Chow Chow puppy pictured at 12-weeks-of-age at the Walnut Grove, Nashville, Tennessee Kennels of Lucile and Gerald Sterling.

There are several paths that will lead you to a litter of puppies where you can find the puppy of your choice. Write to the parent club and ask for the names and addresses of members who have puppies for sale. The addresses of Chow Chow clubs can be obtained by writing the American Kennel Club, 51 Madison Avenue, New York, N.Y. 10010. They keep an accurate, up-to-date list of reputable breeders from whom you can seek information on obtaining a good, healthy puppy. You might also check listings in the classified ads of major newspapers. The various dog magazines also carry listings and usually a column each month which features information and news on the breed.

It is to your advantage to attend a few dog shows in the area where purebred dogs of just about every breed are being exhibited in the show ring. Even if you do not wish to buy a show dog, you should be familiar with what the better specimens look like so that you may at least get a decent looking representative of the breed for your money. You will learn a lot by observing the dogs in action in the show ring, or in a public place where their personalities come to the fore. The dog show catalogue will list the dogs and their owners with local kennel names and breeders whom you can visit to see the types and colors they are breeding and winning with at the shows. Exhibitors at these shows are usually delighted to talk to people about their dogs and the specific characteristics of their particular breed.

Once you have chosen the Chow Chow above all others because you admire its exceptional beauty, intelligence and person-

Shanglo's Prince, pictured at 4 months of age. Owned and bred by Mildred Fairchild of the Shanglo Kennels in Tigard, Oregon.

ality, and because you feel the breed will fit in with your family's way of life, it is wise to do a little research on it. The American Kennel Club library, your local library, bookshops, and the breed clubs can usually supply you with a list of reading matter or written material on the breed, past and present. Then, once you have drenched yourself in the breed's illustrious history and have definitely decided that this is the breed for you, it is time to start writing letters and making phone calls to set up appointments to see litters of puppies.

A blue male puppy of Tamarin breeding, owned by Prudence Baxter of San Anselmo, California.

Ch. Liontamer Kudos as a puppy. He is owned by Mrs. Priscilla St. George Ryan of Tuxedo Park, New York, and is pictured winning under judge Tom Stevenson with handler Ted Young, Jr., at the Boston show in 1972.

Another Liontamer puppy photographed at eight weeks of age.

A word of caution here: don't let your choice of a kennel be determined by its nearness to your home, and then buy the first cute puppy that races up to you or licks the end of your nose. All puppies are cute, and naturally you will have a preference among those you see. But don't let preferences sway you into buying the wrong puppy.

If you are buying your dog as a family pet, a preference might not be a serious offense. But if you have had, say, a color preference since you first considered this breed, you would be wise to stick to it. If you are buying a show dog, all physical features must meet with the Standard for the breed. In considering your purchase you must think clearly, choose carefully, and make the very best possible choice. You will, of course, learn to love whichever puppy you finally decide upon, but a case of "love at first sight" can be disappointing and expensive later on if a show career was your primary objective.

To get the broadest possible concept of what is for sale and the current market

A pair of Belgian imports owned by the Gerald Sterlings of Nashville, Tennessee.

prices, it is recommended that you visit as many kennels and private breeders as you can. With today's reasonably safe, inexpensive and rapid non-stop flights on the major airlines, it is possible to secure dogs from far-off places at nominal additional charges, allowing you to buy the valuable bloodlines of your choice if you have a thought toward a breeding program in the future.

The six-month-old Jade's Dutch Master, bred by Nelson Tardy and owned by Marion Perantoni. The sire is Ch. Mi-Pao's Timang *ex* Ch. Soo-Z's Miss Kee-Zee of Jade.

Dougy Hay and two pals take a ride on a swing. . . A darling picture taken in February, 1958 of Mrs. E. Hay, Jr.'s son and two puppies from a litter of seven. The Hays and their Chows are from Portland, Oregon.

Beau Monde The Shamrock, bred by Larry and Carol Kelly and owned by Thomas F. Roh and Richard Beauchamp, publisher of *Kennel Review* magazine. Blossom is pictured here at three months being handled by Mr. Beauchamp to a Best Junior Puppy win at the Golden State Chow Chow Club Match show in June, 1974. The sire was Ch. Starcrest Mr. Christopher *ex* Don-Lee UR Peaches of Shamrock.

While it is always safest to actually *see* the dog you are buying, there are enough reputable breeders and kennels to be found for you to buy a dog with a minimum of risk once you have made up your mind what you want, and when you have decided whether you will buy in your own country or import to satisfy your concept of the breed Standard. If you are going to breed dogs, breeding Standard type can be a moral obligation, and your concern should be with buying the very best bloodlines and individual animals obtainable, in spite of cost or distance.

It is customary for the purchaser to pay the shipping charges, and the airlines are most willing to supply flight information and prices upon request. Rental on the shipping crate, if the owner does not provide one for the dog, is nominal. While unfortunate incidents have occurred on the airlines in the transporting of animals by air, the major airlines are making improvements in safety measures and have reached the point of reasonable safety and cost. Barring unforeseen circumstances, the safe arrival of a dog you might buy can pretty much be assured if both seller and purchaser adhere to and follow up on even the most minute details from both ends.

THE PUPPY YOU BUY

Let us assume you want to enjoy all the cute antics of a young puppy and decide to buy a six-to-eight-week-old puppy. This is about the age when a puppy is weaned, wormed and ready to go out into

the world with a responsible new owner. It is better not to buy a puppy under six weeks of age; it simply is not yet ready to leave the mother or the security of the other puppies. At eight to twelve weeks of age you will be able to notice much about the appearance and the behavior. Puppies, as they are recalled in our fondest childhood memories, are gay and active and bouncy, as well they should be! The normal

An adorable grouping of puppies owned by the Mil-Gil Kennels in Plainfield, New Jersey.

Betmar's Zorro, never shown but demonstrating great quality, was bred and owned by Betty Schellenberg and Vivian Shryock. Zorro's sire was the famous American and Mexican Ch. Ghat de la Moulaine *ex* Hetai de la Moulaine. Zorro is another part of the "Z" litter.

Three peas in a pod. . . three Liontamer puppies get into their crate on the way to a match show!

puppy should be interested, alert, and curious, especially about a stranger. If a puppy acts a little reserved or distant, however, such act need not be misconstrued as shyness or fear. It merely indicates he hasn't made up his mind whether he likes you as yet! By the same token, he should not be fearful or terrified by a stranger — and especially should not show any fear of his owner!

In direct contrast, the puppy should not be ridiculously over-active either. The puppy that frantically bounds around the room and is never still is not especially desirable. And beware of the "spinners"! Spinners are the puppies or dogs that have become neurotic from being kept in cramped quarters or in crates and behave in an emotionally unstable manner when loosed in adequate space. When let out they run in circles and seemingly "go wild." Puppies with his kind of traumatic background seldom ever regain full composure or adjust to the big outside world. The puppy which has had the proper exercise and appropriate living quarters will have a normal, though spirited, outlook on life and will do his utmost to win you over without having to go into a tailspin.

If the general behavior and appearance of the dog thus far appeal to you, it is time for you to observe him more closely for additional physical requirements. First of all, you cannot expect to find in the puppy all the coat he will bear upon maturity. That will come with time and good food, and will be additionally enhanced by the many wonderful grooming aids which can be found on the market today. Needless to say, the healthy puppy's coat should have a nice shine to it, and the more dense at this age, the better the coat will be when the dog reaches adulthood.

Look for clear, dark, sparkling eyes,

The first time Dr. JoAnne Schmidt O'Brien bred her famous Linnchow line to Dr. Imogene Earle's equally important Pandee line this litter of Chows was produced. From left to right, Ginny Tu Linnchow, Ch. Twinkle Linnchow, and Pandee's Cin Nee Linnchow, a cinnamon. Ginny Tu was to become the mother of Champion Kitty Bear Linnchow and Ch. Scotchow Am I Blu owned by Joan Hannephin of Scotchow Kennels. Cin Nee Linnchow became the mother of Ch. Pandee's Jubilee, a top show dog and sire which was co-owned by Dr. Earle and Dr. O'Brien.

Eight-week-old Gotschall Ringo Star of Jade, bred by Nelson Tardy and owned by Valetta Gotschall. The sire is Ch. Mi-Pao's Timang ex Ch. Soo-Z's Miss Kee-Zee of Jade.

A litter of five sired by Ch. Chang-Shi Zygoto and Ch. Fireball's Black Angel. All five achieved their championships when they were less than one year old. Angel, bred by Willard L. Boehner, produced a total of 8 champions in all. Owners are Gerald and Lucile Sterling of Nashville, Tennessee.

Ky-Lin's Meus, bred by Betty Mae Sewards and owned by Betty Schellenberg of Fort Worth, Texas.

Ch. Cherokee's Nik-Nak, photographed at five weeks of age; whelped December 5, 1965. Nik-Nak's sire was Ken-Wan's Sun Down ex Gin-Ling's Liza of Cherokee. Owned by Mr. and Mrs. Oral E. Crisp of the Cherokee Chow Chow Kennels, Cathlamet, Washington.

Wide Track Bummer, owned and bred by the Thomas Carters, Tag-El's Chow Chow Ranch, Mc-Loud, Oklahoma.

free of discharge. Dark eye rims and lids are indications of good pigmentation, which is important in a breeding program, and even for generally pleasing good looks.

When the time comes to select your puppy, take an experienced breeder along with you if this is possible. If it is not possible, take the Standard for the breed with you. Try to interpret the Standard as best you can by making comparisons between the puppies you see.

Check the bite completely and carefully. While the first set of teeth can be misleading, even the placement of teeth at this young age can be a fairly accurate indication of what the bite will be in the grown dog. The gums should be a good healthy pink in color, and the teeth should be clear, clean and white. Any brown cast to them could mean a past case of distemper and would assuredly count against the dog in the show ring and against the dog's general appearance at maturity.

Puppies take anything and everything into their mouths to chew on while they are teething, and a lot of infectious diseases are transmitted this way. The aforementioned distemper is one, and the brown teeth as a result of this disease never clear. The puppy's breath should not be sour or even unpleasant or strong. Any acrid odor could indicate a poor mixture of food, or low quality of meat, especially if it is being fed raw. Many breeders have compared the breath of a healthy puppy to that of fresh toast, or as being vaguely like garlic. At any rate, a puppy should never be fed just table scraps, but should have a well-balanced diet containing a good dry puppy chow and a good grade of fresh meat. Poor meat and too much cereal or fillers tend to make the puppy too fat. We like puppies to be in good flesh, but not fat from the wrong kind of food.

It goes without saying that we want to find clean puppies. The breeder or owner who shows you a dirty puppy is one from whom to steer away! Look closely at the skin. Rub the fur the wrong way or against the grain; make sure it is not spotted with

A basketful of Chow Chow charm! Two puppies owned and bred by Douglas and Florence Broadhurst, old-time breeders.

insect bites or red, blotchy sores or dry scales. The vent area around the tail should not show evidences of diarrhea or inflammation. By the same token, the puppy's fur should not be matted with dry excrement or smell of urine.

True enough, you can wipe dirty eyes, clean dirty ears and give the puppy a bath when you get it home, but these things are all indications of how the puppy has been cared for during the important formative first months of its life, and can vitally influence its future health and development. There are many reputable breeders raising healthy puppies that have been reared in proper places and under the proper conditions in clean housing, so why take a chance on a series of veterinary bills and a questionable constitution?

MALE OR FEMALE?

The choice of sex in your puppy is also something that must be given serious thought before you buy. For the pet owner, the sex that would best suit the family life you enjoy would be the paramount choice to consider. For the breeder or exhibitor, there are other vital considerations. If you are looking for a stud to establish a kennel, it is essential that you select a dog with both testicles evident, even at a tender age, and verified by a veterinarian before the sale is finalized if there is any doubt.

The visibility of only one testicle, known as monorchidism, automatically disqualifies the dog from the show ring or from a breeding program, though monorchids are capable of siring. Additionally, it must be noted that monorchids frequently

Sitting pretty! Three Ledgelands Chow Chows pose for their picture at their kennel in Tuxedo Park, New York, owned by Mrs. David Wagstaff.

sire dogs with the same deficiency, and to introduce this into a bloodline knowingly is an unwritten sin in the dog fancy. Also, a monorchid can sire dogs that are completely sterile. These are referred to as cryptorchids and have no testicles.

If you want the dog to be a member of the family, the best selection would probably be a female. You can always go out for stud service if you should decide to breed. You can choose the bloodlines doing the most winning because they should be bred true to type, and you will not have to foot the bill for the financing of a show career. You can always keep a male from your first litter that will bear your own "kennel name" if you have decided to proceed in the kennel "business."

An additional consideration in the male versus female decision for the private owner is that with males there might be the problem of leg-lifting and with females there is the inconvenience while they are in season. However, this need not be the problem it used to be—pet shops sell "pants" for both sexes, which help to control the situation.

A nine-week-old Chow Chow puppy which grew up to be American and Mexican Ch. Betmar's Zeus de la Moulaine. Owned by Betty Schellenberg of Fort Worth, Texas.

THE PLANNED PARENTHOOD BEHIND YOUR PUPPY

Never be afraid to ask pertinent questions about the puppy, as well as questions about the sire and dam. Feel free to ask the breeder if you might see the dam, the purpose of your visit to determine her general health and her appearance as a representative of the breed. Ask also to see the sire if the breeder is the owner. Ask what the puppy has been fed and should be fed after weaning. Ask to see the pedigree, and inquire if the litter or the individual puppies have been registered with the American Kennel Club, how many of the temporary and/or permanent inoculations the puppy has had, when and if the puppy has been wormed, and whether it has had any illness, disease or infection.

You need not ask if the puppy is housebroken. . . it won't mean much. He may have gotten the idea as to where "the place" is where he lives now, but he will need new training to learn where "the place" is in his new home! And you can't really expect too much from puppies at this age anyway. Housebreaking is entirely up to the new owner. We know puppies always eliminate when they first awaken and sometimes dribble when they get excited. If friends and relatives are coming over to see the new puppy, make sure he is walked just before he greets them at the front door. This will help.

The normal time period for puppies around three months of age to eliminate is about every two or three hours. As the time draws near, either take the puppy out or indicate the newspapers for the same purpose. Housebreaking is never easy, but anticipation is about 90 per cent of solving the problem. The schools that offer to housebreak your dog are virtually useless. Here again the puppy will learn the "place" at the schoolhouse, but coming home he will need special training for the new location.

A reputable breeder will welcome any and all questions you might ask and will voluntarily offer additional information, if only to brag about the tedious and loving care he has given the litter. He will also sell a puppy on a 24-hour veterinary approval. This means you have a full day to get the puppy to a veterinarian of your choice to get his opinion on the general health of the puppy before you make a final decision. There should also be veterinary certificates and full particulars on the dates and types of inoculations the puppy has been given up to that time.

PUPPIES AND WORMS

Let us give further attention to the unhappy and very unpleasant subject of worms. Generally speaking, most all puppies—even those raised in clean quarters—come into contact with worms early in life. The worms can be passed down from the mother before birth or picked up during the puppies' first encounters with the earth or their kennel facilities. To say that you must not buy a puppy because of an infestation of worms is nonsensical. You might be passing up a fine animal that can be freed of worms in one short treatment, although a heavy infestation of worms of any kind in a young dog is dangerous and debilitating.

The extent of the infection can be readily determined by a veterinarian, and you might take his word as to whether the future health and conformation of the dog has been damaged. He can prescribe the dosage and supply the medication at the time and you will already have one of your problems solved. The kinds and varieties of worms and how to detect them is described in detail elsewhere in this book and we advise you to check the matter out further if there is any doubt in your mind as to the problems of worms in dogs.

VETERINARY INSPECTION

While your veterinarian is going over the puppy you have selected to purchase, you might just as well ask him for his opinion of it as a breed as well as the facts about its general health. While few veterinarians can claim to be breed conformation experts, they usually have a good eye for a worthy specimen and can advise you where to go for further information. Perhaps your veterinarian could also recommend other breeders if you should want another opinion. The veterinarian can point out structural faults or organic problems that affect all breeds and can usually judge whether an animal has been abused or mishandled and whether it is oversized or undersized.

I would like to emphasize here that it is only through this type of close cooperation between owners and veterinarians that we can expect to reap the harvest of modern research in the veterinary field. Most reliable veterinarians are more than eager to learn about various breeds of purebred dogs, and we in turn must acknowledge and apply what they have proved through experience and research in their field. We can buy and breed the best dog in the world, but when disease strikes we are only as safe as our veterinarian is capable—so let's keep them informed breed by breed, and dog by dog. The veterinarian represents the difference between life and death!

An adorable Chow Chow puppy bred by the Starcrest Kennels of Mr. and Mrs. Joel Marston of Sun Valley, California.

THE CONDITIONS OF SALE

While it is customary to pay for the puppy before you take it away with you, you should be able to give the breeder a deposit if there is any doubt about the puppy's health. You might also (depending on local laws) postdate a check to cover the 24-hour veterinary approval. If you decide to take the puppy, the breeder is required to supply you with a pedigree, along with the puppy's registration paper. He is also obliged to supply you with complete information about the inoculations and American Kennel Club instructions on how to transfer ownership of the puppy into your name.

Some breeders will offer buyers time payment plans for convenience if the price on a show dog is very high or if deferred payments are the only way you can purchase the dog. However, any such terms must be worked out between buyer and breeder and should be put in writing to avoid later complications.

You will find most breeders cooperative if they believe you are sincere in your love for the puppy and that you will give it the proper home and the show ring career it deserves (if it is sold as a show quality specimen of the breed). Remember, when buying a show dog, it is impossible to guarantee nature. A breeder can only tell you what he *believes* will develop into a show dog. . . so be sure your breeder is an honest one.

Also, if you purchase a show prospect and promise to show the dog, you definitely should show it! It is a waste to have a beautiful dog that deserves recognition in the show ring sitting at home as a family pet, and it is unfair to the breeder. This is especially true if the breeder offered you a reduced price because of the advertising his kennel and bloodlines would receive by your showing the dog in the ring. If you want a pet, buy a pet. Be honest about it, and let the breeder decide on this basis which is the best dog for you. Your conscience will be clear and you'll both be doing a real service to the breed.

BUYING A SHOW PUPPY

If you are positive about breeding and showing your dog, make it clear that you intend to do so so that the breeder will sell you the best possible puppy. If you are dealing with an established kennel, you will have to rely partially if not entirely on their choice, since they know their bloodlines and what they can expect from the breeding. They know how their stock develops, and it would be foolish of them to sell you a puppy that could not stand up as a show specimen representing their stock in the ring.

However, you must also realize that the breeder may be keeping the best puppy in the litter to show and breed himself. If

Liontamer All-My-Tee and Liontamer Ah-Tum as young puppies, displaying the typical "teddy bear" resemblance that endears them to all!

A trio of Chow Chow puppies blending the famous Starcrest and Shryock's de la Moulaine bloodlines. These puppies were bred by the Shryocks of California.

Wah-Hu's Blooming Luck, sired by Ch. Wah-Hu's Brass Buddha *ex* Ky-Lin's Quintella; on the left is Ky-Lin's Yu Hu of Wah-Hu, sired by Ky-Lin's Quintus Son *ex* Ky-Lin's Monette. Blossom and Yu Hu are owned by the William Chambers, Wah-Hu Kennels, Glen Ellyn, Illinois.

this is the case, you might be wise to select the best puppy of the opposite sex so that the dogs will not be competing against one another in the show rings for their championship title.

THE PURCHASE PRICE

Prices vary on all puppies, of course, but a good show prospect at six weeks to six months of age will sell for several hundred dollars. If the puppy is really outstanding, and the pedigree and parentage is also outstanding, the price will be even higher. Honest breeders, however, will all be around the same figure, so price should not be a deciding factor in your choice. If there is any question as to the current price range, a few telephone calls to different kennels will give you a good average. Breeders will usually stand behind their

Ch. Shoh Dee T'Sing of Farresdale, bred and owned by Mrs. Pearl E. Farres of Charlotte, North Carolina. Pictured at 14 months of age in this July, 1939 photograph. The sire was Ch. Manchu Hung Yao of Farresdale ex Ch. Tung Sen T'Sing of Farresdale.

Two home-bred puppies sired by the Gerald Sterlings' Ch. Chang-Shi Zygoto, whelped in the 1950's. Ch. Chang-Shi Sombre Sambah (M) and Ch. Chang-Shi Bamboo Loo (B).

Liontamer Love and Kisses, whelped in June of 1972. "Impy" makes her show ring debut as Best Junior Puppy in Match at the Ramapo Kennel Club Match show in September, 1972. Desmond Murphy handling. Her sire is Ch. Eastward Liontamer of Elster ex Ch. Westfield Liontamer Athena. "Impy" is co-owned by Mr. and Mrs. Rick Donnelly and Dr. Sam Draper who was co-breeder of Impy with Desmond Murphy.

Ch. Liontamer Bruiser photographed as a puppy. Owned by Mr. and Mrs. Carl Boudreau, Kamara Kennels, Cape Cod, Massachusetts. Bruiser's father is Ch. Eastward Liontamer of Elster; his mother is Pandee's Chin-ky.

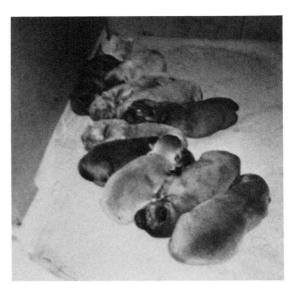

Ten Chow puppies who are five days old represent, according to Dr. Imogene Earle, one of the largest Chow litters on record. This is the Pandee "K" litter which includes Ch. Pandee's Kenya, Pandee's Katanga, and so on. The sire is Ch. Pandee's Jubilee, the mother Pandee's Zip Orah. Dr. Earle is breeder and owner.

Pandee's Little Red, owned and bred by Dr. Earle, was sired by Ch. Pandee's Red Rufus II out of Pandee's Beta Ching. Little Red was subsequently sent to Santiago, Chile.

Mi-Pao Arrogant Bon-Bon, pictured as a three-month-old puppy, owned by David Laverne Owens of Las Vegas, Nevada.

Winsome two-some. . . Mr. Grumps on the left, and Wiggles on the right, both owned by Dr. and Mrs. Edward North, Jr. of the Tsang-Po Kennels in Jackson, Mississippi.

Best of Breed from the Puppy Class over Specials under Frank Haze Burch was Shanglo's Soo-Z's Dar-Lin, handled by Al Lemar and owned by Susan S. Anderson of Santa Rosa, California. The show was the September, 1967 Contra Costa County Kennel Club event.

puppies; should something drastically wrong develop, such as hip dysplasia, etc., their obligation to make an adjustment is usually honored. Therefore, your cost is covered.

THE COST OF BUYING ADULT STOCK

Prices for adult dogs fluctuate greatly. Some grown dogs are offered free of charge to good homes; others are put out with owners on breeders' terms. But don't count on getting a "bargain" if it doesn't cost you anything! Good dogs are always in demand, and worthy studs or brood bitches are expensive. Prices for them can easily go up into the four-figure range. Take an ex-

pert with you if you intend to make this sort of investment. Just make sure the "expert" is free of professional jealousy and will offer unprejudiced opinion. If you are reasonably familiar with the Standard, and get the expert's opinion, between the two you can usually come up with a proper decision.

Buying grown stock does remove some of the risk if you are planning a kennel. You will know exactly what you are getting for your foundation stock and will also save time on getting your kennel started.

10. THE SOCIALIZATION OF THE CHOW CHOW

Chow breeders, exhibitors and devotees of the breed know that the Chow is one of the most handsome as well as one of the most challenging of all breeds. . . and one of the most wonderful, of course! But if we want to succeed in making the breed a little more popular and more widely appreciated and understood, the truth must be faced: the Chow Chow still has a reputation of being bad-tempered, and to combat that stigma, all Chow people must work together to present the Chow to the public in the best possible light. To some degree, we have failed to accomplish excellent public relations in the past, and we must not fail again. We have a deplorable stigma to overcome, a stigma which is widespread, ingrained and stubborn. In the next few years, we must erase the stain of the Chow's "bad reputation" and start again as if we had an entirely new breed to proclaim, the Chow Chow that is friendly, reliable in every sense and completely amenable to handling by all strangers.

One example from a recent show will serve to illustrate the continuing unfortunate reputation the breed must live down as well as to provide evidence that "the new image" of the Chow Chow will hopefully succeed. At a show in Connecticut, nine Chows were entered. Only a small number of spectators watched the judging. Afterwards, an attractive couple, experienced in Afghans and Lhasa Apsos, came over to look at one of our young males who had gone Best of Winners. I took him out of the crate and put him on a grooming table. Wagging his tail heartily as if to say, "Hello! Come on over and get acquainted," he attracted several spectators who were not specifically interested in Chows. The

The five-month-old Ch. Shang-Tai's Sonombre, whelped in October, 1965. Sonombre was Ruby Van Over's first home-bred champion.

Ch. Hetherchow Liontamer Daz-zel, winning a Group as a puppy at a match show under judge Mrs. Cyril Bernfeld. Desmond Murphy handling. A Michael Loconte photo.

Ch. Tsang-Po's Red Commander of Jade, owned by Mr. and Mrs. Nelson Tardy, pictured winning at a show before his tragic death from anesthesia at two years of age. Bred by the Tsang-Po Kennels, Lubbock, Texas. The judge is Charles Hamilton.

Ch. Tsang-Po's Tomiko was bred in 1968 by the Hal Allens of Lubbock, Texas. Mr. and Mrs. Robert Flippo, owners.

Ch. Eastward Liontamer of Elster (handled by Robert A. Hetherington, Jr.) and Ch. Ah Sid Go Go (handled by David Owens) were the judge's Best of Breed and Best of Opposite Sex at a 1967 show under Robert Griffing. Photo by William P. Gilbert.

young husband and wife became smitten with him. The Chow actually gave the lady a juicy kiss which she relished. The husband asked if he might take the dog on a lead for a stroll. Many of those watching were won over by that action because the Chow strode away merrily with the stranger, tail whipping back and forth like it was running with a motor! Just at that moment, when everyone was impressed with the lovable Chow, an older woman, austere and powerfully built, leaned over into our

Cowboy Roy Rogers was on hand at the Lehigh Valley Kennel Club show in 1962 to present the Best in Show trophy which judge Earle T. Adair awarded to the Chow Chow, Ch. Ah Sid's the Dilettante, who is handled by Jane Kamp Forsyth.

Ch. Liontamer All-American pictured here as a puppy. Owned by Mr. and Mrs. R.A. Hetherington, Jr., All-American was whelped in August, 1967.

A lovely portrait of Ch. Cho Co's Kee Jo who attained his championship in just eight shows with 6 Group Placements. To Ko lived to be 13 years of age and gave nothing but pleasure to his owner, Mary Alice Elliott of Denver, Colorado.

Ch. Hetherchow Liontamer Doll-ee, pictured winning Best of Winners under judge Mrs. Paul Silvernail at the Trenton Kennel Club Show in May, 1969. Handler is Doll-ee's breeder, Dr. Samuel Draper. Owners: Mr. and Mrs. Robert Borsuch, Morris, Connecticut.

The cinnamon-colored Chow Chow Ch. Ah Sid's Guardian Knight, pictured going Best of Breed and Group Second under judge Nakada at the Rock Creek Kennel Club show in October, 1960. Guardian Knight is owned by Ottile Hunter of Rockville, Maryland.

coterie and blurted, "Well, that dog's NOT a typical Chow! All the Chows I ever saw were vicious! When I was younger, a hideous red Chow lived down the block. . .", etc., etc., the same old song, the same old platitude. Before that cackling fishwife nearly destroyed all the good image our Chows had demonstrated, I croaked, "But, madam, you'll have to change with the times. You're talking about twenty-five years ago. It is true that some of the Chows then were reprobates, but not any more. We want our Chows to be friendly, reliable in every way, above all happy with everybody and all dogs. In fact, we insist upon it."

"Do you mean this is a different breed?" someone offered.

"No, not a new breed," I continued. "This is a Chow and like nearly all the Chows today has a good, steady temperament. That's the way we're breeding them now. The breeders of today and of the future want their Chows to be friendly, happy, and amenable to handling by all strangers. All of us are striving for that goal."

"And for the most part you're succeeding," said a leading non-sporting judge who came along and joined in. "Chows really aren't like they used to be." With that spoken blessing, the crowd started to break up. But nevertheless, I sensed that the negative, annoying "legend" about the "mean" Chow had sifted down over these people like a pall of black smoke. I wasn't sure whether the crowd believed me or the detractor. But the living proof of my testimony that Chows are friendly, our Chow, had acquitted himself well.

If there had been one Chow there who had growled at a stranger, or backed away from the judge, or objected to having his mouth opened or his body gone over, all the talking in the world on our part would have been useless. And had the young Chow in question balked or growled when invited to go for a walk by the stranger—or even put his tail down—the old "image" would have perpetuated itself.

A Chow Chow, as show dog, stud dog,

and/or companion, is "worthless" unless he is amenable to being handled by strangers. One example will demonstrate: several Chow breeders and I went to see a potential show dog offered for sale. When we saw him, alone in a paddock, we were dumbstruck. We were somewhat breathless as we studied his magnificence. He was one of the greatest Chows any of us had ever seen! "That Chow is worth a fortune," someone offered. Agreeing, we hardly believed our eyes. He looked faultless in every aspect. When we asked the owner how he got along with other Chows, particularly bitches, he retorted, "Oh, you could never use this dog at stud. He'd kill any bitch—in season or out!" We swallowed hard. "Well," we continued, "how's he with people?" "Fair," the owner answered.

We soon learned that we had not discovered the great new Chow of the future. In short, the owner had a difficult time getting his hands on the Chow. When the dog was brought in the house and put on a grooming table in order that we might go over him, he growled and tried repeatedly to go for us. Even the choke chain the owner had to use on him was not able to

The future champion Belgian import whelped August 29, 1950, Ch. Chang-Shi Zygoto, bred by Countess R. de Changy and imported by Lucile and Gerald Sterling of Nashville, Tennessee. Sire of 16 champions, he has set the record in the breed to date. He is 12-weeks-old in this photograph.

Ch. Ah Sid the Dilettante, Best in Show winner at the 1963 Ladies' Kennel Association of America show under judge Anna Katherine Nicholas. The photo features, from left to right, Mrs. Higgins, the judge, Mrs. Alker, handler Jane Forsyth and Mrs. Pyne. The late Joan Wellborn and John Davis of Clinton, Maryland are the owners. The Dilettante is the Best in Show record holder for Chow Chows.

Danny Hetherington with Ch. Liontamer All-American, the first champion sired by the great Ch. Eastward Liontamer of Elster. "Little Louie" was born in August, 1967 and finished his championship in 1968.

subdue the ugly dog. We were very disappointed.

That beautiful Chow was worthless because at two and a half years of age, he was too old to become socialized. He could not be used at stud nor could he be shown. And nobody would have him as a pet, certainly. (*I think he was too set in his ways to become even a guard dog. However, it is my firm belief that the Chow Chow should not be used as a guard dog. If that role has to be assumed again by the Chow, our cause of promoting friendly Chows is lost. The guard dog image is precisely the wrong image. It only adds fuel to the flames that the Chow is a "nasty" dog.*)

Back to the Chow described above. When a dog has never been socialized, it is difficult to make much progress with him as an adult. Some progress can be made, but it is slow and the results are perhaps only temporary. That is why the Chow Chow must be socialized from the time he is a small puppy. The group that went to see this magnificent but useless Chow should have known better, for that particular breeder had a well-known reputation for bad-tempered dogs. None of his Chows

had ever been socialized, and when he tried to show them, it was a disaster for the "promotion" of the friendly Chow Chow. He alone set back the correct "friendly" Chow image many years.

Another reason for socializing the Chow is that the public relations image of the Chow is still bad, and any display of bad temperament in public only contributes to the unfortunate idea that Chows are mean. One such incident is unforgettable: at a Chow Specialty Show several years ago, seven or eight Chows behaved very badly—that is, seven or eight out of the about fifty shown. One or two were aggressively hostile, trying to bite the judge. Several others came into the ring, tails down, behaving as if they had never been on a lead before. They all backed away from the judge; one or two spun around in circles like a whirlwind. Three absolutely refused to allow the judge, an experienced Chow breeder, to touch them at all. It was an outrageous spectacle and would lead, on the part of the spectators, to one conclusion—Chows are temperamental, difficult, unreliable, distrustful of people, and afraid of other dogs! The other well-behaved Chows were examples of Chows that had been "socialized." They behaved as all Chows should in the show ring. Any Chow trained from puppyhood to like people and other dogs will be a happier, more successful show dog, companion and public image.

The Chow Chow must be socialized if we are ever going to be successful in eradicating that insidious, omnipresent legend that Chows are bad tempered. Unfortunately, the legend exists because there is some truth to it; yes, there are some "mean" Chows who have not been socialized. All Chow breeders must work together toward *total socialization*. That must become a rule of life if our breed is going to survive.

To end with, it should be reported that the young Connecticut couple whose introduction to Chows was related earlier came back to our crates toward the end of the day. "We want one of your Chows," beamed the couple. They had never met a

Five sons sired by the fabulous Ch. Ghat de la Moulaine *ex* Jon Ell's Mei Ling, bred and owned by Mrs. M. Maxine Joner of Vancouver, Washington.

Ch. G.R.OW.L Scotchow Laz-A-Rus, bred by Joan M. Hannephin and owned by Gerry M. Rivera and O.K. Leverich of Phoenix, Arizona. The judge is Frank Foster Davis, a one-time Chow breeder. McLaughlin photo.

Chow before and the only one that they had gotten to know was a cordial one, one which they trusted. So, because they are a new generation who had never had a malignant experience with a Chow, they loved the breed immediately. Because there will be many people in Chows as worthy as this young couple, who will build a strong future for our breed, one can be perhaps a bit hopeful. Hopeful, yes, because the new people who come into Chows will insist upon socialization for their Chows.

We must prove the goodness of the breed to the world by showing the public that the Chow is a friendly, steady, stable dog, one that can be loved, trusted, and counted on always to be agreeable with strangers.

A big win in 1973 for Mi-Tu's Han Su Shang under Haskell Schuffman at the Danville, Illinois show. Shang won a four-point major in an entry of 30 Chows toward his American Championship. He was 7 months old at the time of this photo. In February 1974 Shang went Best of Breed over several specials at the Westminster Kennel Club show held in Madison Square Garden in New York City. He was handled at the show pictured here and at the Garden by his co-owner, Mr. John C. Frederick Peddie of Toronto, Canada. Shang's other owners are Mr. and Mrs. Herb Williams.

RULES FOR THE SOCIALIZATION OF THE CHOW CHOW

1. Accept the idea that the Chow Chow must be "socialized" from the time he is a puppy. This philosophy is the most important of all to insure success of your Chow kennel.

2. Socialization is the process by which the Chow puppy is taught to meet and like human beings, other dogs, and situations with steadiness and even, hopefully, enthusiasm.

3. Pick up the Chow puppy as often as possible from the time he is a few days old.

4. Once you have picked up the puppy, pet him, and talk to him quietly. At first, the puppy may cry or whine but as he becomes accustomed to your hands and voice, he will like the experience.

5. Continue to pick up and hold the puppy. By this time, his eyes will be open and he will adjust through his vision to the feeling of being held.

6. Pick up the puppy and hand him to strangers who come in to visit. By now, he will enjoy being held and petted by anybody.

7. If you know any children, ask them to visit you in order to hold and play with the puppy.

8. Encourage your puppy to be openly friendly by romping with him, chasing him in fun, picking him up, and hugging him.

9. By the time your puppy is eight weeks old, start taking him in the car with you. Whenever you meet anyone, let the stranger hold the puppy.

10. From the start of the socialization of your Chow when he is a puppy, begin to open his mouth several times a day. Treat the process as a game, talking to him while you are opening the jaw, and after, praising him for the success. Chow Chows do not like to have their mouths opened, but if you will start the mouth-opening early in his life, he will learn to accept it and hopefully to like it. The dog show judge will appreciate your efforts.

11. In addition to opening your Chow's mouth as part of his socialization, if your Chow is a male, start to touch his testicles rather often to get him accustomed to this idea rather early. If you practice this frequently and consistently, you will have no problem when the judge examines him in this area.

12. Whenever you go to visit your friends, take your puppy with you. By now your puppy may be three months old, and he will be a very steady, friendly puppy who loves people. . . if you follow the above rules. Be sure you take your puppy to as many "new" environments as you can. He may be completely at ease when strangers come into his own home where he is secure. But make sure that he can be taken to the supermarket, the post office, perhaps to a school or park without any discomfort, fear or insecurity. Your puppy's tail should stay up at all times no matter into what "foreign" or unfamiliar environment he may be taken.

13. By the time your puppy is between ten and twelve weeks old, he should be introduced to other puppies and older dogs. (Even before this age, the puppy may become aggressive towards his brothers and sisters, actually attacking them, biting, etc. If this happens, your common sense would indicate that you must separate the offending puppy or puppies.)

14. It is time to take your puppy to his first puppy match. He should be able to accept the experience of seeing all the other puppies and all the people with complete confidence and happiness. He has been preparing and training for this moment all of his life. If you have done your work well, he will be happy and at ease. You will be very proud of him and you can share in that pride.

15. Continue to "socialize" your puppy in every way possible. When you are taking him for a walk, let any person you meet who is interested touch your Chow, pet him, and generally go over him. Presumably you have exposed him early in his life to children so that he not only likes adults but children, too.

16. If for some reason you are not able to continue to socialize your Chow, and he should not see anyone but you (and/or your family) for some length of time, he may regress. You may find that when a stranger comes into your home, your young dog may drop his tail and run into another room, hiding from the social contact. Be patient with your dog and blame yourself, not him. He was socialized, but then he has not been permitted to continue to put into practice what he had already learned earlier. If this happens, begin the "socialization" process over again, and because he had a good social beginning, he should snap out of this temporary lapse once he is able to see people and be exposed to strangers again. Remember he has been taught to like people and dogs, and that friendly pattern will re-establish itself quickly.

17. Should you have a Chow that seems bent on becoming attached to you and your family, a Chow that does not socialize easily because he feels he wants only to be loved by you, perhaps the following idea might be of help. If your Chow starts to become too attached to you when he's between two and three months of age, try to find a friend, a dog person, of course, preferably another Chow breeder, to whom you can give your Chow temporarily. The new "temporary" owner will continue to socialize the puppy in the manner described above. The puppy will very soon transfer his affection to the new owner and his family, thus breaking the original attachment that might well lead to later problems. This process has proved effective in many cases. Finally, the puppy will learn to love everyone, not just one

Plain Acre's Black Fancy, another beautiful black whelped in 1973 at Manota Stertz' kennels in Cincinnati. Sire was Beamer's Oriental Boi *ex* Plain Acres Silhouette. Tammy won a 3-point major at a Springfield, Ohio show in December, 1973, under judge Bursch at the start of her show career.

owner or family. Use as many temporary owners as you need until the puppy can be returned to his "original" owner without becoming overly attached.

18. A "socialized" Chow is a happy, stable, well-adjusted dog. Because he is not only reliable with people and other dogs but also happy with them, you, likewise, can be relaxed and content when your Chow is confronted by a stranger, a dog he doesn't know, or a situation which is new to him. Because you have been wise in your insistence on his socialization, you have made him a happier dog and yourself a happier owner.

11. GROOMING THE CHOW CHOW:
The Adult and the Puppy

A Chow must be groomed if he is to be at his most beautiful. Although your Chow may be of very high quality, if he is not brushed he looks unkempt and disheveled, certainly not his best.

However, one has heard very often "I like Chows but would never own one because they're too much trouble to groom." Surprisingly, the Chow is not difficult or time-consuming to groom. He is perhaps one-tenth as difficult to groom as the very popular Old English Sheepdog. Because of the hard, stiff quality of the adult Chow's coat, it doesn't mat or tangle easily. One short grooming period a week would constitute the minimum time required to keep the Chow well groomed; however, if you can spend even ten minutes each day with a brush plus a weekly session, you will be able to keep your Chow clean and well groomed.

Here is the basic necessary equipment for grooming the adult Chow Chow:

1. A rake-type brush called either a "rake" or a "wire slicker."

2. A pin brush, sometimes called a "Poodle brush."

3. A steel comb.

4. A pair of nail clippers.

5. A pair of barber's scissors for trimming the Chow's feet.

THREE POSITIONS FOR GROOMING THE CHOW
These three positions *must be taught from puppyhood.*

1. The Chow lies on its side. Called the "lying position."

2. The standing position.

3. The sitting position.

BASIC GROOMING OR BRUSHING
If your adult Chow has been trained since his puppyhood to lie on his side, put him in this "lying position." If not, let the Chow stand naturally on the grooming table. Using the pin brush and some commercial coat conditioner in an aerosol spray can or bottle:

1. Start at the neck, with the dog in standing position, and part the hair to the skin, making the part go all across the top of the back. (If the dog is in the lying position, the part will start at the shoulder and go down the side of the dog.)

2. Brush the coat thoroughly along the part from the skin out to the very ends of the hair. Repeat this process spraying as much coat conditioner as you need, brushing the hair on both sides of the part right to the skin.

3. Now move the part one quarter-inch (¼ inch) toward the withers of the dog. Now brush the coat along the part from the skin out to the very ends of the hair; this process as described in step 2 is the secret of correct grooming.

4. Move the part again one quarter-inch (¼ inch) toward the rear of the dog.

GROOMING YOUR CHOW—Step 1.
If you have—as you should have—trained your Chow from puppyhood to lie on a grooming table, you will have no difficulty in putting him in this position for grooming. Part the dog's hair TO THE SKIN in the middle of the Chow or at either end. Brush the coat to the skin THOROUGHLY (over and over) before moving the part toward the dog's head or toward his rear end, depending on which direction you wish to move. Notice that the Chow is relaxed and will stay indefinitely on the grooming table without being held.

All photos in this sequence of grooming photos shown here and on the following pages are by Alexander C. Schwartz, Jr.

GROOMING YOUR CHOW—Step 2.
This is a continuation of Step 1; this shows the owner of the Chow actually brushing the dog's coat to the skin, thoroughly. Repeat this several times brushing the same hair using a pin brush. This particular Chow is being groomed from the middle of his body to the head; you may start at the middle and move toward the head or you may start in the middle and move toward the rear end; no matter where you start you groom the ENTIRE CHOW from head to rear end using this parting and brushing method. When you finish brushing both sides of the dog's part thoroughly, you move the part toward the head or the rear depending on the direction you're working. Here the groomer is moving toward the head.

GROOMING YOUR CHOW—Step 3.
This shows a continuation of Steps 1 and 2. The groomer is moving progressively toward the head with his parting and brushing method. The key to success is to brush thoroughly to the skin before moving the part up or down.

434

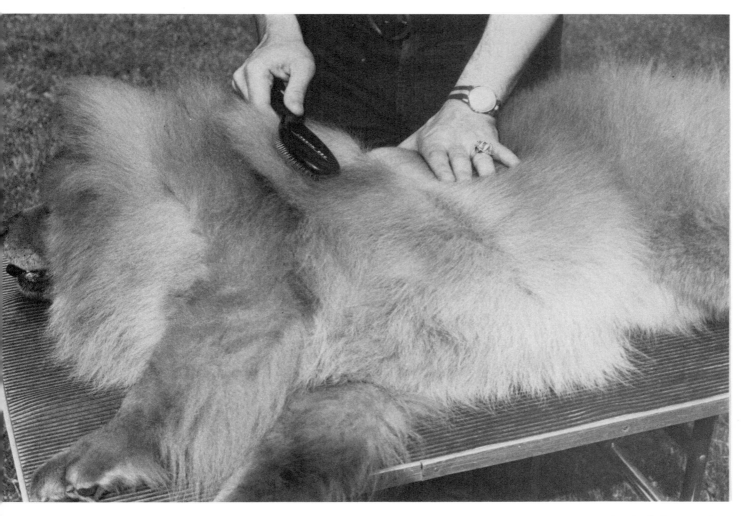

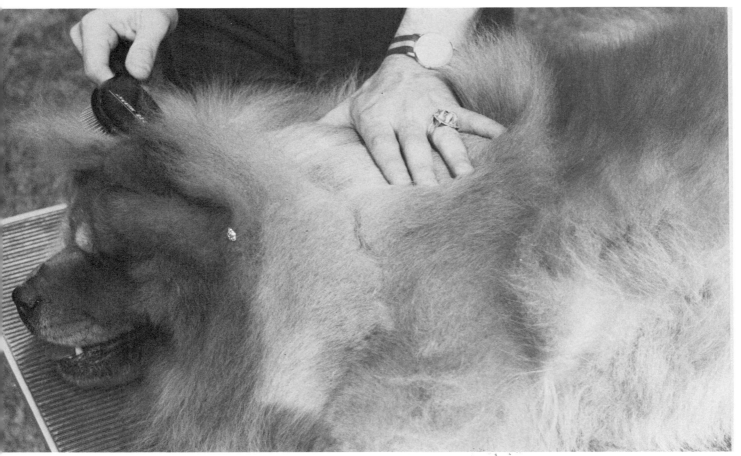

GROOMING YOUR CHOW—Step 4.
Once you have finished, brush your Chow from the middle to the head and from the middle to the rear, or vice versa and then put the dog in a standing position. The groomer has almost finished the brushing of the body coat and the part is still visible.

GROOMING YOUR CHOW—Step 5.
The part is brushed out, and the entire coat is being brushed FORWARD. The Chow's ruff is brushed forward also. Notice that the tail has been thoroughly brushed and is being brushed forward.

GROOMING YOUR CHOW—Step 6.
After you finish grooming the Chow's ruff, start on his chest and brush downward toward the table. You may use the parting and brushing method on the chest if you wish, but finally you must brush downward. And once again, thoroughness is the key to success.

GROOMING YOUR CHOW—Step 7.
Here the ruff or pants on the Chow's leg are being brushed thoroughly. First you may brush in the direction of the Chow head (that is, upward), then finally brush downward toward the table. Groom all four legs thoroughly.

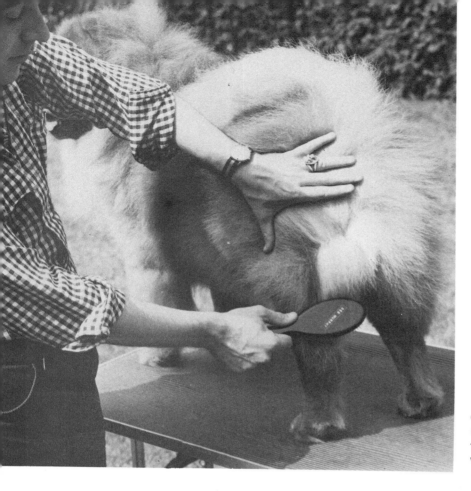

GROOMING YOUR CHOW—Step 8.
Brush the rear end of the Chow downward toward
the table. You may part and brush the rear if you
wish, but finally you will brush downward.

GROOMING YOUR CHOW—Step 9.
Now your Chow has been brushed thoroughly on
all parts of his body. Put the finishing touches of
perfection on him by brushing every hair on his
body forward and all the hair on his legs downward toward the table. Every hair stands out because it has been brushed thoroughly to the
roots. If your Chow is somewhat short of coat,
you can make every hair count by brushing to the
skin or to the roots.

GROOMING YOUR CHOW—Step 10.
You can use a pair of nail clippers similar to those shown here to cut your Chow's toenails or you may use a rotary grinder. The grinder is a noisy instrument and the Chow will not like its buzzing sound unless he has been accustomed to it since he was a puppy. Chows appear to be very sensitive to having their nails cut, but any veterinarian will tell you that no dog, of any breed, relishes his nail cutting experience. In any case, you must keep your Chow's nails short as part of your grooming program.

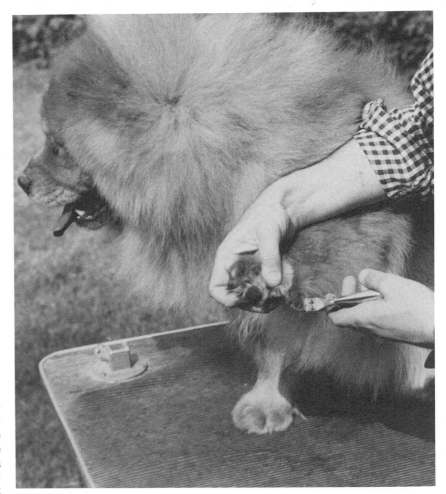

GROOMING YOUR CHOW—Step 11.
Although the official AKC Standard for the Chow Chow speaks of "untouched naturalness," it is an accepted practice among Chow exhibitors to use the scissors in trimming your Chow's feet. The extra long hairs can be cut off to make the foot a rounded, cat-like foot essential to the Chow's leonine appearance. The Chow's coat should not be cut or scissored except for his feet.

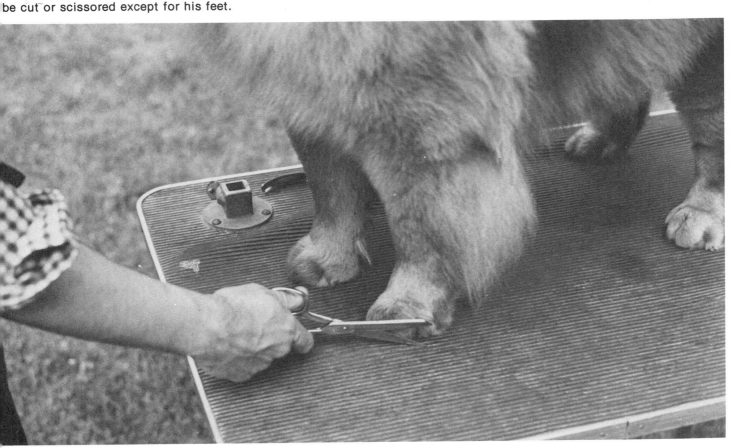

439

Continue the process of parting and brushing to the skin. Then move the part again one-quarter of an inch toward the goal of reaching the tail. If the dog is lying on his side, finish the sides, then the legs, and then turn the dog over and repeat the process. If the dog is standing, the groomer finishes one side and moves to the opposite side of the dog.

5. The process can be summarized as follows: part and brush (and spray if you wish) moving the part toward the direction of accomplishment.

6 Brush the back and sides and stomach first; next are the legs, the tail, pants, then the ruff, and the top of the head, ending with the front.

7. After the Chow has been groomed all over to the skin, the dog may stand (if he has been in the lying position for all the preceding). The dog may be in the sitting position for the grooming of the head, ruff, and front. Since all the above brushing has been done with the pin brush, you may want to switch to the rake to take out any snarls or mats in the soft hair behind the ears.

8. The dog should stand for the final touches in which all the hair is brushed forward toward his head to give that "finished" look, that magnificence that can only be achieved when every hair is groomed to the skin and is "off-standing" shining and unforgettable.

9. If you have brushed thoroughly to the skin, you will be able to put on the finishing touches with the pin brush as described in step 8, or with a steel comb (whose teeth in one part are perhaps 1/4" apart and in another 1/8" apart).

10. Use the scissors to cut the long guard hairs off the feet, rounding them to the compact, round and cat-like shape called for by the Standard.

BATHING

The Chow that has been brushed regularly according to the prescribed method doesn't have to be bathed very often, perhaps only once or twice a year. If you wish to bathe your Chow, you may follow the directions for bathing given in any general dog book.

In addition to the regular brushing, you may keep your Chow clean by rubbing him with a damp towel which has been soaked in a shampoo and water solution. After the wet towel, use a dry one, rubbing briskly.

In addition to the occasional damp towel method as well as the regular "skin deep" brushing, you can use any of the commercially prepared "dry cleaners" sold at all pet stores, supermarkets and at all dog shows. If you wish to use a coat conditioner spray in an aerosol can or bottle as an accompaniment to your daily and weekly brushing, many kinds are available on the market.

GROOMING THE PUPPY

Use the wire rake or the wire slicker to groom your Chow puppy. Use the same method of parting the hair to the skin, brushing thoroughly, but not too hard, along the part to the very ends of the hair. Once the puppy's coat is thoroughly groomed "to the skin," you may use a steel comb, a finer one than that described for use on the adult coat.

One of the most important things you can do to facilitate all the future grooming of your Chow is to begin early. Start your puppy off at an early age (perhaps six to eight weeks) by placing him on his side on a grooming table or card table. Make him lie there by stroking him gently and telling him, "What a good fellow you are." Make his stay on his side the first time for perhaps one minute. Increase the period of time gradually so that in a week or so he is happy to lie on his side and on his back for 10 minutes or longer. You can turn this session of lying on his side into a kind of pleasure period because he is rewarded by getting lots of verbal praise, lots of petting and scratching of his tummy, which he will learn to relish. You will be thankful many times in the future that you trained your

Chart showing the proper method of grooming the Chow Chow. The arrows show the direction in which the hair should be brushed.

puppy to lie on his side and back because he will continue to lie on his side and/or back as a pleasure throughout the rest of his life. Grooming him in this "lying position" is by far the most thorough and easy method in grooming the Chow.

It's a good idea to begin to accustom your Chow puppy to getting his nails trimmed first when he is a baby with man-

icure scissors then later on with either an electric rotary grinder or a pair of professional dog nail clippers. The earlier you start the better, as a Chow seems particularly sensitive to having his feet touched or his nails trimmed. Early insistence on this important grooming will prove very helpful in the future.

12. GENETICS

Miki de la Moulaine, whelped in September, 1961, was sired by Ch. Ghat de la Moulaine *ex* Fluffy Chinese Princess. Bred by Clif and Vivian Shryock and owned by Betty Schellenberg of Fort Worth, Texas.

Tsang-Po's Ho Toi, whelped in June, 1972, is owned by Mr. and Mrs. Burgess and bred by the Hal Allens and Tsang-Po Kennels.

You can't guarantee nature! But with a few facts and theories at your command you can at least, on paper, plan a litter of puppies that should fulfill your fondest expectations. Since the ultimate purpose of breeding is to try to improve the breed, this planning, no matter how uncertain, should be earnestly attempted.

There are a few terms you should be familiar with to help you understand the breeding procedure and the structure of genetics. The first thing that comes to mind is the Mendelian Law — or The Laws of Mendelian Inheritance. Who was Mendel? Gregor Mendel was an Austrian clergyman and botanist born in Brunn, Moravia. He developed his basic theories on heredity while working with peas. Not realizing the full import of his work, he published a paper on his experiments in a scientific journal in the year 1866. That paper went unnoticed for many years, but the laws and theories put forth in it have been tried and proven. Today they are accepted by scientists as well as dog breeders.

To help understand the Mendelian Law as it applies to breeding dogs, we must acquaint ourselves with certain scientific terms and procedures. First of all, dogs possess glands of reproduction; these glands are called gonads. The gonads of the male are in the testicles, which produce sperm, or spermatozoa. The gonads of the female, the ovaries, produce eggs. The bitch is born with these eggs and, when she is old enough to reproduce, she comes into heat. The eggs descend from the ovaries via the Fallopian tubes to the two horns of the uterus. There they either pass on out during the heat cycle or are fertilized by the male sperm in the semen deposited during a mating.

Ch. Scotchow Liontamer Leo, photographed winning under judge Virgil Johnson in August, 1967. Breeder-owner: Joan M. Hannephin of Wheeling, West Virginia.

Ch. Don Lee's Umbo of Chia Hsi is shown at one year of age. His sire is Ch. Don Lee's Prophet and his dam, Livin' Doll of Poppyland. Umbo is owned by Mr. and Mrs. Harold Toudt.

In dog mating there is what we refer to as a tie, which is a time period during which the male pumps about 600 million spermatozoa into the female to fertilize the ripened eggs. When the sperm and the ripe eggs meet, zygotes are created and the little one-celled future puppies descend from the fallopian tubes into the uterus where they attach themselves to the walls of the uterus and begin to develop. With all inherited characteristics determined as the zygote was formed, the dam now must only assume her role as incubator for her babies, which are now organisms in their own right. The bitch has been bred and is now in whelp!

Let us take a closer look at what is happening during the breeding phenomenon. We know that while the male deposits as many as 600 million sperm into the female, the number of ripe eggs she releases will determine the number of puppies in the litter. Therefore, those breeders who advertise their stud as "producer of large litters" do not know the facts. The bitch determines the size of the litter; the male the sex of the puppies. It takes only one sperm of the 600 million to produce a puppy!

Each dog and bitch possesses 39 pairs of chromosomes in each reproductive germ cell. The chromosomes carry the genes, like peas in a pod, and there are approximately 150,000 genes in each chromosome. These chromosomes split apart and unite with half the chromosomes from the other parent and the puppy's looks and temperament are created.

To understand the procedure more thoroughly, we must understand that there are two kinds of genes—dominant and recessive. A dominant gene is one of a pair whose influence is expressed to the exclusion of the effects of the other. A recessive gene is one of a pair whose influence is subdued by the effects of the other. Most of the important qualities we wish to perpetuate in our breeding programs are carried on by the dominant genes. It is the successful breeder who becomes expert at eliminating recessive or undesirable genes and building up the dominant or desirable genes.

There are many excellent books available which will take you deeper into the fascinating subject of canine genetics. You can learn about your chances of getting so many black, so many white, and so many black and white puppies, etc. Avail yourself of this information before your next — or hopefully, first — breeding.

13. BREEDING YOUR CHOW CHOW

Ch. Kinghai Jill, bred and owned by Mr. and Mrs. LeRoy King, is pictured winning at a New England Chow Chow Specialty under the late judge Florence Broadhurst. Her sire was Me-Li San Dee *ex* Kinghai Bo-Peep. Handling for owners is Florence Stanton.

Let us assume the time has come for your dog to be bred, and you have decided you are in a position to enjoy producing a litter of puppies that you hope will make a contribution to the breed. The bitch you purchased is sound, her temperament is excellent and she is a most worthy representative of the breed.

You have taken a calendar and counted off the ten days since the first day of red staining and have determined the tenth to fourteenth day, which will more than likely be the best days for the actual mating. You have additionally counted off 65 to 63 days before the puppies are likely to be born to make sure everything necessary for their arrival will be in good order by that time.

From the moment the idea of having a litter occurred to you, your thoughts should have been given to the correct selection of a proper stud. Here again the novice would do well to seek advice on analyzing pedigrees and tracing bloodlines for your best breedings. As soon as the bitch is in season and you see color (or staining) and a swelling of the vulva, it is time to notify the owner of the stud you selected and make appointments for the breedings. There are several pertinent questions you will want to ask the stud owners after having decided upon the pedigree. The owners, naturally, will also have a few questions they wish to ask you. These questions will concern your bitch's bloodlines, health, age, how many previous litters if any, etc.

THE HEALTH OF THE BREEDING STOCK

Some of your first questions should concern whether or not the stud has already proved himself by siring a normal healthy litter. Also inquire as to whether or not the owners have had a sperm count made to determine just exactly how fertile or potent the stud is. Also ask whether he has been X-rayed for hip dysplasia and found to be clear. Determine for yourself whether the dog has two normal testicles.

When considering your bitch for this mating, you must take into consideration a few important points that lead to a successful breeding. You and the owner of the stud will want to recall whether she has had normal heat cycles, whether there are too many runts in the litter, and whether Caesarean section was every necessary. Has she ever had a vaginal infection? Could she take care of her puppies by herself, or was there a milk shortage? How many surviving puppies were there from the litter, and what did they grow up to be in comparison to the requirements of the breed Standard?

Don't buy a bitch that has problem heats and has never had a litter. But don't be afraid to buy a healthy maiden bitch, since chances are, if she is healthy and from good stock, she will be a healthy producer. Don't buy a monorchid male, and certainly not a cryptorchid. If there is any doubt in your mind about his potency, get a sperm count from the veterinarian. Older dogs that have been good producers and are for sale are usually not too hard to find at good established kennels. If they are not too old and have sired quality show puppies, they can give you some excellent show stock from which to establish your own breeding lines.

THE DAY OF THE MATING

Now that you have decided upon the proper male and female combination to produce what you hope will be — according to the pedigrees — a fine litter of puppies, it is time to set the date. You have selected the two days (with a one day lapse in between) that you feel are best for the breeding, and you call the owner of the stud. The bitch always goes to the stud, unless, of course, there are extenuating circumstances. You set the date and the time and arrive with the bitch *and* the money.

Standard procedure is payment of a stud fee at the time of the first breeding, if there is a tie. For the stud fee, you are entitled to two breedings with ties. Contracts may be written up with specific conditions on breeding terms, of course, but this is general procedure. Often a breeder will take the pick of a litter to protect and maintain his bloodlines. This can be especially desirable if he needs an outcross for his breeding program or if he wishes to continue his own bloodlines if he sold you the bitch to start with, and this mating will continue his line-breeding program. This should all be worked out ahead of time and written and signed before the two dogs are bred. Remember that the payment of the

Ch. Cho Co's Kee Jo, the first show dog owned by Mary Alice Elliott of Denver, Colorado. He is pictured here with her winning the Non-Sporting Group at the 1963 Central Wyoming Kennel Club Show under judge William Pym.

stud fee is for the services of the stud — not for a guarantee of a litter of puppies. This is why it is so important to make sure you are using a proven stud. Bear in mind also that the American Kennel Club will not register a litter of puppies sired by a male that is under eight months of age. In the case of an older dog, they will not register a litter sired by a dog over 12 years of age, unless there is a witness to the breeding in the form of a veterinarian or other responsible person.

Many studs over 12 years of age are still fertile and capable of producing puppies, but if you do not witness the breeding there is always the danger of a "substitute" stud being used to produce a litter. This brings up the subject of sending your bitch away to be bred if you cannot accompany her.

The winsome threesome from the Chia Hsi Kennels of Harold and Adie Toudt in Dousman, Wisconsin. Canadian and American Champion You-Two Ganti Biroe Alves (Holland), Ch. Shanglo's Jill of Chia Hsi, and Champion Elster's Gee Nee of Chia Hsi.

The disadvantages of sending a bitch away to be bred are numerous. First of all, she will not be herself in a strange place, so she'll be difficult to handle. Transportation if she goes by air, while reasonably safe, is still a traumatic experience, and there is the danger of her being put off at the wrong airport, not being fed or watered properly, etc. Some bitches get so upset that they go out of season and the trip, which may prove expensive, especially on top of a substantial stud fee, will have been for nothing.

If at all possible, accompany your bitch so that the experience is as comfortable for her as it can be. In other words, make sure before setting this kind of schedule for a breeding that there is no stud in the area that might be as good for her as the one that is far away. Don't sacrifice the proper breeding for convenience, since bloodlines are so important, but put the safety of the bitch above all else. There is always a risk in traveling, since dogs are considered cargo on a plane.

HOW MUCH DOES THE STUD FEE COST?

The stud fee will vary considerably— the better the bloodlines, the more winning the dog does at shows, the higher the fee. Stud service from a top winning dog could run up to $500.00. Here again, there may be exceptions. Some breeders will take part cash and then, say, third pick of the litter. The fee can be arranged by a private contract rather than the traditional procedure we have described.

Here again, it is wise to get the details of the payment of the stud fee in writing to avoid trouble.

THE ACTUAL MATING

It is always advisable to muzzle the bitch. A terrified bitch may fear-bite the stud, or even one of the people involved, and the wild bitch may snap or attack the stud, to the point where he may become discouraged and lose interest in breeding. Muzzling can be done with a lady's stocking tied around the muzzle with a half knot, crossed under the chin and knotted at the back of the neck. There is enough "give" in the stocking for her to breathe or salivate freely and yet not open her jaws far enough to bite. Place her in front of her owner, who holds onto her collar and talks to her and calms her as much as possible.

If the male will not mount on his own initiative, it may be necessary for the owner to assist in lifting him onto the bitch, perhaps even in guiding him to the proper place. But usually, the tie is accomplished once the male gets the idea. The owner should remain close at hand, however, to make sure the tie is not broken before an adequate breeding has been completed. After a while the stud may get bored and try to break away. This could prove injurious. It may be necessary to hold him in place until the tie is broken.

We must stress at this point that while some bitches carry on physically, and vocally, during the tie, there is no way the bitch can be hurt. However, a stud can be seriously or even permanently damaged by a bad breeding. Therefore the owner of the bitch must be reminded that she must not be alarmed by any commotion. All concentration should be devoted to the stud and a successful and properly executed service.

Many people believe that breeding dogs is simply a matter of placing two dogs, a male and a female, in close proximity, and letting nature take its course. While often this is true, you cannot count on it. Sometimes it is hard work, and in the case of valuable stock it is essential to supervise to be sure of the safety factor, especially if one or both of the dogs are inexperienced. If the owners are also inexperienced it may not take place at all!

ARTIFICIAL INSEMINATION

Breeding by means of artificial insemination is usually unsuccessful, unless under a veterinarian's supervision, and can lead to an infection for the bitch and discomfort for the dog. The American Kennel Club requires a veterinarian's certificate to register puppies from such a breeding. Although the practice has been used for over two decades, it now offers new promise, since research has been conducted to make it a more feasible procedure for the future.

Great dogs may eventually look forward to reproducing themselves years after they have left this earth. There now exists a frozen semen concept that has been tested and found successful. The study, headed by Dr. Stephen W.J. Seager, M.V.B., an instructor at the University of Oregon Medical School, has the financial support of the American Kennel Club, indicating that organization's interest in the work. The study is being monitored by the Morris Animal Foundation of Denver, Colorado.

Dr. Seager announced in 1970 that he had been able to preserve dog semen and to produce litters with the stored semen. The possibilities of selective, world-wide breedings by this method are exciting.

Imagine simply mailing a vial of semen to the bitch! The perfection of line-breeding by storing semen without the threat of death interrupting the breeding program is exciting, also.

As it stands today, the technique for artificial insemination requires the depositing of semen (taken directly from the dog) into the bitch's vagina, past the cervix and into the uterus by syringe. The correct temperature of the semen is vital, and there is no guarantee of success. The storage method, if successfully adopted, will present a new era in the field of purebred dogs.

THE GESTATION PERIOD

Once the breeding has taken place successfully, the seemingly endless waiting period, about 63 days, begins. For the first ten days after the breeding, you do absolutely nothing for the bitch—just spin dreams about the delights you will share with the family when the puppies arrive.

Around the tenth day it is time to begin supplementing the diet of the bitch with vitamins and calcium. We strongly recommend that you take her to your veterinarian for a list of the proper or perhaps

This six-weeks-old trio of Chow Chow puppies was bred by the Liontamer Kennels in Mahwah, New Jersey; included are Scotchow Liontamer Foggy Dew, Scotchow Liontamer Frankee, and Liontamer Forever.

necessary supplements and the correct amounts of each for your particular bitch. Guesses, which may lead to excesses or insufficiencies, can ruin a litter. For the price of a visit to your veterinarian, you will be confident that you are feeding properly.

The bitch should be free of worms, of course, and if there is any doubt in your mind, she should be wormed now, before the third week of pregnancy. Your veterinarian will advise you on the necessity of this and proper dosage as well.

PROBING FOR PUPPIES

Far too many breeders are overanxious about whether the breeding "took" and are inclined to feel for puppies or persuade a veterinarian to radiograph or X-ray their bitches to confirm it. Unless there is reason to doubt the normalcy of a pregnancy, this is risky. Certainly 63 days are not too long to wait, and why risk endangering the litter by probing with your inexperienced hands? Few bitches give no evidence of being in whelp, and there is no need to prove it for yourself by trying to count puppies.

ALERTING YOUR VETERINARIAN

At least a week before the puppies are due, you should telephone your veterinarian and notify him that you expect the litter and give him the date. This way he can make sure that there will be someone available to help, should there be any problems during the whelping. Most veterinarians today have answering services and alternate vets on call when they are not available themselves. Some veterinarians suggest that you call them when the bitch starts labor so that they may further plan their time, should they be needed. Discuss this matter with your veterinarian when you first take the bitch to him for her diet instructions, etc., and establish the method which will best fit in with his schedule.

DO YOU NEED A VETERINARIAN IN ATTENDANCE?

Even if this is your first litter, I would advise that you go through the experience

Ch. Plainacre's Gadabout pictured winning Winners Bitch at the Chow Chow Parent Club Specialty Show in 1973 under judge Isidore Schoenburg. The Specialty was held in conjunction with the Memphis, Tennessee Kennel Club show. Owner and handler is Mrs. Mary L. Wuest of Mason, Ohio.

of whelping without panicking and calling desperately for the veterinarian. Most animal births are accomplished without complications, and you should call for assistance only if you run into trouble.

When having her puppies, your bitch will appreciate as little interference and as few strangers around as possible. A quiet place, with her nest, a single familiar face and her own instincts are all that is necessary for nature to take its course. An audience of curious children squealing and questioning, other family pets nosing around, or strange adults should be avoided. Many a bitch which has been distracted in this way has been known to devour her young. This can be the horrible result of intrusion into the bitch's privacy. There are other ways of teaching children the miracle of birth, and there will be plenty of time later for the whole family to enjoy the puppies.

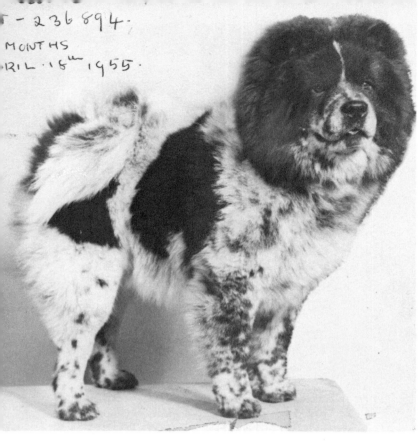

San Kee Atomic, a very rare piebald Chow Chow, bred by Dorothea Rademaker at her San Kee Kennels in Teaneck, New Jersey. Atomic was whelped in April, 1955 and is pictured here at six months of age (sitting) and at nine months of age (standing). The sire was Samurey of El Cher ex San Kee Champion Xoodan Sensation. The sire was a large cream dog from the well-known El Cher kennels of Mrs. Hugo Prinz in Paramus, New Jersey. The name El Cher represented some of the outstanding Chow Chows in the U.S.A. Atomic only lived to be 11 months of age, and therefore was never used in an experimental color breeding program planned by Mrs. Rademaker.

LABOR

Some litters—many first litters—do not run the full term of 63 days. So, at least a week before the puppies are actually due, and at the time you alert your veterinarian as to their arrival, start observing the bitch for signs of the commencement of labor. This will manifest itself in the form of ripples running down the sides of her body, which will come as a revelation to her as well. It is most noticeable when she is lying on her side—and she will be sleeping a great deal as the arrival date comes closer. If she is sitting or walking about, she will perhaps sit down quickly or squat peculiarly. As the ripples become more frequent, birth time is drawing near; you will be wise not to leave her. Usually within 24 hours before whelping, she will stop eating, and as much as a week before she will begin digging a nest. The bitch should be given something resembling a whelping box with layers of newspaper (black and white only) to make her nest. She will dig more and more as birth approaches, and this is the time to begin making your promise to stop interfering unless your help is specifically required. Some bitches whimper and others are silent, but whimpering does not necessarily indicate trouble.

THE ARRIVAL OF THE PUPPIES

The sudden gush of green fluid from the bitch indicates that the water or fluid surrounding the puppies has "broken" and they are about to start down the canal and come into the world. When the water breaks, birth of the first puppy is imminent. The first puppies are usually born within minutes to a half hour of each other, but a couple of hours between the later ones is not uncommon. If you notice the bitch straining constantly without producing a puppy, or if a puppy remains partially in and partially out for too long, it is cause for concern. Breech births (puppies born feet first instead of head first) can often cause delay or hold things up, and this is often a problem which requires veterinarian assistance.

FEEDING THE BITCH BETWEEN BIRTHS

Usually the bitch will not be interested in food for about 24 hours before the arrival of the puppies, and perhaps as long as two or three days after their arrival. The placenta which she cleans up after each puppy is high in food value and will be more than ample to sustain her. This is nature's way of allowing the mother to feed herself and her babies without having to leave the nest and hunt for food during the first crucial days. The mother always cleans up all traces of birth in the wilds so as not to attract other animals to her newborn babies.

However, there are those of us who believe in making food available should the mother feel the need to restore her strength during or after delivery—especially if she whelps a large litter. Raw chopped meat, beef boullion, and milk are all acceptable and may be placed near the whelping box during the first two or three days. After that, the mother will begin to put the babies on a sort of schedule. She will leave the whelping box at frequent intervals, take longer exercise periods, and begin to take interest in other things. This is where the fun begins for you. Now the babies are no longer soggy little pinkish blobs. They begin to crawl around and squeal and hum and grow before your very eyes!

It is at this time, if all has gone normally, that the family can be introduced gradually and great praise and affection given to the mother.

BREECH BIRTHS

Puppies normally are delivered head first. However, some are presented feet first, or in other abnormal positions, and this is referred to as a "breech birth." Assistance is often necessary to get the puppy out of the canal, and great care must be taken not to injure the puppy or the dam.

Aid can be given by grasping the puppy with a piece of turkish toweling and pulling gently during the dam's contractions. Be careful not to squeeze the puppy too hard; merely try to ease it out by moving it gently back and forth. Because even this much delay in delivery may mean the puppy is drowning, do not wait for the bitch to remove the sac. Do it yourself by tearing the sac open to expose the face and head. Then cut the cord anywhere from one-half to three-quarters of an inch away from the navel. If the cord bleeds excessively, pinch the end of it with your fingers and count five. Repeat if necessary. Then pry open the mouth with your finger and hold the puppy upside-down for a moment to drain any fluids from the lungs. Next, rub the puppy briskly with turkish or paper toweling. You should get it wriggling and whimpering by this time.

If the litter is large, this assistance will help conserve the strength of the bitch and will probably be welcomed by her. However, it is best to allow her to take care of at least the first few herself to preserve the natural instinct and to provide the nutritive values obtained by her consumption of the afterbirths.

DRY BIRTHS

Occasionally the sac will break before the delivery of a puppy and will be expelled while the puppy remains inside, thereby depriving the dam of the necessary lubrication to expel the puppy normally. Inserting vaseline or mineral oil via your finger will help the puppy pass down the birth canal. This is why it is essential that you be present during the whelping so that you can count puppies and afterbirths and determine when and if assistance is needed.

THE TWENTY-FOUR-HOUR CHECKUP

It is smart to have a veterinarian check the mother and her puppies within 24 hours after the last puppy is born. The vet can check for cleft palates or umbilical hernia and may wish to give the dam—particularly if she is a show dog—an injection of Pituitin to make sure of the expulsion of all afterbirths and to tighten up the uterus. This can prevent a sagging belly after the puppies are weaned and the bitch is being readied for the show ring.

FALSE PREGNANCY

The disappointment of a false pregnancy is almost as bad for the owner as it is for the bitch. She goes through the gestation period with all the symptoms—swollen stomach, increased appetite, swollen nipples—even makes a nest when the time comes. You may even take an oath that you noticed the ripples on her body from the labor pains. Then, just as suddenly as you made up your mind that she was definitely going to have puppies, you will know that she definitely is not! She may walk around carrying a toy as if it were a puppy for a few days, but she will soon be back to normal and acting just as if nothing happened —and nothing did!

CAESAREAN SECTION

Should the whelping reach the point where there is a complication, such as the bitch's not being capable of whelping the puppies herself, the "moment of truth" is upon you and a Caesarean section may be necessary. The bitch may be too small or too immature to expel the puppies herself; or her cervix may fail to dilate enough to allow the young to come down the birth canal; or there may be torsion of the uterus, a dead or monster puppy, a sideways puppy blocking the canal, or perhaps toxemia. A Caesarean section will be the only solution. No matter what the cause, get the bitch to the veterinarian immediately to insure your chances of saving the mother and/or puppies.

The Caesarean section operation (the name derived from the idea that Julius Caesar was delivered by this method) involves the removal of the unborn young from the uterus of the dam by surgical incision into the walls through the abdomen. The operation is performed when it has been determined that for some reason the puppies cannot be delivered normally. While modern surgical methods have made the operation itself reasonably safe, with the dam being perfectly capable of nursing the puppies shortly after the completion of the surgery, the chief danger lies in the ability to spark life into the puppies immediately upon their removal from the womb. If the mother dies, the time element is even more important in saving the young, since the oxygen supply ceases upon the death of the dam, and the difference between life and death is measured in seconds.

After surgery, when the bitch is home in her whelping box with the babies, she will probably nurse the young without distress. You must be sure that the sutures are kept clean and that no redness or swelling or ooze appears in the wound. Healing will take place naturally, and no salves or ointments should be applied unless prescribed by the veterinarian, for fear the puppies will get it into their systems. If there is any doubt, check the bitch for fever, restlessness (other than the natural concern for her young) or a lack of appetite, but do not anticipate trouble.

EPISIOTOMY

Even though large dogs are generally easy whelpers, any number of reasons might occur to cause the bitch to have a difficult birth. Before automatically resorting to Caesarean section, many veterinarians are now trying the technique known as episiotomy.

Used rather frequently in human deliveries, episiotomy (pronounced a-pease-e-ott-o-me) is the cutting of the membrane between the rear opening of the vagina back almost to the opening of the anus. After delivery it is stitched together, and barring complications, heals easily, presenting no problem in future births.

THE POWER OF PEDIGREES

An old dog philosopher once remarked that the definition of a show prospect puppy is one third the pedigree, one third what you see, and one third what you *hope* it *will* be! Well, no matter how you break down your qualifying percentages, we all quite agree that good breeding is essential if you have any plans at all for a show career for your dog! Many breeders will buy on pedigree alone, counting largely on what they can do with the puppy themselves by way of feeding, conditioning and training. Needless to say, that very important piece of paper commonly referred to as "the pedigree" is mighty reassuring to a breeder or buyer new at the game or to one who has a breeding program in mind and is trying to establish his own bloodline.

One of the most fascinating aspects of tracing pedigrees is the way the names of the really great dogs of the past keep appearing in the pedigrees of the great dogs of today. . . proof positive of the strong influence of heredity and witness to a great deal of truth in the statement that great dogs frequently reproduce themselves, though not necessarily in appearance only. A pedigree represents something of value when one is dedicated to breeding better dogs.

To the novice buyer, or one who is perhaps merely switching to another breed, and sees only a frolicking, leggy, squirming bundle of energy in a fur coat, a pedigree can mean *everything*! To those of us who believe in heredity, a pedigree is more like an insurance policy.

Ch. Starcrest Lemon Drop Kid pictured winning Best of Breed from the classes at the Chow Fanciers Club of Southern California Show held with the Kennel Club of Beverly Hills summer show in 1974. This win was under judge Winifred Heckmann. Mrs. Palmer Boustead, a long-time Chow enthusiast and former handler, is presenting the trophy. June Marston, co-owner of Lemon Drop with her husband Joel, is the handler.

Lli Haven Thundercloud, bred by Bettie Hill and owned by Neva Gaspar of Cupertino, California. Sire was Ch. Storm Cloud of Shang-Hi *ex* Tu Tang's Too.

Ten-weeks-old and ready to go to his new owner, Mrs. Merilyn Bowden of Falls Church, Virginia, is Liontamer Ah-Tum Hetherchow, bred by Samuel Draper and Mr. and Mrs. Robert A. Hetherington, Jr., of Liontamer Kennels in Mahwah, New Jersey. Ah-Tum was whelped August 26, 1967.

Two top dogs at the Gerald Sterling' kennel in Nashville, Tennessee. On the left is Chang-Shi Ki-Foo, Belgian import, and Ch. Chang-Shi Golden Nugget.

Ch. Jo Jo Hanson, owned and bred by Mr. and Mrs. Walter Hanson. The sire was Ch. West's Sun of East *ex* Hanson's Toujours Moi. This bitch was the dam of five champions, two of which were Best in Show winners. Jo Jo himself was the sire of three Best in Show winners—Ch. Li Ching's Chang of Ferg-Sun (3 BIS), Ch. Five Ash Jo Jo and Ch. Miltenberger's Toffee Son of Jo. These were all outstanding Chow Chows in their day.

Ch. Charmar Chatterbox, Best of Breed at Paper City Kennel Club show under judge Frances Holland. She is owned by Mrs. Marjorie Evans of Grand Rapids, Michigan. Photo by Ritter.

Ch. Chang-Shi Careless Coquette, bred by Lucile and Jerry Sterling, pictured winning at the 1960 Southern Chow Chow Club Specialty Show. The sire was Ch. Chang-Shi Zygoto *ex* Be-Luv-Ed Linnchow. Miss C.E. Collette, a well-known English Chow breeder is the judge.

A trio of Chow Chow puppies, owners unknown.

14. BREEDING AND NUTRITION

FEEDING PUPPIES

There are many diets today for young puppies, including all sorts of products on the market for feeding the newborn, for supplementing the feeding of the young and for adding this or that to diets, depending on what is lacking in the way of a complete diet.

When weaning puppies, it is necessary to put them on four meals a day, even while you are tapering off with the mother's milk. Feeding at six in the morning, noontime, six in the evening and midnight is about the best schedule, since it fits in with most human eating plans. Meals for the puppies can be prepared immediately before or after your own meals, without too much of a change in your own schedule.

6 A.M.

Two meat and two milk meals serve best and should be served alternately, of course. Assuming the 6 A.M. feeding is a milk meal, the contents should be as follows: Goat's milk is the very best milk to feed puppies but is expensive and usually available only at drug stores, unless you live in farm country where it could be readily available fresh and still less expensive. If goat's milk is not available, use evaporated milk (which can be changed to powdered milk later on) diluted two parts evaporated milk and one part water, along with raw egg yoke, honey or Karo syrup, sprinkled with a high-protein baby cereal and some wheat germ. As the puppies mature, cottage cheese may be added or, at one of the two milk meals, it can be substituted for the cereal.

NOONTIME

A puppy chow which has been soaked in warm water or beef broth according to the time specified on the wrapper should be mixed with raw or simmered chopped meat in equal proportions with a vitamin powder added.

6 P.M.

Repeat the milk meal—perhaps varying the type of cereal from wheat to oats, or corn or rice.

MIDNIGHT

Repeat the meat meal. If raw meat was fed at noon, the evening meal might be simmered.

Please note that specific proportions on this suggested diet are not given. However, it is safe to say that the most important ingredients are the milk and cereal, and the meat and puppy chow which forms the basis of the diet. Your veterinarian can advise on the portion sizes if there is any doubt in your mind as to how much to use.

If you notice that the puppies are cleaning their plates you are perhaps not feeding enough to keep up with their rate of growth. Increase the amount at the next feeding. Observe them closely; puppies should each "have their fill," because growth is very rapid at this age. If they have not satisfied themselves, increase the amount so that they do not have to fight for the last morsel. They will not overeat if they know there is enough food available. Instinct will usually let them eat to suit their normal capacity.

If there is any doubt in your mind as to any ingrediet you are feeding, ask yourself, "Would I give it to my own baby?" If the answer is no, then don't give it to your puppies. At this age, the comparison between puppies and human babies can be a good guide.

If there is any doubt in your mind, I repeat: ask your veterinarian to be sure.

Many puppies will regurgitate their food, perhaps a couple of times, before they manage to retain it. If they do bring up their food, allow them to eat it again, rather than clean it away. Sometimes additional saliva is necessary for them to digest it, and you do not want them to skip a meal just because it is an unpleasant sight for you to observe.

This same regurgitation process holds true sometimes with the bitch, who will bring up her own food for her puppies every now and then. This is a natural instinct on her part which stems from the days when dogs were giving birth in the wilds. The only food the mother could provide at weaning time was too rough and indigestible for her puppies. Therefore, she took it upon herself to pre-digest the food until it could be taken and retained by her young. Bitches today will sometimes resort to this, especially bitches which love having litters and have a strong maternal instinct. Some dams will help you wean their litters and even give up feeding entirely once they see you are taking over.

WEANING THE PUPPIES

When weaning the puppies the mother is kept away from the little ones for longer and longer periods of time. This is done over a period of several days. At first she is separated from the puppies for several hours, then all day, leaving her with them only at night for comfort and warmth. This gradual separation aids in

Ch. Pandee's Alpha Sing, Joel Marston's magnificent black Chow Chow, shown to perfection by Frank Sabella to another Best In Show award.

helping the mother's milk to dry up gradually, and she suffers less distress after feeding a litter.

If the mother continues to carry a great deal of milk with no signs of its tapering off, consult your veterinarian before she gets too uncomfortable. She may cut the puppies off from her supply of milk too abruptly if she is uncomfortable, before they should be completely on their own.

There are many opinions on the proper age to start weaning puppies. If you plan to start selling them between six and eight weeks, weaning should begin between two and three weeks of age. Here again, each bitch will pose a different situation. The size and weight of the litter should help determine the time, and your veterinarian will have an opinion, as he determines the burden the bitch is carrying by the size of the litter and her general condition. If she is being pulled down by feeding a large litter, he may suggest that you start at two weeks. If she is glorying in her motherhood without any apparent taxing

of her strength, he may suggest three to four weeks. You and he will be the best judges. But remember, there is no substitute that is as perfect as mother's milk—and the longer the puppies benefit from it, the better. Other food yes, but mother's milk first and foremost for the healthiest puppies!

FEEDING THE ADULT DOG

The puppies' schedule of four meals a day should drop to three by six months and then to two by nine months; by the time the dog reaches one year of age, it is eating one meal a day.

The time when you feed the dog each day can be a matter of the dog's preference or your convenience, so long as once in every 24 hours the dog receives a meal that provides him with a complete, balanced diet. In addition, of course, fresh clean water should be available at all times.

There are many brands of dry food, kibbles and biscuits on the market which are all of good quality. There are also

Ch. Shanglo's Jill and Shanglo's Tiga, 18- and 6-months-old, respectively, who are owned by Mildred Fairchild of the Shanglo Kennels in Tigard, Oregon.

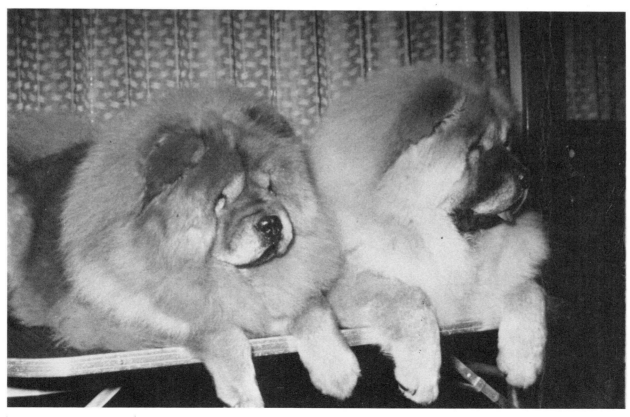

many varieties of canned dog food which are of good quality and provide a balanced diet for your dog. But, for those breeders and exhibitors who show their dogs, additional care is given to providing a few "extras" which enhance the good health and good appearance of show dogs.

A good meal or kibble mixed with water or beef broth and raw meat is perhaps the best ration to provide. In cold weather many breeders add suet or corn oil (or even olive or cooking oil) to the mixture and others make use of the bacon fat after breakfast by pouring it over the dog's food.

Salting a dog's food in the summer helps replace the salt he "pants away" in the heat. Many breeders sprinkle the food with garlic powder to sweeten the dog's breath and prevent gas, especially in breeds that gulp or wolf their food and swallow a lot of air. I prefer garlic powder; the salt is too weak and the cloves (also used) are too strong.

There are those, of course, who cook very elaborately for their dogs, which is not necessary if a good meal and meat mixture is provided. Many prefer to add vegetables, rice, tomatoes, etc., in with everything else they feed. As long as the extras do not throw the nutritional balance off, there is little harm, but no one thing should be fed to excess. Occasionally liver is given as a treat at home. Fish, which most veterinarians no longer recommend even for cats, is fed to puppies, but should not be given in excess of once a week. Always remember that no one thing should be given as a total diet. Balance is most important; a 100 per cent meat diet can kill a dog.

THE ALL MEAT DIET CONTROVERSY

In March of 1971, the National Research Council investigated a great stir in the dog fancy about the all-meat dog-feeding controversy. It was established that meat and meat by-products constitue a complete balanced diet for dogs only when

Princess Misty Ling, whelped in 1969, was sold as a show puppy and later bought back by breeder M.M. Stertz. Misty was being trained for the show ring at two years of age when her death put an end to her career. Sire was Ch. Beamer's Chummy Chinaman *ex* Plain Acre's Belle Chien.

Sam's Sing Fu pictured at four years of age in 1946. Owned by Hazel Gray of Nevada City, California. The sire was Ch. Sing Fu Brilliantine *ex* Nellie Sing Fu. Mrs. Gray judges occasionally.

it is further fortified with vitamins and minerals.

Therefore a good dog chow or meal mixed with meat provides the perfect combination for a dog's diet. While the dry food is a complete diet in itself, the fresh meat additionally satisfies the dog's anatomically and physiologically meat-oriented appetite. While dogs are actually carnivores, it must be remembered that when they were feeding themselves in the wild they ate almost the entire animal they captured including its stomach contents. This provided some of the vitamins and minerals we must now add to the diet.

In the United States, the standards for diets which claim to be "complete and balanced" are set by the Subcommittee on Canine Nutrition of the National Research Council (NRC) of the National Academy of Sciences. This is the official agency for establishing the nutritional requirements

Ch. Ghat de la Moulaine, imported and owned by Clif and Vivian Shryock of Hawaiian Gardens, California. One of the greatest Chow Chows of all time and sire supreme!

of dog foods. Most foods sold for dogs and cats meet these requirements, and manufacturers are proud to say so on their labels, so look for this when you buy. Pet food labels must be approved by the Association of American Feed Control Officials, Pet Foods Committee. Both the Food and Drug Administration and the Federal Trade Commission of the AAFCO define the world "balanced" when referring to dog food as:

"Balanced is a term which may be applied to pet food having all known required nutrients in a proper amount and proportion based upon the recommendations of a recognized authority (The National Research Council is one) in the field of animal nutrition, for a given set of physiological animal requirements."

With this much care given to your dog's diet, there can be little reason for not having happy, well-fed dogs in proper weight and proportions for the show ring.

Ch. Tsang-Po's Wong Gi, whelped in November of 1968, is owned by Walter and Brenda Jones. Bred by the Tsang-Po Kennels. The judge is the late Clara Alford.

A lovely headstudy of Ch. Eastward Liontamer of Elster taken shortly after he arrived from California in 1967 at the Liontamer Kennels in Mahwah, New Jersey.

Ch. Shang-Tai's My Kind of Black pictured finishing his championship at the 1970 Pontiac Kennel Club Show at 13 months of age. Whelped in November, 1968 his sire was Shang-Tai's Cypher of Ky-Lin ex Ch. Shang-Tai's Ebony Empress. Owned by Ruby A. Van Over of Highland, Michigan. Raphael Schulte is the judge.

Two-year-old Jan Petti holds tight to Meddie's Kan Check while two other Chow Chow puppies sit by. A Tri-Foto Studios photograph.

Ch. Balthazar Liontamer Avril pictured winning under judge Mary Nelson Stephenson at the Plainfield Kennel Club show in June, 1971. Mr. Bernard Kennedy is owner-handler. A William P. Gilbert photograph.

OBESITY

As we mentioned above, there are many "perfect" diets for your dogs on the market today. When fed in proper proportions, they should keep your dogs in "full bloom." However, there are those owners who, more often than not, indulge their own appetites and are inclined to overfeed their dogs as well. A study in Great Britain in the early 1970's found that a major percentage of obese people also had obese dogs. The entire family was overfed and suffered from the same condition.

Obesity in dogs is a direct result of the animal's being fed more food than he can properly "burn up" over a period of time, so it is stored as fat or fatty tissue in the body. Pet dogs are more inclined to become obese than show dogs or working dogs, but obesity also is a factor to be considered with the older dog, since his exercise is curtailed.

A lack of "tuck up" on a dog, or not being able to feel the ribs, or great folds of

Ch. Warlord's Chu-Jen, whelped in 1971, was bred by Shirley Nelson. "Lil Dink" is pictured at 14 months of age. He finished his championship under Clif Shryock, well-known breeder-judge, at the North Texas Chow Chow Specialty.

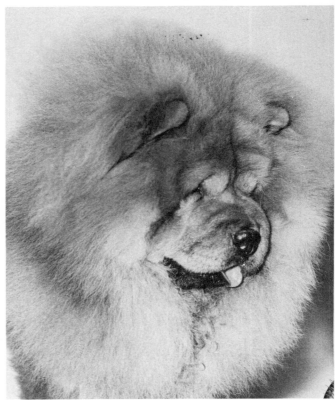

fat which hang from the underside of the dog can all be considered as obesity. Genetic factors may enter into the picture, but usually the owner is at fault.

The life span of the obese dog is decreased on several counts. Excess weight puts undue stress on the heart as well as the joints. The dog becomes a poor anesthetic risk and has less resistance to viral or bacterial infections. Treatment is seldom easy or completely effective, so emphasis should be placed on not letting your dog get FAT in the first place!

ORPHANED PUPPIES

The ideal solution to feeding orphaned puppies is to be able to put them with another nursing dam who will take them on as her own. If this is not possible within your own kennel, or a kennel that you know of, it is up to you to care for and feed the puppies. Survival is possible but requires a great deal of time and effort on your part.

Your substitute formula must be precisely prepared, always served heated to body temperature and refrigerated when not being fed. Esbilac, a vacuum-packed powder with complete feeding instructions on the can, is excellent and about as close to mother's milk as you can get. If you can't get Esbilac, or until you do get Esbilac, there are two alternative formulas that you might use.

Mix one part boiled water with five parts of evaporated milk and add one teaspoonful of di-calcium phosphate per quart of formula. Di-calcium phosphate can be secured at any drug store. If they have it in tablet form only, you can powder the tablets with the back part of a tablespoon. The other formula for newborn puppies is a combination of eight ounces of homogenized milk mixed well with two egg yolks.

You will need baby bottles with three-hole nipples. Sometimes doll bottles can be used for the newborn puppies, which should be fed at six-hour intervals. If they are consuming sufficient amounts, their stomachs should look full, or slightly enlarged, though never distended. The

Ch. Tsang-Po's Soo-Chy finished with four majors in 10 shows at 12½ months. Bred by Hal Allen and owned by S.O. and J.M. Parrish. "Tootie" was whelped in 1968.

Winner of the Southern Chow Chow Specialty Show at the Baltimore County Kennel Club Show in April, 1966, was Ch. Ah Sid the Avant Garde, handled by Jane Kamp Forsyth. "Stuffy" was then owned by Samuel Draper. William P. Gilbert photograph.

463

amount of formula to be fed is proportionate to size and age and growth and weight of the puppy, and is indicated on the can of Esbilac or on the advice of your veterinarian. Many breeders like to keep a baby scale nearby to check the weight of the puppies to be sure they are thriving on the formula.

At two to three weeks you can start adding Pablum or some other high protein baby cereal to the formula. Also, baby beef can be licked from your finger at this age, or added to the formula. At four weeks the surviving puppies should be taken off the diet of Esbilac and put on a more substantial diet, such as wet puppy meal or chopped beef. However, Esbilac powder can still be mixed in with the food for additional nutrition. The jarred baby foods of pureed meats make for a smooth change-over also, and can be blended into the diet.

Ch. Liontamer Bruiser, handled by Robert A. Hetherington, Jr., to a Best of Breed win at the Rhode Island Kennel Club show in 1972 under judge Irene Khatoonian Schlintz. Bruiser was owned by Robert and Jean Hetherington of Mahwah, New Jersey, at the time of this photo. Bruiser is now owned by Mr. and Mrs. Carl Boudreau of East Falmouth, Massachusetts.

HOW TO FEED THE NEWBORN PUPPIES

When the puppy is a newborn, remember that it is vitally important to keep the feeding procedure as close to the natural mother's routine as possible. The newborn puppy should be held in your lap in your hand in an almost upright position with the bottle at an angle to allow the entire nipple area to be full of the formula. Do not hold the bottle upright so the puppy's head has to reach straight up toward the ceiling. Do not let the puppy nurse too quickly or take in too much air and possibly get the colic. Once in a while, take the bottle away and let it rest for a moment and swallow several times. Before feeding, always test the nipple to see that the fluid does not come out too quickly, or by the same token, too slowly so that the puppy gets tired of feeding before he has had enough to eat.

When the puppy is a little older, you can place him on his stomach on a towel to eat, and even allow him to hold on to the

Three-month-old Chow Chow puppies whelped in 1966 by Manota Stertz, who owns the Plain Acre Kennels in Cincinnati, Ohio. The male on the left is Plain Acre's Charman Shoh-Dee (never shown) and the female on the right became Ch. Charman's Fancy of Plain Acre.

bottle or to "come and get it" on his own. Most puppies enjoy eating and this will be a good indication of how strong an appetite he has and his ability to consume the contents of the bottle.

It will be necessary to "burp" the puppy. Place a towel on your shoulder and hold the puppy on your shoulder as if it were a human baby, patting and rubbing it gently. This will also encourage the puppy to defecate. At this time, you should observe for diarrhea or other intestinal disorders. The puppy should eliminate after each feeding with occasional eliminations between times as well. If the puppies do not eliminate on their own after each meal, massage their stomachs and under their tails gently until they do.

You must keep the puppies clean. If there is diarrhea or if they bring up a little formula, they should be washed and dried off. Under no circumstances should fecal matter be allowed to collect on their skin or fur.

All this — plus your determination and perseverance — might save an entire litter of puppies that would otherwise have died without their real mother.

A magnificent headstudy of James R. Facciolii, Jr.'s Ch. Fa-Ci Chinkapin, taken in 1972. Photo by Pastor.

Ch. Pandee's Alpha Sing, whelped in 1959, was bred by Dr. Imogene P. Earle and owned by Joel Marston of Sun Valley, California. He is pictured here winning with his handler Frank Sabella under the late judge Dr. A.A. Mitten. Alpha Sing won several Bests in Show, All Breeds.

The adorable future Champion Mil-Her Sunbonnet of Jade, bred and owned by Nelson and Diane Tardy of Union City, California, and photographed at eight weeks by Johnnie McMillan.

15. TRAINING YOUR CHOW CHOW

There are few things in the world a dog would rather do than please his master! Therefore, obedience training, or even the initial basic training, will be a pleasure for your dog, if taught correctly, and will make him a much nicer animal to live with for the rest of his life.

WHEN TO START TRAINING

The most frequently asked question by those who consider training their dog is, naturally, "What is the best age to begin training?" The answer is, "not before six months." A dog simply cannot be sufficiently or permanently trained before this age and be expected to retain all he has been taught. If too much is expected of him, he can become frustrated and it may

ruin him completely for any serious training later on, or even jeopardize his disposition. Most things a puppy learns and repeats before he is six months of age should be considered habit rather than training.

THE REWARD METHOD

The only proper and acceptable kind of training is the kindness and reward method which will build a strong bond between dog and owner. A dog must have confidence in and respect for his teacher. The most important thing to remember in training any dog is that the quickest way to teach, especially the young dog, is through repetition. Praise him when he does well, and scold him when he does wrong. This will suffice. There is no need or excuse for swinging at a dog with rolled up newspapers, or flailing hands which will only tend to make the dog hand shy the rest of his life. Also, make every word count. Do not give a command unless you intend to see it through. Pronounce distinctly with the fewest possible words, and use the same words for the same command every time.

Include the dog's name every time to make sure you have his undivided attention at the beginning of each command. Do not go on to another command until he has successfully completed the previous one and is praised for it. Of course, you should not mix play with the serious training time. Make sure the dog knows the difference between the two.

In the beginning, it is best to train without any distractions whatsoever. After he has learned to concentrate and is older and more proficient, he should perform the exercises with interference, so that the

Ch. Ah Sid Liontamer Jamboree, pictured as a puppy. Jamboree was purchased by Joan Wellborn before her death and is now owned by Desmond Murphy, who showed him to his championship.

"Pals" at the Tally-Ho Kennels of the late Mrs. Bonney in Oyster Bay, Long Island, pictured in July, 1940 by Percy T. Jones.

dog learns absolute obedience in the face of all distractions. Needless to say, whatever the distractions, you never lose control. You must be in command at all times to earn the respect and attention of your dog.

HOW LONG SHOULD THE LESSONS BE?

The lessons should be brief with a young dog, starting at five minutes, and as the dog ages and becomes adept in the first lessons, increase the time all the way up to one-half hour. Public training classes are usually set for one hour, and this is acceptable since the full hour of concentration is not placed on your dog alone. Working under these conditions with other dogs, you will find that he will not be as intent as

he would be with a private lesson where the commands are directed to him alone for the entire thirty minutes.

If you should notice that your dog is not doing well, or not keeping up with the class, consider putting off training for awhile. Animals, like children, are not always ready for schooling at exactly the same age. It would be a shame to ruin a good obedience dog because you insist on starting his training at six months rather than at, say, nine months, when he would be more apt to be receptive both physically and mentally. If he has particular difficulty in learning one exercise, you might do well to skip to a different one and come back to it again at another session. There are no set rules in this basic training, except, "don't push!"

Liontamer Robinhood wins Best Puppy in Match at the Tri-State Chow Chow Match Show in July, 1971 under renowned breeder Donald Drennan. "Robby," now owned by Edward Zoller, was whelped February 26, 1971. Handler, Desmond Murphy.

WHAT YOU NEED TO START TRAINING

From three to six months of age, use the soft nylon show leads, which are the best and safest. When you get ready for the basic training at six months of age, you will require one of the special metal-link choke chains sold for exactly this purpose. Do not let the word "choke" scare you. It is a soft, smooth chain and should be held slack whenever you are not actually using it to correct the dog. This chain should be put over the dog's head so that the lead can be attached over the dog's neck rather than underneath against his throat. It is wise when you buy your choke collar to ask the salesperson to show you how it is to be put on. Those of you who will be taking your dog to a training class will have an instructor who can show you.

To avoid undue stress on the dog, use both hands on the lead. The dog will be taught to obey commands at your left side, and therefore, your left hand will guide the dog close to this collar on a six-foot training lead. The balance of the lead will be held in your right hand. Learn at the very beginning to handle your choke collar and lead correctly. It is as important in training a dog as is the proper equipment for riding a horse.

WHAT TO TEACH FIRST

The first training actually should be to teach the dog to know his name. This, of course, he can learn at an earlier age than six months, just as he can learn to walk nicely on a leash or lead. Many puppies will at first probably want to walk around with the leash in their mouths. There is no objection to this if the dog will walk while doing it. Rather than cultivating this as a habit, you will find that if you don't make an issue of it, the dog will soon realize that carrying the lead in his mouth is not rewarding and he'll let it fall to his side where it belongs.

We also let the puppy walk around by himself for a while with the lead around his neck. If he wishes to chew on it a little, that's all right too. In other words, let it be something he recognizes and associates with at first. Do not let the lead start out being a harness.

If the dog is at all bright, chances are he has learned to come on command when you call him by name. This is relatively simple with sweet talk and a reward. On lead, without a reward, and on command without a lead is something else again. If there has been, or is now, a problem, the best way to correct it is to put on the choke collar and the six-foot lead. Then walk away from the dog, and call him, "Pirate, come!" and gently start reeling him in until the dog is in front of you. Give him a pat on the head and/or a reward.

Walking, or heeling, next to you is also one of the first and most important things for him to learn. With the soft lead

training starting very early, he should soon take up your pace at your left side. At the command "heel" he should start off with you and continue alongside until you stop. Give the command, "Pirate, sit!" This is taught by leaning over and pushing down on his hindquarters until he sits next to you, while pulling up gently on the collar. When you have this down pat on the **straight away**, then start practicing in circles, with turns and figure eights! When he is an advanced student, you can look forward to the heels and sits being done neatly, spontaneously, and off lead as well!

THE "DOWN" COMMAND

One of the most valuable lessons or commands you can teach your dog is to lie down on command. Some day it may save his life, and is invaluable when traveling with a dog or visiting, if behavior and manners are required even beyond obedience. While repeating the words, "Pirate, down!" lower the dog from a sitting position in front of you by gently pulling his front legs out in front of him. Place your full hand on him while repeating the command, "Pirate, down!" and hold him down to let him know you want him to *stay* down. After he gets the general idea, this can be done from a short distance away on lead along with the command, by pulling the lead down to the floor. Or perhaps, you can slip the lead under your shoe (between the heel and the sole) and pull it directly to the floor. As the dog progresses in training, a hand signal with or without verbal command, or with or without lead, can be given from a considerable distance by raising your arm and extending the hand palm down.

THE "STAY" COMMAND

The stay command eventually can be taught from both a sit and a down position. Start with the sit. With your dog on your left side in the sitting position give the command, "Pirate, stay!" Reach down with the left hand open and palm side to the dog and sweep it in close to his nose. Then walk a short distance away and face him. He will at first, having learned to heel immediately as you start off, more than likely start off with you. The trick in teaching this is to make sure he hears "stay" before you start off. It will take practice. If he breaks, sit him down again, stand next to him, and give the command all over again. As he masters the command, let the distance between you and your dog increase while the dog remains seated. Once the command is learned, advance to the stay command from the down position.

THE STAND FOR EXAMINATION

If you have any intention of going on to advanced training in obedience with your dog, or if you have a show dog which you feel you will enjoy showing yourself, a most important command which should be mastered at six months of age is the stand command. This is essential for a show dog since it is the position used when the show judge goes over your dog. This is taught in the same manner as the stay command, but this time with the dog remaining up on all four feet. He should learn to stand still, without moving his feet and without flinching or breaking when approached by either you or strangers. The hand with palm open wide and facing him should be firmly placed in front of his nose with the command, "Pirate, stand!" After he learns the basic rules and knows the difference between stand and stay, ask friends, relatives,

Identical twins bred by Clif and Vivan Shryock and owned by Betty Schellenberg of Fort Worth, Texas. The sire was Miki de la Moulaine *ex* Heidi de la Moulaine.

and strangers to assist you with this exercise by walking up to the dog and going over him. He should not react physically to their touch. A dog posing in this stance should show all the beauty and pride of being a sterling example of his breed.

FORMAL SCHOOL TRAINING

We mentioned previously about the various training schools and classes given for dogs. Your local kennel club, newspaper, or the yellow pages of the telephone book will put you in touch with organizations in your area where this service is performed. You and your dog will learn a great deal from these classes. Not only do they offer formal training, but the experience for you and your dog in public, with other dogs of approximately the same age and with the same purpose in mind is invaluable. If you intend to show your dog, this training is valuable ring experience for later on. If you are having difficulty with the training, remember, it is either too soon to start—or YOU are doing something wrong!

ADVANCED TRAINING AND OBEDIENCE TRIALS

The A.K.C. obedience trials are divided into three classes: Novice, Open and Utility.

In the Novice Class, the dog will be judged on the following basis:

TEST	MAXIMUM SCORE
Heel on lead	35
Stand for examination	30
Heel free—on lead	45
Recall (come on command)	30
One-minute sit (handler in ring)	30
Three-minute down (handler in ring)	30

Maximum total score *200*

If the dog "qualifies" in three shows by earning at least 50% of the points for each test, with a total of at least 170 for the trial, he has earned the Companion Dog degree and the letters C.D. (Companion Dog) are entered after his name in the A.K.C. records.

After the dog has qualified as a C.D.,

Ten-year-old junior handler Tammy Overturf of Dallas, Texas wins Best Junior Handler in Match at a 1970 event, showing the Chow Chow Ch. Starcrest Autumn Haze Tiawin, co-owned by A.J. Overturf and Richard Inman.

he is eligible to enter the Open Class competition, where he will be judged on this basis:

TEST	MAXIMUM SCORE
Heel free	40
Drop on recall	30
Retrieve (wooden dumbbell) on flat	25
Retrieve over obstacle (hurdle)	35
Broad jump	20
Three-minute sit (handler out of ring)	25
Five-minute down (handler out of ring)	25
Maximum total score	200

Again he must qualify in three shows for the C.D.X. (Companion Dog Excellent) title and then is eligible for the Utility Class, where he can earn the Utility Dog (U.D.) degree in these rugged tests:

TEST	MAXIMUM SCORE
Scent discrimination (picking up article handled by master from group) Article 1	20
Scent discrimination Article 2	20
Scent discrimination Article 3	20

471

Best in Show for Li Ching's Chang of Ferg Sun, the American and Canadian champion owned by Madaline and Perry Ferguson of Long Beach, California. The judge was Beatrice Hopkins Godsol and the show was held at the Sun Maid Kennel Club in Fresno, California, in November, 1948. Chang won two other Bests in Show, all breeds, in Canada.

Seek back (picking up an article
   dropped by handler) 30
Signal exercise (heeling, etc., on
   hand signal) 35
Directed jumping (over hurdle and
   bar jump) 40
Group examination 35
                            —————
Maximum total score *200*

For more complete information about these obedience trials, write for the American Kennel Club's *Regulations and Standars for Obedience Trials*. Dogs that are disqualified from breed shows because of alteration or physical defects are eligible to compete in these trials.

Ch. Dre-Don Sun-King of Craglinden as a puppy at nine months of age. "Sunny" is owned by Samuel Draper, Monroe, New York.

16. THE CHOW CHOW IN OBEDIENCE

Although the Chow Chow has been assigned to the Non-Sporting Group at dog shows, this should not be interpreted as meaning that they do not have the capacity to learn that dogs classified as Working or Hunting Dogs are presumed to have. Many Non-Sporting breeds, most notably the Poodle, are outstanding performers in obedience. Even the more unlikely members of the Non-Sporting Group, such as the Bulldogs, French Bulldogs, Bostons and Schipperkes have earned more of the advanced degrees than our Chow Chows. As of 1973 there were only 10 Chow C.D.X. title

Heel off lead, demonstrated by Ch. Pandee's Katrina, C.D.

holders over a forty-year period—and half of those were acquired more than twenty years ago. Since 1968 there have been four C.D.X. degrees, plus the only U.D. degree ever earned by a Chow Chow. There have been quite a number of C.D. degrees awarded, approximately 40 of these in the last 10 years, which is encouraging.

We should not lose sight of the fact that our Chows always have been considered useful and that they definitely have the background and potential for training. Too many people regard the Chow as non-functional and simply a thing of beauty. Many Chows are excessively pampered and not encouraged to display much physical or mental training. A truly sound dog in any breed should be physically and mentally capable of some degree of training. While some breeds are known to be more receptive than others, there is no reason why a normal healthy Chow Chow can not learn obedience.

The exercises required for the Companion Dog, or C.D. title, are really only what any dog should know in order to live within a family atmosphere. A family dog certainly should be able to walk beside you and sit and stay and lie down and come when called! The C.D. degree requirements are well within the Chow Chow's ability to learn, as is evidenced by the number of Chows which have earned this degree over the years. The reason there have not been more is undoubtedly due to lack of interest on the owners' part rather than any lack of ability on the Chow's part!

The Companion Dog Excellent (C.D.X.) degree is considerably more difficult, since it requires off-lead work and retrieving and jumping. In Companion

Retrieving dumbbell on flat by Katrina.

Broad jump demonstrated by Ch. Hung Jai Lin Fa, U.D., and Canadian C.D.

**Obedience Instruction by
Prudence Baxter**

Scent discrimination, a utility exercise, again demonstrated by Lin Fa.

Returning to handler with correct article. . . you hope!

Directed jumping, utility exercise demonstrated by Lin Fa.

Clearing the bar jump in utility. Lin Fa clears.

Dog Excellent training it is most important to have a dumbbell that fits comfortably into your dog's mouth. The dowel part should fit easily behind the front teeth when being carried or the dog will have the tendency to spit it out. Also, using a dumbbell with smaller shaped ends allows a Chow Chow, with its deep-set eyes and long coat, to have better visibility. One that would be perfectly suitable for say, a Great Dane, with the heavy blocks at the end would definitely limit a Chow Chow's vision. If you have trouble getting your Chow to pick up the dumbbell, you will find he will respond a great deal better if you have taken the trouble to get him a "good fit."

The other exercises for the C.D.X. are retrieving over the high and the broad jumps. Also required is off-lead heeling and the drop on recall, three-minute sits and five-minute downs with the handler out of sight. In the high jump the Chow is required to jump its height plus half again. The broad jump is twice the height of the high jump. The broad jump is not too difficult for Chows, and they can clear it pretty well once they understand what they are meant to do. But the high jump is understandably more difficult for a heavy-boned, short-legged Chow.

Utility exercises for the U.D. degree are the most advanced and intricate. Chows are known for having excellent noses, so this should not be too difficult. In the directed jumping the dog must be sent to the far end of the ring on command; after arriving there, he is told which jump to take on his return. He is then sent out again and must jump the other hurdle on the second return. One of these jumps is a bar jump and one is a high jump, the same as is used in the open exercise for retrieving over the jump. The other exercises for the U.D. are the signal commands in which the dog must do the heeling pattern along with the down, sit, and come—all with hand signals only. The last exercise is the group stand for examination for three minutes. All the dogs in the class are lined up together and the handlers move across the ring. The judge approaches each dog sepa-

rately and goes over it briefly. This can be a challenge for the overly friendly Chow! It is quite different from examination in the breed ring, where you are right with the dog and can reassure it with your presence.

The Tracking degree is entirely separate from the others and is not even performed at a regular dog show or trial. Tracks are laid out in a large open field, and usually only five or six dogs are allowed to compete. Dogs must be certified by a tracking judge and demonstrate to the judge's satisfaction that it can track before it is allowed to enter an actual Tracking Trial. Since a track can only be used once, this prerequisite, hopefully, keeps unqualified dogs from taking the place of one that is ready for the test. Since interest in tracking has increased markedly, many obedience clubs are holding tracking tests along with their obedience trials.

Actually, tracking is the most challenging of all the degrees available to a Non-Sporting dog. Each track is totally different, and the dog must use its *head*, while in the straight obedience work the exercises can be practiced and repeated until they become almost routine. While tracking the dog is on its own from the time it starts out, and any attempt by the handler to direct its course results in the dog's disqualification. The dog must work well in front of you on a thirty-foot lead, and the track must be a minimum of 440 yards, with at least two right angle turns well out in the open where there are no boundaries or fences to guide the dog. The track layer must be a stranger to the dog, and the dog must work continuously once he has started off.

There is no doubt that even the most elementary obedience work will bring you and your Chow much closer together. It is a most rewarding feeling when you and your dog receive a leg toward that obedience degree! Remember, in obedience if your Chow performs the exercises with reasonable skill, he should be recognized and rewarded for it; in the breed ring the final decision of whether you "pass" or not is up to the judge's preference. And working with a Chow can be fun, because invariably the spectators and the judges are surprised to see them there!

Chows do not respond to a heavy hand in training and need a lot of praise while learning. This is true of many breeds, but never more so than when training Chows. It is sometimes very beneficial with a shy dog or one that is giving you trouble in some special area. It is important to be very conscientious about the use of a training lead also, especially if the dog is shown in the breed ring as well. Always use the chain and leather lead *only* when actually working the dog. Then take it off when the session is over. A chain-type collar should never be left on a dog if it could get caught on something or wear away the fur on a show dog. But mostly you want it to associate the chain with the actual training period. Never use the same equipment for obedience and show training. Chows will quickly learn the difference between the two and will know which procedure is expected of them. Consistency is really the key word to successful training; never try to practice with the dog on impulse without the proper equipment. It will confuse the dog and lead to bad habits.

While it may be apparent that Chow Chows are not quite as trainable as some of the other breeds, they are far from *un*trainable. . . as we are proving more and more frequently as the lists of title winners grows. Also, other breeds can at times be equally exasperating as Chows! With the Chow, several five-or ten-minute sessions a day will work better than a half hour period once a day. Forcing them to keep at something they are losing interest in will only make them resent the training. Perhaps Chows do need more "humoring," but they are worth it when you see how really well they *can* work! So never end the session on a bad note. Have your dog do something that he does particularly well as an end to the session, then praise him lavishly for it and give your release command—"Okay," "Finished," "Done," or whatever word or phrase you may use— and he will remember the lesson as a happy, pleasant time with you and look forward eagerly to the next one!

Tracking test. Scenting trail toward the article. Lin Fa demonstrating.

Eureka! It is found! The scented article is located at the end of the track.

Directed retrieve, an exercise in utility.

Clearing the high jump in utility exercise.

Nu Nui Linnchow, C.D.; an early obedience Chow. She was the mother of the famous Chow, Ch. Linnchow Chu Fu II and grandmother of Ch. Pitchi Wu Linnchow. Nu Nui was owned and bred by Mr. and Mrs. H.P. Schmidt of Linnchow Kennels, Tinley Park, Illinois.

Ch. Tamarin Midnight Idol finishing for his championship at a recent Del Monte Kennel Club show under judge Edd Biven. Sire was Ch. Starcrest Matinee Idol *ex* Ch. Pandee's Katrina, C.D. Owner-handler is Prudence Baxter of San Anselmo, California.

17. SHOWING YOUR CHOW CHOW

Let us assume that after a few months of tender loving care, you realize your dog is developing beyond your wildest expectations and that the dog you selected is very definitely a show dog! Of course, every owner is prejudiced. But if you are sincerely interested in going to dog shows with your dog and making a champion of him, now is the time to start casting a critical eye on him from a judge's point of view.

There is no such thing as a perfect dog. Every dog has some faults perhaps even a few serious ones. The best way to appraise your dog's degree of perfection is to compare him with the Standard for the breed, or before a judge in a show ring.

MATCH SHOWS

For the beginner there are "mock" dog shows, called Match Shows, where you and your dog go through many of the procedures of a regular dog show, but do not gain points toward championship. These shows are usually held by kennel clubs, annually or semi-annually, and much ring poise and experience can be gained there. The age limit is reduced to two months at match shows to give puppies four months of training before they compete at the regular shows when they reach six months of age. Classes range from two to four months; four to six months; six to nine months; and nine to twelve months. Puppies compete with others of their own age for comparative purposes. Many breeders evaluate their litters in this manner, choosing which is the most outgoing, which is the most poised, the best showman, etc.

For those seriously interested in showing their dog to full championship, these match shows provide important experience for both the dog and the owner. Class categories may vary slightly, according to number of entries, but basically include all the classes that are included at a regular point show. There is a nominal entry fee and, of course, ribbons and trophies are given for your efforts as well. Unlike the point shows, entries can be made on the day of the show right on the show grounds. They are unbenched and provide an informal, usually congenial atmosphere for the amateur, which helps to make the ordeal of one's first adventures in the show ring a little less nerve-racking.

Balthazar Liontamer Chester gets his show career off to a good start by winning Best Junior Puppy in Match under judge Peter Belmont. Owner-handled by Mr. Robert Borsuch of Morris, Connecticut. W. Bushman photograph.

THE POINT SHOWS

It is not possible to show a puppy at an American Kennel Club sanctioned point show before the age of six months. When your dog reaches this eligible age, your local kennel club can provide you with the names and addresses of the show-giving superintendents in your area who will be staging the club's dog show for them, and where you must write for an entry form.

The forms are mailed in a pamphlet called a premium list. This also includes the names of the judges for each breed, a list of the prizes and trophies, the name and address of the show-giving club and where the show will be held, as well as rules and regulations set up by the American Kennel Club which must be abided by if you are to enter.

A booklet containing the complete set of show rules and regulations may be obtained by writing to the American Kennel Club, Inc., 51 Madison Avenue, New York, N.Y., 10010.

When you write to the Dog Show Superintendent, request not only your premium list for this particular show, but ask that your name be added to their mailing list so that you will automatically receive all premium lists in the future. List your breed or breeds and they will see to it that you receive premium lists for Specialty shows as well.

Unlike the match shows where your dog will be judged on ring behavior, at the point shows he will be judged on conformation to the breed Standard. In addition to being at least six months of age (on the day of the show) he must be a thoroughbred for a point show. This means both of his parents and he are registered with the American Kennel Club. There must be no alterations or falsifications regarding his appearance. Females cannot have been spayed and males must have both testicles in evidence. No dyes or powders may be used to enhance the appearance, and any lameness or deformity or major deviation from the Standard for the breed constitutes a disqualification.

With all these things in mind, groom your dog to the best of your ability in the specified area for this purpose in the show hall and walk into the show ring with great pride of ownership and ready for an appraisal of your dog by the judge.

The presiding judge on that day will allow each and every dog a certain amount of time and consideration before making his decisions. It is never permissible to consult the judge regarding either your dog or his decision while you are in the ring. An exhibitor never speaks unless spoken to, and then only to answer such questions as the judge may ask — the age of the dog, the dog's bite, or to ask you to move your dog around the ring once again.

A proud moment for all Chow lovers! The Best Brace in the Non-Sporting Group was awarded to Ch. Lidice's Ko Ko, right, and to Ch. Lidice's Ki Ki, left, by Mr. Heywood Hartley at the Westminster Kennel Club show in February, 1972 in Madison Square Garden, New York City. The brace is co-owned by Mr. and Mrs. Herb Williams and Mr. John C. Frederick Peddie, all of Toronto, Canada. These partners are the owners of BuDynasty Kennels.

Ch. Ky-Lin's Midas, 1957 Best of Breed winner at the Westminster Kennel Club show under judge Kathleen Staples. Ralph Hellum handling for owner Mrs. Mary MacEachern. Miss Staples owned several important Chows.

However, before you reach the point where you are actually in the ring awaiting the final decisions of the judge, you will have had to decide on which of the five classes in each sex your dog should compete.

Point Show Classes

The regular classes of the AKC are: Puppy, Novice, Bred-by-Exhibitor, American-Bred, Open; if your dog is undefeated in any of the regular classes (divided by sex) in which it is entered, he or she is **required** to enter the Winners Class. If your dog is placed second in the class to the dog which won Winners Dog or Winners Bitch, hold the dog or bitch in readiness as the judge must consider it for Reserve Winners.

Puppy Classes shall be for dogs which are six months of age and over but under twelve months, which were whelped in the U.S.A. or Canada, and which are not champions. Classes are often divided 6 and (under) 9, and 9 and (under) 12 months. The age of a dog shall be calculated up to and inclusive of the first day of a show. For example, a dog whelped on Jan. 1st is eligible to compete in a puppy class on July 1st, and may continue to compete up to and including Dec. 31st of the same year, but is not eligible to compete Jan. 1st of the following year.

The Novice Class shall be for dogs six months of age or over, whelped in the U.S.A. or Canada which have not, prior to the closing of entries, won three first prizes in the Novice Class, a first prize in Bred-by-Exhibitor, American-Bred or Open Class, nor one or more points toward a championship title.

The Bred-by-Exhibitor Class shall be for dogs whelped in the U.S.A. which are six months of age and over, which are not champions, and which are owned wholly or in part by the person or by the spouse of the person who was the breeder or one of the breeders of record. Dogs entered in the BBE Class must be handled by an owner or by a member of the immediate family of an owner, i.e., the husband, wife, father, mother, son, daughter, brother or sister.

The American-Bred Class shall be for all dogs (except champions) six months of age or over, whelped in the U.S.A. by reason of a mating that took place in the U.S.A.

The Open Class is for any dog six months of age or over, except in a member specialty club show held for only American-bred dogs, in which case the class is for American-Bred dogs only.

Winners Dogs and **Winners Bitches:** After the above male classes have been judged, the first-place winners are then **required** to compete in the ring. The dog judged "Winners Dog" is awarded the points toward his championship title.

Reserve Winners are selected immediately after the Winners Dog. In case of a disqualification of a win by the AKC, the Reserve Dog moves up to "Winners" and receives the points. After all male classes are judged, the bitch classes are called.

Best of Breed or Best of Variety Competition is limited to Champions of Record or dogs (with newly acquired points, for a 90-day period prior to AKC confirmation) which have completed championship requirements, and Winners Dog and Winners Bitch (or the dog awarded Winners if only one Winners prize has been awarded), together with any undefeated dogs which have been shown only in non-regular classes. All compete for Best of Breed or Best of Variety (if the breed is divided by size, color, texture or length of coat hair, etc.).

Best of Winners: If the WD or WB earns BOB or BOV, it automatically becomes BOW; otherwise they will be judged together for BOW (following BOB or BOV judging).

Best of Opposite Sex is selected from the remaining dogs of the opposite sex to Best of Breed or Best of Variety.

Other Classes may be approved by the AKC: **Stud Dogs, Brood Bitches, Brace Class, Team Class**; classes consisting of local dogs and bitches may also be included in a show if approved by the AKC (special rules are included in the AKC Rule Book).

The magnificent Ch. Starcrest Spy of Poppyland winning Best in Show in Ensenada, Mexico. Owned by the Howard Kend of California, and handled by Mr. Kendall.

The Miscellaneous Class shall be for purebred dogs of such breeds as may be designated by the AKC. No dog shall be eligible for entry in this class unless the owner has been granted an Indefinite Listing Privilege (ILP) and unless the ILP number is given on the entry form. Application for an ILP shall be made on a form

provided by the AKC and when submitted must be accompanied by a fee set by the Board of Directors.

All Miscellaneous Breeds shall be shown together in a single class except that the class may be divided by sex if so specified in the premium list. There shall be **no** further competition for dogs entered in this class. Ribbons for 1st, 2nd, 3rd and 4th shall be Rose, Brown, Light Green and Gray, respectively. This class is open to the following Miscellaneous Breeds: Akitas, Australian Cattle Dogs, Australian Kelpies, Border Collies, Cavalier King Charles Spaniels, Ibizan Hounds, Miniature Bull Terriers, Shih Tzu (soon to be shown in the toy group), Spinoni Italiani and Tibetan Terriers.

If Your Dog Wins a Class. . .

Study the classes to make certain your dog is entered in a proper class for his or her qualifications. If your dog wins his class, *you are required* to enter classes for Winners, Best of Breed and Best of Winners (no additional entry fees). The rule states, "No eligible dog may be withheld from competition." It is not mandatory that you stay for group judging. *If your dog wins a group, however, you must stay for Best-in-Show competition.*

THE PRIZE RIBBONS AND WHAT THEY STAND FOR

No matter how many entries there are in each class at a dog show, if you place first through fourth position you will receive a ribbon. These ribbons commemorate your win and can be impressive when collected and displayed to prospective buyers when and if you have puppies for sale, or if you intend to use your dog at public stud.

All ribbons from the American Kennel Club licensed dog shows will bear the American Kennel Club seal, the name of the show, the date and the placement. In the classes the colors are Blue for first, Red for second, Yellow for third, and White for fourth. Winners Dog or Winners Bitch ribbons are Purple, while Reserve Dog and Reserve Bitch ribbons are Purple and White. Best of Winners ribbons are Blue and White; Best of Breed, Purple and Gold; and Best of Opposite Sex ribbons are Red and White.

In the six groups, first prize is a Blue rosette or ribbon, second placement is Red, third Yellow, and fourth White. The Best in Show rosette is either Red, White and Blue, or incorporates the colors used in the show-giving club's emblem.

QUALIFYING FOR CHAMPIONSHIP

Championship points are given for Winners Dog and Winners Bitch in accordance with a scale of points established by the American Kennel Club based on the popularity of the breed in entries, and the number of dogs competing in the classes. This scale of points varies in different sections of the country, but the scale is published in front of each dog show catalog. These points may differ between the dogs and the bitches at the same show. You may, however, win additional points by winning Best of Winners, if there are fewer dogs than bitches entered, or vice versa. Points never exceed five at any one show, and a total of fifteen points must be won to constitute a championship. These fifteen points must be won under at least three different judges, and you must acquire at

Ch. Beamer's Kim Lee, owned by Bonnie L. Kane, of Louisville, Kentucky, wins Best of Breed at the Mid-States Chow Chow Club Specialty Show in March, 1958 under judge Major Godsol. Clint Harris handles. A Frasie Studio photograph.

least two major wins. Anything from a three to five point win is a major, while one and two point wins are minor wins. Two major wins must be won under two different judges to meet championship requirements.

OBEDIENCE TRIALS

Some shows also offer Obedience Trials which are considered as separate events. They give the dogs a chance to compete and score on performing a prescribed set of exercises intended to display their training in doing useful work.

There are three obedience titles for which they may compete. First, the Companion Dog or CD title; second, the Companion Dog Excellent or CDX; and third, the Utility Dog or UD. Detailed information on these degrees is contained in a booklet entitled Official Obedience Regulations and may be obtained by writing to the American Kennel Club.

JUNIOR SHOWMANSHIP COMPETITION

Junior Showmanship Competition is for boys and girls in different age groups handling their own dog or one owned by their immediate family. There are four divisions: Novice A, for the ten to 12 year olds; Novice B, for those 13 to 16 years of age, with no previous Junior Showmanship wins; Open C, for ten to 12 year olds; and Open D, for 13 to 16 year olds who have earned one or more JS awards.

As Junior Showmanship at the dog shows increased in popularity, certain changes and improvements had to be made. As of April 1, 1971, the American Kennel Club issues a new booklet containing the Regulations for Junior Showmanship which may be obtained by writing to the A.K.C. at 51 Madison Avenue, New York, N.Y. 10010.

A beautiful photograph of Ch. Dai Fu King of Glenmont, photographed by Evelyn M. Shafer; owned by Mr. and Mrs. John Anderson, old-time Chowists.

DOG SHOW PHOTOGRAPHERS

Every show has at least one official photographer who will be more than happy to take a photograph of your dog with the judge, ribbons and trophies, along with you or your handler. These make marvelous remembrances of your top show wins and are frequently framed along with the ribbons for display purposes. Photographers can be paged at the show over the public address system, if you wish to obtain this service. Prices vary, but you will probably find it costs little to capture these happy moments, and the photos can always be used in the various dog magazines to advertise your dog's wins.

TWO TYPES OF DOG SHOWS

There are two types of dog shows licensed by the American Kennel Club. One is the all-breed show which includes classes for all the recognized breeds, and groups of breeds; i.e., all terriers, all toys, etc. Then there are the Specialty shows for one particular breed which also offer championship points.

BENCHED OR UNBENCHED DOG SHOWS

The show-giving clubs determine, usually on the basis of what facilities are offered by their chosen show site, whether their show will be benched or unbenched. A benched show is one where the dog show superintendent supplies benches (cages for toy dogs). Each bench is numbered and its corresponding number appears on your entry identification slip which is sent to you prior to the show date. The number also appears in the show catalog. Upon entering the show you should take your dog to the bench where he should remain until it is time to groom him before entering the ring to be judged. After judging, he must be returned to the bench until the official time of dismissal from the show. At an unbenched show the club makes no provision whatsoever for your dog other than an enormous tent (if an outdoor show) or an area in a show hall where all crates and grooming equipment must be kept.

Benched or unbenched, the moment you enter the show grounds you are expected to look after your dog and have it under complete control at all times. This means short leads in crowded aisles or getting out of cars. In the case of a benched show, a "bench chain" is needed. It should allow the dog to move around, but not get down off the bench. It is also not considered "cute" to have small tots leading enormous dogs around a dog show where the child might be dragged into the middle of a dog fight.

PROFESSIONAL HANDLERS

If you are new in the fancy and do not know how to handle your dog to his best advantage, or if you are too nervous or physically unable to show your dog, you can hire a licensed professional handler who will do it for you for a specified fee. The more successful or well-known handlers charge slightly higher rates, but generally speaking there is a pretty uniform

Ch. Eastward Liontamer of Elster's first Best In Show win, under judge Mrs. Evelyn Silvernail at the Springfield Kennel Club in May, 1969. Ted Young, Jr. handled for owners Mr. and Mrs. Robert Hetherington, Jr. and Dr. Samuel Draper of Mahwah, New Jersey. Miss Jeannette Williams, club president, presents the trophy tray, and Mr. Vell Brewin, show chairman, presents the bowl. "Louie," one of the top-winning Chow Chows in the history of the breed, figures prominently in the pedigrees of many of today's winning Chow Chows. Photo by Evelyn Shafer.

American and Canadian Ch. Loy-Jean's China Boi pictured winning Best In Show at the Mensona Kennel Club show in November, 1961 under judge Major Godsol. The Loy-Jean Chow Chow Kennels are owned by Floyd and Jeanne Messer.

The moment of truth in the show ring. Judge Anna Katherine Nicholas takes a last look before deciding on the winner. Here she is observing Ch. Dre-Don Sun-King of Craglinden as a young dog at the Westchester Kennel Club Show in 1967. Miss Nicholas drew a large entry of twenty Chows, remarkable for the time. Samuel Draper is handling Sun-King.

charge for this service. As the dog progresses with his wins in the show ring, the fee increases proportionately. Included in this service is professional advice on when and where to show your dog, grooming, a statement of your wins at each show, and all trophies and ribbons that the dog accumulates. Any cash award is kept by the handler as a sort of "bonus."

When engaging a handler, it is advisable to select one that does not take more dogs to a show than he can properly and comfortably handle. You want your dog to receive his individual attention and not be rushed into the ring at the last moment,

because the handler has been busy with too many other dogs in other rings. Some handlers require that you deliver the dog to their establishment a few days ahead of the show so they have ample time to groom and train him. Others will accept well-behaved and previously trained and groomed dogs at ringside, if they are familiar with the dog and the owner. This should be determined well in advance of the show date. NEVER expect a handler to accept a dog at ringside that is not groomed to perfection!

There are several sources for locating a professional handler. Dog magazines

Eastward Josie posing for her first photograph at the age of three months. Her sire was Ch. Starcrest Eastward Roman; her dam was Liontamer Ah-Tum Hetherchow. Her owner is Merilyn Morgan of Falls Church, Virginia.

Ch. Nor-Ton's Kim Sing winning Best in Show at 4½ years of age in April, 1959 at the Atlanta Kennel Club show. His sire was Ch. Nor-Ton's Silver Moon *ex* Nor-Ton's Chikee Fu. Owned by Fanny B. Smith of Charlotte, North Carolina.

carry their classified advertising; a note or telephone call to the American Kennel Club will put you in touch with several in your area. Usually, you will be billed after the day of the show.

DO YOU REALLY NEED A HANDLER?

The answer to the above question is sometimes yes! However, the answer most exhibitors give is, "But I can't *afford* a professional handler!" or, "I want to show my dog myself! Does that mean my dog will never do any big winning?"

Do you *really* need a handler to win? If you are mishandling a good dog that should be winning and isn't, because it is made to look simply terrible in the ring by its owner, the answer is yes. If you don't know how to handle a dog properly, why make your dog look bad when a handler could show it to its best advantage?

Some owners simply cannot handle a dog well and still wonder why their dogs aren't winning in the ring, no matter how hard they try. Others are nervous and this nervousness travels down the leash to the dog and the dog behaves accordingly. Some people are extroverts by nature, and these are the people who usually make excellent handlers. Of course, the biggest winning dogs at the shows usually have a lot of "show off" in their nature, too, and this helps a great deal!

THE COST OF CAMPAIGNING A DOG WITH A HANDLER

Many Chow champions are shown an average of 25 times before completing a championship. In entry fees at today's prices, that adds up to about $200. This does not include motel bills, traveling expenses, or food. There have been Chow champions finished in less shows, say five to ten shows, but this is the exception rather than the rule. When and where to show should be thought out carefully so that you can perhaps save money on entries. Here is one of the services a professional handler provides that can mean a considerable saving. Hiring a handler can save money in the long run if you just wish to make a cham-

An exquisite headstudy of what has been reported to be one of the best Chow Chow heads in the history of the breed — Ch. Eastward Liontamer of Elster, owned by the Robert Hetheringtons and co-author Dr. Samuel Draper. This photograph was used as the front cover of *Popular Dogs* magazine for the August, 1970 special Non-Sporting Dog issue while co-author Joan Brearley was editor.

Ch. Lyle's Age of Aquarius winning the Non-Sporting Group at the 1972 San Fernando Kennel Club Show under judge Miss Melba M. Jones, John and Ora Woodard presenting trophies. Blu is owned by Cliff and Vivian Shryock of Hawaiian Gardens, California.

pion. If your dog has been winning reserves and not taking the points and a handler can finish him in five to ten shows, you would be ahead financially. If your dog is not really top quality, the length of time it takes even a handler to finish it (depending upon competition in the area) could add up to a large amount of money.

Campaigning a show specimen that not only captures the wins in his breed but wins group and Best in Show awards gets up into the big money. To cover the nation's major shows and rack up a record as one of the top dogs in the nation usually costs an owner between ten and fifteen thousand dollars a year. This includes not only the professional handler's fees for taking the dog into the ring, but the cost of conditioning and grooming, board, advertising in the dog magazines, photographs, etc.

There is great satisfaction in winning with your own dog, especially if you have trained and cared for it yourself. With today's enormous entries at the dog shows and so many worthy dogs competing for top wins, many owners who said, "I'd rather do it myself!" and meant it, became discouraged and eventually hired a handler anyway!

However, if you really are in it just for the sport, you can and should handle your own dog if you want to! You can learn the tricks by attending training classes, and you can learn a lot by carefully observing the more successful professional handlers as they perform in the ring. Model yourself after the ones that command respect as being the leaders in their profession. But, if you find you'd really rather be at ringside looking on, then do get a handler so that your worthy dog gets his deserved recognition in the ring. To own a good dog and win with it is a thrill, so good luck, no matter how you do it.

A lovely head study of Ch. Plain Acre's Charman Fella which was featured on Chow Chow notepaper. Photographed by Creszentia Allen. Charman Fella is owned by Mr. and Mrs. Richard Meaney, Connecticut.

America's top-winning Chow Chow for 1959, Ch. Chang-Shi Choonam Kwong. This home-bred, whelped in 1956 by Lucile and Jerry Sterling of Nashville, Tennessee, was sired by Ch. Chang-Shi Zygoto ex Ch. Fireball's Black Angel. His show record was three Group Firsts, 1 Group Second, 1 Group Third, and 1 Group Fourth.

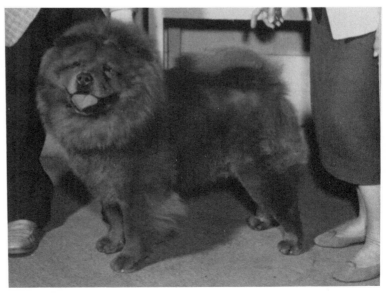

18. TOP-WINNING CHOW CHOWS AND THEIR RECORDS

While records are made to be broken, as we hopefully improve our breed with each succeeding generation, there are a few records which should go down in history along with the names of the winners.

We consider the most important of records to be the Chow Chows which have won at the Specialty Shows over the years and the dogs which have won at the prestigious Westminster Kennel Club Show at Madison Square Garden in New York City. We present a partial list of both in this chapter along with, in some cases, the entry and other pertinent facts of interest, in list form for easier reference.

Also, we present the Top Ten Chow Chows in the United States according to the Phillips System rating of show dogs. With their listing of first through tenth, we also include the number of points garnered to attain this rating. Each number stands for another dog defeated in all breeds if the win represented a Best in Show, or victory over all other Non-Sporting breeds if the win represented a Group or Group Placement. One can appreciate the amount of winning and the number of dog shows attended when you see the points climb up into the thousands. And all the more to their credit!

We salute our Top Winning Chow Chows for their past records and look toward the following generations for the glories yet to come!

PARTIAL LIST OF CHOW CHOW WINNERS AT WESTMINSTER

1890 TAKYA. Born: Oct. 18, 1888. Owned by Miss A.C. Derby, New York City. Imported from England. Entered in Miscellaneous Class of 25 dogs as Chinese Chow Chow Dog; placed Third. Judges: Mr. R.F. Mayhew and Mr. John Davidson.

1914 CH. EASTERN STAR. Born: July 5, 1907 in the U.S. Owned by Greenacre Kennels. Judge: Mr. John Sergeant Price, Jr. *Entries: 52.*

1919 No judging of Best of Breed. Judge: John Z. Adams. Winners Dog: CH. YUEY, owned by Coassock Kennels. Winners Bitch: SHOCKHEADED SADIE, no owner listed. No birth dates listed. *Entries: 99.*

1928 CH. SU T'SUN OF FIVE ASH. Born: July 31, 1925. Owned by Greenacre Kennels. Judge: Dr. William S. Baer. *Entries: 77.*

1929 GREENACRE AH LING. Born: August 29, 1924. Owned by Greenacre Kennels. Judge: Mr. Ormond Deignan. *Entries: 66.*

1930 RED CLOUD III. Born: October 29, 1928. Owned by Mr. and Mrs. C.H. Quereaux. *Entries: 67.*

1931 YANG FU TANG. Born: October 10, 1929. Owned by Mr. and Mrs. Arthur E. Hoffman. Judge: Mrs. David Wagstaff. *Entries: 55.*

1932 CH. YANG FU TANG. Born: October 10, 1929. Owned by Mrs. Louise C. Seamer. Judge: Mr. Frank H. Addyman. *Entries: 60.*

1933 CH. FAR LAND THUNDERGUST. Born: August 29, 1930. Owned by Far Land Kennels. Judge: Miss Alice M. Deignan. *Entries: 32.*

1934 CH. CLAREDALE SON TOO. Born: December 13, 1927. Owned by Clairedale Kennels. Judge: Mrs. Grace G. Neyhart. *Entries: 49.*

1935 CH. FAR LAND THUNDERGUST. Born: August 29, 1930. Owned by Mrs. William MacFarland. Judge: Dr. Henry Jarrett, Jr. *Entries: 72.*

1936 CH. FAR LAND THUNDERGUST. Born: August 29, 1930. Owned by Mrs. William MacFarland. Judge: Mrs. L.W. Bonney. *Entries: 58.*

1937 CH. FAR LAND THUNDERGUST. Born: August 29, 1930. Owned by Mrs. William McFarland. Judge: Mrs. A.F. Messmore. *Entries: 44.*

1938 CH. LLE WOL LAH SON. Born: December 7, 1936. Owned by Mrs. A.V. Hallowell. Judge: Mrs. Grace G. Neyhart. *Entries: 24.*

1939 CH. LLE WOL LAH SON. Born: December 7, 1936. Owned by Mrs. A.V. Hallowell. Judge: Mr. Livingston E. Osborne. *Entries: 35.*

1940 CH. LLE WOL LAH SON. Born: December 7, 1936. Owned by Mrs. A.V. Hallowell. Judge: Mr. Walter H. Reeves. *Entries: 24.*

1941 CH. LLE WOL LAH SON. Born: Dec. 7, 1936. Owned by Mrs. A.V. Hallowell. Judge: Mrs. Grace G. Neyhart. *Entries: 26.*

1942 LEDGELANDS' BLUEBERRY. Born: February 2, 1939. Owned by Ledgelands' Kennels. Judge: Dr. A.V. Hallowell. *Entries: 15.*

1943 CH. EL CHER GEISHA GIRL OF TALLY-HO. Born: Oct. 14, 1937. Owned by Tally-Ho Kennels. Judge: Edward H. Goodwin. *Entries: 11.*

1944 CH. JIMMEE BOY. Born: February 20, 1936. Owned by Miss Kathleen Staples. Judge: Dr. Thomas D. Buck. *Entries: 29.*

1945 CH. HO-HAN CHU-GLO. BORN: May 14, 1940. Owned by Mr. George H. Armitage. Judge: Mrs. L.W. Bonney. *Entries: 30.*

1946 CH. STORM CLOUD OF SHANG-HI. Born: June 25, 1936. Owned by Tally-Ho Kennels. Judge: Mrs. John G. Anderson. *Entries: 24.*

1947 CH. RASK'S KAR-LEE. Born: May 8, 1940. Owned by Noa-Doi Kennels. Judge: Mr. Chris Shuttleworth. *Entries: 14.*

1948 GE-NI'S HAN-YU. Owned by Mrs. Nina L. Armitage. Judge: Mrs. William L. Fitzgerald. *Entries: 21.*

1949 CH. LINNCHOW YU HUSO. Born: August 25, 1945. Owned by Mr. Logan N. Paton. Judge: Mr. Walter H. Reeves. *Entries: 13.*

1950 CH. LINNCHOW YU HUSSO. Born: August 25, 1945. Owned by Mr. Logan N. Patton. Judge: Miss Ruth Stillman. *Entries: 21.*

1951 CH. LINNCHOW MING LOO YET. Born: Feb. 16, 1946. Owned by Mr. and Mrs. William D. Ross. Judge: Mr. William L. Kendrick. *Entries: 22.*

1952 CH. OWHYO WAG-GEE. Born: March 16, 1947. Owned by Mr. and Mrs. Steven G. Gillich. Judge: Mr. Mervin F. Rosenbaum. *Entries: 14.*

1953 CH. OWHYO WAG-GEE. Born: March 16, 1947. Owned by Mr. and Mrs. Steven G. Gillich. Judge: Mrs. David Wagstaff. *Entries: 9.*

1954 CH. OWHYO WAG-GEE. Born: March 16, 1947. Owned by Mr. and Mrs. Steven G. Gillich. Judge: Mrs. Winifred L. Heckmann. *Entries: 16.*

1955 CH. AL EDI'S SENSATION. Born: April 16, 1950. Owned by Noa-Doi Kennels. Judge: Mrs. John G. Anderson. *Entries: 13.*

1956 CH. WUPEI NAGYUR TUT. Born: April 21, 1952. Owned by Mr. and Mrs. David Wagstaff. Judge: Miss Adele S. Colgate. *Entries: 17.*

1957 CH. KY-LIN'S MIDAS. Born: June 6, 1955. Owned by Mr. and Mrs. Russell MacEachern. Judge: Miss Kathleen Staples. *Entries: 10.*

1958 CH. NOR-TON'S YIM-LEE. Born: July 4, 1952. Owned by Mrs. Betty-Mae Sewards. Judge: Dr. Malcolm E. Phelps. *Entries: 9.*

1959 CH. CHUM YONG FU FUN. Born: Nov. 30, 1954. Owned by Mrs. Earl F.

Humphries. Judge: Virgil Johnson. *Entries: 11.*

1960 CH. LOY-JEAN'S CHINA BOI. Born: Sept. 29, 1955. Owned by Mr. and Mrs. F.B. Messer. Judge: Edward H. Goodwin. *Entries: 21.*

1961 CH. AH SID THE DILETTANTE. Born: April 2, 1958. Owned by Miss Sidney Joan Wellborn and Mr. John Davis. Judge: Mr. J.J. Duncan. *Entries: 11.*

1962 CH. LILBERN'S CHINESE RED ROBIN. Born: Sept. 1, 1956. Owned by Mrs. Carole R. Whitlock. Judge: Mr. William H. Ackland. *Entries: 17.*

1963 CH. LOY-JEAN'S CHINA BOI. Born: Sept. 29, 1955. Owned by Mr. and Mrs. F.B. Messer. Judge: Mr. George M. Beckett. *Entries: 19.*

1964 CH. LOY-JEAN'S BEAU MONTY. Born: August 29, 1961. Owned by Mr. and Mrs. Eldon McCormack. Judge: Mr. Phil Marsh. *Entries: 16.*

1965 CH. LOY-JEAN'S BEAU MONTY. Born: August 29, 1961. Owned by Mr. and Mrs. Eldon McCormack. Judge: Mr. Frank Landgraf. *Entries: 11.*

1966 CH. LOY-JEAN'S BEAU MONTY. Born: Aug. 29, 1961. Owned by Mr. and Mrs. Eldon McCormack. Judge: Mr. Major B. Godsol. *Entries: 16.*

1967 CH. GOTSCHALL'S VAN VAN. Born: July 2, 1963. Owned by Donald L. Drennan and Mrs. Valetta L. Gotschall. Judge: Mr. Albert E. Van Court. *Entries: 15.*

1968 CH. FIVE ASH VICKI JO. Born: Aug. 1, 1964. Owned by Ah Sid and Pennyworth Kennels. Judge: Mr. R.J. Schulte. *Entries: 15.*

1969 CH. GOTSCHALL'S VAN VAN. Born: July 2, 1963. Owned by Donald L. Drennan and Mrs. Valetta L. Gotschall. Judge: Mr. Joseph Faigel. *Entries: 15.*

1970 CH. EASTWARD LIONTAMER OF ELSTER. Born: Nov. 27, 1964. Owned by Mr. and Mrs. Robert A. Hetherington, Jr. and Dr. Samuel Draper. *Entries: 12.*

1971 CH. KY-LIN'S BLACK POWER.

Born: Aug. 17, 1967. Owned by John P. and Dusten Cox. Judge: Mrs. Florence W. Broadhurst. *Entries: 15.*

1972 CH. LAKEVIEW'S MR. LU-KEE. Born: Aug. 29, 1967. Owned by Mr. David S. Reynolds and Mr. Don Aull. Judge: Mr. William W. Fetner. *Entries: 11.*

1973 CH. EASTWARD LIONTAMER OF ELSTER. Born: Nov. 27, 1964. Owned by Mr. and Mrs. Robert A. Hetherington, Jr., and Dr. Samuel Draper. Judge: Dr. David Green Doane. *Entries: 14.*

1974 MI TU'S HAN SU-SHANG (Open Dog). Born: December 6, 1972 in Canada. Owned by Mr. and Mrs. Herbert Williams and Mr. John C. Frederick Peddie. Judge: Joseph Faigel. *Entries: 17.*

The great Ch. Liontamer winning the Non-Sporting Group at the Newton Kennel Club Show in 1969 under judge Mrs. S.J. Fishman. Handled by co-owner Samuel Draper of Liontamer Kennels, Mahwah, New Jersey. A William P. Gilbert photo.

Ch. Gotschall's Van Van, a Best In Show-winning Chow Chow owned by Donald Drennan and Mrs. Valetta Gotschall of Getzville, New York, winning under judge Robert Waters at a Sugarbush Kennel Club show. A Norton of Kent photo. Handled by Bud Moser.

THE CHOW CHOW CLUB'S SPECIALTY WINNERS
[*The Parent Organization*]

1920—New York City. 198 entries. Judge, Theo. Crane. BOB, *Ning Poo*, a son of Ch. Win Sum Min T'Sing.

1921—New York City. 196 entries. Judge, Vinton P. Breese. No BOB record.

1922—New York City. 155 entries. Judge, Wallace McMonnies. No BOB record.

1923—Chicago. 98 entries. Judge, Dr. Wm. S. Baer. No BOB record.

1924—New York City. 160 entries, 98 benched. Judge, Theo. Crane. Mrs. Earl Hoover's *Ch. Victorious of Tien H'Sia*.

1925—Tuxedo, N.Y. 96 entries. Judge, Alva Rosenberg. No. BOB record.

1926—Baltimore. 120 entries. Judge, Mrs. Neyhart. No BOB record.

1927—New York City. 223 entries. Judge, Wm. Scriven (England). G.L. Radcliffe's *Wende Foo Sunleigh*.

1928—New York City. 113 entries. Judge, Andrew Albright. *Ch. Son of Min T'Sing*.

1929—Englewood, N.J. 106 entries. Judge, Eugene Byfield. *Ch. Clairedale Son Too*.

1930—New York City. 177 entries. Judge, Mrs. David Wagstaff. *Ch. Clairedale Son Too*.

1931—New York City. 139 entries. Judge, C.E. Libbey. Ormond Deignan's *Ch. Greenacre Ah Ling*.

1932—New York City. 167 entries. Judge, Mrs. Wm. Fitzgerald. *Ch. Yang Fu Tang*.

1933—Madison, N.J. (M. & E.). 112 entries. Judge, Andrew Albright. *Ch. Farland Thundergust*.

1934—Madison, N.J. 107 entries. Judge Anton Rost substituted for W.O. Penney. Mrs. F.R. Humpage's *Ch. Blue Cheriton of Dingley Dell*.

1934—New York City. 101 entries. Judge, Chas. G. Hopton. *Ch. Wende Foo Sunleigh*.

1935—Madison. 94 entries. Judge, Livingston Osborne. *Ch. Farland Thundergust*.

1935—New York City. 92 entries. Art Hoffmann, judge. *Ledgeland's Tuff-Fei*, owner-bred.

1936—Madison. 95 entries. Judge, W.O. Penney. *Ch. Shanghai Chief*, Mrs. B.J. Houston's home-bred.

1936—New York City. 74 entries. Judge, Mrs. W.O. Penney. *Honorable Mr. Lu Tang*.

1937—Madison. 88 entries. Judge, Mrs. L.W. Bonney. *Ch. Farland Thundergust*.

1937—New York City. 109 entries. Judge, Mrs. B.J. Houston. *Lle Wol Lah Son*, owner-bred of Mrs. A.V. Hallowell.

1938—Madison, N.J. (Morris & Essex). 63 class dogs benched. Judge, Mrs. W.S. Mears. *Wyndcrest Handsome*, bred by Katherine Kandra, owned by W.A. McElwaine.

1938—Far Hills, N.J. 32 dogs benched. Judge Ernest Wells substituted for D. Wagstaff. *Ch. Lle Wol Lah Son*.

1939—Madison. 51 class dogs benched. Judge, Mrs. Wm. Fitzgerald. *Ch. Lle Wol Lah Son*.

1939—White Plains, N.Y. Entry 75, 66 benched. Judge, Mrs. R.W. Spike. *Ch. Tally-Ho Black Image of Storm*, home-bred by Mrs. Bonney.

1940—Madison, N.J. (Morris & Essex). 85 entries. Judge, Dr. Henry Jarrett. *Ch. Jimmee Boy*, owner-bred of Miss K. Staples.

1941—Katonah, N.Y. 88 entries. Judge, Gaston Valcourt. *Ch. Ho Han Beautiful*, bred by Eva Chase, owned by the Wm. Dawes of Massachusetts.

1942—war year. No specialty records.

1943—Rye, N.Y. 21 class dogs present. Judge, Mrs. L.W. Bonney. *Ch. Ledgeland's Tuff-Fei*, owner-bred of Ledgelands Kennels.

1944—South Orange, N.J. 33 entries. Judge, Ralph Spike. *Ch. Ledgeland's Blueberry*, bred by Livingston Osborne.

1945—No specialty records.

1946—Plainfield, N.J. 27 entries. Judge, David Wagstaff. *Ch. Lu Tang's Ski Mas-*

ter. Bred by Ernest Muller. Owned by H.J. Carroll of Washington state.

1947—Plainfield, N.J. No available record of number of entries. (Entry 44 the previous day at Morris & Essex.) Judge, Mrs. K. Humpage. *Ch. Dai Fu King of Glenmont*, bred by Maro Evans.

1948—St. Louis. 67 entries. Judge, Mrs. David Wagstaff. *Ch. Copper Topper II*, bred by J. Melvin Reid, owned by Dr. Cuber.

1949—Long Beach, California. 208 entries. Judge, Mrs. John G. Anderson. *Ch. Hanson's Hooper Du*, home-bred. Owned by Claire Hanson.

1950—Plainfield, N.J. 50 entries. Judge, R. Hoffmann. *Ch. Owhyo Wag-Gee*, bred by Stewart, owned by the Steven Gillichs.

1951—Detroit (with Progressive). 66 entries. Judge, Miss K. Staples. *Ch. Al-Edi's Black Magic*, bred by Todter. Owned by Florence Stanton.

Tauskey headstudy of Ch. Tally-Ho Black Image of Storm, circa '39. This great Chow was owned by Mrs L.W. Bonney, Long Island, New York.

1952—Santa Monica, Cal. (with Beverly-Riviera). 62 entries. Judge, Art Hoffmann. *Ch. Wah Gee of Dover*, home-bred of R. Reeves.

1953—Ladies KC of America, L.I. 28 entries. Judge, Mrs. C. Humpage. *Ch. Owhy Wag-Gee*.

1954—Milwaukee. 46 entries. Judge, Miss Staples. *Ch. Flagg's Chubby Chinaman*, owned by Merle Thompson of St. Louis.

1955—Long Beach, Cal. (with Harbor Cities). 78 entries. Judge, Mrs. L.W. Bonney. *Ch. Five Ash Victory*, home-bred of Florence W. Graham.

1956—Greenwich, Conn. KC. 48 entries. Judge, H.F. Howell. *Ch. Wupei Nagyur Tut*. Owned by Mrs. David Wagstaff.

1957—St. Louis. 25 entries. Judge, Howard C. Bogue. *Ch. Trojan of Poppyland*. Owned by Mr. and Mrs. L. Howard Kendall. Bred by Joe Felt.

1958—Lubbock, Texas. Judge, Mrs. L.W. Bonney. *Ch. Chum Yong Fu Fun*. Owned by Mrs. Earl Humphries. Bred by J.D. Carter.

1959—Pikesville, Md. 33 entries. Judge, H. Foster Howell. *Ch. Chum Yong Fu Fun*. Owned by Mrs. Earl Humphries. Bred by J.D. Carter.

1960—Ravenna, Ohio. 40 entries. L. Howard Kendall, judge. *Ch. Ah Sid's Guardian Knight*. Owned by Ottilie R. Hunter.

1961—12 entries. Judge, L. Howard Kendall. *Ch. Ah Sid's the Dilettante*.

1962—Seattle. *Ch. Spy of Poppyland*. Owned by Mr. and Mrs. L. Howard Kendall.

1963—43 entries. Judge, Mrs. Aggripina Anderson. *Ch. Ah Sid's the Dilettante*.

1964—Cleveland. *Ch. Spy of Poppyland*.

1965—Judge, Erica Huggins. *Ch. Starcrest Spy of Poppyland*.

1966—Annapolis, Md. *Ch. Ah Sid the Avant Garde*. Judge, Mrs. Florence Broadhurst. Owned by Dr. Samuel Draper.

1967—30 entries. Judge, Earle T. Adair.

Loy-Jean's Shoe Shine Boi. Owned by Mrs. Bertha Smith.

1968—Trenton. Judge, Mrs. Margaret Shoemaker. *Ch. Eastward Liontamer of Elster.* Mr. and Mrs. Robert A. Hetherington, Jr. and Dr. Samuel Draper, owners.

1969—Santa Ana Valley. *Ch. Eastward Liontamer of Elster.* Judge, Marjorie Siebern.

1970—Illinois. Judge, Virgil Johnson. *Ch. Eastward Liontamer of Elster.*

1971—Northern Virginia. Judge, Harold Lee. *Ch. Eastward Liontamer of Elster.*

1972—Santa Ana Valley. *Ch. Five Ash Kissin' George.* Owned by Mrs. Florence Wilson Graham.

1973—Dallas. Judge, Max Riddle. *Ch. Eastward Liontamer of Elster.*

TOP TEN CHOW CHOWS—1960-1973
1960
1. CH. GHAT de la MOULAINE; 2730 points. Owners: Clif and Vivian Shryock.
2. CH. CHIANG LeMAR; 887 points. Owners: Mr. and Mrs. Alfred LeMar.
3. CH. LOY-JEAN'S CHINA BOI; 855 points. Owners: Mr. and Mrs. Floyd B. Messer.
4. CH. CHUM YONG FU FUN; 657 points. Owner: Mrs. Earl Humphries.
5. CH. AH SID'S THE DILETTANTE; 503 points. Owner: Ah Sid Kennels.
6. CH. KY-LIN'S MIDAS; 412 points. Owners: Mr. and Mrs. Russell Mac-Eachern.
7. CH. TANG'S SONG OF CHAR-LEE. Owner: Mrs. F.A. Thomas.
8. CH. LOY-JEAN'S RED AVENGER. Owners: Charles and Vesta Stromberg.
9. CHARMAR DELILAH. Owners: Mr. and Mrs. Charles Evans.
10. CH. CHARMAR GALLANT SON. Owners: Mr. and Mrs. Charles Evans.

1961
1. CH. LOY-JEAN'S CHINA BOI; 2092 points. Owners: Mr. and Mrs. Floyd B. Messer.
2. CH. GHAT de la MOULAINE; 1857 points. Owners: Clif and Vivian Shryock.
3. CH. CHUM YONG FU FUN; 907 points. Owner: Mrs. Earl Humphries.
4. CH. PANDEE'S RED SING; 559 points. Owner: I.P. Earle.
5. CH. KY-LIN'S MIDAS; 472 points. Owners: Mr. and Mrs. Russell Mac-Eachern.
6. CH. LOY-JEAN'S RED AVENGER; 445 points. Owners: Charles and Vesta Stromberg.
7. CH. CHIANG LeMAR; 389 points. Owners: Mr. and Mrs. Alfred LeMar.
8. CH. AH SID'S THE DILETTANTE; 354 points. Owner: Ah Sid Kennels.
9. CH. CHENG LEE'S JUNG LUNG OF FIVE ASH; 228 points. Owners: Mr. and Mrs. Harold E. Lee.
10. CH. JEAN'S WAN WOO; 163 points. Owner: Jean Ferguson.

1962
1. CH. AH SID'S THE DILETTANTE; 10,659 points. Owner: Ah Sid Kennels.
2. CH. LOY-JEAN'S CHINA BOI; 2962 points. Owners: Mr. and Mrs. Floyd B. Messer.
3. CH. STARCREST SPY OF POPPYLAND; 946 points. Owners: Mr. and Mrs. L. Howard Kendall.
4. CH. JEAN'S WAN WOO; 701 points. Owner: Jean Ferguson.
5. CH. GHAT de la MOULAINE; 559 points. Owners: Clif and Vivian Shryock.
6. CH. CHUM YONG FU FUN; 526 points. Owner: Mrs. Earl Humphries.
7. CH. CHARMAR DUKE; 153 points. Owners: Mr. and Mrs. Charles Evans.
8. CH. FIVE ASH B.B. DANCER; 143 points. Owner: Florence Wilson Graham.
9. CH. STARCREST DART OF POPPYLAND; 134 points. Owner: Florence Stanton.
10. CH. KY-LIN'S MAGNUS; 120 points.

Owner: Betty-Mae Sewards.

1963

1. CH. AH SID'S THE DILETTANTE; 7267 points. Owner: Ah Sid Kennels.
2. CH. PANDEE'S ALPHA SING; 2155 points. Owner: Joel Marston.
3. CH. LOY-JEAN'S CHINA BOI; 2040 points. Owners: Mr. and Mrs. Floyd B. Messer.
4. CH. LILBERN'S CHINESE RED ROBIN; 1544 points. Owner: Carole R. Whitlock.
5. CH. KY-LIN'S CIRCUS; 441 points. Owner: Betty-Mae Sewards.
6. CH. LOY-JEAN'S CHI YAN KID; 353 points. Owner: Donald L. Drennan.
7. CH. STARCREST SPY OF POPPY-LAND; 339 points. Owners: Mr. and Mrs. L. Howard Kendall.
8. CH. CHUM YONG FU FUN; 301 points. Owner: Mrs. Earl Humphries.
9. CH. MARTONGE JO JO OF PEKE-CHOW; 185 points. Owners: Mr. and Mrs. George Curzon.
10. CH. GHAT de la MOULAINE; 163 points. Owners: Clif and Vivian Shryock.

1964

1. CH. AH SID'S THE DILETTANTE; 4682 points. Owner: Ah Sid Kennels.
2. CH. LOY-JEAN'S BEAU MONTY; 1422 points. Owners: Mr. and Mrs. Eldon McCormack.
3. CH. LILBERN'S CHINESE RED ROBIN; 1323. Owner: Carole R. Whitlock.
4. CH. STARCREST SPY OF POPPY-LAND; 981 points. Owners: Mr. and Mrs. L. Howard Kendall.
5. CH. LOY-JEAN'S CHINA BEAU; 452 points. Owners: Mr. and Mrs. Alfred LeMar.
6. CH. CARLEE'S FANCY DAN; 376 points. Owner: Carole R. Whitlock.
7. CH. LOY-JEAN'S CHI YAN KID; 352 points. Owner: Donald L. Drennan.
8. CH. KY-LIN'S JUSTUS; 286 points. Owner: Mrs. E. Sutton.
9. CH. PANDEE'S ALPHA SING; 265 points. Owner: Joel Marston.
10. CH. KWAY FIRE FLAME; 174 points. Owner: Brockway Crouch.

1965

1. CH. AH SID'S THE AIDE de KAMP; 1372 points. Owner: Dr. W.J. Fritz.
2. CH. STARCREST SPY OF POPPY-LAND; 1349 points. Owners: Mr. and Mrs. L. Howard Kendall.
3. CH. LAKEVIEW'S HAN SUM; 1255 points. Owner: Mamie R. Gregory.
4. CH. LOY-JEAN'S BEAU MONTY; 1163 points. Owners: Mr. and Mrs. Floyd B. Messer.
5. CH. SCOTCHOW SUM WUN OF LAKEVIEW; 598 points. Owner: Joan M. Hannephin.
6. CH. GOTSCHALL'S VAN VAN; 524 points. Owners: Valetta E. Gotschall and Donald L. Drennan.
7. CH KWAY FIRE FLAME; 489 points. Owner: Brockway Crouch.
8. CH. LAKEVIEW'S GOLDEN EMPEROR; 443 points. Owner: Dr. W. Oriville Mayfield.
9. CH. KY-LIN'S MITHRAS; 418 points. Owner: Betty-Mae Sewards.
10. CH. AH SID'S THE AVANT GARDE; 386 points. Owner: Dr. Samuel J. Draper.

1966

1. CH. LAKEVIEW'S HAN SUM; 1730 points. Owner: Mamie R. Gregory.
2. CH. STARCREST SPY OF POPPY-LAND; 1721 points. Owners: Mr. and Mrs. L. Howard Kendall.
3. CH. GOTSCHALL'S VAN VAN; 1632 points. Owners: Valetta E. Gotschall and Donald L. Drennan.
4. CH. AH SID'S THE AVANT GARDE; 1482 points. Owner: Dr. W.J. Fritz.
5. CH. LOY-JEAN'S BEAU MONTY; 1345. Owners: Mr. and Mrs. Eldon McCormack.
6. CH. SCOTCHOW'S SUM WUN OF LAKEVIEW; 1082. Owner: Joan M. Hannephin.
7. CH. EASTWARD LIONTAMER OF ELSTER; 1000 points. Owner: Merilyn Bowden.
8. CH. CHARLIE O'SUCCESS; 692 points. Owners: Mariam and Dan Frederick.
9. CH. CHARMAR CHATTERBOX;

359 points. Owners: Mr. and Mrs. Charles Evans.

10. CH. TSANG-PA-LI-CHO LI-KU-TU; 349 points. Owners: Dan and Mariam Frederick.

1967

1. CH. LAKEVIEW'S HAN SUM; 1274 points. Owner: Mamie Gregory.
2. CH. EASTWARD LIONTAMER OF ELSTER; 1245 points. Owner: Merilyn Bowden.
3. CH. GOTSCHALL'S VAN VAN; 989 points. Owners: D.L. Drennan and Mrs. V.E. Gotschall.
4. CH. FIVE ASK VIKI JO; 890 points. Owners: Ah Sid and Pennyworth Kennels.
5. CH. LOY-JEAN'S CHINA BEAU; 917 points. Owners: A.R. and M.M. LeMar.
6. CH. TSANG-PA-LI-CHO LI-KU-TU; 602 points. Owner: D. Frederick.
7. CH. STARCREST SPY OF POPPYLAND; 470 points. Owners: Mr. and Mrs. L.H. Kendall.
8. CH. SCOTCHOW SUM WUN OF LAKEVIEW; 425 points. Owner: J.M. Hannephin.
9. THE WESTERN BEAU; 251 points. Owners: Mr. and Mrs. E. McCormack.
10. CH. KANKING'S BINGO; 249 points. Owner: E.M. Gandt.

1968

1. CH. FIVE ASH VICKI JO; 5929 points. Owners: Pennyworth and Ah Sid Kennels.
2. CH. LAKEVIEW'S HAN SUM; 1597 points. Owner: Mamie R. Gregory.
3. CH. GOTSCHALL'S VAN VAN; 1204 points. Owners: Valetta E. Gotschall and Donald L. Drennan.
4. CH. EASTWARD LIONTAMER OF ELSTER; 891 points. Owners: Mr. and Mrs. Robert A Hetherington, Jr., and Dr. Samuel Draper.
5. CH. SHANG TAI'S SANDY PRINCE; 575 points. Owner: E. Kladja.
6. CH. THE WESTERN BEAU; 531 points. Owners: Mr. and Mrs. Eldon McCormack.

7. CH. CHEROKEE NIK NAK; 425 points. Owners: Mr. and Mrs. O.E. Crisp.
8. CH. SCOTCHOW LIONTAMER LOUISE; 369 points. Owner: Joan M. Hannephin.
9. CH. PLAIN ACRES WUN DAI DREAM; 322 points. Owners: Sanford and Ruth Little.
10. CH. KY-LIN'S RED BUDDHA; 223 points. Owners: William and Mary Chambers.

1969

1. CH. EASTWARD LIONTAMER OF ELSTER; 7252 points. Owners: Mr. and Mrs. Robert A. Hetherington, Jr., and Dr. Samuel Draper.
2. CH KY LIN'S BLACK POWER; 2593 points. Owners: J. and D. Cox.
3. CH. GOTSCHALL'S VAN VAN; 1744 points. Owners: D. Drennan and V.E. Gotschall.
4. CH. LAKEVIEW'S HAN SUM; 1714 points. Owner: Mamie Gregory.
5. CH. FIVE ASH VICKI JO; 1279 points. Owners: Ah Sid and Pennyworth Kennels.
6. PANDEE'S JUBILEE; 1105 points. Owner: I. Earle.
7. CH. LIONTAMER MARDI GRAS; 1045 points. Owner: M. Elliott.
8. CH. CARLEE'S EMPEROR CHU; 942 points. Owner: C. Whitlock.
9. CH. PLAIN ACRES WUN DAE DREAM; 903 points. Owners: R. and S. Little.
10. CH. DRE DON'S VAN ACE; 519 points. Owner: V. Gotschall.

1970

1. CH. EASTWARD LIONTAMER OF ELSTER; 10,186 points. Owners: Mr. and Mrs. Robert A. Hetherington, Jr., and Dr. Samuel Draper.
2. CH. LAKEVIEW'S HAN SUM; 5323 points. Owner: Mamie Gregory.
3. CH. LIONTAMER MARDI GRAS; 1386 points. Owner: M. Elliot.
4. CH. DRE-DON'S VAN ACE; 800 points. Owner: V. Gotschall.
5. CH. LAKEVIEW JO JO; 729 points. Owner: N. Scott.
6. CH. MI-PAO'S BATOE KETJIL; 716

points. Owner: J. Murphy.

7. CH. SCOTCHOW LIONTAMER FRANKEE; 701 points. Owner: J. Hannephin.
8. CH. WUN DAE DREAM KIKKO JADE; 680 points. Owner: M. King.
9. CH. KEE-ZEE KEESAMAN OF CHENG LEE; 553 points. Owners: Mr. and Mrs. R. Keesaman.
10. CH. SCHILLING'S SIR LANCE; 357 Points.

1971

1. CH. EASTWARD LIONTAMER OF ELSTER; 7087 points. Owners: Mr. and Mrs. R.A. Hetherington, Jr., and Dr. Samuel Draper.
2. CH. GOTSCHALL'S CHANG KON CHIAN; 5079 points. Owner: T.A. Cassidy.
3. CH. LIONTAMER MARDI GRAS; 1595 points. Owner: M.A. Eliott.
4. CH. MI-PAO'S BATOE KETJIL; 1464 points. Owner: J.B. Murphy.
5. CH. LAKEVIEW'S JO JO; 1289 points. Owner: N. Scott.
6. CH. FAHSONDI BLACK XPO; 631 points. Owner: Mrs. E. Ellwanger.
7. CH. STARCREST MR. CHRISTO-PHER; 499 points. Owner: J. Marston.
8. CH. SCHILLING SIR LANCE; 473 points. Owners: R.H. and M.E. Schilling.
9. CH. KY LIN'S BLACK POWER; 459 points. Owners: J.P. and D. Cox.
10. CH. LAKEVIEW'S MR. LU KEE; 449 points.

1972

1. CH. GOTSCHALL'S CHANG KOU CHIAN; 4351 points. Owner: T.A. Cassidy.
2. CH. LAKEVIEW'S MR. LU KEE; 2618 points. Owners: D.S. Reynolds and D. Aull.
3. CH. LIONTAMER MARDI GRAS; 2231. Owner: M.A. Eliott.
4. CH. STARCREST MR. CHRISTO-PHER; 1866 points. Owners: F. and M. Schilling.
5. CH. KY LIN'S BLACK POWER; 1808 points. Owners: D. and J. Cox.
6. CH. LAKEVIEW'S JO JO; 1561

points. Owner: N. Scott.

7. CH. SAM KU SON ONE; 891 points. Owner: S. Brumbaugh.
8. CH. SCOTCHOW LIONTAMER FRANKEE; 829 points. Owner: J.M. Hannephin.
9. CH. EASTWARD LIONTAMER OF ELSTER; 629 points. Owners: Mr. and Mrs. R.A. Hetherington, Jr., and Dr. Samuel Draper.
10. CH. DRE DON'S VAN ACE; 505 points. Owners: Mrs. V.E. Gotschall and C.R. Whitlock.

1973

1. CH. LAKEVIEW'S MR. LU KEE; 3779 points. Owners: David S. Reynolds and Don Auli.
2. CH. SAM KU SON ONE; 2758 points. Owner: Mrs. Suzanne Brumbaugh.
3. CH. GOTSCHALL'S CHANG KOU CHIAN; 2627 points. Owner: Thomas A. Kennedy.
4. CH. STARCREST MR. CHRISTO-PHER; 2108 points. Owner: Joel Marston.
5. CH. LAKEVIEW'S HAN SUM; 1306 points. Owner: Mamie R. Gregory.
6. CH. AH SID LIONTAMER JAM-BOREE; 1280 points. Owners: Desmond J. Murphy and Dr. Samuel Draper.
7. CH. LIONTAMER MARDI GRAS; 1181 points. Owner: Mary Alice Elliott.
8. CH. KY-LIN'S BLACK POWER; 701 points. Owners: John and Dustin Cox.
9. CH. CARLEE'S GENERAL FA-CI; 568 points.
10. CH. SCOTCHOW LIONTAMER FRANKEE; 468 points. Owner: Joan M. Hannephin.

(See Appendix A for list of the top ten Chow Chows for 1974 and 1975.)

19. GENERAL CARE AND MANAGEMENT

Ch. Betmar's Leesa of Shanglo winning a 3-point major at a 1966 kennel club show under judge Langdon Skarda. Bred by the Shanglo Kennels, she is owned by Betty Schellenberg of Fort Worth, Texas.

TATTOOING

Ninety per cent success has been reported on the return of stolen or lost dogs that have been tattooed! More and more this simple, painless, inexpensive method of positive identification for dogs is being reported all over the United States. Long popular in Canada, along with nose prints, the idea gained interest in this country when dognapping started to soar as unscrupulous people began stealing dogs for resale to research laboratories. Pet dogs that wander off and lost hunting dogs have always been a problem. The success of tattooing has been significant.

Tattooing can be done by the veterinarian for a minor fee. There are several dog "registries" that will record your dog's number and help you locate it should it be lost or stolen. The number of the dog's American Kennel Club registration is most often used on thoroughbred dogs, or the owner's Social Security number in the case of mixed breeds. The best place for the tattoo is the groin. Some prefer the inside of an ear, and the American Kennel Club has rules that the judges officiating at the AKC dog shows not penalize the dog for the tattoo mark.

The tattoo mark serves not only to identify your dog should it be lost or stolen, but offers positive identification in large kennels where several litters of the same approximate age are on the premises. It is a safety measure against unscrupulous breeders "switching" puppies. Any age is a proper age to tattoo, but for safety's sake, the sooner the better.

The buzz of the needle might cause your dog to be apprehensive, but the pricking of the needle is virtually painless. The risk of infection is negligible when done properly, and the return of your beloved pet may be the reward for taking the time to insure positive identification for your dog! Your local kennel club will know of a dog registry in your area.

OUTDOOR HOUSEBREAKING

If you are particular about your dog's behavior in the house, where you expect him to be clean and respecful of the carpets and furniture, you should also want him to have proper manners outdoors. Just because the property belongs to you doesn't necessarily mean he should be allowed to empty himself any place he chooses. Before long the entire yard will be fouled and odorous and the dog will be completely irresponsible on other people's property as well. Dogs seldom recognize property lines!

If your dog does not have his own yard fenced in, he should be walked on leash before being allowed to run free and before being penned up in his own yard. He will appreciate his own run being kept clean. You will find that if he has learned his manners outside, his manners inside will be better. Good manners in "toilet training" are especially important with big dogs!

OTHER IMPORTANT OUTDOOR MANNERS

Excessive barking is perhaps the most objectionable habit a dog indulges in out of doors. It annoys neighbors and makes for a noisy dog in the house as well. A sharp jerk on the leash will stop a dog from excessive barking while walking; trees and shrubs around a dog run will cut down on barking if a dog is in his own run. However, it is unfair to block off his view entirely. Give him some view — preferably of his own home — to keep his interest. Needless to say, do not leave a dog that barks excessively out all night.

You will want your dog to bark at strangers, so allow him this privilege. Then after a few "alerting" barks tell the dog to be quiet (with the same word command each time). If he doesn't get the idea, put him on leash and let him greet callers with you at the door until he does get the idea.

Do not let your dog jump on visitors either. Leash training may be necessary to break this habit as well. As the dog jumps in the air, pull back on the lead so that the dog is returned to the floor abruptly. If he attempts to jump up on you, carefully raise your knee and push him away by leaning against his chest.

Do not let your dog roam free in the neighborhood no matter how well he knows his way home. Especially do not let your dog roam free to empty himself on the neighbor's property or gardens!

A positive invitation to danger is to allow your dog to chase cars or bicycles. Throwing tin cans or chains out of car windows at them has been suggested as a cure, but can also be dangerous if they hit the

Headstudy of a great Chow, Champion Five Ash Jo Jo, a Group and Best in Show winner. He was the sire of many champions. His sire was Ch. Jo Jo Hanson out of Five Ash Gloming, and his breeders were Mickey and Dorothy Miltenberger. Florence Wilson Graham purchased him as a young dog and campaigned him to national fame.

Ch. Sharbo's Satanya, bred by Ed and Les Candy and owned by Robert and Sharon Gilb of Illinois. The sire was Ch. Charmar Cho-Sen ex Charmar China Doll.

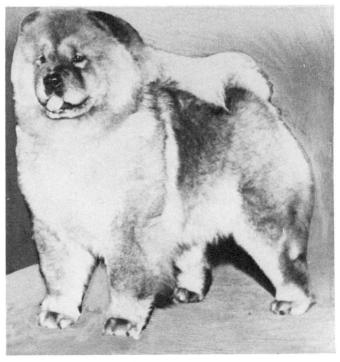

Ch. Starcrest Twilight Idol, outstanding example of a true blue male. Sired by Ch. Starcrest Matinee Idol *ex* Ch. Pandee's Katrina, C.D. Owned and bred by Prudence Baxter, California.

dog instead of the street. Streams of water from a garden hose or water pistol are the least dangerous, but leash control is still the most scientific and most effective!

If neighbors report that your dog barks or howls or runs from window to window while you are away, crate training or room training for short periods of time may be indicated. If you expect to be away for longer periods of time, put the dog in the basement or a single room where he can do the least damage. The best solution of all is to buy him another dog or cat for companionship. Let them enjoy each other

while you are away and have them both welcome you home!

GERIATRICS

If you originally purchased good healthy stock and cared for your dog throughout his life, there is no reason why you cannot expect your dog to live to a ripe old age. With research and the remarkable foods produced for dogs, especially this past decade or so, his chances of longevity have increased considerably. If you have cared for him well, your dog will be a sheer delight in his old age, just as he was while in his prime.

We can assume you have fed him properly, if he is not too fat! Have you ever noticed how fat people usually have fat dogs because they indulge their dogs' appetite as they do their own? If there has been no great illness, then you will find that very little additional care and attention are needed to keep him well. Exercise is still essential, as is proper food, booster shots, and tender loving care.

Even if a heart condition develops, there is still no reason to believe your dog cannot live to an old age. A diet may be necessary, along with medication, and limited exercise, to keep the condition under control. In the case of deafness, or partial blindness, additional care must be taken to protect the dog, but neither infirmity will in any way shorten his life. Prolonged exposure to temperature variances, overeating, excessive exercise, lack of sleep, or being housed with younger, more active dogs may take an unnecessary toll on the dog's energies and introduce serious trouble. Good judgment, periodic veterinary checkups and individual attention will keep your dog with you for many added years.

When discussing geriatrics, the question of when a dog becomes old or aged usually is asked. We have all heard the old saying that one year of a dog's life is equal to seven years in a human. This theory is strictly a matter of opinion, and must remain so, since so many outside factors enter into how quickly each individual dog "ages." Recently, a new chart was devised which is more realistically equivalent:

DOG	MAN
6 months	10 years
1 year	15 years
2 years	24 years
3 years	28 years
4 years	32 years
5 years	36 years
6 years	40 years
7 years	44 years
8 years	48 years
9 years	52 years
10 years	56 years
15 years	76 years
21 years	100 years

It must be remembered that such things as serious illnesses, poor food and housing, general neglect and poor beginnings as puppies will all take their toll on a dog's general health and age him more quickly than a dog that has led a normal, healthy life. Let your veterinarian help you determine an age bracket for your dog in his later years.

While good care should prolong your dog's life, there are several "old age" disorders to be on the lookout for no matter how well he may be doing. The tendency toward obesity is the most common, but constipation is another. Aging teeth and a slowing down of the digestive processes may hinder digestion and cause constipation, just as any major change in diet can bring on diarrhea. There is also the possibility of loss or impairment of hearing or eyesight which will also tend to make the dog wary and distrustful. Other behavioral changes may result as well, such as crankiness, loss of patience and lack of interest; these are the most obvious changes. Other

Ch. Carr's Hop-You-Lik-Me, owned by the William Carrs of Louisiana, pictured here winning a 5-point major under judge Frank Booth at the Calcasieu Kennel Club show. "Happy" went on to win Group Fourth and also has other Group placings to his credit.

Chang-Shi A-Go-Go pictured winning Winners Bitch and Best of Opposite Sex at the Reston, Virginia show a few years ago.

K-Lee's Aristotle, whelped November 26, 1970, is owned by Kay Thomas of Denver, Colorado. Sire was Ch. Pandee's Jubilee *ex* Ch. Hetherchow Liontamer Daizi.

Pictured at 5 months of age, the delightful Chang-Shi Gala Holiday. The sire was Chang-Shi Xabu *ex* Chang-Shi Phoebe. Owners are the Gerald Sterlings of Nashville, Tennessee.

Quad. International and American Ch. Chang-Shi Rolly Polly imported and owned by the Gerald Sterlings of Nashville, Tennessee. Bred by the late Comtesse R. de Changy of Brussels, Belgium, this beautiful bitch, born in 1943, was the winner of a Group First—at the time a super triumph for a bitch.

ailments may manifest themselves in the form of rheumatism, arthritis, tumors and warts, heart disease, kidney infections, male prostatism and female disorders. Of course, all of these require a veterinarian's checking the degree of seriousness and proper treatment.

Take care to avoid infectious diseases. When these hit the older dog, they can debilitate him to an alarming degree, leaving them open to more serious complications and a shorter life.

DOG INSURANCE

Much has been said for and against canine insurance, and much more will be said before this kind of protection for a dog becomes universal and/or practical. There has been talk of establishing a Blue Cross-type plan similar to that now existing for

Champion Charmar Air Express, bred and owned by Mr. and Mrs. Charles Evans of the Charmar Kennels in Grand Rapids, Michigan. The Charmar Kennels, established in 1939, are known for their show-winning Chow Chows; this E.H. Frank photograph features Air Express winning at a recent show under judge Benny D'Amico.

humans. However, the best insurance for your dog is *you*! Nothing compensates for tender, loving care. Like the insurance policies for humans, there will be a lot of fine print in the contracts revealing that the dog is not covered after all. These limited conditions usually make the acquisition of dog insurance expensive and virtually worthless.

Blanket coverage policies for kennels or establishments which board or groom dogs can be an advantage, especially in transporting dogs to and from their premises. For the one dog owner, however, whose dog is a constant companion, the cost for limited coverage is not necessary.

THE HIGH COST OF BURIAL

Pet cemeteries are mushrooming across the nation. Here, as with humans, the sky can be the limit for those who wish to bury their pets ceremoniously. The costs of satin-lined caskets, grave stones, flowers, etc. run the gamut of prices to match the

On the way to her championship, Balthazar Liontamer Avril wins Best of Winners under judge Erica Huggins at the Harrisburg Kennel Club show in 1971. Avril was shown by his co-owner, Mr. Bernard Kennedy. An Ashbey photo.

emotions and means of the owner. This is strictly a matter of what the bereaved owner wishes to do.

IN THE EVENT OF YOUR DEATH

This is a morbid thought perhaps, but ask yourself the question, "If death were to strike at his moment, what would become of my beloved dogs?"

Perhaps you are fortunate enough to have a relative, friend or spouse who could take over immediately, if only on a temporary basis. Perhaps you have already left instructions in your last will and testament for your pet's dispensation, as well as a stipend for their perpetual care.

Providing definite instructions before a disaster occurs and your dogs are carted off to the pound or stolen by commercially minded neighbors with "resale" in mind is a must. It is a simple thing to instruct your lawyer about your wishes in the event of sickness or death. Leave instructions on feeding, etc., posted on your kennel room or kitchen bulletin board, or wherever your kennel records are kept. Also, tell several people what you are doing and why. If you prefer to keep such instructions private, merely place them in sealed envelopes in a known place with directions that they are to be opened only in the event of your demise. Eliminate the danger of your animals suffering in the event of an emergency that prevents your personal care of them.

Sharbo Fancy, bred by the Robert Gilbs and owned by the Justamere Kennels. Fancy's sire was Ch. Starcrest By Jupiter O'Sharbo *ex* Sharbo Pocha.

Ch. Tsang-Po's Ai Tse of Starcrest finished his championship at 9½ months of age. He is pictured here winning under judge Frank Haze Birch. Bred by Dr. and Mrs. Edward North, Jr., Ai Tse is owned by Dick and Suzanne Marshall of Dallas, Texas. Twomey photo.

KEEPING RECORDS

Whether you have one dog or a kennel full of them, it is wise to keep written records. It takes only a few moments to record dates of inoculations, trips to the vet, tests for worms, etc. It can avoid confusion or mistakes, or having your dog not covered with immunization if too much time lapses between shots because you have to guess at the last shot.

In an emergency, these records may prove their value if your veterinarian cannot be reached and you have to use another, or if you move and have no case history on your dog for the new veterinarian. In emergencies, you do not always think clearly or accurately, and if dates, and types of serums used, etc., are a matter of record, the veterinarian can act more quickly and with more confidence.

20. THE BLIGHT OF PARASITES

Anyone who has ever spent countless hours peering down intently at his dog's warm, pink stomach waiting for a flea to appear will readily understand why we call this chapter "the blight of parasites." For it is that dreaded onslaught of the pesky flea that heralds the subsequent arrival of worms.

If you have seen even one flea scoot across that vulnerable expanse of skin you can be sure there are more fleas lurking on other favorite areas of your dog. They seldom travel alone. So it is now an established fact that *La puce*, as the French would say when referring to the flea, has set up housekeeping on your dog and it is going to demand a great deal of your time before you manage to evict them completely, and probably just temporarily, no matter which species your dog is harboring.

Fleas are not always choosy about their host, but chances are your dog has what is commonly known as *Ctenocephalides canis*, the dog flea. If you are a lover of cats also, your dog might even be playing host to a few *Ctenocephalides felis*, the cat flea, or vice versa! The only thing you can be really sure of is that your dog is supporting an entire community of them, all hungry and all sexually oriented, and you are going to have to be persistent in your campaign to get rid of them.

One of the chief reasons they are so difficult to catch is that what they lack in beauty and eyesight (they are blind at birth, throughout infancy and see very poorly or are blind during adulthood), they make up for in their fantastic ability to jump and scurry about.

While this remarkable ability to jump—some say 150 times the length of

their bodies—stands them in good stead with circus entrepeneurs and has given the flea claim to fame as chariot pullers and acrobats in side show attractions, the dog owner can be reduced to tears at the very thought of the onset of fleas.

Modern research has provided a remedy in the form of flea sprays, dips, collars and tags which can be successful in varying degrees. But there are those who swear by the good old-fashioned method of removing them by hand, which can be a challenge to your sanity as well as your dexterity.

Since the fleas' conformation (they are built like envelopes, long and flat) with their spiny skeletal system on the outside of their bodies is specifically provided for slithering through hair forests, they are given a distinct advantage to start with. Two antennae on the head select the best spot for digging and then two mandibles penetrate the skin and hit a blood vessel. It is also at this moment that the flea brings into play his spiny contours to prop himself against a few surrounding hairs which prevent him from being scratched off as he puts the bite on your dog. A small tubular tongue is then lowered into the hole to draw out blood and another tube is injected into the hole to pump the saliva of the flea into the wound which prevents the blood from clotting. This allows the flea to drink freely. Simultaneously your dog jumps into the air and gets one of those back legs into action scratching endlessly and in vain.

Now while you may catch an itinerant flea as he mistakenly shortcuts across your dog's stomach, the best hunting grounds are usually in the deep fur down along the

Quad-International Ch. Schilds Xanda, imported from Belgium by Lucile and Jerry Sterling. Xanda holds championships in Belgium, France, Holland and America. She was bred by Comtesse de Changy and won a Group and a Specialty in this country as well. Handler is Jerry Sterling; the judge is the late Florence Broadhurst.

dog's back from the neck to the base of the tail. However, the flea like every other creature on earth must have water, so several times during its residency it will make its way to the moister areas of your dog, such as the corners of the mouth, the eyes or the genital areas. This is when the flea

collars and tags are useful. The fumes from them prevent the fleas from passing the neck to get to the head of your dog.

Your dog can usually support several generations of fleas if he doesn't scratch himself to death or go out of his mind with the itching in the interim. The population of the flea is insured by the strong mating instinct and the wise personal decision of the female flea as to the best time to deposit her eggs. She has the useful capacity to store semen until the time is right to lay the eggs after some previous brief encounter with a passing member of the opposite sex.

When that times comes for her to lay the eggs, she does so without so much as a backward glance and moves on. The dog, during a normal day's wandering, shakes the eggs off along his way, and there the eggs remain until hatched and the baby fleas are ready to jump back on the dog. If any of the eggs remain on the dog, chances are your dog will help them emerge from their shells with his scratching when some adult flea passes in the vicinity.

Larval fleas look like very small and slender maggots; they begin their lives feasting off their own egg shells until your dog comes along and offers the return to the world of adult fleas, whose excrement provides the predigested blood pellets they must have to thrive. They cannot survive on fresh blood, nor are they capable at this tender age of digging for it themselves. We are certain that the expression "two can eat as cheaply as one" originated after some curious scientist made a detailed study of the life cycle of the flea.

After a couple of weeks of this free loading, the baby flea makes his own cocoon and becomes a pupa. This stage lasts long enough for the larval flea to grow legs, mandibles, and sharp spines and to flatten out and in general get to be identifiable as the commonly known and obnoxious *Ctenocephalides canis*. The process can take several weeks or several months, depending on weather conditions, heat, moisture, etc., but generally three weeks is all that is required to enable it to start chomping on your dog in its own right.

And so the life of the flea is renewed and begun again, and if you don't have plans to stem the tide, you will certainly see a population explosion that will make the human one resemble an endangered species. Getting rid of fleas can be accom-plished by the aforementioned spraying of the dog, or the flea collars and tags, but air, sunshine and a good shaking out of beds, bedding, carpets, cushions, etc., certainly must be undertaken to get rid of the eggs or larvae lying around the premises.

However, if you love the thrill of the chase, and have the stomach for it, you can still try to catch them on safari across your dog's stomach. Your dog will love the attention, that is, if you don't keep pinching a bit of skin instead of that little blackish critter. Chances are great you will come up with skin rather than the flea and your dog will lose interest and patience.

Should you be lucky enough to get hold of one, you must either squeeze it to death (which isn't likely) or break it in two with a sharp, strong fingernail (which also isn't likely) or you must release it *under-water* in the toilet bowl and flush immediately. This prospect is only slightly more likely. We strongly suggest that you shape up, clean up, shake out and spray—on a regular basis.

There are those people, however, who are much more philosophical about the flea, since, like the cockroach, it has been around since the beginning of the world.

A 1960 photograph of the magnificent Ch. Ghat de la Moulaine. This photograph shows the imported French dog winning yet another Best In Show award, this time under judge Derek Rayne. The "Great Ghat" is owned by the Clif Shryocks, with Mr. Shryock handling here.

For instance, that old-time philosopher, David Harum, who has been much quoted with his remark, "A reasonable amount of fleas is good for a dog. They keep him from broodin' on bein' a dog." We would rather agree with John Donne who in his *Devotions* reveals that, "The flea, though he kill none, he does all the harm he can." This is especially true if your dog is a show dog! If the scratching doesn't ruin the coat, the inevitable infestations of the parasites the fleas will leave with your dog will!

So we readily see that dogs can be afflicted by both internal and external parasites. The external parasites are known as the aforementioned fleas, plus ticks and lice; while all of these are bothersome, they can be treated. However, the internal parasites, or worms of various kinds, are usually well-infested before discovery and require more substantial means of ridding the dog of them completely.

INTERNAL PARASITES

The most common worms are the round worms. These, like many other worms, are carried and spread by the flea and go through a cycle within the dog host. They are excreted in egg or larval form and passed on to other dogs in this manner.

Worm medicine should be prescribed by a veterinarian, and dogs should be checked for worms at least twice a year, or every three months if there is a known epidemic in your area, and during the summer months when fleas are plentiful.

Major types of worms are hookworms, whipworms, tapeworms (the only non-round worm in this list), ascarids (the "typical" round worms), heartworms, kidney and lung worms. Each can be peculiar to a part of the country or may be carried by a dog from one area to another. Kidney and lung worms are quite rare, fortunately.

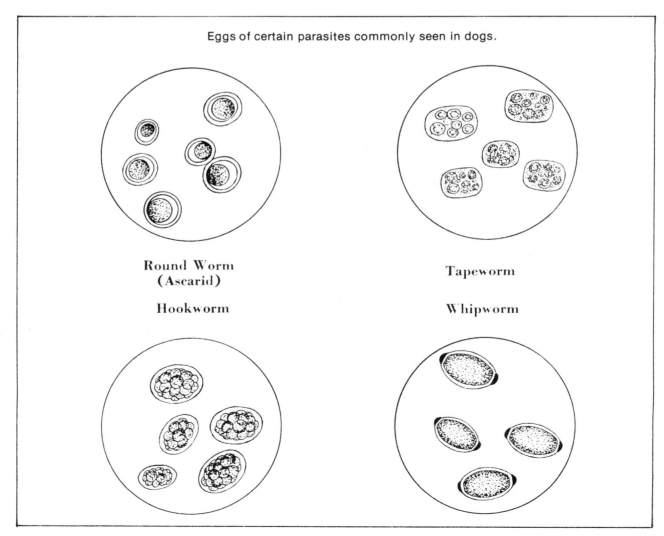

Eggs of certain parasites commonly seen in dogs.

Round Worm
(Ascarid)

Tapeworm

Hookworm

Whipworm

The others are not. Symptoms for worms might be vomiting intermittently, eating grass, lack of pep, bloated stomach, rubbing their tail along the ground, loss of weight, dull coat, anemia and pale gums, eye discharge, or unexplained nervousness and irritability. A dog with worms will usually eat twice as much as he normally would, also.

Never worm a sick dog, or a pregnant bitch after the first two weeks she has been bred, and never worm a constipated dog . . . it will retain the strong medicine within the body for too long a time. The best, safest way to determine the presence of worms is to test for them before they do excessive damage.

HOW TO TEST FOR WORMS

Worms can kill your dog if the infestation is severe enough. Even light infestations of worms can debilitate a dog to the point where he is more susceptible to other serious diseases that can kill, if the worms do not.

Today's medication for worming is relatively safe and mild, and worming is no longer the traumatic experience for either dog or owner that it used to be. Great care must be given, however, to the proper administration of the drugs. Correct dosage is a "must" and clean quarters are essential to find an animal that is completely free of parasites, so we must consider worming as a necessary evil.

However mild today's medicines may be, it is inadvisable to worm a dog unnecessarily. There are simple tests to determine the presence of worms and this chapter is designed to help you learn how to make these tests yourself. Veterinarians charge a nominal fee for this service, if it is not part of their regular office visit examination. It is a simple matter to prepare fecal slides that you can read yourself on a periodic basis. Over the years it will save you much time and money, especially if you have more than one dog or a large kennel.

All that is needed by way of equipment is a microscope with 100x power. These can be purchased in the toy department in a department or regular toy store for a few dollars, depending on what else you want to get with it, but the basic, least expensive sets come with the necessary glass slides and attachments.

After the dog has defecated, take an applicator stick, or a toothpick with a flat end, or even an old-fashioned wooden matchstick, and gouge off a piece of the stool about the size of a small pea. Have one of the glass slides ready with a large drop of water on it. Mix the two together until you have a cloudy film over a large area of the slide. This smear should be covered with another slide, or a cover slip—though it is possible to obtain readings with just the one open slide. Place your slide under the microscope and prepare to focus in on it. To read the slide you will find that your eye should follow a certain pattern. Start at the top and read from left to right, then right back to the left side and then left over to the right side once again until you have looked at every portion of the slide from the top left to the bottom right side, as illustrated here:

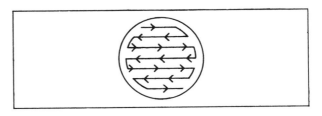

A darling Chow Chow puppy sired by You-Two's Commander Black ex Ch. Tsang-Po's Yum Yum. Owned by Mr. and Mrs. H.A. Allen.

517

An historic family scene in American Chowdom photographed at the Pasadena Kennel Club show, June 1965, is represented here by the first show ever attended by Eastward Liontamer of Elster, on the left, with then owner-handler Merilyn Bowden Morgan, and Don-Lee's Petunio of Elster shown by owner Rick Donnelly. Liontamer and Petunia, litter brother and sister, were sired by Ch. Starcrest Spy of Poppyland, center, presented by his owner Howard Kendall.

Make sure that your smear is not too thick or watery or the reading will be too dark and confused to make proper identification. Included in this chapter are drawings which will show you what to look for when reading the slides to identify the four most common varieties of worms. If you decide you would rather not make your own fecal examinations, but would prefer to have the veterinarian do it, the proper way to present a segment of the stool for him to examine is as follows:

After the dog has defecated, a portion of the stool, say a square inch from different sections of it, should be placed in a glass jar or plastic container, and labeled with the dog's name and address of the owner. If the sample cannot be examined within three to four hours after passage, it should be refrigerated. Your opinion as to what variety of worms you suspect is sometimes helpful to the veterinarian and may be noted on the label of the jar you submit to him for the examination.

Checking for worms on a regular basis is advisable not only for the welfare of the dog but for the protection of your family, since most worms are transmissible, under certain circumstances, to humans.

21. YOUR DOG, YOUR VETERINARIAN AND YOU

The purpose of this chapter is to explain why you should never attempt to be your own veterinarian. Quite the contrary, we urge emphatically that you establish good liaison with a reputable veterinarian who will help you maintain happy, healthy dogs. Our purpose is to bring you up to date on the discoveries made in modern canine medicine and to help you work with your veterinarian by applying these new developments to your own animals.

We have provided here "thumbnail" histories of many of the most common types of diseases your dog is apt to come in contact with during his lifetime. We feel that if you know a little something about the diseases and how to recognize their symptoms, your chances of catching them in the preliminary stages will help you and your veterinarian effect a cure before a serious condition develops.

Today's dog owner is a realistic, intelligent person who learns more and more about his dog—inside and out—so that he can care for and enjoy the animal to the fullest. He uses technical terms for parts of the anatomy, has a fleeting knowledge of the miracles of surgery and is fully prepared to administer clinical care for his animals at home. This chapter is designed for study and/or reference and we hope you will use it to full advantage.

We repeat, we *do not* advocate your playing "doctor." This includes administering medication without veterinary supervision, or even doing your own inoculations. General knowledge of diseases, their symptoms and side effects will assist you in diagnosing diseases for your veterinarian. He does not expect you to be an expert, but will appreciate your efforts in getting a sick dog to him before it is too late and he cannot save its life.

ASPIRIN: A DANGER

There is a common joke about doctors telling their patients, when they telephone with a complaint, to take an aspirin, go to bed and let him know how things are in the morning! Unfortunately, that is exactly the way it turns out with a lot of dog owners who think aspirins are cure-alls and give them to their dogs indiscriminately. Then they call the veterinarian when the dog has an unfavorable reaction.

Aspirins are not panaceas for everything—certainly not for every dog. In an experiment, fatalities in cats treated with aspirin in one laboratory alone numbered ten out of thirteen within a two-week period. Dogs' tolerance was somewhat better, as far as actual fatalities, but there was considerable evidence of ulceration in varying degrees on the stomach linings when necropsy was performed.

Aspirin has been held in the past to be almost as effective for dogs as for people when given for many of the everyday aches and pains. The fact remains, however, that medication of any kind should be administered only after veterinary consultation and a specific dosage suitable to the condition is recommended.

While aspirin is chiefly effective in reducing fever, relieving minor pains and cutting down on inflammation, the acid has been proven harmful to the stomach when given in strong doses. Only your veterinarian is qualified to determine what the dosage is, or whether it should be administered to your particular dog at all.

Judge James Trullinger awards the coveted Best In Show rosette to Ch. Ah Sid's the Dilettante at the Wilmington Kennel Club show in April, 1962. Handled by Jane Kamp Forsyth, Dilettante was shown 207 times and won 26 Bests In Show, 91 Group Firsts and 193 Best of Breed, as well as numerous other Group placements. He was top Chow Chow in America for 1958, 1960, 1961, 1962, 1963, and 1964. Sire of nine champions, the Dilettante is one of the top Chow Chows of all time; he is owned by the Ah Sid Kennels of John Davis and the late Sidney Joan Wellborn, Clinton, Maryland.

Ch. Lyle's Age of Aquarius, photographed at 16 months of age. Blu is owned by Cliff and Vivian Shryock of Hawaiian Gardens, California.

WHAT THE THERMOMETER CAN TELL YOU

You will notice in reading this chapter dealing with the diseases of dogs that practically everything a dog might contract in the way of sickness has basically the same set of symptoms. Loss of appetite, diarrhea, dull eyes, dull coat, warm and/or runny nose, and FEVER!

Therefore, it is most advisable to have a thermometer on hand for checking temperature. There are several inexpensive metal rectal-type thermometers that are accurate and safer than the glass variety which can be broken. This may happen either by dropping, or perhaps even breaking off in the dog because of improper insertion or an aggravated condition with the dog that makes him violently resist the injection of the thermometer. Either kind should be lubricated with Vaseline to make the insertion as easy as possible, after it has been sterilized with alcohol.

The normal temperature for a dog is 101.5° Fahrenheit, as compared to the human 98.6°. Excitement as well as illness can cause this to vary a degree or two, but any sudden or extensive rise in body temperature must be considered as cause for alarm. Your first indication will be that your dog feels unduly "warm" and this is the time to take the temperature, not when the dog becomes very ill or manifests additional serious symptoms. With a thermometer on hand, you can check temperatures quickly and perhaps prevent illness from becoming serious.

COPROPHAGY

Perhaps the most unpleasant of all dog phases of dog breeding is to come up

Ch. Sterncrest Jade of Starcrest photographed as a puppy. Owned by the Joel Marstons of Sun Valley, Cal.

Shanglo's Choo Choo, whelped in 1965 and bred by the Shanglo Kennels of Mildred Fairchild in Tigard, Oregon, sired by Ch. Shanglo's Kodee out of Shanglo's Black Magic.

Ch. Carchow Gudi Tu Shuz, bred by the Howard Kendalls and owned by the William Carrs of Alexandria, Louisiana. She is pictured winning under judge Forest Hall, completing her championship with a 5-point major win. She produced two champion daughters out of her first litter.

with a dog that takes to eating stool. This practice, which is referred to politely as coprophagy, is one of the unsolved mysteries in the dog world. There simply is no explanation to why some dogs do it.

However, there are several logical theories, all or any of which may be the cause. Some say nutritional deficiencies; another says that dogs inclined to gulp their food (which passes through them not entirely digested) find it still partially palatable. There is another theory that the preservatives used in some meat are responsible for an appealing odor that remains through the digestive process. Then again poor quality meat can be so tough and unchewable that dogs swallow it whole and it passes through them in large undigested chunks.

There are others who believe the habit is strictly psychological, the result of a nervous condition or insecurity. Others believe the dog cleans up after itself because it is afraid of being punished as it was when it made a mistake on the carpet as a puppy. Others claim boredom is the reason, or even spite. Others will tell you a dog does not want its personal odor on the premises for fear of attracting other hostile animals to itself or its home.

The most logical of all explanations and the one most veterinarians are inclined to accept is that it is a deficiency of dietary enzymes. Too much dry food can be bad and many veterinarians suggest trying meat tenderizers, monosodium glutamate, or garlic powder which gives the stool a bad odor and discourages the dog. Yeast or certain vitamins or a complete change of diet are even more often suggested. By the time you try each of the above you will probably discover that the dog has outgrown the habit anyway. However, the condition cannot be ignored if you are to enjoy your dog to the fullest.

There is no set length of time that the problem persists, and the only real cure is to walk the dog on leash, morning and night and after every meal. In other words, set up a definite eating and exercising schedule before coprophagy is an established pattern.

Starcrest Sterling Silver, bred by June Marston and sired by Ch. Starcrest Mr. Christofer *ex* Starcrest Lemon Twist, shown here handled by Richard Inman. He is co-owned by Mr. Inmon and A.J. Overturf of Dallas, Texas.

Ch. Charlie O'Success, a consistent Group winner and rated in the Top Ten Chow Chows in the nation. Whelped in 1965, he is pictured winning second in the Non-Sporting Group under judge Maxwell Riddle at the 1966 Houston, Texas Kennel Club show, handled by Richard Vaughn. Owners are Mr. and Mrs. Dan Frederick of Baton Rouge, Louisiana.

Ch. Kway Star Moulaine Rou-Dee, whelped in 1964, was bred by Brockway Crouch. Owner is Mrs. Sarah Parrish of Cantonment, Florida.

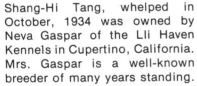

Shang-Hi Tang, whelped in October, 1934 was owned by Neva Gaspar of the Lli Haven Kennels in Cupertino, California. Mrs. Gaspar is a well-known breeder of many years standing.

Sire of the world-famous Ch. Ghat de la Moulaine, Duang-Lai de la Moulaine, owned by Clif and Vivian Shryock of Hawaiian Gardens, California. Ghat holds the record for being the sire of the most champions.

Hanoi Glorianna, British-bred bitch whelped in December of 1971 and bred by Dulcie Smith. Sire was U'Kwong Zenith *ex* Hanoi Honey. Owned by the Gerald Sterlings of Nashville, Tennessee.

Marion Grissom of Kannapolis, North Carolina with Mai Woh Gee, whelped in 1969. The breeder was J.R. Facciolli.

A typical Starcrest puppy, the future Ch. Starcrest Autumn Haze Tiawin. Sired by Ch. Starcrest Mr. Christofer *ex* Pandee's Blu Witching, Haze is owned by A.J. Overturf of Tiawin Kennels, Dallas, Texas.

MASTURBATION

A source of embarrassment to many dog owners, masturbation can be eliminated with a minimum of training.

The dog which is constantly breeding anything and everything, including the leg of the piano or perhaps the leg of your favorite guest, can be broken of the habit by stopping its cause.

The over-sexed dog—if truly that is what he is—which will never be used for breeding can be castrated. The kennel stud dog can be broken of the habit by removing any furniture from his quarters or keeping him on leash and on verbal command when he is around people, or in the house where he might be tempted to breed pillows, people, etc.

Hormone imbalance may be another cause and your veterinarian may advise injections. Exercise can be of tremendous help. Keeping the dog's mind occupied by physical play when he is around people will also help relieve the situation.

Females might indulge in sexual abnormalities like masturbation during their heat cycle, or again, because of a hormone imbalance. But if they behave this way because of a more serious problem, a hysterectomy may be indicated.

A sharp "no!" command when you can anticipate the act, or a sharp "no!" when

caught in the act will deter most dogs if you are consistent in your correction. Hitting or other physical abuse will only confuse a dog.

Dr. Samuel Draper judges Canorwall Bamboo Best of Breed at the 1973 Putnam Kennel Club show. Bamboo is owned by Mr. and Mrs. Harry Brock of Chester, New York.

Ch. Ro-Don Samson with his owner Ron Ewing.

Ch. Tsang-Po's Red Commander Jade, bred by Hal Allen and owned by Nelson and Diane Tardy of Union City, California. The sire was You-Two's Black Commander *ex* Ch. Tsang-Po's Yum Yum. Photo by Clif.

The top-winning cinnamon Chow Chow on the West Coast for 1973 was Ch. Jade's Dr. Strange-Love of Mil-Her. Bred by Russell Herman and sired by Ch. Tsang-Po's Red Commander of Jade ex Ch. Mil-Her Sunbonnet of Jade, his owners are Diane and Nelson Tardy of Union City, California. Langdon photo.

RABIES

The greatest fear in the dog fancy today is still the great fear it has always been—rabies!

What has always held true about this dreadful disease still holds true today. The only way rabies can be contracted is through the saliva of a rabid dog entering the bloodstream of another animal or person. There is, of course, the Pasteur treatment for rabies which is very effective. There was of late the incident of a little boy

Ch. Tsang Po's Chu Fu Chu finishing his championship at the Jackson, Mississippi Kennel Club show under judge W.W. Fetner. Whelped in 1971, he is owned by Mrs. Mariam Frederick of Baton Rouge, Louisiana. The sire was Ch. Tsang Po's Linn's Fu-Yi *ex* Ch. Tsang Po's Ming Lee. Photo by Twomey.

bitten by a rabid bat having survived the disease. However, the Pasteur treatment is administered immediately if there is any question of exposure. Even more than dogs being found to be rabid, we now know that the biggest carriers are bats, skunks, foxes, raccoons and other fur-bearing animals, which pass it from one to another, since they do not have the benefit of inoculation. Dogs that run free should be inoculated for protection against these animals. For city or house dogs that never leave their owner's side, it may not be as necessary.

For many years, Great Britain, because it is an island and because of the country's strictly enforced six-month quarantine, was entirely free of rabies. But in 1969, a British officer brought back his dog from foreign duty and the dog was found to have the disease soon after being released from quarantine. There was a

great uproar about it, with Britain killing off wild and domestic animals in a great scare campaign, but the quarantine is once again down to six months and things seem to have returned to a normal, sensible attitude.

Health departments in rural towns usually provide rabies inoculations free of charge. If your dog is outdoors a great deal, or exposed to other animals that are, you might wish to call the town hall and get information on the program in your area. One cannot be too cautious about this dread.disease. While the number of cases diminishes each year, there are still thousands being reported and there is still the constant threat of an outbreak where animals roam free. And never forget, there is no cure.

Rabies is caused by a neurotropic virus which can be found in the saliva, brain and sometimes the blood of the warm-blooded animal afflicted. The incubation period is usually two weeks or as long as six months, which means you can be exposed to it without any visible symptoms. As we have said, while there is still no known cure, it can be controlled. It is up to every individual to help effect this control by reporting animal bites, educating the public to the dangers and symptoms and prevention of it, so that we may reduce the fatalities.

There are two kinds of rabies; one form is called "furious," and the other is referred to as "dumb." The mad dog goes through several stages of the disease. His disposition and behavior change radically and suddenly; he becomes irritable and vicious; the eating habits alter, and he rejects food for things like stones and sticks; he becomes exhausted and drools saliva out of his mouth almost constantly. He may hide in corners, look glassy-eyed and suspicious, bite at the air as he races around snarling and attacking with his tongue hanging out. At this point paralysis sets in, starting at the throat so that he can no longer drink water though he desires it desperately; hence, the term hydrophobia is given. He begins to stagger and eventually convulse and death is imminent.

In "dumb" rabies paralysis is swift; the dog seeks dark, sheltered places and is abnormally quiet. Paralysis starts with the jaws, spreads down the body and death is quick. Contact by humans or other animals with the drool from either of these types of rabies on open skin can produce the fatal disease, so extreme haste and proper diagnosis is essential. In other words, you do not have to be bitten by a rabid dog to have the virus enter your system. An open wound or cut that comes in touch with the saliva is all that is needed.

The incubation and degree of infection can vary. You usually contract the disease faster if the wound is near the head, since the virus travels to the brain through the spinal cord. The deeper the wound, the more saliva is injected into the body, the more serious the infection. So, if bitten by a dog under any circumstances—or any warm-blooded animal for that matter—

immediately wash out the wound with soap and water, bleed it profusely, and see your doctor as soon as possible.

Also, be sure to keep track of the animal that bit, if at all possible. When rabies is suspected the public health officer will need to send the animal's head away to be analyzed. If it is found to be rabies free, you will not need to undergo treatment. Otherwise, your doctor may advise that you have the Pasteur treatment, which is extremely painful. It is rather simple, however, to have the veterinarian examine a dog for rabies without having the dog sent away for positive diagnosis of the disease. A ten-day quarantine is usually all that is necessary for everyone's peace of mind.

Rabies is no respecter of age, sex or geographical location. It is found all over the world from North Pole to South Pole, and has nothing to do with the old wives' tale of dogs going mad in the hot summer

The gang at the Cissy Boo Kennels. From left to right: Nancy and Melissa Hodges holding Tsang-Po's Tai Wan, Merle Hodges holding Pandee's Cissy Boo. On the floor from left to right: Cissy Boo's Atlas, Cissy Boo's John-John, and Boo Hodges holding Blocky, a pet, and the black Cissy Boo's Grundoon.

Ch. Kan Kings Charlie Wong, dark red Chow Chow born in August, 1967, who is the foundation stud at Earl and Mae Palm's kennel in Helenville, Wisconsin. Sired by Ky-Lin's Cupid ex Kan Kings Bunny.

Justameres Delft Cordon Bleu, owned by the Justamere Kennels of Don Foster and Jim Pierson of Monrovia, California. The sire is Ch. Starcrest Dandy Lion *ex* Starcrest Blue China. Cordon Bleu was whelped in September of 1972.

Don-Lee's Corky wins Best of Breed under judge Ellsworth Gamble at the 1968 Orange Empire Dog Club show. Bred by Rick and Reba Donnelly of the Don-Lee Kennels, he is owned by Wayne and Marion Byrne of San Bernardino, California.

Ch. Tsang-Po's Chu-Fu-Chu, bred by Dr. and Mrs. Edward North, Jr. and owned by Dan and Miriam Fredericks of Baton Rouge, Louisiana. Charles Nelson is the judge.

Champion Beeson's Thunderstorm, bred by Frank and Lydia Beeson. The sire was Yen Chee's Tiger of Poppyland *ex* Madam Darlyn. This magnificent black dog is a Group winner from the classes. Roberts portrait.

Ch. Fahsondu Black Xpo, whelped in 1967 and imported from England by breeder Mrs. F.A. Hudson. Xpo's sire was English Champion Tiko-Ling of Hanoi *ex* Fahsondu Jade Lady. Owner: Eleanor Ellwanger of Brockport, New York. Xpo is a Best in Show, all breeds, winner.

months. True, there is an increase in reported cases during summer, but only because that is the time of the year for animals to roam free in good weather and during the mating season when the battle of the sexes is taking place. Inoculation and a keen eye for symptoms and bites on our dogs and other pets will help control the disease until the cure is found.

VACCINATIONS

If you are to raise a puppy, or a litter of puppies, successfully, you must adhere to a realistic and strict schedule of vaccination. Many puppyhood diseases can be fatal—all of them are debilitating. According to the latest statistics, 98 per cent of all puppies are being inoculated after 12 weeks of age against the dread distemper, hepatitis and leptospirosis and manage to escape these horrible infections. Orphaned puppies should be vaccinated every two weeks until the age of 12 weeks. Distemper and hepatitis live-virus vaccine should be used, since they are not protected with the colostrum normally supplied to them through the mother's milk. Puppies weaned at six to seven weeks should also be inoculated repeatedly because they will no longer be receiving mother's milk. While

not all will receive protection from the serum at this early age, it should be given and they should be vaccinated once again at both nine and 12 weeks of age.

Leptospirosis vaccination should be given at four months of age with thought given to booster shots if the disease is known in the area, or in the case of show dogs which are exposed on a regular basis to many dogs from far and wide. While annual boosters are in order for distemper and hepatitis, every two or three years is sufficient for leptospirosis, unless there is an outbreak in your immediate area. The one exception should be the pregnant bitch since there is reason to believe that inoculation might cause damage to the fetus.

Strict observance of such a vaccination schedule will not only keep your dog free of these debilitating diseases, but will prevent an epidemic in your kennel, or in your locality, or to the dogs which are competing at the shows.

Ch. Pandee's Double Jubilee, owner-handled by Brenda Jones of the Tao-Ming Kennels in Memphis, Tennessee, is pictured here winning the Non-Sporting Group at the 1972 Ozarks Kennel Club. Always owner-handled, Jubilee finished his championship in February, 1972 and has won Chow Chow Specialty as well as Groups.

Tamerins Pekeo of Jade, bred by Prudence Baxter and owned by Diane Tardy and Pru Baxter, is pictured winning at a recent show. The sire was Jade's Cicso Kid *ex* Ch. Pandee's Katrina, C.D.

American and Canadian Ch. Hanoi Tiko Topper, whelped in 1970 and bred by Dulcie Smith of Birmingham, England. Topper completed his canadian title in 3 shows something no other American Chow Chow has done before. He won two Group Firsts and 6 other Group Placements. In 11 shows he placed in 8 Groups. Sire was Ch. Hanoi Damon of Kalamunda *ex* Heyville's Francesca. Imported by Lucile and Jerry Sterling of Nashville, Tennessee.

Tag-El's Keiko-China Boi, whelped October 6, 1970, is pictured here winning at the 1972 Lawton-Ft. Sill Kennel Club show under judge Ramona Van Court. This Best of Breed win was with owner and handler Evelyn E. Carter of the Tag-El's Kennels in McLoud, Oklahoma. Sire was Keiki King Carter ex Utzmoor's China Doll.

Ch. Pitchi Wu Linnchow is pictured in the front yard of Linnchow Kennels, Mr. and Mrs. H.P. Schmidt, owners, Tinley Park, Illinois. She was an outstanding bitch of her day and the mother of six champions.

Ch. Mil-Her Sun Bonnet of Jade, bred by Nelson and Diane Tardy and owned by Russell Herman, a Chow Chow judge.

Tsang-Po Chung-Kiang Chan, pictured in January, 1972, at 9 months of age. Owned by Betty Poteet and bred by the Tsang-Po Kennels, Texas.

SNAKEBITE

As field trials and hunts and the like become more and more popular with dog enthusiasts, the incident of snakebite becomes more of a likelihood. Dogs that are kept outdoors in runs or dogs that work the fields and roam on large estates are also likely victims.

Most veterinarians carry snakebite serum, and snakebite kits are sold to dog owners for just such purpose. To catch a snakebite in time might mean the difference between life and death, and whether your area is populated with snakes or not, it behooves you to know what to do in case it happens to you or your dog.

Your primary concern should be to get to a doctor or veterinarian immediately. The victim should be kept as quiet as possible (excitement or activity spreads the venom through the body more quickly) and if possible the wound should be bled enough to clean it out before applying a tourniquet, if the bite is severe.

First of all, it must be determined if the bite is from a poisonous or non-poisonous snake. If the bite carries two horse-shoe-shaped pinpoints of a double row of teeth, the bite can be assumed to be non-poisonous. If the bite leaves two punctures or holes—the result of the two fangs carrying venom—the bite is very definitely poisonous and time is of the essence.

Recently, physicians have come up with an added help in the case of snakebite. A first aid treatment referred to as hypothermia, which is the application of ice to the wound to lower body temperature to a point where the venom spreads less quickly, minimizes swelling, helps prevent infection and has some influence on numbing the pain. If ice is not readily available, the bite may be soaked in ice-cold water. But even more urgent is the need to get the victim to a hospital or a veterinarian for additional treatment.

Ch. Cherokee's Nik-Nak, photographed winning at a show in December, 1965. This Best of Breed win was garnered under judge Derek Rayne. Nik-Nak went on to third in the Non-Sporting Group the same day. Owned by Mr. and Mrs. Oral E. Crisp of Washington.

Starcrest Apollo, a very young dog bred and owned by Mr. and Mrs. Joel Marston who own the Starcrest Kennels in Sun Valley, California.

T'Waga Royal Lion, owned and bred by E.H. Stanton. The Royal Lion was photographed here at two years of age.

Ch. Loy-Jean's Chi-Yan Kid, sire of 22 champions. Son of the famous Ch. Ghat de la Moulaine *ex* Ch. Loy-Jean's Princess of Hai-Nan. Owned by Donald L. Drennan, Dre-Don Kennels, Getzville, New York.

EMERGENCIES

No matter how well you run your kennel or keep an eye on an individual dog, there will almost invariably be some emergency at some time that will require quick treatment until you get the animal to the veterinarian. The first and most important thing to remember is to keep calm! You will think more clearly and your animal will need to know he can depend on you to take care of him. However, he will be frightened and you must beware of fear biting. Therefore, do not shower him with kisses and endearments at this time, no matter how sympathetic you feel. Comfort him reassuringly, but keep your wits about you. Before getting him to the veterinarian try to alleviate the pain and shock.

If you can take even a minor step in this direction it will be a help toward the final cure. Listed here are a few of the emergencies which might occur and what you can do AFTER you have called the vet and told him you are coming.

Ch. Fu San Queen Victoria, bred and owned by Ernest L. Shook of Burlington, Wisconsin. The sire was Manchu Prince Charming *ex* Ch. Sandunes Pa Glo.

536

Three Chow Chow champions during a show training session. Left to right: Mrs. John E. Baggus with Moss' Katmandu, Ellen Moss with Ch. Warlord's Counter Spy and Clarence Moss with Ch. Chu Fu Mein.

BURNS

If you have been foolish enough to turn your pot handles toward the back of the stove—for your children's sake as well as your dog's—and the dog is burned, apply ice or cold water and treat for shock. Electrical or chemical burns are treated the same; but with an acid or alkali burn use, respectively, a bicarbonate of soda or vinegar solution. Check the advisability of covering the burn when you call the veterinarian.

DROWNING

Most animals love the water, but sometimes get in "over their heads." Should your dog take in too much water, hold him upside down and open his mouth so that water can empty from the lungs, then apply artificial respiration or mouth-to-mouth resuscitation. Then treat for shock by covering him with a blanket, administering a stimulant such as coffee with sugar, and soothing him with voice and hand.

Ch. Scotchow Me and My Shadow, sired by Ch. Scotchow Home By Dark *ex* Scotchow Red Ching Ching. Bred and owned by Joan M. Hannephin of Wheeling, West Virginia.

bite set in, thaw out the affected area slowly with a circulatory motion and stimulation. Use Vaseline to help keep the skin from peeling off and/or drying out.

HEART ATTACK

Be sure the animal keeps breathing by applying artificial respiration. A mild stimulant may be used and give him plenty of air. Treat for shock as well, and get to the veterinarian quickly.

SUFFOCATION

Artificial respiration and treat for shock with plenty of air.

SUN STROKE

Cooling the dog off immediately is essential. Ice packs, submersion in ice water, and plenty of cool air are needed.

WOUNDS

Open wounds or cuts which produce bleeding must be treated with hydrogen peroxide and tourniquets should be used if bleeding is excessive. Also, shock treatment must be given, and the animal must be kept warm.

FITS AND CONVULSIONS

Prevent the dog from thrashing about and injuring himself, cover with a blanket and hold down until you can get him to the veterinarian.

FROSTBITE

There is no excuse for an animal getting frostbite if you are on your toes and care for the animal. However, should frost-

Sharbo Black Sabbeth, owned and bred by Robert and Sharon Gilb of Round Lake, Illinois. The sire was Ch. Ky-Lin's Black Panther *ex* Sharbo Pocha.

538

THE FIRST AID KIT

It would be sheer folly to try to operate a kennel or to keep a dog without providing for certain emergencies that are bound to crop up when there are active dogs around. Just as you would provide a first aid kit for people you should also provide a first aid kit for the animals on the premises.

The first aid kit should contain the following items:

> BFI or other medicated powder
> jar of Vaseline
> Q-tips
> bandage—1 inch gauze
> adhesive tape
> band-aids
> cotton
> boric acid powder

A trip to your veterinarian is always safest, but there are certain preliminaries for cuts and bruises of a minor nature that you can care for yourself.

Cuts, for instance, should be washed out and medicated powder or Vaseline applied with a bandage. The lighter the bandage the better so that the most air possible can reach the wound. Q-tips can be used for removing debris from the eyes after which a mild solution of boric acid wash can be applied. Burns can be assuaged by an application of Vaseline. As for sores, use dry powder on wet sores, and Vaseline on dry sores. Use cotton for washing out wounds and drying them.

A particular caution must be given here on bandaging. Make sure that the bandage is not too tight to hamper the dog's circulation. Also, make sure the bandage is made correctly so that the dog does not bite at it trying to get it off. A great deal of damage can be done to a wound by a dog tearing at a bandage to get it off. If you notice the dog is starting to bite at it, do it over or put something on the bandage that smells and tastes bad to him. Make sure, however, that the solution does not soak through the bandage and enter the wound. Sometimes, if it is a leg wound, a sock or stocking slipped on the dog's leg will cover the bandage edges and will also keep it clean.

HOW NOT TO POISON YOUR DOG

Ever since the appearance of Rachel Carson's book, *The Silent Spring*, people have been asking, "Just how dangerous are chemicals?" In the animal world where disinfectants, room deodorants, parasitic sprays, solutions and aerosols are so widely used, the question has taken on even more meaning. Veterinarians are beginning to ask, "What kind of disinfectant do you use?" or "Have you any fruit trees that have been sprayed recently?" When animals are brought in to their offices in a toxic condition, or for unexplained death, or when entire litters of puppies die mysteriously, there is good reason to ask such questions.

The popular practice of protecting animals against parasites has given way to their being exposed to an alarming number of commercial products, some of which are dangerous to their very lives. Even flea collars can be dangerous, especially if they get wet or somehow touch the genital regions or eyes. While some products are a great deal more poisonous than others, great care must be taken that they be applied in proportion to the size of the dog and the area to be covered. Many a dog has been taken to the vet with an unusual skin problem that was a direct result of having been bathed with a detergent rather than a proper shampoo. Certain products that are safe for dogs can be fatal for cats. Extreme care must be taken to read all ingredients and instructions carefully before use on any animal.

The same caution must be given to outdoor chemicals. Dog owners must question the use of fertilizers on their lawns. Lime, for instance, can be harmful to a dog's feet. The unleashed dog that covers the neighborhood on his daily rounds is open to all sorts of tree and lawn sprays and insecticides that may prove harmful to him, if not as a poison, as a producer of an allergy. Many puppy fatalities are reported when they consume mothballs.

There are various products found around the house which can be lethal, such

Ch. Balthazar Liontamer Avril, owned by the Bernard Kennedys, is pictured winning points at the Trenton Kennel Club in 1971 under judge Margaret Shoemaker, well-known Chow breeder. Avril was sired by Ch. Pandee's Jubilee *ex* Ch. Hetherchow Liontamer Doll-ee.

Ch. Tsang-Po's Ai Tso, owned by Mr. and Mrs. Wayne Martin of White Heath, Illinois, and bred by the H.A. Allens of the Tsang-Po Kennels in Texas.

Ch. Starcrest Dart of Poppyland, a litter brother to one of the most famous of all Chow Chows, Ch. Starcrest Spy of Poppyland. Owned by the Starcrest Kennels of Mr. and Mrs. Joel Marston, Sun Valley, California.

A Storm Cloud daughter photographed at 7 months of age. The sire was Ch. Storm Cloud of Shang-Hi *ex* Lli Haven Black Cloud. Owner, Neva Gaspar of Cupertino, California.

Ch. Chang Si Tang, owned by Neva Gaspar of the Lli Haven Kennels in Cupertino, California. The sire was Ch. Yang Fu Tang *ex* Tang's Son Poppy. Yang Fu Tang was the greatest Chow of the 1930's.

as rat poison, boric acid, hand soap, detergents, and insecticides. The garage too may provide dangers: antifreeze for the car, lawn, garden and tree sprays, paints, etc., are all available for tipping over and consuming. All poisons should be placed on high shelves for the sake of your children as well as your animals.

Perhaps the most readily available of all household poisons are plants. Household plants are almost all poisonous, even if taken in small quantities. Some of the most dangerous are the elephant ear, the narcissus bulb, any kind of ivy leaves, burning bush leaves, the jimson weed, the dumb cane weed, mock orange fruit, cas-

tor beans, Scotch broom seeds; the root or seed of the plant called four o'clock, cyclamen, pimpernel, lily of the valley, the stem of the sweet pea, rhododendrons of any kind, spider lily bulbs, bayonet root, foxglove leaves, tulip bulbs, monkshood roots, azalea, wisteria, poinsettia leaves, mistletoe, hemlock, locoweed and arrowglove. In all, there are over 500 poisonous plants in the United States. Peach, elderberry and cherry trees can cause cyanide poisoning if the bark is consumed. Rhubarb leaves either raw or cooked can cause death or violent convulsions. Check out your closets, fields and grounds around your home to see what might be of danger to your pets.

SYMPTOMS OF POISONING

Be on the lookout for vomiting, hard or labored breathing, whimpering, stomach cramps, and trembling as a prelude to convulsions. Any delay in a visit to your veterinarian can mean death. Take along the bottle or package or a sample of the plant you suspect to be the cause to help the veterinarian determine the correct antidote.

The most common type of poisoning which accounts for nearly one-fourth of all animal victims is staphylococcic-infected food. Salmonella ranks third. These can be avoided by serving fresh food and not letting it lie around in hot weather.

There are also many insect poisonings caused by animals eating cockroaches, spiders, flys, butterflies, etc. Toads and some frogs give off a fluid which can make a dog foam at the mouth—and even kill him—if he bites just a little too hard!

Some misguided dog owners think it is "cute" to let their dogs enjoy a cocktail with them before dinner. There can be serious effects resulting from encouraging a dog to drink—sneezing fits, injuries as a result of intoxication, and heart stoppage are just a few. Whiskey for medicinal purposes or beer for brood bitches should be administered only on the advice of your veterinarian.

There have been cases of severe damage and death when dogs emptied ash trays and consumed cigarettes, resulting in nicotine poisoning. Leaving a dog alone all day in a house where there are cigarettes available on a coffee table is asking for trouble. Needless to say, the same applies to marijuana. The narcotic addict who takes his dog along with him on a "trip" does not deserve to have a dog. All the ghastly side effects are as possible for the dog as for the addict, and for a person to submit an animal to this indignity is indeed despicable. Don't think it doesn't happen. Ask the veterinarians that practice near some of your major hippie havens! Unfortunately, in all our major cities the practice is becoming more and more of a problem for the veterinarian.

Be on the alert and remember that in the case of any type of poisoning, the best treatment is prevention!

Tag-el's Lionora Kamara at six months of age. Owners, Mr. and Mrs. Carl Boudreau, Kamara Kennels, Massachusetts.

On a bright Southern California day, the camera caught Starcrest Q.P. Doll of Don-Lee as she posed for her owners Mr. and Mrs. Robert Burk of San Pedro, California. Q.P. Doll was sired by Ch. Starcrest Mr. Christopher out of Livin' Doll of Poppyland.

Ch. Chang-Shi Poppy Western Style in full bloom. This beautiful bitch was whelped on May 8, 1964, and was bred by William and Florence Elster. The sire was Ch. Starcrest Spy of Poppy-land *ex* Ken-Wan's Tagh Along. Owners are Lucile and Jerry Sterling, Nashville, Tennessee.

THE CURSE OF ALLERGY

The heartbreak of a child being forced to give up a beloved pet because he is suddenly found to be allergic to it is a sad but true story. Many families claim to be unable to have dogs at all; others seem to be able only to enjoy them on a restricted basis. Many children know animals only through occasional visits to a friend's house or the zoo.

While modern veterinary science has produced some brilliant allergists, such as Dr. Edward Baker of New Jersey, the field is still working on a solution for those who suffer from exposure to their pets. There is no permanent cure as yet.

Over the last quarter of a century there have been many attempts at a permanent cure, but none has proven successful, because the treatment was needed too frequently, or was too expensive to maintain over extended periods of time.

However, we find that most people who are allergic to their animals are also allergic to a variety of other things as well. By eliminating the other irritants, and by taking medication given for the control of allergies in general, many are able to keep pets on a restricted basis. This may necessitate the dog's living outside the house, being groomed at a professional grooming parlor instead of by the owner, or merely being kept out of the bedroom at night. A discussion of this "balance" factor with your medical and veterinary doctors may give new hope to those willing to try.

A paper presented by Mathilde M. Gould, M.D., a New York allergist, before the American Academy of Allergists in the 1960's, and reported in the September-October 1964 issue of the *National Humane Review* magazine, offered new hope to those who are allergic by a method referred to as hyposensitization. You may wish to write to the magazine and request the article for discussion with your medical and veterinary doctors on your individual problem.

DO ALL DOGS CHEW?

All young dogs chew! Chewing is the best possible method of cutting teeth and exercising gums. Every puppy goes through this teething process. True, it can be destructive if not watched carefully, and it is really the responsibility of every owner to prevent the damage before it occurs.

When you see a puppy pick up an object to chew, immediately remove it from his mouth with a sharp "No!" and replace the object with a toy or a rawhide bone which should be provided for him to do his serious chewing. Puppies take anything and everything into their mouths so they should be provided with proper toys which they cannot chew up and swallow.

BONES

There are many opinions on the kind of bones a dog should have. Anyone who has lost a puppy or dog because of a bone chip puncturing the stomach or intestinal wall will say "no bones" except for the processed rawhide or nylon kind you buy in pet shops. There are those who say shank or knuckle bones are permissible. Use your

Ch. Nor-Ton's Lim Lee, a champion in Canada and the United States. Bred and owned by Bessie Volkstadt of North Tonawanda, New York.

Ch. Chang-Shi Jamaica, whelped in December, 1957, and owned by the Gerald Sterlings of Nashville, Tennessee. The sire was Ch. Chang-Shi Zygoto ex Ch. Chang-Shi Miss Mis-Be-Having.

Ch. Liontamer Bruiser shown here winning Group 4 at the Kennel Club of Northern New Jersey, April, 1974, with his owner-handler, Carl Boudreau, Kamara Kennels, East Falmouth, Massachusetts. The judge is Dr. Malcolm E. Phelps.

Shia's Starcrest Kway Replica pictured winning at the 1 Winston-Salem Kennel Club show under judge Rap Schulte. Replica needed just two points for his title at time, and is shown by his breeder-owner, Mrs. Pearl E. res, Farresdale Chows, Charlotte, North Carolina. The was Ch. Starcrest Kway ex Shia-Ken, a Canadian im bitch.

Ch. Loy-Jean's Princess Mauri, whelped in 1963 by breeders Floyd and Jeanne Messer. Mauri was sired by the great Ch. Loy-Jean's China Boi *ex* Ch. Loy-Jean's Princess of Hai-Nan. She is owned by Fred and Eleanor Ellwanger of Brockport, New York.

T'Waga Fortune Cookie at 21 months of age who has both majors toward her championship. She is a granddaughter of Ch. Ghat de la Moulaine and was bred by E.H. Stanton, her owner.

Famous Chow Chow breeder and judge Mrs. Armitage places Mary MacEachern's Int. Ch. Ky-Lin's Midas Best of Breed at a June, 1958 kennel club show. Mrs. MacEachern is owner of the Wu San Kennels in Sodus, New York. Mrs. Armitage was a pillar of the Chow breed.

Liontamer Firecracker at 18 months of age. Owner is Marion Grissom of Kannapolis, North Carolina. Sire was Ch. Liontamer of Elster *ex* Gotschall's Velvet Nite. Firecracker is litter brother to Ch. Liontamer Mardi Gras, a Best in Show winner owned by Mary Alice Elliott, Denver.

Plain Acre's Belle Chien, one of Manota Stertz' top brood bitches at the Plain Acre Kennels in Cincinnati, Ohio. The sire was Beamer's Beau Chien *ex* Beamer's Scarlet Imp. Belle was whelped February 19th, 1965.

own judgment, but when there are adequate processed bones which you know to be safe, why risk a valuable animal? Cooked bones soft enough to be pulverized and put in the food can be fed if they are reduced almost to a powder. If you have the patience for this sort of thing, okay. Otherwise, stick to the commercial products.

As for dogs and puppies chewing furniture, shoes, etc., replace the object with something allowable and safe and put yourself on record as remembering to close closet doors. Keep the puppy in the same room with you so you can stand guard over the furniture!

Electrical cords and sockets, or wires of any kind, present a dangerous threat to chewers. Glass dishes which can be broken are hazardous if not picked up right after feeding.

Chewing can also be a form of frustration or nervousness. Dogs sometimes chew for spite, if owners leave them alone too long or too often. Bitches will sometimes chew if their puppies are taken away from them too soon; insecure puppies often chew thinking they're nursing. Puppies which chew wool or blankets or carpet corners or certain types of materials may have a nutritional deficiency or something lacking in their diet, such as craving the starch that might be left in material after washing. Perhaps the articles have been near something that tastes good and they retain the odor.

The act of chewing has no connection with particular breeds or ages, any more than there is a logical reason for dogs to dig holes outdoors or dig on wooden floors indoors.

So we repeat, it is up to you to be on guard at all times until the need—or habit—passes!

HIP DYSPLASIA

Hip dysplasia, or HD, is one of the most widely discussed of all animal afflictions, since it has appeared in varying degrees in just about every breed of dog. True, the larger breeds seem most susceptible, but it has hit the small breeds and is beginning to be recognized in cats as well.

While HD in man has been recorded as far back as 370 B.C., HD in dogs was more than likely referred to as rheumatism until veterinary research came into the picture. In 1935, Dr. Otto Schales, at Angell Memorial Hospital in Boston, wrote a paper on hip dysplasia and classified the four degrees of dysplasia of the hip joint as follows:

Grade 1—Slight (poor fit between ball and socket).

Grade 2—Moderate (moderate but obvious shallowness of the socket).

Grade 3—Severe (socket quite flat).

Grade 4—Very severe (complete displacement of head of femur at early age).

HD is an incurable, hereditary, though not congenital disease of the hip sockets. It is transmitted as a dominant trait with irregular manifestations. Puppies appear normal at birth but the constant wearing away of the socket means the animal moves more and more on muscle, thereby presenting a lameness, a difficulty in getting up and severe pain in advanced cases.

Ch. West's Sun of East, sired by Ch. East is West *ex* Lady Agatha, was owned by Mr. and Mrs. Ted Holleman.

The degree of severity can be determined around six months of age, but its presence can be noticed from two months of age. The problem is determined by X-ray, and if pain is present it can be relieved temporarily by medication. Exercise should be avoided since motion encourages the wearing away of the bone surfaces.

Dogs with HD should not be shown or bred, if quality in the breed is to be maintained. It is essential to check a pedigree for dogs known to be dysplastic before breeding, since this disease can be dormant for many generations.

ELBOW DYSPLASIA

The same condition can also affect the elbow joints and is known as elbow dyspla-

Ch. Pandee's Jubilee captured the Best In Show award at the 1969 Valley Forge Kennel Club show under judge Frank Landraf. Club President Russell Jackson presents the trophy. Jubilee is co-owned by Dr. I.P. Earle and Dr. J.A. O'Brien. A William P. Gilbert photo.

sia. This also causes lameness, and dogs so affected should not be used for breeding.

PATELLA DYSPLASIA

Some of the smaller breeds of dogs also suffer from patella dysplasia, or dislocation of the knee. This can be treated surgically, but the surgery by no means abolishes the hereditary factor. Therefore, these dogs should not be used for breeding.

All dogs—in any breed—should be X-rayed before being used for breeding. The X-ray should be read by a competent veterinarian, and the dog declared free and clear.

HD PROGRAM IN GREAT BRITAIN

The British Veterinary Association (BVA) has made an attempt to control the spread of HD by appointing a panel of members of their profession who have made a special study of the disease, to read X-rays. Dogs over one year of age may be X-rayed and certified as free. Forms are completed in triplicate to verify the tests. One copy remains with the panel, one copy is for the owner's veterinarian, and one for the owner. A record is also sent to the British Kennel Club for those wishing to check on a particular dog for breeding purposes.

THE UNITED STATES REGISTRY

In the United States we have a central hip dysplasia foundation, known as the OFA (Orthopedic Foundation for Animals). This HD control registry was formed in 1966. X-rays are sent for expert evaluation by qualified radiologists.

All you need do for complete information on getting an X-ray for your dog is to write to the Orthopedic Foundation for Animals at 817 Virginia Ave., Columbia, Mo. 65201, and request their dysplasia packet. There is no charge for this kit. It contains an envelope large enough to hold your X-ray film (which you will have taken by your own veterinarian), and a drawing showing how to position the dog properly for X-ray. There is also an application card for proper identification of the dog. Then, hopefully, your dog will be certified "normal." You will be given a registry number which you can put on his pedigree, use in your advertising, and rest assured your breeding program is in good order.

All X-rays should be sent to the address above. Any other information you might wish to have may be requested from Mrs. Robert Bower, OFA, Route 1, Constantine, Mo. 49042.

We cannot urge strongly enough the importance of doing this. While it involves time and effort, the reward in the long run will more than pay for your trouble. To see the heartbreak of parents and children when their beloved dog has to be put to sleep because of severe hip dysplasia as the result of bad breeding is a sad experience. Don't let this happen to you or those who will purchase your puppies!

Additionally, we should mention that there is a method of palpation to determine the extent of affliction. This can be painful if the animal is not properly prepared for the examination. There have also been attempts to replace the animal's femur and socket. This is not only expensive, but the percentage of success is small.

For those who refuse to put their dog down, there is a new surgical technique which can relieve pain, but in no way constitutes a cure. This technique involves the severing of the pectinius muscle which, for some unknown reason brings relief from pain over a period of many months—even up to two years. Two veterinary colleges in the United States are performing this operation at the present time. However, the owner must also give permission to "desex" the dog at the time of the muscle severance. This is a safety measure to help stamp out hip dysplasia, since obviously the condition itself remains and can be passed on.

While this is by no means any kind of cure, at least it is respite for families who cannot bear to lose their beloved pets.

Ch. Soo-Z's Miss Kee-Zee of Jade pictured winning at a recent show. She is owned by Nelson Tardy and Susan S. Anderson of California.

22. PURSUING A CAREER IN DOGS

One of the biggest joys for those of us who love dogs is to see someone we know or someone in our family grow up in the fancy and go on to enjoy the sport of dogs in later life. Many dog lovers, in addition to leaving codicils in their wills, are providing in other ways for veterinary scholarships for deserving youngsters who wish to make their association with dogs their profession.

Unfortunately, many children who have this earnest desire are not always able to afford the expense of an education that will take them through veterinary school, and they are not eligible for scholarships. In recent years, however, we have had a great innovation in this field—a college course for those interested in earning an Animal Science degree, which costs less than half of what it costs to complete veterinary courses. These students have been a boon to the veterinarians, and a number of colleges are now offering the program.

With each passing year, the waiting rooms of veterinarians have become more crowded, and the demands on the doctors' time for research, consultation, surgery and treatment have consumed more and more of the working hours over and above his regular office hours. The tremendous increase in the number of dogs and cats and other domestic animals, both in cities and in the suburbs, has resulted in an almost overwhelming consumption of veterinarians' time.

Until recently most veterinary help consisted of kennel men or women who were restricted to services more properly classified as office maintenance rather than actual veterinary assistance. Needless to say, their part in the operation of a veterinary office is both essential and appreciated, as are the endless details and volumes of paperwork capably handled by office secretaries and receptionists. However, still more of a veterinarian's duties could be handled by properly trained semiprofessionals.

With exactly this additional service in mind, many colleges are now conducting two-year courses in animal science for the training of such semiprofessionals, thereby opening a new field for animal technologists. The time saved by the assistance of these trained semiprofessionals will relieve veterinarians of the more mechanical chores and will allow them more time for diagnosing and general servicing of their clients.

"Delhi Tech," the State University Agricultural and Technical College at Delhi, New York, has recently graduated several classes of these technologists, and many other institutions of learning are offering comparable two-year courses at the college level. Entry requirements are usually that each applicant must be a graduate of an approved high school or have taken the State University admissions examination. In addition, each applicant for the Animal Science Technology program must have some previous credits in mathematics and science, with chemistry as an important part of the science background.

The program at Delhi was a new educational venture dedicated to the training of competent technicians for employment in the biochemical field and has been generously supported by a five-year grant, designated as a "Pilot Development Program in Animal Science." This grant provided both personal and scientific equipment with such obvious good results when

Jade's Rough and Ready, owned by Karen Tardy and Trudy Shawger of California. The sire was Ch. Tsang-Po's Red Commander Jade *ex* Ch. Mil-Her Sunbonnet of Jade. Handler is Al LeMar, a Chow breeder.

it was done originally pursuant to a contract with the United States Department of Health, Education, and Welfare. Delhi is a unit of the State University of New York and is accredited by the Middle States Association of Colleges and Secondary Schools. The campus provides offices, laboratories and animal quarters and is equipped with modern instruments to train technicians in laboratory animal care, physiology, pathology, microbiology, anesthesia, X-ray and germ-free techniques. Sizable animal colonies are maintained in air-conditioned quarters: animals housed include mice, rats, hamsters, guinea-pigs, gerbils and rabbits, as well as dogs and cats.

First-year students are given such courses as livestock production, dairy food science, general, organic and biological chemistry, mammalian anatomy, histology and physiology, pathogenic microbiology and quantitative and instrumental analysis, to name a few. Second year students matriculate in general pathology, animal parasitology, animal care and anesthesia,

A lovely formal study of Ch. Balthazar Liontamer Avril, photographed by the famous photographer. Tauskey for owners Mr. and Mrs. Bernard Kennedy of Wallingford, Connecticut.

introductory psychology, animal breeding, animal nutrition, hematology and urinalysis, radiology, genetics, food sanitation and meat inspection, histological techniques, animal laboratory practices and other techniques. These, of course, may be supported by electives that prepare the student for contact with the public in the administration of these duties. Such recommended electives include public speaking, botany, animal reproduction and other related subjects.

In addition to Delhi and the colleges which got in early on the presentation of these courses, more and more universities are offering training for animal technologists. Students at the State University of Maine, for instance, receive part of their practical training at the Animal Medical Center in New York City, and after this actual experience can perform professionally immediately upon entering a veterinarian's employ.

Under direct veterinary supervision they are able to perform all of the following procedures as a semi-professional:

- Recording of vital information relative to a case. This would include such information as the client's name, address, telephone number and other facts pertinent to the visit. The case history would include the breed, age of the animal, its sex, temperature, etc.
- Preparation of the animal for surgery.
- Preparation of equipment and medicaments to be used in surgery.
- Preparation of medicaments for dispensing to clients on prescription of the attending veterinarian.
- Administration and application of certain medicines.
- Administration of colonic irrigations.
- Application or changing of wound dressings.
- Cleaning of kennels, exercise runs and kitchen utensils.
- Preparation of food and the feeding of patients.
- Explanation to clients on the handling and restraint of their pets, including needs for exercise, house training and elementary obedience training.

- First-aid treatment for hemorrhage, including the proper use of tourniquets.
- Preservation of blood, urine and pathologic material for the purpose of laboratory examination.
- General care and supervision of the hospital or clinic patients to insure their comfort.
- Nail trimming and grooming of patients.

High school graduates with a sincere affection and regard for animals and a desire to work with veterinarians and perform such clinical duties as mentioned above will find they fit in especially well. Women particularly will be useful since, over and beyond the strong maternal instinct that goes so far in the care and the recovery phase when dealing with animals, women will find the majority of their duties well within their physical capabilities. Since a majority of the positions will be in the small animal field, their dexterity will also fit in well. Students having financial restrictions that preclude their education and licensing as full-fledged veterinarians can in this way pursue careers in an area close to their actual desire. Their assistance in the pharmaceutical field, where drug concerns deal with laboratory animals, covers another wide area for trained assistance. The career opportunities are varied and reach into job opportunities in medical centers, research institutions and government health agencies; at present, the demand for graduates far exceeds the current supply of trained personnel.

As far as the financial remunerations, yearly salaries are estimated at an average of $5,000.00 for a starting point. As for the estimate of basic college education expenses, they range from $1800.00 to $2200.00 per year for out-of-state residents, and include tuition, room and board, college fees, essential textbooks and limited personal expenses. These personal expenses, of course, will vary with individual students, as well as the other expenses, but we present an average. It is obvious that the costs are about half of the costs involved in becoming a full-fledged veterinarian, however.

Ch. Starcrest Tsong of Selwonk, owned by the Rev. Harold Frank Knowles II and bred by Starcrest Kennels, Sun Valley, California. Tsong was whelped in April, 1970.

PART TIME KENNEL WORK

Youngsters who do not wish to go on to become veterinarians or animal technicians can get valuable experience and extra money by working part-time after school and weekends, or full-time during summer vacations, in a veterinarian's office. The exposure to animals and office procedure will be time well spent.

Another great help to veterinarians has been the housewife who loves animals and wishes to put in some time at a job away from the house, especially if her children are grown or away at college. If she can clean up in her own kennel she can certainly clean up in a veterinarian's office, and she will learn much about handling and caring for her own animals while she is making money.

Kennel help is also an area that is wide open for retired men. They are able to help out in many areas where they can learn and stay active, and most of the work allows them to set their own pace. The gentility that age and experience brings is also beneficial to the animals they will deal with; for their part, the men find great reward in their contribution to animals and will be keeping their hand in the business world as well.

At left is Robert Wright with Ch. Bob-Bet's Chan, bred by Mr. and Mrs. Wright. This lovely dog was sired by the famous American and Mexican Ch. Ghat de la Moulaine ex Beeson's Nu Ying. In the middle is Grace Luckey of Seattle with her Luck-ee U'Kwong Prunella, Chan's Daughter, and on the right is Bob Childress with Noel and Lillian Bergh's R-K-Dea Lee Han Sum Sun, now a champion. He is a Chan son out of R-K-Dea Tsassee Missee

PROFESSIONAL HANDLERS

For those who wish to participate in the sport of dogs and whose interests or abilities do not center around the clinical aspects of the fancy, there is yet another avenue of involvement.

For those who excel in the show ring, who enjoy being in the limelight and putting their dogs through their paces, a career in professional handling may be the answer. Handling may include a weekend of showing a few dogs for special clients, or it may be a full-time career which can also include boarding, training, conditioning, breeding and showing of dogs for several clients.

Depending on how deeply your interest runs, the issue can be solved by a lot of preliminary consideration before it becomes necessary to make a decision. The first move would be to have a long, serious talk with a successful professional handler to learn the pros and cons of such a profession. Watching handlers in action from ringside as they perform their duties can be revealing. A visit to their kennels for an on-the-spot revelation of the behind-the-scenes responsibilities is essential! And working for them full or part time would be the best way of all to resolve any doubt you might have!

Professional handling is not all glamour in the show ring. There is plenty of "dirty work" behind the scenes 24 hours of every day. You must have the necessary ability and patience for this work, as well as the ability and patience to deal with the CLIENTS—the dog owners who value their animals above almost anything else and would expect a great deal from you in the way of care and handling. The big question you must ask yourself first of all is: do you *really* love dogs enough to handle it. . .

DOG TRAINING

Like the professional handler, the professional dog trainer has a most responsible job! You not only need to be thoroughly familiar with the correct and successful methods of training a dog but also must have the ability to communicate with dogs. True, it is very rewarding work, but training for the show ring, obedience, or guard dog work must be done exactly right

Ch. Tag-El's Little Rock and Mi-Pao's Teratai, owned and shown by Evelyn E. Carter of the Tag-El's Chow Chow Ranch in McLoud, Oklahoma.

Another show win for Ch. Scotchow Liontamer's Louise, one of the few Chow Chow bitches to win Groups. The judge is Edwin Pickhardt; Louise's handler is Dr. Nancy Lenfestey for owner Miss Joan Hannephin. An Evelyn Shafer photograph.

for successful results to maintain a business reputation.

Training schools are quite the vogue nowadays, with all of them claiming success. But careful investigation should be made before enrolling a dog. . . and even more careful investigation should be made of their methods and of their actual successes before becoming associated with them.

GROOMING PARLORS

If you do not wish the 24-hour a day job which is required by a professional handler or professional trainer, but still love working with and caring for dogs, there is always the very profitable grooming business. Poodles started the ball rolling for the swanky, plush grooming establishments which sprang up like mushrooms all over the major cities, many of which seem to be doing very well. Here again, handling dogs and the public is necessary for a successful operation, as well as skill in the actual grooming of the dogs, and of all breeds.

While shops flourish in the cities, some of the suburban areas are now featuring mobile units which by appointment will visit your home with a completely equipped shop on wheels and will groom your dog right in your own driveway!

Ch. Chang-Shi Zip, bred in Belgium and imported by the Gerald Sterlings of Nashville, Tennessee. This beautiful black bitch received a Top Brood Bitch award from *Popular Dogs* magazine for having produced 4 Chows which completed their championships in 1958. Bred by the late Comtesse R. de Changy of Belgium, Zip is the littermate to the fabulous Ch. Chang-Shi Zygoto. She has a Group First and Group Placings to her credit as well.

Ch. Burton's Wong Dai, owned by Mrs. Bee Burton, and bred by the Walter Hansons. The sire was Ch. Cheng Lee's Waugee of Poppyland *ex* Hanson's Toujours Moi. He is a Best in Show winner.

Ch. Farresdale Yang Ping Yu photographed winning Best of Breed, Group Second, and Best Local Dog at the 1960 Charlotte, North Carolina Kennel Club show with his breeder-owner, Mrs. Pearl E. Farres, Farresdale Chows. The judge is William Kendrick.

Wah-Hu's Chutzpah, owned by William and Mary Ann Chambers, Wah-Hu Chow Chows, Glen Ellyn, Illinois.

THE PET SHOP

Part-time or full-time work in a pet shop can help you make up your mind rather quickly as to whether or not you would like to have a shop of your own. For those who love animals and are concerned with their care and feeding, the pet shop can be a profitable and satisfying association. Supplies which are available for sale in these shops are almost limitless, and a nice living can be garnered from pet supplies if the location and population of the city you choose warrant it.

DOG JUDGING

There are also those whose professions or age or health prevent them from owning or breeding or showing dogs, and who turn to judging at dog shows after their active years in the show ring are no longer possible. Breeder-judges make a valuable contribution to the fancy by judging in accordance with their years of experience in the fancy, and the assignments are enjoyable. Judging requires experience, a good eye for dogs and an appreciation of a good animal.

MISCELLANEOUS

If you find all of the aforementioned too demanding or not within your abilities, there are still other aspects of the sport for you to enjoy and participate in at will. Writing for the various dog magazines, books or club newsletters, dog photography, portrait painting, club activities, making dog coats, or needlework featuring dogs, typing pedigrees or perhaps dog walking. All, in their own way, contribute to the sport of dogs and give great satisfaction.

557

Governor of Pennsylvania Milton Shapp and his wife are photographed with their black Chow Chow, Cleo. Cleo made national headlines in the early 1970's during the severe floods when Governor Shapp insisted on personally returning to the flooded executive mansion to rescue Cleo.

23. CHOW-MANIA

Over the years, the authors, as Chow lovers are inclined to do, have collected a list of Chow Chow owners, breeders and admirers which we are also inclined to share with our readers. . .

For instance, did you know that Sigmund Freud owned a Chow Chow to which he was particularly devoted? There are many photographs of Freud with Chows, including one appearing in *The Dog* by Fernard Mery. The photograph is from the collection of Hans Casparius, whom we could not, unfortunately, contact for permission to reproduce in this book. Another was sent to us by Mary Alice Elliott; most unfortunately, this one also was not reproducible. It featured Dr. Freud on his balcony with a Chow.

Needless to say, scholars of the Chow Chow breed can attest to the prominence of the Chow Chow in the classic book *King Solomon's Ring*, by Konrad Lorenz, who both owned and bred Chows. Another literary great who adored the Chow was Virginia Woolf. Not only did she own them, but her novel *Mrs. Dalloway* starred a Chow Chow as one of the characters; she was perhaps best known in literary circles for her book *Flush*, the tale of Elizabeth Browning's Cocker Spaniel, one of the most touching dog stories ever told. Eugene O'Neill was another literary genius who owned a Chow Chow; he included one in *Marco's Millions*.

Among royalty Queen Victoria ranks at the top for her devotion to dogs. Though many claim she seemed to have housed in "the castles of olde" one of just about every breed available at the time, she is known to have included a Chow Chow in her personal menagerie, as did President Calvin Coolidge.

After the turn of the century, the movie stars seemed to take a fancy to the furry China balls from the Orient. Clara Bow, who was touted as having "It," also had good dog sense, for she not only owned but also bred some Chows. Mary Pickford, another luminary in the film industry at the time, along with Charlie Chaplin, was attracted to the breed. There also were several opera singers who professed great admiration for our breed. Among them Birgit Nilsson and Kirsten Flagstad, friends of co-author Sam Draper, who can attest to their affection and elaborates on the subject further along in this chapter.

Mrs. Speyer, who was responsible for the world-famous Speyer Animal Hospital in New York City, was a Chow Chow owner and breeder, as is Senator Howard Baker, of the Watergate hearings. Herbert von Karajan, musical director of the Vienna State Opera, has also joined the ranks of Chow enthusiasts. The authors were particularly impressed with the devotion of Governor and Mrs. Milton Shapp of Pennsylvania. During the devastating flooding

Two Hong Kong stamps featuring the Chow Chow. This 1970 issue commemorates the February 6th Lunar New Year.

of the executive mansion during the 1972 floods, they refused to evacuate the mansion without personally rescuing their pet Chow Chow! We were additionally pleased when the Governor sent us a photograph of him and his wife with Cleo.

From a painting titled *Gentleman-at-Arms*, by Richard Marientreu. This Chang-Shi Chow Chow is a major portion of the painting of young Christopher Needham.

ABOUT BIRGIT NILSSON AND "LITTLE LOUIE"

Several years ago when "Little Louie" (Liontamer All-American) was a puppy, Sam Draper took him to Thanksgiving dinner at the home of Robert Herman, Artistic Director of the Metropolitan Opera for twenty-three years during Rudolf Bing's tenure. As master and puppy came into the large entry hall of the Herman estate, the walls of which were covered with autographed photos and letters of the world's great singers and conductors, the "Love Duet" from *Tristan und Isolde* poured forth from the omnipresent audio system, waves of sound from the incomparable Kirsten Flagstad and Lauritz Melchior. This particular music had been planned for Sam's arrival, Bob Herman being well aware that Sam had been a close friend of Madame Flagstad for many years.

But even a more unexpected surprise than the transcendental music of Richard Wagner was the presence in the living room of Birgit Nilsson, one of the greatest living operatic sopranos! At the same time, she extended her hand in greeting to Sam and reached for "Little Louie," an adorable eight-week-old stuffed toy of soft blond fur, exclaiming, "I don't believe it! I don't believe it!"

That Thanksgiving occasion was spent in listening to a lot of opera (before, during, and after the dinner), including several recordings of Nilsson herself. The Chow puppy was scarcely ever out of the arms or sight of the Swedish diva. She wanted to take him with her, but despite the flattering offer, Sam and his partners, Bob and Jean Hetherington, could not part with this puppy who, they were certain, would become Liontamer's first champion son. However, Bob Herman reports that Birgit Nilsson often asks about the little Chow Chow puppy with whom she fell so much in love at Thanksgiving. In correspondence between Dr. Draper and Madame Flagstad, she answered his question about her degree of familiarity with Chows this way:

"You asked me about whether I had even seen a Chow Chow. Yes, I have. In fact, I had a close friend who owned a Chow many years ago which was imported from England. I loved her Chow and I always wanted one. But as you know, one has to give up many things when one has a demanding career."

VIRGINIA WOOLF AND CHOWS

Sam Draper has taught an Honors Literature Seminar on Virginia Woolf at Rockland Community College, State University of New York, Suffern, where he is Professor of English. He relishes English and European literature greatly and has taught courses on Tolstoy, Dostoevsky, Flaubert, Hardy, Lawrence, Gide, Proust, Ibsen, Strindberg, Chekhov and others. One of his favorites is Virginia Woolf, perhaps the most difficult novelist in English. It was only in 1973 that the students in his Honors Literature Seminar elected to study the life and work of Virginia Woolf. Although Sam had read most of Virginia's novels, he had never attempted *Mrs. Dalloway*. When he came across three references in the novel to Chow Chows, he was surprised—and delighted, of course. And so

A needlepoint tapestry purchased in Bermuda of the old type Chow Chow, worked by Joan Brearley and presented to her co-author, Dr. Draper, as a gift while working on *The Book of the Chow Chow*.

were the students, who were well aware of Sam's interest in this ancient breed. As most dog lovers know, Virginia Woolf loved dogs and owned several; her book *Flush*, a biography of the English Cocker Spaniel that belonged to Elizabeth Barrett Browning, is a perennial favorite.

In the Harcourt, Brace & World edition of *Mrs. Dalloway* there are at least three separate references to Chows. In two cases (page 82 and 168) the references are non-committal, as the dogs are mentioned in passing as parts of the background scenery. One reference, however (page 270), is remarkably to the point and characterizes the dogs as "adorable."

GEORGIA O'KEEFFE VISITS THE CHOWS IN MONROE

Sam Draper's home in Monroe, Orange County, in the foothills of the Catskills in New York State, was purchased because of its trees, grass, and kennel space for the Chow Chows. Inside the house there is scarcely any furniture; one notices mostly the white walls which are the background for a collection of modern abstract expressionistic paintings, a Dufy flower, a small collage by Jackson Pollock, a scarlet and black abstraction by Dorchy, an enormous Mesibov of blue, yellow, orange, red, pink, violet, and green abstraction covering one large wall, as well as many others.

Since 1944 when Sam first visited the Metropolitan Museum in New York City (he was still a California resident then), he fell in love with "Black Iris," one of the first modern paintings in America done by Georgia O'Keeffe, whom Picasso and others have called America's greatest painter. Following her career and her art, Sam became aware that Georgia O'Keeffe owned a couple of Chow Chows whose photos appeared along with their distinguished owner in the March, 1968 *Life* magazine cover story titled: "Georgia O'Keeffe in New Mexico—Stark Visions of a Pioneer Painter."

Sam first met Georgia O'Keeffe and her companion-friend and agent, Doris Bry, in 1973 at Fort Worth, Texas, where they had traveled to attend the parent club

Zsa Zsa Gabor and the famous Ch. Starcrest Spy of Poppyland. Owner Howard Kendall completes the photo.

Chow Specialty. An acquaintanceship developed which was climaxed by Miss O'Keeffe's and Miss Bry's visit to Liontamer Kennels in Mahwah, New Jersey and in Monroe, New York. When Miss O'Keeffe entered Sam's living room, she said softly, "Oh, this is a country museum!" "Yes," Sam replied, "With Chows everywhere!" She and Miss Bry liked the paintings, but they liked the Chows even more. Miss O'Keeffe expressed her desire to take each Chow home with her as introductions were made. "This dog's head is a giant orange chrysanthemum," she remarked. . . "And this one is a magnificent scarlet pin cushion." Her reactions to the Chows were dramatic and original, and her presence in Sam's world of Chows and modern art will never be forgotten.

The world-famous painter Georgia O'Keeffe with her Chow Chow Pandee's Jingo of Abiquiu, just 11 months old. Miss O'Keeffe was the subject of a "cover story" in *Life* magazine March 1, 1968, in which several Chows were shown with their celebrated owner. A Doris Bry photo.

The Far East Kennels of Lothar R. Zifferer in Columbia, Pennsylvania.

FROM OUR NOSTALGIA DEPARTMENT

To many the "Roaring Twenties" mean one thing—to Chow lovers, the Roaring Twenties mean a time when the Chow Chow was "coming of age" in America. The dog fancy was roaring as loudly as any enterprise in the American system, and among dog aficionados we had a lot to yell about! Some of the most famous and elaborate kennels in the history of the fancy were emerging to make history as the leaders in the breed of their choice. Many of these great kennels are mentioned in this book, but we feel we must also make special mention of one of the most lavish and ornate kennels of all—any breed!

We are talking about the Far East Kennels of Lothar R. Zifferer. Mr. Zifferer had a penchant for doing everything in a bigger, better and more spectacular way than anyone else he knew, and this didn't stop at his kennels. He loved the Chow Chow and bought the best from the leading kennels of the day to establish his Far East Kennels on Lincoln Highway in Columbia, Pennsylvania. Mr. Zifferer, had he lived to an old age, might have become one of the most formidable breeders of his time, for he bred many quality Chows. He did, perhaps more than any other Chowist, more to make the dog fancy believe that there is nothing too good for a dog. He presented them in a lavish setting, erected with no regard for expense, in a way that no one could deny that good things came

with good dogs. They were one and the same. . .

In a November, 1927 issue of the *American Kennel Gazette* the remarkable Arthur Frederick Jones devoted an article to Zifferer's enterprise, entitled "In Far East's Temple of the Chow," referring to it as America's most beautiful kennel. The enormous, high-ceilinged hall was neither temple nor ballroom, but rather a reception room for visitors to the kennels in which the owner wished to present his beloved Oriental dogs in their proper Oriental surroundings. Travelers along the Lincoln Highway never ceased to be amazed at the fantastic Oriental setting against a background of Pennsylvania smokestacks and smog! Having adored the Chow before he ever owned one, Zifferer was determined to obtain one, and then another— and then another—and another. He studied the breed, then bloodlines—and then in his mind's eye he began to divine the perfect Chow. Soon the Far East Kennels, with all these things in mind, became a reality. The Far East Kennels were said to be the most beautifully planned and finished kennels in the world at the time. Let's not forget, however, that our Mr. Zifferer was always cognizant of the value of advertising. A huge neon sign blazed above the formidable ediface of the Oriental architecture. He knew that it pays to advertise, and he devoted himself to publicizing his Chow Chows! Corners of the roof were adorned with Chinese lanterns weighing over 200 pounds, and necessitating special roof braces, and even the kennel rooms over the main buildings were decorated with authentic Oriental decor.

In spite of its spaciousness, the edifice would accommodate only 33 kennels, and each day each Chow Chow was lead to the bathing room where its eyes were washed and it was groomed and brushed just as if it were going into the show ring! While this was going on, each kennel was being washed and disinfected! Each kennel bore a receptacle which held the complete record of the dog housed within and was a duplicate of a master file kept in the office itself. Blue cards for boys and pink for girls, of course!

One of the most fascinating formalities of the kennel was that each kennel facility had an iron dish that had been rusted before being put into the kennel. This was done on scientific advice to aid the dogs in acquiring the proper amount of iron for their systems. It was done as a supplemental additive to their very carefully prepared dietary procedure. All the meat, we might add, was killed on the property and preserved in a special refrigerator room. (Goat's milk was used exclusively, a practice still adhered to by many dog fanciers today!) Steers were bought, inspected by a veterinarian, and killed on the premises. A hospital was maintained also, complete with isolation quarters. There was also a special room in the kennel where the dogs returning from the dog shows were disinfected with a special pressure spray and dried with an electric dryer. . . which was quite an addition in the 1920's. One girl was hired by the kennel on a full-time basis to do nothing but wash the eyes of the Chows each day with boric acid! The diet served at the Far East Kennels was as carefully planned and prepared as that of any gourmet restaurant. The morning meal consisted of shredded wheat and milk with corn flakes as an alternate, buttermilk for lunch and a 4:30 dinner, or main meal consisting of cooked beef on three days of the week, raw the rest. Vegetables, taken fresh from a 15-acre garden, compliments of the owner, were cooked with the meat, and included tomatoes, lettuce, and spinach. It was cooked in a pressure cooker, which was also an innovation at the time. Approximately one pound of meat a day was fed to each Chow. Puppies were fed five times a day.

Speaking of puppies, the Far East Kennels of our devoted Mr. Zifferer produced the first litter of pure white Chow Chows (with jet black pigmentation) in America. First, and ONLY! A photograph of the four white balls of fluff appeared in the article in the *American Kennel Club Gazette*. We can only surmise what would happen today if one of our well-known breeders announced the arrival of a litter of four white Chow Chows!!!

View of the Far East Kennels from Lincoln Highway.

This Chow Chow painting hangs in the National Gallery of Art in Washington, D.C., and is entitled *"THE DOG, by an Unknown American Artist."* A reproduction of this fascinating painting was loaned to the authors by the National Gallery especially for this book, and we are most grateful. We urge all Chow enthusiasts to see this great painting in full color on their next visit to the nation's capitol.

Ch. Plain Acre's Melody Me is shown here in a charcoal drawing by Rakestraw. She is owned by Judy Tarpley of Chatsworth, Georgia.

Carol Moorland Marshall's remarkably accurate and beautiful rendition of a Chow Chow in porcelain, from the collection of Joan Brearley. Notice the perfect balance of this Chow

Artist Marjorie Walker's beautiful pastel of the red Chow Chow Champion Jimmie Boy, which she produced in 1940; this Chow was owned by Miss Kathleen Staples, now of Hopewell Junction, New York.

Puppy portrait of eight-week-old Chows named Charlie, Kiki, Kalhoun and Kikmal that were sired by Ch. Don-Lee's Prophet *ex* Starcrest Caja of Jo-Lew. They are owned by Mr. and Mrs. Tom Lewis of Santa Ana, California. This unique painting was done by Jean Perrin.

HOW TO PHOTOGRAPH A CHOW CORRECTLY

The Chow is very often photographed incorrectly. The Chow should be photographed with his body turned in a three-quarter position toward the camera with his head looking more or less toward the photographer. In this manner the four legs and feet can be seen, the length of the back is shown somewhat, and the head is emphasized with the dog's ears, eyes, scowl, and muzzle seen straight on.

The Chow must not be photographed in body profile, as the only part of the dog that is stressed in that position is the body length and height of the Chow. He is not pictured to his best advantage in this manner.

Platforms that are furnished by the dog show superintendents on which group winners and the Best in Show winner must appear to have their pictures taken are most unflattering for the posing of a Chow. Owing to the platform's construction, the Chow is forced to stand in profile with his head facing left or right, so that only the dog's side is shown. Generally, this stance makes the Chow look longer than he is and does not show off his legs and head to advantage. Posing the Chow on this platform is the wrong way to photograph a Chow.

What the Chow owner or handler should do in this circumstance is to ask the photographer to take two pictures: 1. The official pose on the platform, and 2. A second photo on the ground or floor taken from the three-quarter body position of the Chow, which is the proper and preferable way to photograph our breed.

A trophy annually presented by The Chinese Chow Breeders Club was won by one of the English imported Chow Chows owned by Mrs. E.K. Lincoln of the Greenacre Kennels in Fairfield, Connecticut, one of the largest and most prominent of the early American kennels. The name of the English Chow who won this magnificent award is not known.

Arrogant Melody of Nor-ton pictured winning a three-point major on the way to her championship at the Hunterdon Hills Kennel Club show in 1967. Owners are Samuel Draper and Robert A Hetherington, Jr., who handled her to this win. William P. Gilbert photo.

Liontamer Butterfingers, whelped November 10, 1969 and pictured here at eight months of age. The beautiful Butterfingers is owned by Mr. Edward Zoller of New Jersey.

Ch. Dre-Don Sun King of Craglinden wins Best of Breed under judge Anna Katherine Nicholas at the Bronx County Kennel Club show in March, 1967. Sun King went on to third place in the Non-Sporting Group at the same show. Dr. Samuel Draper is owner-handler. An Evelyn Shafer photograph.

Mr. and Mrs. E. Berry Wall whose Chow, Chi-Chi had many celebrities as friends including several reigning monarchs and a prime minister. When Chi died in 1924 several French newspapers published a complete obituary for Chi. The scene of this photo is Monte Carlo where the Walls and Chi had many friends.

The bronze sculpture shown here of Chi-Chi, owned by Mr. and Mrs. E. Berry Wall, was done by Prince Troubetzkoy who cherished this famous Chow and has immortalized Chi.

This photo of a stuffed Chow is a replica of Chi Chi, often represented wearing long, highly starched collars like his master, E. Berry Wall, who along with his wife offered this Chow souvenir as a favor at a magnificent New Year's Eve party at Ciro's in Paris in 1920, to which many famous people came.

THE MEMOIRES OF CHI-CHI
A FAMOUS CHOW

WHO HAS WRITTEN HIS
AUTOBIOGRAPHY

WITH THE ASSISTANCE OF
MADAME E. BERRY WALL

OFFICER OF THE
FRENCH LEGION OF HONOR

Paris 1933

The above represents the title page of one of the most interesting bits of Chow-Mania in world history, a full book dedicated to the life of a celebrated dog, a Chow Chow who lived and traveled with his American millionaire owners, whose life and friends read like a fairy tale of beautiful trips, homes, servants, luxuries of all kinds and with many of the famous people of the world as friends.

According to Chi-Chi's AKC official pedigree, his birth was in 1908, his Stud Book number being 143,350. His sire was Patoo, his dam San Toy. Chi-Chi's breeder was Miss Ladew of Glen Cove, Long Island, New York. It was in Miss Ladew's stately mansion, called Elsinore, that Chi-Chi was born. He mentions the spacious lawns and flowerbeds tended by dozens of gardeners. His early playmates were two Cairn Terriers, Roddie and Sandy.

Chi-Chi says that there were so few Chows in the United States in the first years of this century that he caused quite a stir with his flaming scarlet coat and blueberry-colored tongue!

Chi-Chi relates his first trip to the Westminster show at Madison Square Garden. When Chi-Chi gave the austere judge his paw to shake, the judge told Mrs. Wall, Chi-Chi's owner-handler, "This is not a circus!" After Mrs. Wall said something to the judge, the exact words unfortunately unreported, the judge apologized and gave Chi the blue ribbon.

Chi-Chi writes about his first sea voyage, a trip from New York to Monte Carlo on *The Adriatic*, a crossing requiring fifteen days. Naturally, Chi stayed with his master and mistress in their sumptuous stateroom and was granted all the privileges of First Class. Aboard the ship was a friend, Mr. Henry C. Frick, the millionaire philanthropist and lover of art, whose son was a neighbor of Chi-Chi at Elsinore in Glen Cove.

When Chi arrived with his owners in Paris for the first time, he created quite a sensation as few, if any, Frenchmen had ever seen a Chow Chow in the flesh! The Walls and Chi-Chi took a suite at the Hotel Meurice, one of Paris's most elegant stopping places, where much of European royalty stayed while visiting the French capital.

Chi reports on a dog show held at the Paris Polo Club to which the American Ambassador to France, Myron T. Herrick, had brought his own Schnauzer, and the Baron Rothschild had brought twelve Chow Chows. Chi-Chi writes, "When my breed was called, a glance at the other Chows reassured me that I had nothing to fear from the twelve others! I knew I would win the first prize and I did, a magnificent silver cup."

One evening at Aix-les-Bains an outdoor performance of *Aïda* was presented, and Chi-Chi lay under the Walls' table listening to one of his favorite operas. Afterwards when Chi came out from his hiding place, some of the audience exclaimed, "How is it possible? Chi-Chi was under the table, and he never moved. That's extraordinary!"

"Not extraordinary at all," Chi-Chi wrote, "because I adore music!"

Chi-Chi relates many stories about his trip to Spain, where he became a close friend of King Alfonso XIII. Once on a trip to the Alhambra, Chi was photographed with several medieval statues of Lions whom he resembled much to everyone's amusement.

One fascinating letter concerns the special treatment Chi-Chi received when it came to traveling on trains in the United States with his owners. The letter from the Pennsylvania Railroad is addressed to Mr. E. Berry Wall, Hotel Plaza, New York City. "Dear Mr. Wall: With reference to taking your dog Chi-Chi to Washington on your trip, arrangements have been made to see that you are accommodated in this respect. If you will call Mr. William Eagan, Stationmaster at the Pennsylvania Terminal, New York City, notifying him of the day and the hour you wish to leave New York for Washington, Mr. Eagan will notify Mr. C.M. Schaffer, Chief of Transportation of the Pennsylvania Railroad, so that you can take your dog in the drawing room of whatever chair car your accommodation calls for. This will apply also upon your return from Washington.

"Will you kindly consider this entire matter confidential as these courtesies are not generally extended, and in your case, it is due to the very friendly feeling the Pennsylvania Railroad management has toward you personally. Yours truly, John B. Given, President." Indeed, Chi-Chi and his wonderful owners had many friends in many walks of life.

The book ends in 1924, when Chi-Chi was sixteen years old. He becomes very tired, he reports, and all he wishes after his departure from this earth is that his beloved Master and Mistress would say that he had been a good doggy. His last words were, "I am sleepy. . . I want to rest. . . I just had a terrible dream in which I was alone. When I woke up from the nightmare, I yelped a bit with joy to find that my Master and Mistress were seated on the ground beside me. My Mistress took me in her arms. . ."

Then as a kind of epilogue, Mrs. Wall wrote, "A large void has come into our lives. Chi, our faithful, dear and good companion no longer waits for us. His joyful welcome whenever we returned home and his sixteen years of friendship are destined to become only a memory. This worthy little dog was loved by everyone who knew him, and his obituary was published

Mr. E. Berry Wall, a famous American expatriate, is shown here with his Chow, Chi-Chi, which is the only Chow in history to be the subject of an entire book.

in many newspapers. One reported, 'Monte Carlo is entirely in mourning not for an emperor or king but for Chi-Chi, the Chow we love so much.' The mortal remains of Chi-Chi rest in Asniere, just outside Paris, in a dog cemetery. Surrounding his grave are many other graves belonging to dogs who are likewise missed by their owners, with touching inscriptions such as, 'Man's best friend is his dog.' "

The newspaper said at the time of Chi-Chi's death that no one would ever forget this lovable Chow Chow.

We will not forget him either.

This cartoon by Sem shows one of America's and France's great socialite "dandies," E. Berry Wall, famous for his aristocratic dress and mostly for his pointed starched collars, with his equally well-known Chow, Chi-Chi, who had more important people for friends than any other Chow in history.

Mrs. Calvin Coolidge and a black Chow Chow, Timmy, photographed in 1929. Timmy was the brother to Mary Alice Elliott's red female, Ching.

APPENDIX

TOP TEN CHOW CHOWS FOR 1974

1. CH. TAMARIN MIDNIGHT IDOL; owned by Prudence Baxter.
2. AM. AND CAN. CH. MI-TU'S HAN SU SHANG; owned by Mr. and Mrs. Herbert Williams and John C. Frederick Peddie.
3. CH. SAM KU SON ONE; owned by Suzanne Brumbaugh.
4. CH. LAKEVIEW'S MR.-LUKEE; owned by David Reynolds and Don Aull.
5. CH. RO-JO'S JERI LU LING; owned by Robert and Roberta Jones.
6. CH. GRIFFCHOW'S MAR JA'S SHOU LING; owned by Mr. and Mrs. James Griffith.
7. CH. STARCREST DANDY LION; owned by James Pierson and G. Don Foster.
8. CH. GOTSCHALL'S CHANG KOU CHIAN; owned by Thomas A. Cassidy.
9. CH. LAKEVIEW'S JO JO; owned by Mrs. Naomi Scott.
10. CH. AH SID LIONTAMER JAMBOREE; owned by Desmond Murphy and Dr. Samuel Draper.

TOP TEN CHOW CHOWS FOR 1975

1. CH. STARCREST LEMON DROP KID; owned by Mr. and Mrs. Joel Marston.
2. CH. GRIFFCHOW'S MAR JA'S SHOU LING; owned by Mr. and Mrs. James Griffith.
3. AM. AND CAN. CH. MI-TU'S HAN SU SHANG; owned by Mr. and Mrs. Herbert Williams and John C. Frederick Peddie.
4. CH. TAMARIN MIDNIGHT IDOL; owned by Prudence Baxter.
5. CH. RODON'S MR. CHIPS; owned by Ron Ewing.
6. CH. LAKEVIEW'S DR. JIM; owned by David Reynolds, Mrs. Naomi Scott, and Don Aull.
7. CH. LO-JA'S RED DRAGON OF SHARBO; owned by Mrs. Loretta Caywood.
8. CH. AH SID LIONTAMER JAMBOREE; owned by Desmond Murphy and Dr. Samuel Draper.
9. CH. PENNDONNA LITTLE WOUIE; owned by Gloria Stevens.
10. CH. SMOKY SHANG-TAI O'SNOWDEN; owned by Max and Dorothy Moore.

Index

A

Advanced Training and Obedience Trials, 470-472, 474-479
American Chow Chow, The, 174
American Kennel Club (A.K.C.), 11, 167
Artificial Insemination, 447
Audrich, 248
Autumn-Sun, 248, 250

B

Back, American Standard for, 383

Bathing, for grooming, 440
Belgium (history of breed and owners), 97, 100
Betmar, 250, 251
Body, American Standard for, 383
British Standard for, 404
German Standard for, 405
Breech Births, 451, 452
Breeding Stock, Health of, 444
Brood Bitch Records (English), 84
Budynasty, 362, 363, 366

C

Carchow, 251
Carlee, 251, 252
Certificat d'Aptitude au Championat
    (C.A.C.), 95
Certificat d'Aptitude au Championat
    Internationale de Beaute
    (C.A.C.I.B.), 95
Champad, 366
Championship, qualifying for, 487, 488
Chang-Shi, 259
Characteristics, British Standard for, 404
Charmar, 259, 260
Cheng Lee, 262, 264
Cherokee, 260, 261
Chia Hsi, 261, 262
Chi-Kwang, 368
Chow Chow, The, 11, 95, 387
Clar-Ell-Mo, 264
Coat, American Standard for, 383
    British Standard for, 404
    German Standard for, 405
Color, British Standard for, 404
    German Standard for, 405
Committee of the Chow Chow Club, 24
Complete Dog Book, The, 11
Coprophagy, 521, 522

D

De La Moulaine, 319, 322, 323
Denmark, history of the breed and
    owners, 137-139
Don-Lee, 264, 265, 269
Don-Ray, 274
Dre-Don, 274, 278

E

Ears, British Standard for, 404
    German Standard for, 405
Eastward, 278, 279
Elbow dysplasia, 547, 548
Ellwanger, 290, 292
English Kennel Club Stud Book, 18
Eyes, British Standard for, 404
    German Standard for, 405

F

Fa-Ci, 292
Farresdale, 292
Faults, British Standard for, 404
    German Standard for, 405

Federation Cynologique Internationale
    (F.C.I.), 93, 96
Feet, British Standard for, 404
    German Standard for, 405
Five Ash, 292-294
Foo H'Sing, 368, 372
Forehand, German Standard for, 405
Forelegs, American Standard for, 383
Forequarters, British Standard for, 404
France, history of the breed and owners,
    128, 135

G

Gait, American Standard for, 383
General Appearance, American
    Standard for, 383
    British Standard for, 404
    German Standard for, 405
Germany, history of the breed and
    owners, 142-159
Gestation period, 448
Gotschall, 294, 295
Grooming, basic, 433, 440
Grooming, for puppy, 440
Grooming parlors, 556

H

Hanchow, 372
Han Dynasty, 11
Head, American Standard for, 383
Head and Skull, British Standard for,
    404
    German Standard for, 405
Hindquarters, British Standard for, 404
    German Standard for, 405
Hip dysplasia, 547
Holland, history of the breed and
    owners, 100-126

I

Insurance, for dog, 511
International Chow Chow Congress, 93
Italy, history of the breed and owners,
    136

J

Jon-Ell, 296-297
Junior Showmanship Competition, 488

K

Keba-Yan, 374

Keesaman, 300
Ky-Lin, 301

L

Lakeview Kennels, 303, 305
Liontamer, 307-309
Lli Haven, 306
Lonsdale Trophy, 22
Luck-EE, 312, 313
Luxembourg, history of the breed and
    owners, 126-128

M

Magi, 314
Mardi Me, 315
Martange, 317
Match Shows, 482
Midland Club show, 57
Minhow, 78
Mi-Pao, 375, 378
Mi-Tu, 380

N

Neck, American Standard for, 383
    British Standard for, 404
    German Standard for, 405
Nor-Ton, 326
Norway and Sweden, history of the
    breed and owners, 162-165
Notable All-Breed Chow Winners
    (English), 86

O

Obedience Trials, 488
Outdoor Housebreaking, 506

P

Pandee, 328, 330, 334
Parasites, internal, 516-518
Patella dysplasia, 548
Pi dog, 20
Plainacre, 334, 338
Point Shows, 483-487
Popular Dogs, 314
Present Day English Record Holders,
    86-90
Puppy,
    buying a show puppy, 418, 419
    conditions of sale, 418
    feeding, 456-457
    feeding newborn, 464, 465
    male or female?, 415-416
    purchase of, 407-422
    weaning, 457

R

Rabies, 527-532
Reward Method, for training, 466-467
"Royal Dogs of China," 13
Ru-Bil, 338

S

San Kee, 339
Scotchow, 341
Shamrock, 339
Shanglo, 338
Sinkiang, 380
Socialization of Chow Chow, rules for,
    430-432
Soo-Z, 339, 340
Standard, American, 383
Standard, American, Interpretation,
    of, 386-403
Standard, British, 404
Standard, German, 404
Stud Dog Records (English), 84
Stud Fee, 447
Suyan, 380, 381
Switzerland, history of the breed and
    owners, 139-142

T

Tag-El, 351
Tamarin, 352
Tsang-Po (The Allens), 354
Tsang-Po (The Norths), 356

U

United States, history of the breed and
    early owners, 167-213

V

Vaccinations, 532

W

Weight and Size, British Standard for,
    404
World War I, history of the breed
    during, 28
World War II, history of the breed
    during, 57
Wu San, 360